RIVER BEND CHRONICLE

RIVER BEND CHRONICLE

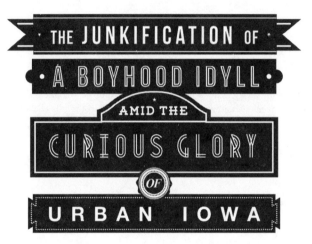

THE JUNKIFICATION OF
· A BOYHOOD IDYLL ·
AMID THE
CURIOUS GLORY
OF
URBAN IOWA

WITH PHOTOGRAPHS BY ROBERT CAMPAGNA

BEN MILLER

LOOKOUT BOOKS
University of North Carolina Wilmington

First printing, March 2013
ISBN: 978-0-9849000-0-8

Cover and divider pages by Matthew Kavan Brooks
Interior design by Arianne Beros, Lee Cannon, Meg Reid, Anna Sutton,
and Ethan Warren for The Publishing Laboratory
Photographs © Robert Campagna

This is a work of literary nonfiction, based on the author's experiences and
memories. Some names and characteristics have been purposefully changed
to protect the identities of those whose lives intersected with his.

Library of Congress Control Number: 2013931543

ART WORKS.
arts.gov

www.ncarts.org

Lookout Books gratefully acknowledges support from the University of
North Carolina Wilmington, the North Carolina Arts Council, and
the National Endowment for the Arts.

Lookout Books
Department of Creative Writing
University of North Carolina Wilmington
601 S. College Road
Wilmington, NC 28403
www.lookout.org

This book is dedicated to a wife,

Anne Pierson Wiese,

and also to a sister,

Marianna Rose Miller,

with love and reverence

I know this vicious minute's hour;

It is a sour motion in the blood,

That, like a tree, has roots in you,

And buds in you.

DYLAN THOMAS

This book presents the finite—if sprawling—locale of one consciousness, as the forces of memory, opinion, intuition, and imagination alternately collude and war to record. My dream of a comprehensive (all inclusive, all embracing) expression is inevitably inspired by the very authorial limitations which make such an achievement elusive.

The imperfectness of recreated dialogue is obvious and acknowledged, and in some cases names have been changed. The portraits etched here are mine alone, definitive only in the sense that they are the particular faces I always find looking back at me when I peer into the past, seeking an improbable purchase on dissolution and shadows.

CONTENTS

GHOSTS
OF THE
Mississippi

GHOSTS OF THE MISSISSIPPI

In DAVENPORT, IOWA, WHERE I GREW UP, there was an elderly
woman who had encountered Flannery O'Connor at the Iowa
Writers' Workshop in the late 1940s. I heard Blanche's side of the
story many times but never tired of it, partially because she did
not take any relish in the telling, always pushing her water glass
aside, as though the liquid might become infected by the dirty
details. Blanche lived in the Mississippi Hotel with her twin sister,
Sadie. Their rooms offered a quizzical view of what downtown
Davenport offered: infantry of parking meters, granite hulls of
department stores weathering poor sales, levee mélange, and the

tugboat-pushed barges riding one of those bends in the Mississippi River that lend eastern Iowa the silhouette of ruptured fruit.
Jazz genius and cornetist Bix Beiderbecke, the city's most famous
native, had once described it all by raising his horn and walking
out the notes of his winsome composition "Davenport Blues."
Blanche and Sadie must have heard the tune, though Blanche
was sure to have dismissed it. In winter, when sidewalks were
icy, these tiny sisters clung to the building bricks, creeping like
paisley-scarfed mountain climbers with a disdain for the vertical. Neither had married. Both smoked like factory chimneys and
sported fine coats of facial down that appeared blond or brown,
depending on whether the shades were drawn. From a distance
of twenty feet, one might have thought they were identical twins.
But to get up close was to note only differences. Sadie's blue eyes,
Blanche's green ones. Sadie's wide smile, Blanche's thin frown.
Sadie's lilting voice, Blanche's academic drone. Once I had occasion to fetch Blanche from the hotel, whose lobby was scary with
couch cushions squashed into the shapes of those no longer on
the planet. The elevator shivered, clanked, arrived on the right
floor, the edgy hall. I knocked on the metal apartment door. Sadie
answered, wearing a robe, and as I was asking her to tell Blanche
that her ride was waiting downstairs, Blanche popped out from
behind the robe. It was like seeing an atom split. After graduating from the University of Iowa with an MA in English literature,
Blanche had immediately enrolled in business school and, a few
years later, received an accounting degree—smart move, given
her attachment to formal verse, a kind of writing she never gave
up, continually testing herself against the sonnet, the sestina, the
villanelle, and reading the results at meetings of various writing
groups. One of these, Writers' Studio, is where we met in the
autumn of 1978, when I was fourteen.

I JOINED THE CLUB DURING MY RECOVERY from the starvation diet that had halved my weight, from a high of more than two hundred pounds, and granted me a first ghost, the fat boy whispering in my ear: "Did I deserve that? I ate only what you told me to." I had found the meeting time and place listed in the *Quad-City Times* and asked my mother to drop me off there, in front of a tenement on a side street in deserted downtown Rock Island, Illinois, across the river from Davenport. It was night: she was glad to do things like that at night. It made things exciting. For some of her children it worked out better than for others. She sped away. A newer car pulled up, parked, and out climbed a man in a tan belted overcoat. He wore a cap, carried a briefcase, smoked a sweet-smelling pipe: awesome. "Here to attend the meeting?" he asked. I said I was. He looked surprised, but extended his pink hand. "I'm Howard Koenig. What's yours?" I forced it out, loud. Howard nodded and produced an old key that opened the door to the rest of my life. It was dark inside, and still pretty dark even after he'd flicked a switch. Together we climbed a narrow creaking staircase to another door off a hall with all the charisma of an Alcatraz tunnel. Howard, enveloped in maroon pipe haze, unlocked that door, too. We entered the musty room rented by the club. More lights, brighter lights, were flicked on, and I saw that steam heat had cooked the colors out of the walls. The meeting table was crooked. But such sad details, one after another, failed to temper my jubilation. I had shaken the hand of one Howard Koenig. He had taken off the coat to reveal a green chiffon suit and tie that went with. He was relating things I should know. He worked in a civilian capacity for the Army Armament Materiel Readiness Command at the Rock Island Arsenal (the military compound situated on an actual island, as the city of Rock Island was not). His favorite author was Edgar Allan Poe, with whom he shared a birthday. His first wife had died in a car accident out East and after that he had moved to the Midwest. He had remarried. Her name was Rita. They had children.

I WAS DECADES YOUNGER than any other club member. This did not seem strange to me. I had long been the outgoing misfit who found acceptance only in unconventional social circles, befriending school janitors, parking lot guards, neighborhood shut-ins—those ruminating fragile retirees. But I was a novelty to Writers' Studio. Members stared happily as they settled onto the folding chairs. Bifocals abounded, and every pair welcomed my long stringy hair and the scar-like facial niches that dieting had cut. No one said a thing about the yellow scampish T-shirt bearing the white iron-on letters I had requested at the mall kiosk where a man would put any words on any rag you handed him. I had picked the Bob Dylan song title: DESOLATION ROW. I returned the smiles of my welcomers. Howard, club president, waived the dollar attendance fee in my case. The lady who introduced herself as Blanche lit a cigarette in approval of the move, before qualifying her enthusiasm, snapping: "We shall see." We shall, I thought. Some strangers were mysteries inviolate and other strangers were mysteries you felt like you knew, despite knowing nothing. I saw ballpoint pens astride notepads, spiral and bound—it was one of the oldest sights in my life, the blank page to fill with colors and then, soon enough, embroider with letters and words, with a will to seek answers if not necessarily to find, and accept, them. "What have you brought to read us?" Howard asked me right off, and when I said I had come to listen—*this time*—there were appreciative murmurs. It meant, they thought, that I was polite. I let it

mean that, too. Their affection, any love—good or bad—had me.
I was the fool for love. I fell all the way, with no strings attached to
their warmth to keep me from falling. They had spotted a fellow
traveler. At the end of the first meeting of rhymes I was admonished to come back the following Thursday for more grins that
were genuine (even if the teeth might not have been). How could
I refuse? Iowa City had its aloof workshop, open only to geniuses
imported and later exported, like a secret trade in diamonds, but
in the most bizarre and comical way Writers' Studio was more
exclusive. Who, seeing our figures spill out of the building, could

have imagined what we had been doing up there? Previously I had had but two allies I could totally trust: stroke-stricken Granny Stanley and our neighbor the widower Mr. Hickey, clad in a clip-on bow tie, polka-dotted or striped. Sitting beside Granny's four-poster bed, and in Mr. Hickey's immaculate kitchen, had taught me the rhythm and substance of genial patter with the aged, training that had come in handy on this night. I liked acting as if I hailed from an era when I wasn't born yet. It was the most reliable way of briefly lightening the load that had come of being born to a certain couple on November 5, 1963, a few weeks before JFK's assassination. "See you later, alligator," I chirped at worried club members after convincing each, individually, that it was permissible to drive off to a post-meeting snack and leave me in the dark at a pay phone across from the extinguished glow of the Walgreens drugstore cursive. "My mother'll come . . ." "Aren't you hungry?" No, I lied. "She'll come . . . soon." "You could call her from the place." But I didn't have money for a snack, nor did I feel I'd earned the right to dine with writers who had published in *Highlights* and *Guideposts*. I was in awe of their old-school grammar, marketing tips, typescripts. "See you later, alligator!"

AFTER A MOTHERLY VOICE ANSWERED my call at Granny Stanley's house up on the hill, piping "I'll be there right away," I stood for another half hour in the close and cavernous night. Little lights here and there cast little flares that in the sky, over dark streets, formed an oily shimmer which blotted out all but the brightest stars. It was a map-bending fact that many Iowans in the Mississippi River Valley spent half their time in Illinois, running errands, visiting relatives. The Rock Island of spittle-laced Grandpa

Stanley, uncivil civil engineer, who let family in mostly to curse their bad choices in careers and stocks; of gelid Dr. Miller, with his suede driving gloves and silver Tiffany chip bowls and London vacations at The Ritz, who sent birthday gifts down to the parking lot of his Steepmeadow luxury condo with Grandmother Rose so as not to be bothered by the children of his poorest son, David. The Rock Island of the brand-new but already eternally failed brick pedestrian mall that had erased parking spots and hurt business. Mayor Jim Davis liked it—one of the few. I missed the linear camaraderie of sidewalks. Sidewalks—whether teal-blue in rain or silvered with snow or cratered as the moon—were a reliable way forward, maybe the only way, whereas diagonal mall bricks reflected no lunar light and led shoes only to the end of the mall, a few short blocks away. Rock Island's downtown, behind its corrugated floodwall, lacked the energy that an unobstructed river view lent to Davenport. Still, vagabonds couldn't be choosers, and I strained to appreciate my private audience with the ill-fated project stretching between the minor cliffs of office buildings. The mall had cost taxpayers millions. It had the charm, at least, of not being a slum. The slum, below the hill where my grandfathers followed the stock market, started south of downtown, separated from it by traffic spilling off the Centennial Bridge. Across the river, Davenport's poorest area existed atop its hill and was airier and livelier, a centrality overlooking downtown, and more of a piece with it all, sandwiched between the east side's old money, the west side's bungalows, and the new money to the north, where the Windsor Crest subdivision, and others like it, were loosely enclosed by the lope of Interstate 80. A castaway on the mall, a fly in Illinois aspic, I was finding myself increasingly thrilled to claim my hometown of Davenport—a big recognition—when I heard the honking.

As the passenger's side door swung open, the spurt of light, like a camera flash, caught my mother's flushed damp jowls and bowl-cut hair and eyes in their own world. (Granny called her Tommy Lynn.) I said hi and she belted out greetings. We were both thankful, truly thankful, I had not been mugged or stabbed or shot and dumped in the river while pursuing my writing dream. Pedal met metal. She began to detail Grandpa's drunken antics, her voice sharp in the center and on the edges soft, regretful, insecure, a sigh. "Dad disinherited Deena again!" she said. Deena, mother's sister, the chemist, lived in Pittsburgh and seldom returned to take guff. Mother could not conceal her joy. In most ways the ride home from my first Writers' Studio meeting was the same ride I had been on countless times following a visit to Wayne's Comic Book Store in Moline, or some other local trove of cultural dust that I considered nutritious. Her torpid rhetoric, my fidgeting on the soiled upholstery, the eau de exhaust and engine chortles and Mississippi River churned into it all. The car's worn tires expertly translated the idiosyncrasies of land estranged from its soil, the piecemeal stanzas of pavement: the smooth the grooved the grated the creamy the chunky. Each jolt got us, and good. The dashboard library of poetry anthologies and true-crime accounts shifted as the chassis creaked and the car, a beater perpetually on its last legs and soon to cough its fnal cough, cantered onto a ramp leading to one of the bridges over the river. I thought I glimpsed, behind us, the orange and black ILLINOIS OIL sign painted on a warehouse facing the railroad tracks. Night thickened over the water. The car felt lighter, though just as bogged with the funk of conflicts. Dare we return home, where my father, exhaling daisy chains of smoke, and five angry younger brothers and sisters waited? Reflections fattened on the hood and vanished. I was bones and ink in the passenger's seat, the driver a migrating fifty-cent rummage sale dress. As long as possible she would put off asking: "How did things go?" She was afraid to hear. She did not want to be jealous, but would be anyway. She could see I was smiling and less in tune with her frequent contention that life was a "lonely, lonely journey." She had always been quick to spot serious rivals for my attention, but that tendency had been exacerbated in the wake of my recently eliminating the fat boy she'd been so close to for so long. I had starved him to death, going on what amounted to a prison-style hunger strike to get her off his back. I'd never be the fat boy again, though it seemed I'd be stuck with his vociferous echo as long as I lived. When I had finally begun eating again, after dipping below 105 pounds, my mother told herself I had given up the strike not for my own sake, but for hers! I had gained twenty pounds in what seemed like an instant, thanks to honey, peanut butter, tuna and Miracle Whip. I had put on another twenty pounds since and though still gaunt, my frame was filling out, finally alluding more to life aboveground than to graves below. Heads no longer turned when my mother and I strolled the fluorescent infernos of Kmart, Target, and Woolworths. She wished to forget the months of being trailed by the skeleton of the boy she had once played the "kidnapping game" with. (In the kitchen she would whisper, "Sneak out, meet me on Fulton Street, none of the other children help me...your father, he...I'll be around with the car in a few minutes...we'll go to Granny's, Big Boy for a burger, the Paperback Exchange—you and I..." Then, skidding to the pickup spot, she would wail, "Get in the back!" I got in, got down. It was one big tease. We never escaped for long. But she liked it.) She had wanted more years of low-octane mother-son odyssey, when our loneliness granted us acres of adjacent darkness—only now our darks, if not detached, had ceased communicating well.

She couldn't forget, or forgive, what I had done to her partner in crime. Why had I hurt myself to hurt her? her eyes asked, but I thought she had a clue. She was too numb to feel any direct strike. Pain might be inflicted only by wrenching from her grip a child she thought she had brainwashed. I had never battled her before, had often edited my conversation so as not to shatter her illusions about her prospects. I had only rarely rebuffed her inappropriate touching in the dark upstairs bedroom as she talked about her marital problems and the famous murders she had read of, and described—in the most bizarre twist, while kneading the balls of my feet or applying salve to my buttocks—the various ways that a child could fend off an attack, either by being perfectly quiet and still (like the student nurse, who had hid under the dorm bunk during the Speck massacre in Chicago) or by screaming and pissing and all else. On my tummy, spread-eagled, I chose the former. I listened to the leaves rustling outside the window and to her voice inside, also rustling. She requested permission before every infraction—"Can I rub . . . can I put on . . . ?"—and I complied. She asked with such need and desperation that I sympathized with her more than with myself. Her hurting me became me helping her, being with her in her darkest moments, or trying to be there—as the voice telling me what to do were I attacked was at least a hundred miles from the hands doing the squeezing. In those mad moments she offered her oldest son the mad choice either to believe in her as a protector or to revile her as an enemy, and if I knew the best choice (I could not afford to lose a parent— not then!) and tried to make it, I also knew the truth. Actually she was enemy and protector in one slippery form—and it was a story of truth devouring truth. Anyone who peeked in and saw us, who saw what was happening in that bedroom, would have faced the same dilemma of having to fathom an implausible reality or make do with a half-truth—or a half-lie, really—but no one cared to see or hear. Mother carefully picked her spots—when I was eleven, and she had put infant Nathan down for the night; when I was twelve, and thirteen—but then, near the end of a miserable seventh-grade year, I had finally refused her advances. I went on strike. When we visited the public clinic, the frizzy-haired doctor warned me: "Your body is eating its muscle to survive." I liked that idea for a time, the body slipping into itself as if down a drain and one day leaving behind no trace save a few mid-air cells. One clean—and permanent—exit from the family mire.

I RECALLED A VOICE, HER VOICE, begging the rib cage on the stairs to eat. "Please, you've got to … for me … " The cage would not eat. I stood on the laundry-strewn step, gazing through bars of filament-infested sunlight that streaked the living room as in the old days, when I had stayed home from school for weeks to watch *The Price Is Right* with her, and to cheer her recitations of Emily Dickinson: "How dreary—to be—Somebody! / How public—like a Frog." I left her wiping her bloodshot eyes on the landing and returned to my room to resume slicing me in half. I got credit for it from other people. My disfigurement, astonishingly, made me more appealing and acceptable to tubby neighbors who had been fighting, and losing, the so-called Battle of the Bulge. "Lookin' good!" they cried from yards and driveways. School officials, and most teachers, seeing me shrink, were relieved to be no longer confronted with a child there was no place for, the fat boy bereft of "team spirit." I ate a Granny Smith apple for lunch in the junior high cafeteria—the variety of green apple depicted on the Beatles record labels, a fact I had learned from the Beatles quiz book that was one of the lowercase bibles I read over and over during this ordeal—and a three-hundred-calorie beef or chicken pot pie for dinner each night, plus the skin of my lips that I nibbled in bed in a trance as the plastic stylus of my suitcase player slid off a side of the White Album and hit the spindle, *thu-thup*, *thu-thup*, flip disc, *thu-thup*, *thu-thup*, flip disc. "Mother Nature's Son" and "Dear Prudence" and "Wild Honey Pie" fed me on the hungriest nights so I did not have to eat anything else. These songs blanketed the ruined room, and its terror-wracked occupant, with melancholy serenity. No nitrates of bologna, no ice cream, no cashew bits, no margarine, no Fritos, no Pop-Ts, no frozen tacos, no Banquet TV dinners. And now? Now, though eating again out of cans and boxes and foil trays, and willingly visiting McDonald's and Big Boy, the point I had made was sticking her. It was sticking me, too, making me write like never before, in a flea-sized script. What was wrong was our bond, whereas before it had been the one thing we considered right. It had never been right, though. The bond was her gyres of energy and strategy and purse strings, and my hapless capitulation to it all. Even with her control over my fate diminished, I yet filled the car with tacit concessions to her rule over the family and its future. I had not defeated her antic force. I had only briefly resisted its weight like never before. Now we had our truce, instituted without anything having been figured out between us—a war waiting to happen. Each second on the bridge stretched its legs like a year. Finally, she fired the brusque lawyerly questions about the how, what, and why of Writers' Studio. I answered as she yanked the wheel about. I wanted to let her in on it. I knew her well enough to know that she *wanted* to want for me what she'd never be truly generous enough to want for me. I could tell she wished at once for me never to go back to Writers' Studio and for me to become the darling of the group. One wish checkmated the other, and she was relieved of the intense responsibilities of dreaming. She despised herself, I had learned, above all. Sourly she chirped: "How wonderful you found that Writerly Studio!" Then silence. But any gap in conversation now was a turbulent inlet where truth lurked, fang-toothed like a fifteen-foot sturgeon swishing below the lock and dam parallel to this endless bridge. She had to say more! She filled the car with praise for members of Writers' Studio whom she had never met. I had told her their names, which she mispronounced, making them her own. "Heyward" for Howard. I didn't correct her. I remained a glutton for humiliation. If eager to be clear of her currents of pain, I was equally horrified of any final rejection and detachment, which promised, at least at the start, to fling me into another state of unprecedented incoherence, the confusion wrought by bitter yellow light hitting darkest spaces never before lit. While she *Heyward*ed about Howard, I listened to the warm whistles of cool river wind, noted the blue and purplish gleams bejeweling the levees.

THE JUNKER GALLOPED OFF THE END of the vibrating bridge grating and landed with a double thump. Urban Iowa hummed under our wheels. We shed the trestle shadows and veered onto River Drive. There was the modular Clayton House hotel, where a neighbor lady, Buddy's mother, had once been arrested for turning tricks. There loomed the sooty French and Hecht factory, where Lonnie had once worked the line—Lonnie the red-haired live-at-home son of a Tennessee minister who had come north to study chiropractic science at Palmer College, wanting to combine preaching with medicine, and who, after graduating, had sold that brown house to Buddy's mother and her husband in the raccoon coat, who, in turn, sold the place to the driver of a Frito-Lay delivery truck. There were the winks of the TIME & TEMP billboard, the bulb chorus blinking, blinking, blurting staccato notes of light. Inside me I carried that meeting-room circle of pens, humble faces, "how-to" articles—a counterbalance to the jungle of grandiose and absurd conceits holding sway at home. The family myths were shields at times, armaments at other times, cheap amusements or desperate prayers at still others, but most often ineffective salves for wounded egos. "That Writerly Studio of yours, it reminds me of Brook Farm," swerving mother murmured, oblivious now to Al's Wineburger restaurant on the left, the Robin Hood Flour factory silos on the right. I braced. I could see where things were going. She was glad to hand back anything of yours real nice after first stomping on it real good. Over that meeting room, my smile, my notebook, over the rungs of my bones, she spread the winding sheet of "At Brook Farm, honey, they…" She ignored the white lines of the road. The tires straddled them. She was expert at that—living on the edge without going over. Most of the time, when she did cross big lines, she veered back quick and became, again, merely the eccentric forging forth in an inhospitable world of conformity. In so doing, she delivered to the family the sort of heroine that misfit kids could cheer for. The heroine who spread her steam of ridiculous idealism and hapless bombast was useful to all of us, and in that hypercharismatic atmosphere we could stow, and hide, the deeply aberrant bouts of her behavior. It was vital that our forgetting keep up with our knowing. Truths too heavy to be constantly borne must be denied for the sake of one's sanity. But that wasn't the only reason I could sit there in the car with her, smiling. I smiled because I was determined that my life be about more than my worst hours on earth. I had snapped under the pressure of her eerie routines, but there was more to me than simply broken pieces—I believed there was more. Why? Because the dark had asked me for light. The generation of light. The scavenging of light from streets and the faces of strangers and neighbors and even from mother's lectures on culture and reading. She was still a lot of what I had. I had no father to see me through, really. Even now I let her sit at night on the edge of my bed and caress my feet, as long as her hands stayed below the ankles, and they did. I had showed her that they must. In the gloom she sadly quoted A. E. Housman poems to let me know how much any boundary killed her. I absorbed the lines oozing from her head. The light I needed—it was there, hiding in the family dark, embedded, encoded, awaiting extraction. We were more than our worst hours, right? I, at least, had been through the worst hours, and now sought something else. It felt as if the car were suspended between industrial lots, as if we weren't moving at all, as if instead it was the glaring night passing through us at a high speed that stilled everything. The river a blacker night flowing through thinner city dark. The river night of Mark Twain and Jack Kerouac, who had first glimpsed the Mississippi at this spot, crossing from Rock Island into Davenport in *On the Road*.

THE GHOST ROAD TO 15 CRESTWOOD TERRACE, the nowhere road to a nowhere place, often passed the only farm I knew of in urban Iowa, her reinvented "Brook Farm"—a distant, fantastical relative of the real 1840s settlement of utopian transcendental leanings, of philosophy and hay raking. Dorothy Day lived there, and Emerson, Mailer, Thoreau, Jackie O., Bertrand Russell, Margaret Mead, the Alcotts, Brendan Behan, and a motley host of other free thinkers and/or free-love advocates who could never

have met except in her aching skull. The concept was so addled
I had to take it seriously. Her chant of *Brook Farm* this, *Brook
Farm* that, seemed shorthand for every family delusion. On the
bridge I had told her I would attend the next meeting of Writers'
Studio if I had to swim to Rock Island. That was a mistake. She
would try to convince me out of it. Not out of attending, but out
of attending in a way that hinted at any exchange of her, of the
family, for something better. There was nothing better than us—if
we would only realize it. Her children, she insisted, were little
Brook Farm geniuses on caffeine destined in their intellectual
restlessness to hunt down enrichment wherever it existed—and

find it incredibly disappointing. Her husband, though suffering from emotional stuff and apparent mental shutdown, had written unpublished novels as a young man—a feat that had made him a Brook Farm hand, too. Our address stunk of failure's fertility: a barnyard of illusions seeking to displace our difficult, unacceptable realities. Her huckster's voice, the hustler's voice I knew best and despised the most, clanged like deck bells during a storm warning. *But, honey, at Brook Farm they*...sure, they raised cattle on verbs alone, and pigs on nouns, and they...She would do her damnedest to minimize the uniqueness of my Writers' Studio experience and thus diffuse its threatening attraction. She was saying, yet again: *Don't think you can get away, you can't.* Was it possible she would prefer six dead interesting kids to six live boring kids who said "please" and "thank you"? She tilted over the wheel and stared into the dark where all her dreams had led. Good choices no less than bad ones had come back to haunt her. She had gone to college, and then to law school in the 1950s, when few women did, and ended up pining wildly behind this cola-yucked car wheel. She had found another eccentric to marry and it had turned ugly. When all else failed, she had given birth to six children, but those children, each one, tormented her with hungers, expectations. She could raise a family only by dividing it up, day after day, into the few with her, the majority left behind, abandoned. Crisis containment was the obsession to which all her obsessions were naturally dedicated. She would happily let me live in the attic with my books and records until I was sixty—if I asked. It was disturbing how fetching I sometimes found that horrifying notion. Yes, I, too, desired containment. But there was none. There was the spreading of trouble far and farther. The caring too much and not caring a bit—yin and yang of oversensitivity and numbness. At last she *Brook Farm*ed herself out. She groaned, trope-less for a minute. Groggy, I sank back into the seat as the tires juggled more pavements and seemed to drop off the end of the world, but really we were just hydroplaning again on the runoff of excuses. Anyway, I had heard worse from the bully pulpit. In the house her frequent screams implied that clean sheets and towels and kitty litter and coats with buttons and mittens that matched were made for unintellectual *consumers* addicted to needless conveniences. Our dwelling was superior to others on the block precisely because it was neglected, the carpet clutter redeemed for being crowned with stacks of classic literature published by Signet, Knopf, and Anchor. She had yet to equate a plugged-up toilet with Walden Pond but might. To do regular chores was to live the robotic "Hallmark" lifestyle of clichés and administrative duties that squelched creativity and passion. And excuses always had believers—even if cynical or chagrined believers—as it was easier to accept the craziest alibis than to fathom the voids of humiliation and guilt that hatched them. In the car there was everything left to be said, but nothing more to say about it. When this happened, the exhausted driver often muttered a store name. The best mode of survival at our disposal, other than fairy tales or coffee refills, was a shopping trip with few if any purchases. In twenty minutes we were prospecting the Target aisles, digging for bargains on tube socks and hard candy.

No one in the family except my oldest younger sister, Elizabeth (blue bags under her eyes), could have guessed how serious I was about the Writers' Studio business. No one in the family but she, another snakebitten striver and collector of the tragedies of strangers, could understand it was necessary to *live for writing*, because your life alone could not make the volume of suffering seen, and felt, worth its heavy toll. Nor could anyone but she understand that tic of mine to respond to family debacles not by patently rejecting them but by dragging them with me, out of their vile hole and into arenas, like Writers' Studio, where the Brook Farm fantasia—that dream of mental and emotional freedom unconstricted by community—might be tempered, refined, and, instead of destroyed, lent the solidity of reality. Like me, Elizabeth dressed in carefully chosen vintage clothing from St. Vincent de Paul and the Salvation Army. She also cleaved to Social Security recipients for similar reasons, I guessed. Those old hands had seen more things and, to a degree, accepted what things meant. Our shut-in neighbor Mr. Hickey, Coast Guard veteran, at the helm of a kitchen table, would study a chipped mug rim—knowing, unlike our parents, that it wasn't the defeat that defeated you. What defeated you was not grasping, and absorbing, the small and big lessons of defeat. Thirteen-year-old Elizabeth no longer had much time for visits to Hickey's house—she studied constantly, obsessed with good grades as her way out, her end run. Elizabeth did not have much time for anyone but teachers and Granny Stanley. She never forgot Granny over in Rock Island, trapped in the back bedroom by Grandpa's curses, fully dressed on a high mattress, listening to a soothing recording of soft rain, awaiting our next visit. Once, though, Elizabeth and I had shared a world of Granny, Hickey, mother, writing. When Elizabeth was ten, I eleven, we had made a pact in the upstairs bedroom to be writers, pricking our fingers with a needle (teeth clenched) and signing a piece of wide-ruled Mead notebook paper in blood. We had been—and still were—severe romantics, smitten by, say, bare winter trees, whose countless stripped branches crisscrossed in gray light. We doted on the legless GI selling poppies, the detergent-scented nursing home resident, the stammering wallflowers at square dances. We loved gift store wooden nickels and front-yard wishing wells and dime store "grab bags" and wrought-iron fences—the more spears to impale the gaze, the better. We trusted that life must hurt and hurt, then hurt more. In our house we had learned that with any dream, no matter how simple, must come the puncturing needle. Days were races to keep dreaming new dreams. If you could dream one last dream and sleep before it was punctured, it was a good day, and that was the startling goal of a life of pain, right? To have one more dream than devastating punctures? We were inveterately childish in the way of the aged. Teenage spinster, teenage confirmed bachelor, coffee sippers and doily appreciators and twine fanciers and listeners to music from previous decades, the dated rock and roll. This shared outlook had not changed a whit. What had changed was logistical. The ambulances of our dire minds had taken different dire off-ramps. We were still the two oldest, still the helpers, the EMS paramedics, but we saw rescues differently—our own rescue and the rescue of family pride. There were so many ways to view, and puzzle over, deprivations rooted in the inability of our mother, a lawyer, and our father, a lawyer, to live lives of reason. Why was it so often impossible for these schooled people to keep the refrigerator fully stocked? Or even more to the point—what were Elizabeth and I to do about it? We understood that *proving ourselves* to a group of influential people could be vital to survival, but such different groups we picked, such different assignments. Elizabeth's choice to be a browbeaten handmaiden of stifling teachers and sanctimonious textbooks amounted to her version of starving for her own good: *get an A or I am nothing.* But each triumph was fueled by stress and a fear of failure that gave her raccoon eyes and deprived her of her humor and imagination—as writing would not. I blamed myself for not having encouraged her poetry more. She thrived on it, couldn't get enough. How I wanted Elizabeth there with me at the next Writers' Studio meeting, where exploration counted as much as perfection, where failure was welcome! She'd never be a nothing there. She'd be a budding artist, always. Those members knew *not-knowing* and, I had seen, made scant effort to cover up deficiencies. Insoluble stanzas and plots were shamelessly offered up to the circle. That circle knew, and respected, the value of displaying craft's mess. At that first meeting I sensed I could read anything to these tolerant people, be all my selves, in turn, without terror. In the weeks after that, it turned out to be true. Elizabeth would feed off such a feeling, I knew, but, collared to academic excellence, she had no time for the fluff of cinquains and haikus read in halting voices in a tenement across the river. Occasionally, for selfish reasons, I silently derided her choices. Elizabeth's company would have made me less a target on mean detour-twisted rides to and from meetings. But there were other reasons too. Couldn't she see that education alone hadn't cured mother or father of their insecurities and doubts?

ELIZABETH GROUND HER TEETH while sleeping in the bottom bunk beneath Marianna, my middle sister, in the room the three girls shared. Elizabeth hardly ate or went outdoors and yet had a mysterious tan, as if she were toasted from within by her fiery worries. A few times I did cajole her into attending club meetings, with predictably disastrous results. She read poems about winter trees and graveyards and felt that no one liked them *enough*. I revered the lines, though. I also revered her mastering of the violin and the flute, French and then Latin. She quoted Virgil faster and faster until the pale scroll of her thrift store dress seemed to illuminate, yellow flower by yellow flower. But though she seemed to believe there was no future in literature for any human born after the incineration of Caesar, she apprehended why I would be crazy serious about creation: she had been once. This unspoken empathy preserved a consoling hint of that sweet bygone notion of ours that we were a family of two within a gone family. Anyway, her homework obsession and my writing had one important thing in common: both were about a sister and a brother feeling a responsibility to help the family but not knowing enough to help. We lacked answers and were missing tools. We were driven by a livid curiosity that our neediness bred, serially suspending our disbelief as we traveled between the garish theaters of our family drama, where clues were concealed behind curtains whose eerie fluttering was the show itself. Who were we to judge? We did—at times. But we hated ourselves for it. Our parents had obviously been judged enough already by their contemporaries. As father's ailing legal practice brought us near to poverty again and again, and mother's ailing self-esteem made a charade of any serious project she undertook, it was natural that the explanations which Elizabeth and I found most appealing were the more clever myths handed to us, or the classic ones we found on our own and revived, or the dramatic new tales we invented out of iffy fabric. Myths could protect *and* expose. They were reservoirs of hope spawned by confusion. The holes in our lives were so large that only the weirdest fables could span and momentarily repair them. Beyond the myths there was one other constant. There was the unassailable given that Elizabeth and I would remain on that bloody domestic stage until the last scene of the last act, despite being qualm-riddled, plagued by overexertions and breakdowns. We were not the sort to leave anyone behind. And in our own ways, we have not. Elizabeth remains front and center in the family playhouse. I know why. I am sympathetic with her reasons. You remain in a cross fire when you have no exit, stage left. If long ago I located an exit—if I am not now soliloquizing beside her—she is with me nevertheless. I have everyone near, echo and profile. Daily I navigate the stormy presences of deep absences. Estrangement has not corrupted love, nor made it less vital, but sharpened the awareness of what is at stake when one loves, what is to be gained and lost, proving again and again how irreplaceable, and elusive, loved ones are.

WRITERS' STUDIO MEMBERS SOON did not have to ask "Have you brought something to read tonight?" They could see I had. Throughout that first year I brought long poems copied out at the Davenport Public Library or up in my bedroom as the rugged vinyl spun on the wobbling turntable, creating a protective barrier of harmony between me and the dissonance of 15 Crestwood Terrace. *Harvest*, Neil Young. *Leon Russell and the Shelter People*. *Time Loves a Hero*, Little Feat. It all poured into what I wrote, drove my hand across the page. One political poem called "Sequel" told the story of the impoverished widow of Eddie Slovak, the only U.S. soldier to be executed for desertion during World War II. Some TV movie had inspired the idea. I recited the epic like a good composer of free verse: quick, while rocking. Blanche winced but said naught. Other members suggested I enter the monstrosity in the Mississippi Valley Poetry Contest in the high school division. I did, and the ladies checking in entries figured no youth would dare write a five-page poem, and it was added to the pile of poems submitted by adults, and won the seventy-five dollar grand prize handed out in late October at the Butterworth

Center, located in a mansion. Oak-paneled library. Cosmic chandeliers. The beige and otherwise bleak program benefiting from the glitter of judge Robert Dana's biography. Poet-in-Residence: the rare Iowa Workshop graduate who skipped the flight to New York and stayed in the state to teach. Author of *Some Versions of Silence* and *The Power of the Visible*. Hobbies: traveling, swimming. Swimming! I had only heard of poets drowning, one way or the other. At the punch-bowl reception following the to-do, feathered hats told me "congrats" and gave me "kudos." I spilled punch on my dark blue velour jacket—the best clothing I owned. I shook hands with buoyant poet Dana. His goatee-festooned chin dipped, and a voice of grit and gravity said: "Let me know when you're ready to go to college." I promised and then went out and blew the prize money at Kmart and Ben Franklin, buying forgettable plastic Christmas presents for my deserving brothers and sisters and parents. Cornell, the small Iowa college where Robert Dana taught, was incidentally the very one my mother had attended before her life broke into the pieces I grew up with— sharp, sharper, sharpest.

IN ADDITION TO BLANCHE AND HOWARD, the other regular Writers' Studio attenders were roly-poly accomplished Dave, who had published dozens of inspirational biographies for the juvenile audience; Betty, wife of a car mechanic, working on a biography of the eighteenth-century poet Phyllis Wheatley; Cozie, the devout Catholic—and by day technical writer for the government—who each week read a poem about cats; Norm, the retired Rock Island Lines employee who wrote only about trains; Faith, who always nearly died of a heart attack while climbing the stairs, then recovered to wail hymns she had written years ago; John, the haiku writer who lived with his mother, the heart surgeon; Karen, the red-haired fourth-grade teacher who worshipped Joyce Carol Oates and Stephen Crane; and Carole, formerly of Alabama, who had married young, divorced too late, and worked weekdays in the hosiery department of Younkers, standing still as the mannequins. The second-floor meeting room was impossibly hot in the summer. One slender window stuck in the down position. A ceiling fan that moved only when the haiku writer stood on his chair and gave it a spin. John got all the hard assignments—treasurer for a group with virtually no money. Each penny he reported in that shy, monotonous voice of his, words quavering as the rest of him dare not, could not. He was profoundly stuck, and starched. Had his mother ironed his suit with him in it? His eyes bulged to mothball size when he read his 5-7-5 haiku—the hardest of all the hard jobs he had to do. Meanwhile, the Kelvinator buzzed by the dusty window. For a quarter, members could purchase a bottle of warm cola from John. Few did. When better "digs" (as Cozie put it) were eventually located in Davenport, the beverages were left behind for the next thirsting tenant.

If the club had moved meetings to the top of Everest I would have found a way to get there. I wanted to make it in the Beauty and Truth racket. Dear Maxwell Perkins, I did. I had the bug bad, having caught it from a father who had written those unpublished constipated novels and a mother who misquoted the world's loveliest poets (Yeats, Dickinson, Tennyson, Housman), delivered Ogden Nash drivel perfectly, and wished, I knew, to write outlandish odes of her own. Walk into any room in our home and you encountered evidence of quashed literariness: the discarded notebooks, the capless pens, the anthologies butterflied on coffee tables—the luscious pulp innards of Dylan Thomas spilling out of butchered bindings. Attending Writers' Studio meetings helped me understand what had gone wrong. My parents had the art equation backward. They wanted to make great work only—to hell with all else. But before the creation of Beauty and Truth had to come the living out of Beauty and Truth, and if club members never got around to the genius part, they made up for the lack of masterpieces with their perfect intent to do nothing they could not do—to be who they were, without apology or any fudging of logic. Their lack of airs elevated me. I discovered I was as thrilled by the supreme modesty of John's haiku about his long driveway and Cozie's newest blurry cat poem as I was by the grand achievements of Emerson, O'Neill, and Whitman. The voices reading the crap were not crap, that's why. They vibrated with humanity and conviction. They showered the plainest rented rooms with that warm, rich, otherworldly ordinariness that nourished those stray seeds of integrity I gathered in Mr. Hickey's kitchen and Granny Stanley's bedroom.

P<small>ICTURE THE GYM OF A DEFUNCT CATHOLIC SCHOOL</small> half-heartedly converted into a community center. It was located on top of the hill in west Davenport, right off Locust Street. With these "new digs" came the many new members: obese Roy, who rode The Harley to meetings in January wearing no coat, only a vest; Gene, the satirist and hypnotist; Stahl, the taciturn poet, who as a youth had excelled at gymnastics, using a farm fence as his pommel horse; BJ, the single mother of many genres; Jack, the Vietnam vet and softball player who would eventually offer me a joint in the parking lot; one Lucille Eye, who never read anything; and Gordon, with his novel about a white couple who adopted a Mexican woman (Maria) whose house has burned down. A folding table of banquet length stood in the middle of a floor marred with skid marks made decades earlier by the children of German immigrants. The voice of each reader echoed and when I closed my eyes to listen, the sensation was of hearing rhymed shouts at a great, muting distance. Poets somehow dominated meetings though always in the minority. Nature was the topic of choice— flowers, trees, birds. Fiction writers targeted the juvenile audience and dreamed of publishing in *Boys' Life*, *Reader's Digest,* and *Guideposts*—except Roy, who submitted his stories of abducted tied-up women to *Playboy*. It excited me to hear any member report the smallest sale of any kind. Many pieces were placed in church newsletters. Some members brought out books. Betty with a press called Avalon. Dave with many presses. (His goal was to publish fifty books by the time he was fifty, and he did it.) Imagine that: money for words! One Writers' Studio member who shall remain nameless sold the same story more than a dozen times. She dared not write another sentence, for fear it would tarnish her reputation as one of the club's most successful submitters. When it came time to read she simply reported current earnings of "Mallie and the Snail," which over the years climbed to a total in excess of two hundred dollars. Blanche, the most serious, never considered her poems good enough, and submitted to the trash can alone. She rewrote constantly—on the way to the club in the back of Carole's Datsun, and while sitting at the folding table, erasing and replacing words right up until the last moment. And then, quaking, with the down of her lip sweat-shimmered, she would lift the legal pad and apologize profusely for the inept result of her labor. Not one "hill of beans" did the mountain of effort amount to. And if *she* could do no right, well, it would naturally be difficult for others to do better. Each week she brutally took us to task for our linguistic and grammatical inadequacies, quoting *The Elements of Style* while waving an ember-tipped Pall Mall. As little as one hanging clause or misplaced noun could set her off, and special ire was reserved for the incorrect use of "lay." Rather than be subjected to a ten-minute lecture on that subject, the rest of us kept all derivations of that word out of our stories and poems. (And even now, more than thirty years later, I'm still reluctant to have a character take a nap—much better he drink a cup of coffee.) After the meetings in the gym there was a caravan to Riefe's, the diner famous for serving the platters of onion rings heaped like Medusa's hair. Karen bought me an order each week, though things were getting tougher and tougher for her—she had lost her job as a teacher, and was working as a clerk at Woolworths. At Reife's I pled with Blanche to tell me about her famous Iowa City classmate until at last the water glass was pushed aside and her features cleaved toward an invisible center point. First of all, I must know Flannery spoke with such an accent that Paul Engle, workshop director, had to read her stories to the class himself. Second, Flannery did not keep appointments, having promised to meet Blanche at a movie theater one winter afternoon and never showing up, preferring to stay home with "that typewriter and hot pot."

In the basement father surprised me. It was the summer after I had won the Mississippi Valley poetry contest, almost two years into my time at Writers' Studio. He asked if I would be so kind as bring one of his venerable unpublished novels to the club and read it to the other members. He did not say which manuscript: was I to choose? I had halted on the narrow stairs when I saw his hobbled hulking figure at the bottom: smoke, slippers, a fluster of newspaper sections in one hand. He was preparing to make a painful climb after taking care of his business on the toilet with the pedestal cracked where my middle brother, Howard, had struck it with a bowling ball. He also drove golf balls off the terrace and over the roofs below. Howard, despite being just twelve, was the Miller out of a movie, girlfriends and a leading-man tan; father and I were custodians in comparison. "What do you think, Benny?" he asked, wanting in on my good thing. My hand grazed the flimsy pipe railing which, like the stairs, was covered with gray peeling latex paint. The cave-like basement walls of foundation stone were frosted with old white lead paint, now in the news for being poison. The concrete floor was red, where the red had not worn off, that is. "What about it? What do you think?" I was still thinking. An interesting request, but the most intriguing aspects of parents, I had learned, were often their most troublesome or dangerous. I hated to be the next person who rejected him … but no Writers' Studio member read writing not her own. If a writer was not present to receive feedback on her work there was little use in providing the feedback. "Don't you think they'd like it?" he asked. He wore the uniform that typically accompanied him to the recliner: tan slacks boating high around the waist, short-sleeved shirt, wire-rim glasses that made fish of his eyes behind the bowls of the lenses. Around us wafted the antique reek of pigeon shit dating to Howard's failed experiment to raise fifty or so birds in the basement. A crap-speckled coop remained below the broken window the creatures had escaped from. The fruit of father's "novelist period," typed pages bound in expensive leather, lined a shelf of the pea-green metal bookcase behind him, propped against the outer wall of the least-entered room in the house. It was the basement room for storing coal. There was no light fixture, and on the floor just the webbed remnants of the final coal delivery, made fifty or more years earlier. That bookcase also held my father's growing collection of get-rich-quick stock guides. In the side yard, boxes of files from his law practice lived, molting and rotting. He had ordered the delivery man to dump them there to be rained on! But father kept his make-a-million guides and failed novels inside, warm and dry. These choices fascinated me. They said something awful about the man, and something hopeful, and the incompatible feelings he aroused in me were certainly matched by those I aroused in him. He looked up to me because I was mother's favorite. He looked down on me because of the same. "You don't want to *present* my writing?" I shrugged. He opened his mouth again, that shovel of a mouth, and was, I thought, about to dish me lines about his salad days in Iowa City, when, as an older-than-average undergraduate, he had lived over a typewriter shop and attended a John Dos Passos reading, and another by James T. Farrell of Studs Lonigan fame, and, with a group of gadflies, had drunk beer with Wright Morris. I felt all that coming but he said nothing. I recalled the Ruth Azel Agency letterhead that had fluttered out of one of his novels like a squashed moth when I opened it one night, feeling brave. The rejection was cordial and completely discouraging. For many reasons I tried not to crack the books, and usually succeeded, but sometimes not. He had once informed me that many of his works were set in the same mythical county, à la Faulkner. I had turned hundreds of pages looking for the name of father's county and failed to find it. "The club might appreciate my writing," he persisted. I had descended, drawn down by his gravity. He backed toward the cold furnace. "What's the big deal about taking one chapter the next time...?" Bugs traversed the dirty laundry under the chute. I bumbled through an explanation that it would be better if he read his own writing next Thursday. Then a shock. I smiled and *invited* him to come to a meeting *with me*. It amazed me that I meant it. He and I spent too much time apart: in exile from each other in our own home. Writers' Studio might be one thing—the only?—that could unite us. "You'll love it!" I yelped, building up the case for his coming. My voice new, shiny, resolute. Words burst out. "There's a guy Howard . . ." I told him what I knew about Howard. I told him about Blanche. I was picturing us at the folding table together, our injured texts elbow to elbow. There would be plenty of feedback to go around. Dave Collins would say in the nicest way to father: "Show, don't tell." Dave would add that even if you hadn't the time or inspiration to write on a given day it was essential to do something writing related like reading Welty or buying a new pen. Father had no friends and would leave the first meeting with ten. Their support and encouragement might lead him to write new novels better than the ones typed after he had dropped out of Columbia and Notre Dame in quick succession in the fifties and returned home to Rock Island to endure the mockery of Dr. Miller, and the almost-as-painful pity of his mother, Rose. "They'd be thrilled if you came with me. New members are"—that new big voice leaping out leaped higher—"the group's lifeblood!" He started, staring at me like I was a lunatic. We said nothing more—he lost in his basement of emotion and me lost in mine. The shake of a shirt shrug—the swishing plummet of his eyes—telegraphed the message that I had failed him again. He clop-clop-clopped up the stairs to the recliner and the snows of bad TV reception.

FOR A WEAK MAN, MY FATHER had the broadest and strongest-looking back. Watching it that day, I thought, as often before, what a perfect wall. What a great barrier *he* might have made between me and a mother's anger and desire. He was the ally I really needed; I was the son he had lost to her. Our grief wandered in useless and faltering circles. I turned toward the brown on brown of the book bindings in half-light. He would not, could not read his novels to the group...because he did not like the books enough. It could be he even feared the books by now. Dreaded their power to retain the dream they had ended. But making art meant taking responsibility for the choices involved in the making, the club had taught me that much. Without feeling the responsibility for your flubbed plots and botched iambics, you had nothing at stake, nothing to write for. Father was sapped. Little energy for responsibilities. If not really ruined, he felt ruined. I regretted saying no to the request, but was not sorry about it. I dearly wanted something to work out for him—even more than for myself sometimes—but nothing could work out for you without your doing some work, putting yourself in places that weren't exactly comfortable and working forward from there, crawling into the new territory. This was also the year he drove the family to the outskirts of Davenport where community garden plots were for rent below a shuttered asylum on a hill. This father whose bad hip prevented him from bending had gotten a sud-den notion that a garden plot was what the family needed. He was right—right not to think for an hour about the hip pain that dominated his days—and he was right that we needed fresh food rather than the flash-frozen dinners and the powdered soups, but again a surprising ploy fizzled. He had not prepared well enough. He had never before mentioned gardening to any family member. When we arrived, we saw diffident hippies digging around behind the fence that Howard and Marianna immediately began yanking and rattling, and my father himself appeared to forget why it was so important that we come "take a look." One of the Jesus-hair diggers glared at us like a manager who senses a shoplifter. Plots were separated by vampire stakes with rags tied to them. Father puffed. He had a puzzled, heartbroken look. He wanted to grow books, grow rich and own a Lincoln, not grow tomatoes. Why had we come? his vacant eyes asked. Mother, getting off on the pathos of the plot's proximity to the hilltop asylum, kept pointing at that crenellated building and alluding to Zelda Fitzgerald, one of her role models. A kerchiefed digger set aside his trowel and approached the fence and quoted the high price for a summer rental of five feet of soil. It was disorienting. It was all wrong. City outskirts, where the land should have opened up to reveal Grant Wood vistas of rural Iowa, felt more cramped than the city center, where there existed plenty of vacant lots to plow for free and plant with whatever vegetables thrived on broken glass and gravel. We melted back into the car and it grumbled and coughed and we fled to a fast-food joint for the succor of bubble-beaded colas and french fries bent in supplication to oil. Wind whipped the frail restaurant-lot trees and they bent double. We never went out that way again.

BLANCHE AND JOHN AND COZIE and Howard and Karen and Gordon and Norm and Betty and Dick had no sure cures for what afflicted their art other than grammar correctives and repeating after Dave Collins: "Show, don't tell." They repeated this to each other, and kept telling. But however badly we failed to convey our experiences, we still had our experiences—no disaster on the page could strip away the life that had been lived, and its integrity. There was the solace of working, the next time, to get it less wrong. And for four years Writers' Studio members heard a little extra damage in my voice. They understood that scathing criticism was not what was needed—yet. They heard I was trying hard, attempting to learn to live with the mind I had—and to mine my heart of hearts. The technical particulars of struggle could be egregious, but the vigorous effort was noble. They had gone "through it" themselves, their open eyes said. They gathered up the fragments of my shattered voice and held them close and reported what they "got out of it." That was grace. That was faith in time's power to smooth things out—misplaced faith, but I loved that vision of healing. For all the group could not do for me, they did a child of chaos a sweet favor by just being there, week after week, when I showed up with my broken lines—fables that were half poems, poems that were half fables: "The Sand Mountain," "The Tiger in the Rose Garden," "Cat Bread," "Mya's Wind," "At Night the Ballerina Dances," an elegy called "The English Teacher," about the Sudlow High staff member who shut the door of a garage and started her car. I wrote one piece a week, at least. There we were again every Thursday, as the rest of America slumped in front of sitcoms. We showed up for the challenge of facing down oblivion. Though near to clueless and befuddled by the relentless demands of literary craft, we exchanged "tips." Show, don't tell, of course, if at all possible, but if not, well, telling was better than the ineptness of complete capitulation to silence. Like Mr. Hickey, the weathered ring of stymied rhymers showed me how to "stick in there," how to be lost without becoming totally lost. It was better to show up at seven and stumble anew than not to show up for fear of stumbling. Because if you were to make anything of yourself, if anything even mildly good was ever to work out, you must—usually in isolation and under duress—find a way to take yourself seriously when few others did. The ambition alone could add fertile layers to an existence, and generate answers out of almost nothing. Shaky and on edge when I entered meetings, I left knowing the most important writing you ever did was the writing done when things seemed hopeless, as it required the investment of courage. Action thus imbued made you real to yourself. I took that with me into the parking lot after weekly good-byes and, in the end, also cradled a "going away" basket members had packed with pens, pads, a toothbrush, toothpaste, shavers, and other toiletries they figured I would need.

M~Y NEIGHBORHOOD~—like Writers' Studio membership— demanded much from the heart. The hills, some seeming to stretch halfway to heaven, were the ideal place to train for the long-distance cycling trips that I eventually embarked on with another loner named Randy. If you were not pedaling or driving up one precipitous incline, you were sailing downhill (fishtailing, in winter). The frolic of elevations was partially natural and par- tially created. Tiers of terraced blocks rose from glacier-cut dips shaded by arcing trees whose leafy branches rowed like massive oars when lapped by winds off the Mississippi. The relatively modest dwellings on Crestwood Terrace were part of the first addition to the droves of magnificent mansions of industrialists that lined the ridges leading to the water. McClellan Heights— referred to locally as "The Heights"—was in the 1970s populated by successful doctors and lawyers, and the congressman with the appropriate last name of Leach. His riverfront palace contained a ballroom. The place had been built by Mr. French, founder of the French and Hecht metals company and brother of Alice French, who had written short stories under the pen name of Octave Thanet and consorted with William Dean Howells in the early 1900s. When I was a teenager I liked to walk past the storied compound in the summer, when shadows processed like silk gowns across the lawn. Often no Leach was home, but early one sumpy evening I made the climb up from

McClellan Boulevard with my mother and we stopped in our
tracks like characters in Writers' Studio stories did. The low stone
wall that encircled the hillside property was lined with homemade
lanterns set out by organizers of a Leach fund-raiser—hundreds
of paper bags, each sand-weighted and containing a candle. The
glows stretched up and down the adjoining streets, ending at the
litter-strewn River Drive sidewalk, across from the railroad tracks
and the pewter river reaching to Illinois. Guests in fancy cars sped
through the front gate toward the mansion. They missed this
Candlemas under the plum clouds. My mysterious and pained

mother swayed at my side, giggling as if to ward off the import of a solemn sign. Candles looked like your best friend. Candles were God even to the godless. You trusted candles, though they could burn down your house as sure as an acetylene torch.

On our block each house occupied a cramped plane of its own. Below us lived the driver of a Budweiser truck and his phlegmatic wife, a bartender at the nearby dive called Lindsay Park Lounge. Above, in a small but stately white house, lived Mr. Hickey, the retired Realtor and widower with a bad heart, worse vision, and a little pug. We arrived at the tail end of 1968, when I was five, and for a few years after that, Mr. Hickey—who insisted we call him "John" (and we tried, but often forgot)—continued to appear every noon on his glassed-in back porch, like a svelte apparition dressed for inclemency. Black overcoat and polka-dot bow tie. Black fedora on his bald head and, in his right hand, Mikey's chain-link leash. After John, or Mr. Hickey, had exited the porch and hooked the leash to the backyard clothesline, the drooling snuffling dog would commence running back and forth, an activity which would not stop until John reappeared hours later, his face pearled in the late light. He was a proud, pristine man, an award-winning gardener. His rose bushes were wilder by this time but still produced large blooms. Then Mikey died, and our courtly neighbor grew too weak to go outside. The enclosed back porch became the very end of the world, but he made it there often to open the door for visitors, and remained spry of eye, ever hopeful that his demise was only a passing phase—that strength would return if he took the pills and cut down on salt and periodically squeezed the red plastic hand grip. Every Saturday John's sister, Alice, and her husband, Eddie, a retired tugboat captain, drove down from Le Claire, Iowa, and brought John groceries: oatmeal, Lipton tea, low sodium soup—and a pan of Alice's homemade salmon loaf. My mother replenished what perishables ran out during the week and often I was asked to run up the hill to deliver the carton of milk or eggs, the bunch of bananas, the box of Tiparillo cigars. This I did not mind. Being trusted to deliver cigars after dark seemed a task akin to smuggling contraband over the Mexican border. I'd stuff the brown bag under my arm and lumber up the hill toward the back steps, which were illuminated by a spotlight affixed under the eaves. John would be waiting on the back porch to make the pickup, cued by the phone call I'd made a few minutes earlier—no hat or jacket after dark, just the polka-dot bow tie and a red or green sweater vest hanging loosely on his thin shoulders. After the transfer of the bag came the invitation to step inside for a 7UP. I never refused. In fact, had he ever forgotten to invite me in, I would have reminded him to do so, as I was enchanted with his orderly, air-conditioned house. The door leading from the porch to the kitchen had a five-dollar bill taped to it. This was for a burglar. If John ever came back after chaining up Mikey and found the money gone, he would know it was not safe to enter—that someone had sneaked into the house during the five minutes he was off the glassed-in porch. I thought the ploy incredibly clever, as I did his use of old undershirts as rags and flattened soap boxes as coasters. He had cable TV and if it was summer, and daytime, we watched the Cubs bumble and persevere on WGN. Billy Williams could usually be counted on to get a hit. (I had sent him that compliment; he had sent me an autographed photo.) During the Chicago commercials for Canfield's soda and Dominick's supermarkets, Mr. Hickey reminded me to jump rope to improve my reflexes. If no game was on, we'd sit in the kitchen and make conversation as best we could in a harrowing world that took the right words right out of your mouth. He squeezed a red plastic hand grip to strengthen his arthritic fingers. He passed the grip to me and I pumped it. At least a hundred times, over the years, he offered to nominate me for the Junior Achievement program that matched children up with business-man mentors. Had any of those store owners been in the Beauty and Truth racket I'd have been gung-ho. I sensed that none were. But Mr. Hickey, yes. He was my Virgil repeating advice designed to guide me safely out of hell and into the clear. "Hit the rope, Benny," he chanted.

Mr. HICKEY TOLD STORIES in the same terse and tantalizing fashion that Blanche did—leaving out everything but one or two crackling details (as opposed to my habit of spraying words). Be-tween us on the table: his tea mug emblazoned with the crimson mandible of the Cincinnati Reds logo (gift from an ancient friend in Ohio), my green mottled bottle of 7UP, a box of Archway sugar cookies, numerous pill bottles, the red hand grip, a plastic pill counter, a five-band radio, and a pistol with a long black barrel. My eyes rarely left the last item. The grain of the handle gleamed and the trigger too was shiny, as if it had been pulled many times. John claimed Alice had badgered him into accepting her gift of the gun after the first heart attack, worried he wouldn't have the strength to fend off an intruder. This was a fact, but I noted how comfortable John was around the weapon. He carried it from room to room like a water glass, with an impressive nonchalance that spoke of his wild life story prior to the domestication of becoming a real estate agent. In the 1940s there had been Coast Guard service in New Orleans. And before that: shoe shining and newspaper selling in the small town of Tipton, Iowa; a stint on the Midwest boxing circuit ("barnstorming," he called it); a job running numbers for a cigar shop in the lobby of the Kahl Building, in downtown Davenport. This may sound like the makings of a robust life narrative but John did not indulge in romance. Each time I scooted to the edge of my seat to ask for the glorious details of his younger days, he'd press the plastic tip of the cigar to his lips and exhale a twig of smoke, and then another, and another, until those twigs weaved together to seclude his bald head in its own secret grove. Then I shut up and the whining became internal. Why did some people with zilch to talk about grab your shoulder and yak for what seemed like hours while Blanche and John, who had real stories to tell, say next to nothing—reduce the juiciest subject matter to a few dry drops? The torture was most extreme when John would relax a tiny bit and tell of his two encounters with celebrity. The first had occurred at a hotel in Keokuk, Iowa, far south down the river, in the 1930s. The elevator opened and out strode Primo Carnera, heavyweight champion of the world. John approached the Italian giant. They shook hands. And then? And then John reached for the cigar in the ashtray, and added another nutty-smelling smoky bough to the forest. Whatever words he and Carnera had exchanged, I would not be privy to. And neither would I get a clear picture of cornetist Bix Beiderbecke, whom John had frequently glimpsed rushing through the lobby of the Kahl, toward the stairs leading up to the musicians' union. Was Bix's face as ivory and elegant as it appeared in the photos? Was the hair slicked back? What kind of coat, hat, shirt? Carrying a horn? If so, was the case leather or wood? On one occasion I kept questing until I drove John to the stove, where he put on a pot of water for tea and pondered the blue eyes in the enamel between the burners until the whistle blew. Black-rimmed blue eyes. Stubbornness, I thought it was. Old-timey wholesale modesty. But now I know better—why his stories failed to compound into either a satisfying, filled-out narrative or a soaring myth, both of which I needed in equal degree to dose my confusion. It wasn't the glitter of the years John carried with him but the haunting littleness of experiences. The scrape of the calluses on Carnera's right hand. The wan, hopeful faces of the men at the cigar store counter, putting down the family money.

AT TIMES BLANCHE AND MR. HICKEY could not hide their disgust at what they regarded as my 1970s illusions regarding the influence of celebrity. Blanche's lips would protrude, forming a chapped pale platter under her sniffing nose. John's bald head would sink and dart back and forth, as if ducking punches in slow motion. In me they saw the future, and it flickered like a cheap screen. Your life wasn't your own until someone famous led you to it. What they could not know, however, was that I did not represent my generation. Other kids coveted trivia about idols, but those boys and girls, unlike me, spent much of the day outside. They gave each other nicknames. They competed and chased and kissed, more than kissed. Their passion for Cher, Shaun Cassidy, and Reggie Jackson *supplemented* life, that gush of air into the lungs, the heat of sun on skin. They came to their gods out of power, as budding equals. You could see the confidence in the batter in the park focusing his eyes on the coming fastball and in the girl in a car window brushing hair that fell around her shoulders like sunshine. These American teenagers believed themselves to be blessed, unimaginably talented and beautiful. But I was different. For one thing, my heroes were outdated, always. Frequently dead. Their genius came with an expiration date. My mind was like a dissolving attic box, the past spilling into the present, and the present into the past. It was a struggle to get any date right, because only one calendar held fast: Fat Years and Thin

Years. Usually I could recall being obese and desperate when a thing happened, or gaunt and haunted. When making even that broad distinction proved impossible, I was deepest in the abyss of years and feeling their impact most fully, if abstractly. My family was different in that we smashed the clock to pieces each day with our words and deeds. We did not use less truth to tell more truth, like Mr. Hickey did. We told less truth because we had no control over our complex story, and, to a large degree, lived in mortal fear of getting any handle on the truths roaring within. Get a hold on that and we would be carried far away, or drowned. Ours was the family of supposedly aspiring artists who had produced little art in two generations and were prone to think the great art that might have been was just around the next bend. There was a logic to that irrationality. What else would redeem our ugly and artless lives but art? I dreamed I wrung the dirty rag in the kitchen and out tumbled stars. Each week my father saw three or four "flicks," as he called them, exchanging a lonely law office lacking clients for the crowded matinee at mall theaters. Mother came and went through the screen door five or six times a night before finally settling down to study poetry and the paperback accounts of the Manson massacre, the Clutter murders, the Speck case, and the Sheppard controversy. My five younger siblings escaped through drugs, sports, dating, or, in the case of Elizabeth, catatonically playing Claude Bolling's *Suite for Flute and Jazz Piano Trio* for hours on end. Starting very young, I had writing. I wrote. And wrote. No stopping, season after season, during the Fat Years and Thin Years. First I printed spacious looping letters in the Big Chief notebooks, then I filled Mead notebooks with flat-lined starvation script. Each page a freaky raft carrying me farther away from the chaos of the household and into a predicament of my own making. Any form I chose sought more and more expression until it ate its shape and left me with no story and no poem but an amoeba oozing between genres, trying to fuse them to create the larger mirror of realities that had overwhelmed a boy, flooded him, made him him. There existed in me a sense that to get one little thing right—the thing that counted: my version of the Carnera handshake, say—I had to pry open my history entire and reexperience the totality of its murk to be worthy of that gift of clarity, to understand what it could and could not mean, and to know how to use it. Coming from a family of artless artists—cheaters and cheapeners—I had to doubt that authenticity could come easily or even naturally. Like a fervent paddlewheel my Bic pen churned in rooms and in cars and in parks and in stations and everywhere in between, trying to dredge up what was at bottom of it all, what I was really meant to reap from time's vexing currents.

ONE OF MY EARLY TALES concerned Flannery O'Connor's love affair with Bix Beiderbecke. Could never have happened. Flannery was only six when Bix died of pneumonia in Jackson Heights, Queens. But the details fell neatly into place and still adhere—for me—many decades later. A narrative with no beginning or middle. A story all happy ending, a temporary antidote to the confounding complexity of existence. Flannery's stern kisses curing Bix of alcoholism. Bix's tender hugs curing Flannery of lupus. The two moving to New York and renting the smallest-possible apartment so as to be constantly on top of each other. Bix getting a steady job at the Cotton Club with Duke Ellington and then quitting to start his own band at the dawn of the Swing Era. Flannery's drawl quickly diluting as a result of long stoop conversations with a Hell's Kitchen landlady by the name of Gigi. Flannery practicing newly learned Northern words on the manager of Alp's Drugstore and the members of Bix's band, including Jack

Teagarden. Bix completing his first classical composition since "In a Mist." Flannery finishing a story set at the Cotton Club. The two sitting in the Rainbow Room, sipping each other's eyes. The two holding hands in Central Park. The two at the Polo Grounds, munching popcorn. The two exchanging corny Christmas gifts: *To Flannery, my bird of paradise. To Bix, my horn of plenty.* The two dining at the Park Avenue home of Flannery's publisher and being toasted as "the couple of the century!" Count Basie kissing Flannery's ruby wedding ring. Katherine Anne Porter hugging Bix. Flannery's mother coming to visit and lifting the rag rugs, trying to find where Flannery's accent has gone. Mother only too happy to get back to Georgia and Bix laughing when her plane lifts off from Idlewild. Flannery volunteering at the Bronx Zoo and bringing Bix with her one afternoon and introducing him to all the exotic fowl: "Teelie, meet someone who blows even louder than you do." Bix warning Chet Baker about his drinking and Chet Baker listening, cleaning up for good at the age of twenty-five. Bix and Flannery hosting a party at which Louis Armstrong and Robert Penn Warren are introduced. Bix and Flannery starting a family late, after fifteen years of trepidation. The birth of a little boy named Frank, in honor of the late saxophone player Frankie Trumbauer. The birth of a little girl named Maple, in honor of the Iowa City street on which the two met. Bix with one child on each knee. Flannery singing "Froggie Went A-Courtin'." Bix sliding in the mute and playing "Stardust" after the children have gone to bed. Flannery getting up early the next morning and writing her first love story, typing until the end of this sentence: *The darkness wasn't in him, it was around him, black wings nesting in the creases of an ill-fitting dinner jacket.*

BOOK ONE

The

GREAT IDEAS

Club

TWIGMAS

Wisemen lot — The family, illustrated — "An idea, gang-a-roonie!" —
Dumb all-conquering love — KRVR — Miracle number four —
Harpsichord Overindulgence Syndrome — Marc's Big Boy —
Recliners and the moods they put men in — *Miller anti-arithmetic —*
Festival of Slights — *Branches pointed to the larger truth*

WITH CHRISTMAS JUST DAYS AWAY, and each passing minute resonating in our woolen caps like Poe's tintinnabulating bells, the issue of the treeless living room had to be pushed. Children surrounded the recliner and beseeched the spread and smoking newspaper for a simple answer to a simple question. "When are we getting a tree? They'll be gone if we don't go tonight! Time's running out!" At twelve I was the oldest of six, and the most needy—an outcome of continually doting on the desires of others—my voice the loudest, half screech and half gurgle, song of a psychotic drain. "The Wisemen lot is open till ten! We won't fight over which one is best! I'll pick the tree out and carry it so you don't hurt your hip more!" The tan slacks extending across the upraised leg rest seemed appreciative of that offer, shifting just a bit, an important bit, as it would take many such incremental shifts for the stiff man to rise off the upholstered bier and enter our lives again. "I'm gonna pick it out. Not you, fatso!" cried competitors too many to name. At the dining room table mother giggled over a Pierre Trudeau gossip item in a *Cosmo* snatched from the library's free box. A beloved poinsettia next to her elbow spread its leaves like open wounds. To have any hope of survival, that morbid plant must be kept clear of the heat blasting through tarnished wall vents, heat that conversely breathed odious life into the couch stains, and carpet cat dung, and damp canvas tennies leaned against the vent and draped with slush-soaked bobby socks I wore as mittens since nothing better could be found in the kitchen broom closet full of suspect muffs, single galoshes, combs, crusts. (My tougher brother, Howard, went without mittens; my three sisters remained indoors.) A shadow—whose?—cried: "There's no place for Santa to put presents if there isn't a tree! We gots to go to the Wisemen lot!" The lot on busy Brady Street that lodged in the mind like a dream. The lot not there in October but then, after Turkey Day, the ball field behind Madison Elementary School became a forest overnight. *Perfect lines of northern pines arranged by height on the urban Iowa tundra. Scribbles of festive lights stretching between speaker-topped poles. Generator singing a buzzing duet with Bing and Nat King Cole. Booted tree buyers crunching blue snow no one had written a carol about yet. The three Wisemen continuing their eternal journey on the plastic banner lashed to the chain-link fence. And amid the sudden forestation the scrumptiously ramshackle hut of Santa-capped Kiwanis Club members, one handing out candy canes, another counting*

*cigar box proceeds, a third thrusting a purchased tree through the
funnel that bound the limbs in netting as though they were the fins
of a green dolphin harvested from a frozen sea of air.* "The Wisemen lot! The Wisemen lot!" went our frenetic chant. Cigarette
smoke responded: it compiled above the Metro section, ghost of
a snowcapped mountain that swelled until an avalanche occurred.
The paper slid down aching legs that had not been right since
a teenage injury. Revealed was the buzz-cut encased in fumes.
And below: black eye-frames, ochre gaze, classic schnoz, plump

puffing lips, slack stubble-darkened cheeks and neck dough pouring into the undone collar of a tight ketchup-splotched Van Heusen shirt tucked too deep. Or were the slacks yanked too high? Anyway, the belt's dark loop, like a surreal lasso, threatened to capture the two horn-like tips of the chest bucking against striped cotton. Our father, in early decline, hallowed be his agony. We cheered. Beauty being in the eyes of kids who beheld someone who could give them what they must have: a Christmas tree. He smirked and snorted—cruelly, I thought then, but not now, understanding he must have been as desperate and frazzled as we were, if not more so. Surely more. For there was no money for a tree from the Wisemen lot, he thought sourly, and then he faced a mob that would get limbs, one way or another. With twisting effort he wrenched a partly moist, partly phlegm-crisp hankie from a nether pocket, and snotted afresh. Surely his sinuses would explode and eject his eyes from their sockets, but no, the pupils were still typeset like periods on the yellow blankness trying not to take note of us and failing at that failure—seeing more than he ever wanted to see. I glared at the scuffed slippers swinging an inch to the left, inch to the right, keeping time to a show tune we weren't hearing. Beetle-browed Howard cast his ruffian stare at the ceiling, which told our story in a Chinese of cracks, then meanly (but bravely: even I, her favorite, had to admit) berated mother: "What are you laughing at?" She kept laughing, hovering like a coroner beside the bloody leaves of her poinsettia. (My favorite flower, the blue morning glory, had the good sense to close up at night: night I knew to be dangerous.) Wizened Elizabeth, tremulous, olive-skinned, pinched a millimeter of flab, oblivious to father foolery, lost in a gothic dreamworld—but fair-haired Marianna, plush of face and scarily wide-eyed, considered the phenomenon of daddy's belly shelves and abrupt mammaries. *Was he a mommy too?* The family's baby, Nathan, tubby and freckled, sat blinking on the floor next to petite Nanette, the second-youngest, features carved by emotion into an ivory fineness. *No money for a tree?* The thought echoed in every internal canyon of every startled on-looker. *No tree on Christmas morning?* It was more troubling than finding three lumps of coal in your sock. Were we that bad? It was Charles Dickens times ten. We had once belonged to the Arsenal country club. Not fully belonged—no putting, no dining, no dancing—but belonged enough to visit the swimming pool above the men's locker room and golf cart stable. Was the year that much worse than recent difficult years when there was a tall (if lopsided) winking spruce teasing our cats with minty needles? It was—said his next clattering cough.

NO MOOLAH FOR A TREE? ("Moolah" Elizabeth called money because she liked her words not to be the words of anyone else. I understood. I was the same way, and mother too—language as much-needed currency, voodoo charm to fling in the path of approaching demons.) No cashola, lettuce, scratch, dough, bread, bucks to buy a tree? Yet somehow doubloons existed to buy Spanish peanuts and the poinsettia and bologna ("bow-log-nah" in Elizabeth-speak) and red boxes of Mead envelopes ("in-vuh-lops"). Stationery was as necessary as saltine crackers in a family of word-junkies. And the means to pay for it often came from Grandpa Stanley, who lived across the river in Rock Island. Grandpa who listed on swollen gout feet, stalking bottles, and then collapsed in a purplish snoring heap, only to wake with the goat's snort, and then pass out again, while Granny occupied a dark back bedroom, trying to make her stroke symptoms last—the perfect escape. Grandpa's bathrobe pockets were our plaid flannel bank. In order to make a withdrawal, however, we must endure the stifling air of that chill brick house, where windows were never opened, where I swear the furnace and the central air-conditioning ran simultaneously, one machine trying to fry Stanleys and the other trying to freeze them to death. A stale snowless Siberian Hades populated by one monster and ten thousand fears, and we visited it almost every night, mother and I, and sometimes Elizabeth too, and sometimes just mother and Elizabeth, but not usually. We were Granny's lifeline, along with Uncle Eubie, my mother's brother. Grandpa asleep in his chair was no less an assault than Grandpa awake. He wheezed violently, slumped forward as if he'd been bludgeoned by the cone of Tiffany lamp light. The leather tack-studded chair was wedged between two tables. On the higher of these, the long one against the wall, a Salem cigarette burned in a butt-filled ashtray. The small table on the other side held a shot glass, the latest empty pint of Canadian Club, and a tall boy can of Old Style beer. A sot, Grandpa, and what a job that was. The grizzled fishermen faces on mantel meerschaums were virginal compared to his visage. From the neck up he resembled a gigantic plum dissolving into end-of-the-world colors. The face was all jowls—jowls that had co-opted and hideously fattened the lips, nostrils, eye sacks. The whole mess hung at chest level, and dandruff-flecked cowlicks uncoiled off the scalp. That belted robe was not belted enough, open above the knot, and open below. A hair-mossed red chest. Scabrous legs appended to the feet with their blue balloon toes. Other exposed features my eyes usually managed to avoid. It was my job to sit there, on the couch, at the ready to talk Chicago Cubs baseball (and distract him) while mother tended Granny. I listened to the breathing climb and ebb, and climb again. I stared at the coffee table, with its fanned *Forbes* magazines, and *Fortunes*, and the cheddar-cheese hue of the proudly placed *History of the Stanleys* genealogy pamphlet. Night after night, it went this way. It was ordinary to me; in a way, better than home. No bugs. Clean carpet. And a pay-off for the abuse taken. Granny's bedroom door was open a crack, making it possible to hear the manic lilt of my mother dramatically reading aloud the *Crittenden County Express*, the not-new news from a rural area in northern Kentucky that Granny had made the mistake of leaving long ago—some red-dirt paradise where apparently people mostly played Uno and Rook, drank coffee, ate caramel sheet cake and peach cobbler, then let the editor know about it. My granny took my hand once a visit, her grip a frail five-bar cage I could have broken out of, but I liked Granny to take my hand, she meant no harm to anyone, her brittle little voice praised "lilies of the valley," flowers her mind was full of, and on her bedside table was the candy bowl. She never left that room unless she had a guard with her—my mother, Uncle Eubie, or Beatrice, the maid—which meant she rarely left, an invalid by choice, lying on the covers in her faded daisy dress, listening to the rain record Eubie had gotten her to drown out Grandpa's ranting about "Stanley royalty" he was related to, and the castles that were his birthright, and the luxurious Olds he was going to buy just because its picture had zoomed across the thirty-six-inch television console on the floor next to the slate fireplace with its gilled bellows and rack of iron pokers. When asleep, Grandpa often stopped breathing—"ape-knee-uh" mother said it was—then he gasp-grunted with such medieval violence that he would have been catapulted headfirst onto the floor had his robe pockets not been weighted down with moolah and doubloons that would become our grocery money if we stayed for three hours, allowing him to complete a rinse cycle of rage. His

jaws juicily chomped, and his flaking spotted lips loosed tides of
rage at Granny for marrying him, rage at Uncle Eubie for being a
sissy schoolteacher, rage at Aunt Deena, my mother's sister (the
chemistry professor), for living far away in Pittsburgh, rage at my
mother for grinning mockingly at his rage and marrying a lawyer
who could not put much food on the table. Foul waves of rhetoric
...followed finally by a trickle of tears when we were half out the
door and had been for ten or fifteen minutes, waiting for him to
realize the moment for pity had come—waiting, waiting, for the
right claw to plunge into the pocket where the tenners were. He

always came through. It allowed him to be the good guy after all, which made his badness more complete. He played us every which way: up, down, sideways. *Grandpa so smart he passed the state civil engineering test without attending college and cofounded a local engineering firm that constructed highways and bridges across Illinois... a builder now in the full-time business of destroying himself, dismantling relatives.*

"SO WHY DON'T YOU GO OVER TO GRANDPA'S and borrow tree money?" I asked father. He failed to appreciate the suggestion. (If I even made it. Maybe I only thought it, keeping my lips bitten—what a fantasy, my father on the begging couch in the wheezy dim. But he and my mother had been married at that very house, in that very living room, on January 26, 1963, after meeting a few months before at the Great Ideas book club event hosted by a Blackhawk Junior College professor. As far as I knew, my father had never been back to visit Mr. and Mrs. Stanley since the vows, ring, kiss, and cake on the table under that oil painting of fox-hunting dogs bursting into a hut, shocking two knitting peasants. Dr. Miller, my father's father, must have been at the cheap ceremony in his Yves Saint Laurent suit with white-gloved soft-spoken Grandma Rose, another improbable concept...but it would have been harder to picture my idiosyncratic parents being married in a proper church, under the watchful eye of a benevolent God.) Father repocketed the hankie, torso writhing in the process as if he were a patient being turned by a rough invisible caregiver. Who did take care of this damaged man? Only himself, and low-level care it was. He straightened as much as it was possible to straighten while remaining recliner-prone, and scowled that arrogant Miller scowl, a major stroke of a scowl—mouth eyes lips attempting to crawl past the ear lobes. *Beg? I'm Dr. Miller's son. I don't beg.* That's right, I wanted to reply, because we do it for you, lowercase parent—one of two. The lucre he made filing divorce papers for caddies and finalizing dowager wills went first to pay for rent on his office with the view of downtown rooftops and the bending river. Then the mean plodge of his ponderous face relaxed, less shadowed somehow, and the front teeth rabbited out of the mouth's gray hutch. It was his dreamiest, most hopeful, and by far most interesting expression. It offered a glimpse of a star-crossed creator: the writer of those unpublished novels from the 1950s, while still a single man (the row filed on the basement shelf included *Nicholson's Last Game*, *The Red Faucet*, and *Osage Orange*) and the painter of the abstract oils hanging at angles of dejection behind the Y of the television antenna: blue splotch, green splotch, yellow splotch. I balled my fists. The novels, the paintings, were not right. I wanted them to be, I needed them to be. Outside, I could hear, over the babble of brothers and sisters, tire chains rattle up Crestwood Terrace, which wound through the neighborhood like a river, our house clinging to one bend of the continually branching east side geography. Cars labored up hills, down hills, their engines choked on violent transitions. That noise faded out. And through the cigarette fog of the living room wafted a charred but slightly melodious voice—a faint but audible echo of the gifted tenor our father had been at Rock Island High School: "I've got an idea, gang-a-roonie!" The tone tickled Nanette and she responded as the tickled do. I smiled, and Marianna too. It was the voice to love—flying on the whimsical wings of a suffix that proved he was not totally dismissive of the possibilities innate to existence. It was also his most perilous voice—his variation on our word contagion, which probably would not lead anyplace good—but this disease cured the other, the depression. He almost chuckled and that tendril of light in his attitude offered an enticing hint of the art he might have made, his lost art, the art that even if bad would at least be authentically bad, off-kilter in an honest way, non-formulaic, striated with stray gems from the deep shaft of his heart. He snuffed, he puffed, and came out with an idea, stumblingly. Since "your old dad" did not have to go into "the office" tomorrow—the bank-building suite where napping was practiced instead of law (when you asked him how his day was, he mentioned only a nap, although there would also be those moments of horrific wakefulness, scorching alertness, recalling his heyday as the thirty-two-year-old county attorney, one of the rising young Democratic pols, days no less vanished for their temporal proximity)—well, cough, exhale, since it was *the case* that he could take the day off tomorrow, that meant…meant he could use the long-handled cutter from Sears, and the hack-saw, to harvest a Christmas tree in the backyard. Complete silence greeted the suggestion. The house had not been so quiet since before we bought it. We lived in the middle of a city. No harvestable trees grew on the back terrace. From the dining room, mother hollered: "Don't dare touch my lilac bush, Dave! Leave the trumpet vine alone, too!" (Last time he grabbed the cutter—the summer before—he had chopped the vine down to nothing, only to watch it grow back wilder than ever, reasserting its squid-grip on the pillars that supported the small roof over the back stoop, with its love seat and the rusty Bakers Dairy box underneath.) "Aw, go on with ya! I'm after *a tree!*" And he really meant it, we found out.

NEXT MORNING HE DID NOT GO TO WORK to sleep and suffer sporadic bouts of guilt. He did, like usual, rise in rigid sections at dawn and perform the standard pre-office "cleaning-up" (his word) in the untidy upstairs bathroom (cheeks Aqua

Velva splashed, ears Q-Tip reamed, nostril hairs trimmed), and take his usual vaporous recliner breakfast of Camel cigarettes and newsprint and Hills Bros. coffee (black so black it was red), but then he buttoned the buttons left on the heavy black coat dating to a disingenuous flirtation with seminary school and donned *matching* leather gloves and an elastic neck warmer called a dickey (a yarn python), and despite the severe indications of a.m. normalcy, the weirdest thing happened. Without a pause he did what he hesitated most to do. He diverged from a monotonous, deceptively simple, life-saving and life-ruining routine. He did *exactly what he said he was going to do*, when he never did what he promised, or hardly ever. Our father extricated the hack-saw and the stick with snipper tip (steel toucan beak) from the roach-infested basement. Each step down, and up, hurt. He made it, though. He reached the backyard with ample armaments and attacked our overgrown hedges next to the pebbled concrete wall that supported the terrace above, where a Santa blinked on a sill and homebound Mr. Hickey sat at a Formica table in his sweater vest and red bow tie, contemplating a LOW SODIUM can of tomato soup, the dietary plunge to be, or not to be, taken. "What the H-E-double-toothpicks is dad doing?" snapped Elizabeth, peeping through a porthole rubbed in kitchen-window steam. "This is an outer utterage!" Or utter outrage. "He's out of his mind! Shrubs aren't trees!" What would Mrs. Spratt across the alley in her kimono think? And Mr. Dankert, beer truck driver, who dominated the terrace below? We listened for sirens, watched for the men in white coats, and F-14s too. Wreaths of breath swirled around the head of the hulking shrub harvester. His face, in the winter light, was a splendid silver, and pasted across it—from end to end—a look of ecstatic distress, of strategic focus on particular fronds of greenery. "Who does he think he is?" mother said. "Paul Bunyan?" Father seemed to be having a ball out there: the struggling lawyer reborn as woodsman, and working hard. Unlike Elizabeth and my mother, I was starting to fall for father's quirky new act. Each time he leaned to reach a frosty branch, a straight aching leg rose behind him and above the coat's hump, his frame at an equi-awkward-distance from land and sky. Because of his ailing hip, bending or reaching was always painful. The back of the preposterous fulcrum of him upended as the front strained to add another twig to the pile accumulating on frozen ground. He had no touch for bladework like the famous murderers whom mother often mentioned (at my bedtime, in her rustling-leaves voice), a rogue's gallery including Richard Speck, the "drifter" who had filleted nursing students in a Chicago dorm (except the one hiding under the blood-soaked bunk). Father was no Speck, and yet he did collect blades: those he was now inflicting on shrubs, and the electric razor he butched us boys with, and the scythe obtained after neighbors called the cops to report the ten-inch length of our lawn, and a curved pink-handled drug store oddity called a "grapefruit knife." Did this obsession have to do with Dr. Miller, pom-pom-hat Rotarian, who purportedly made a mistake when setting the broken leg of his teenage son? My father had limped to the podium to sing a solo at his graduation, my mother said. She returned often—with relish—to the notion that he had been maimed by his own father and the allegation—true or not—became morbid gospel in my mind. For it went well with things I could see with my own eyes. The way Dr. Miller doted on his other sons at my father's expense. My father's inability to heal even after his hip was replaced. "Your father thinks of himself as a cripple," she whispered. "And has since..." According to her—the true crime historian—the blades father purchased were close relatives of Dr. Miller's negligent scalpels. It was history's circle tightening. It was symbolism worthy of Hitchcock, or the Bible: the story of Isaac and Abraham. "H-E-double-toothpicks!"

Elizabeth yelped again. "He's collecting branches! What for?" We found out when he lugged the bough bundle inside and wired it to the old tree stand, forming an evergreen morass quickly christened "Twigmas!" by Nanette, who was not yet old enough to be appalled by every askew thing she saw. As soon as she chirped the name, the atmosphere lightened. The word was perfect—full of a dumb all-conquering love. She got it right by getting it wrong, rescuing a season that belonged to her. Nanette was born in mid-December, and seen in the paper a few days later, balding head sticking out of a fur-trimmed nursery stocking. She was another imagination battling the scourge of family reality, beating it back briefly, winning never-to-be-forgotten victories. All hail "Twigmas!" Any Davenport family could visit the Wisemen lot and net a tree, only we had a tree from our lot. More cheers of: "Twigmas! Twigmas! Twigmas!"

HIS MISSION ACCOMPLISHED, the immoderate woodsman collapsed behind the *Quad-City Times*, and stayed there, taking surprisingly little credit for his triumph. Whenever Nanette tugged the newspaper, he groaned: "Not in the holiday spirit yet, goozie. Long way to go…" His leg bone's unnatural position continued to ruin the hip socket, which had already been replaced once, at the Mayo Clinic, right before family fortunes took their most precipitous dip. Father had metal in him like a soldier. It hadn't helped. His leg still dragged. From the Ozark Airlines trip to the Minnesota hospital he got, in the end, what? His tacky pride in having had a serious operation unknown to many Americans (though tens of millions would have it by the 1990s). And a rare plastic card to show to airport officials when the metal detector went off, the card proving he was not a hijacker of Pan Am jets. He did not go to airports, though. He stayed home in an armchair better called a leg-chair, a half bed for his broken half, and moped behind the epidermis of current events. Any knock on the door (the bell had long been broken) caused him to scream: "No one answer it!" If I was bitter about his injury, and I was certainly bitter, very early bitter, it was because the hip prevented him from showing up at my choir concerts (he said the folding chairs were too hard) and from playing catch with me in the backyard. It could take him as long as two minutes to get in or out of the car seat that had been altered by a mechanic to go back an extra six inches and pancake the knees of whoever sat behind him. "What about now?" Nanette tried again. "Are you in the spire-rut?" He exhaled a cliff of smoke, and the words "No pep." The man did, though, have a few *Yep*s in him. There were, over the years, some drives to view light strings on west side ranch houses, reindeer on roofs, the front-yard nativity scenes—but he spaced these *Yep*s out very carefully. A friend could know me for years and not see my father and understandably doubt I had one. His reclusiveness was a self-medication, like those cigarettes. Above the smoky mountains, on a fireplace mantel cluttered with junk mail and poetry anthologies, stood a greasy clock radio tuned to KRVR, an easy listening station that employed no announcers, playing the schmaltziest Christmas music around the clock. He himself had put the radio up there to jump-start his stalled spirit, although asking Howard or me to kick him in the chest would have been wiser. The songs sounded like they had been arranged by a sanitation worker for a garbage-compactor choir, manger and baby disposed of, liquefied. It made me wonder: what depressed father most? Money problems? Marriage problems? Dr. Miller's alleged crime of incompetence in the medical office after a son had broken his leg while pushing a friend's car out of a snow bank? Or were *all* those severe realities swirling bluely inside him at once, like cigarette smoke, one trouble obscuring another, a blinding blizzard of misfortune that usually paralyzed him, but also could inspire stunted expressions such as *Nicholson's Last Game* and *Oil Paintings #1–10* and Twigmas? Only *stunted* was a relative term. Twigmas seemed an impressive advance, bad in a better way, some unique and useful way, unlike the unpublished novels. What good were they? When my faith in him wavered daily, they served as his chief defense. He pointed me to the dusty gold embossed bindings, challenged me to read the unreadable books: experience their Faulkner genius, unrecognized, yet awaiting Stockholm. The extreme obvious ineptness of Twigmas protected it from his fatuous tendency to brag and my tendency to insult. The pine contraption provoked only natural sweet responses—the creator felt sorry for his creation, and those he had made it for, we children, had a tender empathy for the creator's wild mistakes. Father had taken the sacred central symbol of the American consumer Christmas, and, though meaning well, done a hack job on it that the Grinch (or Dr. Miller or Grandpa Stanley) would envy. Six drooping moping aborted limbs, each pointing a different low direction at room shadows that no joy could ever penetrate. And he had had such a whistling good time slapping the malformation together, yearning to prove he was an "artist of the beautiful" capable of weaving life's rawness into meaningful new forms. The mess of Twigmas impressed mother. Her perversity and audacity had been, for a minute, topped. Jealousy brought out the satirist. "Oh, Dave. It reminds me of the Watts Towers. How inventive! Now let's deh-core-ate!" Her every exaggerated expression was framed starkly by bowl-cut bangs plastered to a worry-ribbed forehead.

She cradled a candy bag that had fallen onto the drug store floor and been stepped on and—complete with treadmarks—placed in the half-off bin for her to find and appreciate. The treadmarks made the butterscotches taste fantastic to her. It was like she was eating the bottoms of the boots of all the enemies that had stepped on her, every enemy except the one who did her the most injury—herself. She had earned admirable degrees, undergraduate and law, and somehow made out of them a girlish squeal over half-off candy. That descent tormented me. I mulled it incessantly. But defeats were all that seemed to inspire her. "Who wants to deh-core-ate? 'Tis the season to be merry!" Scared cats leaped. "It's a holly molly folly jolly Christmas!" The month-long sugar high made looking into her eyes like a bowling alley visit, balls rolling toward white pins. Side to side she rippled and jiggled, barely contained by the tight blue wool dress even stickier than her forehead—traced with feline fur, cellophane bits, newspaper filaments. Howard, Elizabeth, Marianna disappeared. Nanette and Nathan clapped, hooted. "Come on, Benji Angel! Help me bring down deh-core-aye-shuns." No Twigmas boughs looked strong enough to support an ornament, let alone one string of lights, but "deh-core-ate" we would, I heard it in her stubborn voice. "Ho-ho-ho mistletoe!" She snatched a plastic spoon off a couch cushion and held it above my head and smooched me, tongue leading. The kiss tasted of coffee and midnight. We mounted the carpeted stairs and stomped dirty laundry that had not made it to the basement washer, dryer. The ornament boxes were in the attic, where my cat Whitey had turned yellow and died of liver cancer in a Famous Footwear shoe box. She felt safe nowhere else. I buried her underneath the lilac bush, having made the hole with a gravy spoon. (Not a sooty white cat, a pristine snow drift of a cat sleeping on a summer porch of memory.) I did not favor visiting the mephitic attic stench of piss-poop-fur-dust mixing with the chemical odor of fiberglass insulation loosely installed by father, trying to be creative again. The ceiling vomited pink fluffs. A bare dangling bulb cast interrogating light on overturned boxes spilling shirts cords mags and long-overdue library books. (We were a plague on Miss Rochelle Murray, the children's librarian.) "There's a box!" I cried—eager to exit before ceiling fluffs joined to form an abominable fireproof snowman with bologna breath. "There's the other box!" hollered mother. Green tinsel tentacles trailed from both boxes. We holly-jollied our way down the narrow dark stairs to the stifling second-floor room—father's— where he went to bed but did not sleep, would lie awake under mangy polyester blankets and eerie serrations of smoke, sipping coffee from the mug that painted the impression of the rings of hell on the bedside table. The upstairs hallway was brighter, thanks to light that had crawled up the stairs from the landing window, which offered a view of Mr. Hickey's side hill, not bathed in sunshine but appearing sewn into a fabric of glimmers by white needles of busy rays. Symphonic coughing greeted our return to the living room, followed by aggressive sports-section rattling. Translation: *Leave me out of this new holiday nonsense. I'm not in the spirit yet, and might not ever be.* "Who wants to deh-core-ate besides Benji Boy!?" Everyone did—except Howard. He winged the threadbare styrofoam ball at Twigmas, then a gingerbread-man head, then a cat, then two kittens, then tennis shoes. "Rascal!" scolded mother, proud of him. "Look what you did." He looked, sneered, fled upstairs to the bathroom, its crap-blackened toilet bowl, his *Tor* comic books. We surrounded the victimized tree. Twigmas had survived. It had toppled but had lost none of the limbs wired together by a master of domestic bondage, the Man in the Ink Mask. He grunted along with the KRVR music grind: another forlorn and fatal rendition of "Away in a Manger." Mother and I righted Twigmas. Hooraying Nanette danced. Elizabeth whispered in my ear: "It's not the worst I've seen in the living room. The worst was when dad put the Donald Duck baby pool under the ceiling leak." He had, I nodded, good point. Elizabeth made only good points. Marianna tugged the spread newspaper, asking: "Are you in the Christmas spirit yet?" "Afraid not, goozie!" father barked, and then: "Can't say I'm there yet, muffin!" He was, suddenly, overjoyed at one thing—the cozy feel of his own gloom. (The life ahead so much more painful and difficult to accept than the fact of mortality itself. What to do with that life? How to answer the challenge of days that yawned open like a universe in need of stars? How to star in your own life, fill that void with a glitter?) I closed my eyes and sniffed Twigmas and reported, "It smells like a ten-footer." Miracle number one. Then KRVR broadcast a ten-minute calliope version of "Silent Night," proving that carnival instrument belonged in both heaven *and* hell. (Wouldn't it be nice—one silent night, at least one in a lifetime.) Then Elizabeth hung aluminum balls at regular intervals on the haggard boughs (Elizabeth did things only in regular intervals), and Twigmas did not collapse. Miracle number two. Then Nathan ate tinsel. Then Nanette and I wrapped an aluminum garland around and around and around and around the corroded tree stand, totally hiding it. "What a wonderful job," crunched mother, mouth full of candy ribbons. "But we're not done!" I admonished. Twigmas had no star, nor any lights. Elizabeth cradled Twigmas while I tried in vain to find a place for the cardboard star. Poor Twigmas had no defined top, wider than it was tall. Its ragged branches forked in more directions than a compass could dream of pointing. "Forget the damn star," advised my sister. "Watch your language!" yodeled mother, who never swore because she could make almost any word sound obscene, and, as if that weren't enough, also bent everything you told her into a shape that advanced her paranoid view of the world as a sick degraded place where your son was likely as not to be a murderer of the innocent (because you showed him how) and exhibitionism was the only acceptable lifestyle. "Oh, go wash your hair!" snarled Elizabeth. Mother giggled to show she had no feelings, could not be hurt. Was it another act? It was ridiculous, it was all true: the true act of her. I inhaled father's exhaled smoke

(smoke to become world-famous within ten years—the deadly secondhand variety). I set the star aside, but lights Twigmas must have or our Christmas would not be plugged into the Christmas the rest of the nation was celebrating while lamenting and deploring. How would we get the lights to stay on frail limbs? I had another of my cockamamie thoughts, the sort that swiftly became addled notions. Borrowing heavily from daft machinery in cartoon panels encountered in the Rube Goldberg library compilations I had checked out, I envisioned hooking a clothes hanger to father's pine contraption and winding a string of antique bulbs around the wire. It turned out, though, that nothing of the kind was necessary, because the lights—unbelievable as this might sound—*wanted* to be hung after a depressing year in the attic. They simply refused to slip off after being gingerly slung on Twigmas by wincing pagans on tiptoes. Miracle number three. "It looks so be-you-tie-ful, kids! Elizabeth, turn off the overhead light. Benji, plug in the string." I located the socket, parting heaps of Hart Crane, jungles of Conrad. And Twigmas throbbed like succulent Tastee-Freez neon on a mid-summer night, its lime green and cherry glows basting the room with a blessedness it had lacked before: energy not our own.

THE OBVIOUS CONNECTION between this emaciated pine and Charlie Brown's unfortunate tree-lot pick was not voiced by anyone. Or, I should say, could not be voiced, lest we admit our life was a cartoon, and ridiculous as circumstances often were, always, on some level, they remained serious, too. This was the life we had been given to lead, the only existence, and thus priceless, whatever the markdown on reality's tag. "Five cheers for

Twigmas!" I shouted after the lighting, and everyone agreed: it was miraculous to see winking lights and heirloom ornaments on wired-together shrub limbs. Twigmas quivered, on the brink of tipping over, but Twigmas did not tip, rooted—I had to think—by our deep desire for the tree to work out, since it really was the sole option this lean year. "That's the ticket! Wowsa wowsa!" added father, lowering his newspaper to just below nose level. Often it seemed like that nose was all the face his face needed. The nostrils stared at you and, in their way, listened to you, and certainly they made more noise than the average novel. "Beautissimo!" A formidable dignity was to be attained merely by breaking any speech pattern inherited from the previous generation. "Right-a-roonie! Nuts. Spilled my coffee. Mother, a rag!" Like Blackstone the magician, she yanked three rags out of the patent leather gullet of Moby Purse, flopped next to the bobby-sock-frying wall vent. "Blast it! A clean rag! These smell like"—just what he could not say, the 1950s had him by the throat again—"they—um—aw. Go on with ya! To the devil with you monkeyshiners! Wiseacres!" Lucifer's street address was probably hidden in the purse's belly, but there were more important places to stop (even for pagans) on this day before the day before Christ's birth. We must, for starters, visit the bank teller behind the pea green drive-through window decorated with snowflakes and elves and Santas. This slight squeamish bachelor (and child at heart) was a legend to us. He wore the reindeer tie. He offered customers candy canes from a red bucket, the last of three buckets (he had eaten the contents of the others during breaks). He loved Christmas so much it made him sick to his tummy. Every family member but father—who claimed not to accept charity—rushed now toward the next bank teller hand-out, screen door slamming a separate slam for us each, the frame shuddering as brothers and sisters zagged across snow clumps, dead grass, and frosting swirls of mud. The purse-dragging orchestrator of Yuletide mischief brought up the rear: one coat button but it was a big glossy onion-like button and it was in the best place, the middle. I was struck on my way out not just by Howard's elbow but also by the fact that the holiday's momentum had barely been slowed by the low and faintly lit tree with no trunk in a corner of the living room. Miracle number four. Twigmas had increased our appreciation of the unchanged elements of Christmas—the silly teller Mr. Krill and the street decorations and the department store window displays we would visit after draining the teller of hospitality. Better make the most of familiar holiday rituals before they vanished also, possibly taking the entire season with them.

WE PILED INTO THE CAR sticking halfway out of the tiny garage that had been designed, I think, for horses. Mother turned the key and the car wheezed. The car died. Then we children stomped on the floor mats and the engine started and we took credit and mother imitated Jackie Gleason, bellowing "How sweet it is! And away we go!" (she thought it was a literary allusion, and she was right) while angling the dented boat out of the garage cottage and down down down the steep alley to the ice skating rink called Jersey Ridge Road. We almost hit a telephone pole. A second pole jumped out of the way, then a third. Those frisky poles. It was day. In the house it had been hard to tell. The many windows, smudge mosaics, were never washed. It was dusk inside, but outside—a new day at a time of year when days were shortest and most precious. Bald tires slid onto River Drive, and ahead, under the trestle beam Xs, loomed that tricky S curve—the

S that had resisted every effort to straighten it—the S that I guessed stood for Society. The car and all in it lurched left and right and onto the straightaway alongside the wide Mississippi, which had become a huge freshwater jigsaw puzzle, as it did each December, its gray-blue ice slabs stacked like flapjacks or pushed into teepee formations by the frigid cocoa current. Sewage plant. Hostess Twinkie factory. Robin Hood Flour plant. Al's Wine-burger restaurant. KSTT, home of DJ Spike at the Mike. From a distance the emaciated skyline of downtown Davenport prom-ised nothing sweet—but don't be fooled, below was the teller's cube. We reaped our crinkly cellophane-wrapped booty from his beige drawer, filled to the brim. He tried to smile a smile that could serve seven moochers and almost did it. His fingers flut-tered like crabs waving good-bye to high tide. I could tell mother had wanted the "experience" of yelling into the speaker hole to last longer. She never liked to relinquish a stage, and especially not a stage where she could play opposite a shy nostalgic fellow who was willing to let her have all the lines. For the next fifteen minutes she talked about nothing but Mr. Krill, which was not his name, but the one she thought he should have. "Mr. Krill!" she said too loudly, as if we in the car were separated from her by plate glass (and in a way we were). So overjoyed at the holidays that he looked pallid and underjoyed because of a sore tummy-tum-tum, Krill was one of those "in-die-vidge-u-ales" whose frequent minor illnesses forced them to concentrate on their health, which helped them to live longer. What? "Valley-tude-in-air-eons" such lucky skeletons were called. My goodness, Christmas was a time of mys-terious restorative afflictions as well as the terminal illness of hope and other diseases that cheer-spreading spread. Flu. High blood pressure, Harpsichord Overindulgence Syndrome. Not to men-tion suicidal thoughts inspired by electronic yule log gluey glow and brass angels that flew in wobbly uncertain circles when you lit candles under them. Fewer and fewer citizens shopped downtown now that NorthPark Mall had opened on the outskirts, joining popular discount barns Kmart and Target, but eccentrics (the seekers, the nomads, the unpublished poets) who did make the epic jaunt to the city's former center were greeted by the tumid lamppost wreaths and flickering sleighs of lights suspended by no visible means over streets so empty that the most shocking thing was to see another downtown shopper like you, marching east or west, festively inconsolable or inconsolably festive, no bag in hand because no mind had been made up about a gift. How could a mind be made up when thoughts of autopsies danced in one's brain? When the deluge of candy canes prompted apocolyptic visions of red-striped hooks clicking against the levee wall and other canes placed, like omens of disability, into the palms of seemingly healthy children? When sales merchandise was too often sold out, if it had ever really been available? 'Twas the season when even "well-adjusted" Americans came close to resembling my unright parents, paralyzed yet restless, forever searching for new ways to be stuck. The holiday refined a life's diffuse troubles into one big concentrated difficulty sporting antlers plus a white beard, and in doing so—season of rebirth or not—Christmas delivered you back to your anonymous meandering existence, on Third Street, and the feeling nothing was good enough for you, nor you good enough for it.

BUT AT NORTHPARK MALL, and at Marc's Big Boy restaurant near Interstate 80, December was even uglier—uglier because indoors the power of ugliness was concentrated by walls and ceilings and shut doors. I was thankful we were in downtown with gentle Mr. Krill and clumsy old buildings, and not out there, enduring the antiseptic willies. I had been to Big Boy with mother many times at night, at all ages, escaping smoking father, escaping screaming children, escaping any true chance of escape, joining the mass of incompatible couples slouched in Day-Glo booths and ordering grease. In the parking lot stood a sculpture of the only Big Boy in the city goofier than me, and I was glad he made the effort. Red shoes, orange overalls, cowlick and a look of…put it this way: he should not challenge even Li'l Abner to a chess match. Vertebrae rattle of coat hangers when you entered. Stern truckers on counter stools eating breakfast at nine at night, and the lone man at a two-person booth, walrus mustache, shirt with too many pockets, gaze feasting on weapons in a gun-collector magazine. The waist-high catacomb of the larger orange booths culminating in the Plexiglas casket of the salad bar, lemon JELL-O halo and charnel bacon bits and aluminum soup kettle coated with black plastic. Husbands and wives stared at uneaten fries, unable to think of a civil word to say, or any word. Stuck for the sake of "the children" their stuckness tormented. Stuck in obedience to vows they could not remember the wording of. Stuck because everyone in their card circle was stuck with a bad hand and who were they to be better? Loyal to the point where loyalty became a betrayal of reality: blood-treason. Heart-stuck and mind-stuck, faces extra rigid during holidays, nearly ceramic expressions of self-pity, shame, confusion at being caught in an impossible fix for doing a most possible and understandable thing. Union: that's what creatures desired. People wanted to join and to be joined, tried to join together and suffered uncommonly for making perhaps the world's most common error. Couples of all types, but mired in a similar swamp of surreal ordinariness.

When my mother arrived home, she found herself trapped in a car trapped in a garage so tight it was not possible to open the door unless the handle was aligned with a hole punched into the wall to provide the necessary clearance. All the infuriating inching back and forth—brake, accelerator, brake, accelerator—for her to fit herself perfectly into the perfect jail. She always complained about the ordeal to me in the passenger's seat, but she always kept pressing the pedals, and not for nothing. It was what she knew how to do. It was what life had made her expert at—the tight spot, being cornered and hopeless, but amazingly undaunted. I more than knew the routine. I had come down with the feeling of entrapment quite young—as I had come down with the language contagion. From her I got the most active strain of both infections, I caught it during our intense outings to obscure parks, popular burger chains and discount stores, and Grandpa Stanley's home. At seven, I was obsessively drawing stick figures plunging into flame-filled gorges. I drew a figure, drew an X through the figure, and then drew another figure, another X, dozens of cascading Xed-out figures, each one bent, each one as fractured and partial as the lines I would scribble in the hundreds of notebooks I cradled to my chest in succeeding years, those notebooks to which I fed ink, three words followed by a new line, four more words and another new line, always the same breaks whether it was a poem or story. The America that stretched sense to the breaking point could only be sketched in this broken way, in fragments, in this flow of devolved images and snippets of dialogue descending across a page corpulent with whiteness and negations . . . You did not have to be old or wise to know when you were in danger. What was my mother's plan? She had one, right? I believed I was part of it—all us children were. But the plan was not to form and nurture a family. Maybe it had been once, maybe she had tricked herself into thinking that was what her marriage would be about on the day she said "I do" in Grandpa Stanley's living room, but the marriage was not about that now. She had no wish to hold a family together now that she had a large one. Each night she returned home, but with her returned the stormy ambivalence about most every domestic detail—dishes to cat litter to the man in the recliner. Why had she had kids? She had many uses for kids. We were, in turn, her gossip absorbers, her shoulders to lean on when father barked, her sympathetic jury when she put assistant store managers on trial in the checkout line, her sure way of garnering sympathy from strangers who could then be asked for favors, her couriers carrying bananas to the dapper shut-in on the terrace above ("Tell Mr. Hickey I'll bring him his change later tonight"), her unhappy waiters and waitresses bringing requested treats (condensed milk, pretzel logs) while she lounged on the couch reading Don Marquis satire aloud, and we were also, I guessed, her way of explaining to herself the mystery of why she had been unable to do anything with the law degree she had worked hard to earn. We were an alibi (interesting how the word echoes *lullaby*) and a poisonous curative—a disaster added to another disaster, the one predating us, as if two immense calamities were easier for her to bear than one. But that couldn't be all there was to mother's plan, could it? To go on and on adding disaster to disaster, spreading ever-denser static and fog? It seemed impossible she would not have a better plan—being such a great plotter of plans: three a day, five, six—but then again, in the final analysis, the only thing big about her plans was that they amounted to another trip to the Big Boy. I looked into her mask of grief, seeking the parent I thought I could not live without. What I waited for, dangerously—what I watched for, crazily—was a crack in the garish regalia of her set expressions, a twitch of a persona struggling to shed nonsense and reestablish order. And I listened to the gossip about neighbors, and to misquotations, her wrenching apart famous poems by Edna St. Vincent Millay and Dylan Thomas in a vain attempt to make them her own, one with her particular trauma. (The creative butchery of common words was more successful in my opinion: "in-die-vidge-u-ales" came from her gut.) And when I tired of waiting for her reconstitution from the ashes, I observed the fire-and-ice faces of other Big Boy customers, waiting for their reconstitution instead, and when none occurred after an hour or two (we did the refill thing), I again had an important choice to make. I could choose to believe that what I saw was what I got, was all I could get—hollowness, shallowness and mockery—or I could decide, as I frequently did, to believe I was not a good enough or lucky enough seer, and that the next day, or the day after, I might be a better or luckier seer, able to perceive the actual people who made the mistakes, rather than merely being blinded by the incinerating travesty of their results. I did get lucky once in a while, even with my defensive mother. There were certain moments when her charade frayed, when she fell silent across the table or behind the car's sticky wheel, and I sensed that if I knew the right word or words to say, then a loose thread—any of the many loose threads—could be tugged, and her grotesqueness would dissolve, or peel apart, revealing the mask's soft living lining, a tender face that a violent circumstance had driven into hiding. (Her own self driven into her like a stake.) But what words unlocked rusty Greek masks of the Midwest? I kept saying the four-letter *L* word, but it was not up to the job: L-O-V-E. I had to wait then—watch for the flashes of human beings inside monsters and robots. It was a religion with me. The reason was simple. I did not want to be alone any longer.

"WE'LL VISIT MR. KRILL AGAIN after going to the department store. He'll scare up more candy canes somewhere! Plenty of Santas around to mug. Look for a parking space, kids." There were hundreds, if not thousands, of spaces, and Salvation Army Santa bell-ringers. "Yell if you see a space!" What was the problem finding one? We yelled, pointed. She drove past our choices, convinced—like her husband—that parking downtown could never be easy. "Guess I'll have to drive around the block again." More circles that would get us nowhere but back to the place where we'd started. Each day was rife with circles. Circles around ghostly blocks that appeared abandoned by history while also serving as its most graphic definition. And the driver's mind, like a buzzard, circling around some ancient debilitating wound which she had learned to exploit with such expertise that though she made life hell, it was often easier to feel sorry for her than for yourself. (She dripped pain at high speed, and back then, as now, I associated the traveling massacre of her with a fragment of autobiography she often repeated late at night: "Jumped out of a car when I was a girl in Dixon, rolled into a ditch . . . next to railroad tracks . . . next to the canal . . .") She overshot free space after free space. The smallest errand was the impetus to dive into the core of the city's crisis and from there—so we didn't miss one juicy bit of urban-Iowa trouble—to methodically work our way to the suburbs and NorthPark Mall and the off-ramps, those curving alleys of death. "There's a spot in front of Major Art & Hobby!" She passed it. The sun was nice, though. Light was never nicer than it was downtown, where it had the canvas of stone and brick to brush across. The more neglected a property was, I noticed, the more work light had to do, filling in the gaps and fleetingly making a ruin—or near ruin—appear to have a future ready to be identified. If we ever did park, and get out, I would stare at the sidewalk concrete like it was soil sown with seeds. The cracks were the furrows. They were the slits of the city that always sleeps, or appears always to be sleeping, until a hand reached out of the window of the Dempsey Hotel for a carton of milk on the sill and awakened your eyes to the fact that there were people stowed and stirring behind bricks—the fixed-income hordes who had not cooked a meal for themselves in years, the invisible shuffling people who ate at invisible restaurants called "holes in the wall" serving oatmeal and salty stew. Sidewalk cracks were the trail markers leading to these holes in the wall, proof of the terrific force of humbleness that only the softest footsteps could convey. I looked for more hands reaching for cartons on SRO sills. Who had taped red-nosed Rudolph to a pane? Who dressed a fire escape in baubles? Elizabeth looked for flea markets perhaps—she collected rag dolls and "miniatures," teensy tiny desks and harps. Howard, I'd guess, looked for girls. But what, exactly, did I know about brothers and sisters? We lived in our own worlds of dreams and desires—those worlds clashing one moment but the next as separate as if existing in different galaxies. All I could do was *want* to know them and, alternately, be afraid of knowing their unique version of the fear that bound us together while pushing us apart. But for the moment we were still in our junker, rumbling by the new library partially paid for by our overdue fines, our pennies. It was hard to believe. Palatial two-story windows, white marble verandah. Then past Simon and Landauer Men's Wear, Source Book Store, The Hungry Hobo Sub Shop, Woolworths, the Davenport Bank Building. My eyes climbed to the window of father's office and entered like a burglar. *Only there was nothing there I wanted. He could keep the outer office flag that had once flown in front of the courthouse when he was county attorney. He could keep the three framed degrees on the wall and watercolor of*

Gettysburg and the desk where a secretary, Mrs. White, had once typed. He could keep the creepy brown bulk of uncracked law books and the West Law Supplements and mahogany desk and vibrating recliner. The only question was whether I should torch the recliner because I was sick of recliners and the moods they put men in. In my worst nightmares I battled recliners with black squirrel tails and fanged cushions. In front of Shannon's Cafeteria—the Shangri-La of chicken dumplings—stood a tall finely decorated tree. With a telescope of curled fingers I spied a Twigmas hidden in the center of the shapely greenery. Twigmas was the new heart of the holiday—Noel lessons and Noel passion needed to be mangled, too, if they were to reflect any truth about a mangled planet.

"There's a place!" I shouted. "Right in front of Petersen's Christmas windows!" Mother finally parked. We had seen these displays ten times already but must walk past them once again, followed by a few well-wrapped long-lipped elderly downtown residents complaining of lumbago. They were done having nervous breakdowns and I envied them for that. Mother, me, Elizabeth, Howard, Marianna, Nanette, and Nathan reveled in seeing the sole moving part of each display perform on cue. Here was proof that the world had at least one working part. Skirted skater skating. Sleigh gliding into the snowy Bavarian village. Toy-shop elf hammering and Santa's roly-poly belly undulating and reindeer soaring over rooftops. We pressed our faces close to the glass as a test and the serene skater kept at it, unafraid. The department store St. Nick was off-duty, possibly recovering from injuries incurred when the six of us had sat on his lap the previous week, but the waxed aisles were haunted by interesting seedy temporary employees in ill-fitting suits. They offered the green-striped candy canes to good boys, and good boys said no. "God Rest Ye Merry Gentlemen" and "Greensleeves," my favorite songs of the season, seeped from speakers, aching correctly as a bone, melancholy in a way that inspired the best long thoughtful walks. These were songs in a minor key. They moaned but not like my mother or father. They moaned proper and stoical. In England a bad day would still somehow continue to be a jolly good, and productive, day. I pictured top hats and cobblestones and Mary Queen of Scots in the locked barred towers and wood-beam inns with horses stomping outside, robes of breath flowing from their nostrils. I hummed along. Mother gripped my shoulder. I was her one and only oldest best helper son, she meant. I got that. It was clear. Then, well, she needed no excuse to change the subject. She felt the need to keep even me, her ally, constantly off-balance with a barrage of non sequiturs. She leaned and whispered, apropos of who or what I did not know, the phrase "John Bircher," alluding to that organization of vanilla men who wanted to keep the country as vanilla as possible. (Hearing the phrase, I imagined plotting scions in bark canoes on an estate lake.) She raised her aching head and railed against the price of French perfume and then lurched into an excoriation of the crooner Andy Williams. "That awful Christmas special! Who does that man think he is?" Andy Williams he thought he was, and he was right, he was Andy Williams: plenty of people agreed. But the network holiday special had a gross way of exaggerating the flaws of the star, whoever he or she was. Goony smiles multiplied and polyester sweaters multiplied, fake snow falling behind the polished figure of the croaking crooner backed by an unseen eunuch choir, various fireplaces roaring as if roasting more than chestnuts, possibly burning the immigration papers of Americans this American tradition excluded, except during the dancing seg-ments. ("John Bircher" references had tainted my vision.) Christ-mas seemed more false when Vegas crooners were involved. It had to do with their heartbeat, I thought. It was too slow: nothing got to them. "Then comes Perry Como, who's even worse!" He was worse, though it was hard to finger why: same red V-neck sweater, identical back-up singers in white loafers, similar set of chunky ski lodge furniture. I kept thinking about it as we spilled out of the store to look at the windows again. What could top the tiny ice skater spinning on the mirror in that snug Mr. Krill world, wonderfully and safely contained? I hoped for the best, knew it was best to prepare for the worst. I had a strong (and correct) feeling this excursion would end at National Grocery, we children running up and down the cereal aisle while the woman trained as a lawyer, but struggling to take society's pretensions seriously, swigged free coffee and stared at rotisserie chickens revolving in their heat lamp torture chamber.

RETHINKING THE TWIGMAS MEMORY, I realize a major mistake. During that holiday we were not as young as depicted. True: Christmas evokes the child in us. Bells ring, channels are changed to tune in passions old for having been young so long. But it's not just that. It's also the fact that the weight of my twelfth year—or the force of its crisis—unbalances the whole of my history by anchoring it in the most turbulent waters. In any case, I would have been a fifteen-year-old ninth grader the Twigmas year—a diet-sliced sliver of the troubled child I was at the start of this chapter, and the newest warbling member of Writers' Studio. Nathan, the youngest, would have been a tubby five (having already had his stomach pumped after eating a poinsettia leaf), and Nanette an eight-year-old pixie with vampire choppers. But the house was the same disaster scene, and I was still a mother's boy (albeit a more nervous sycophant) and all else is accurate as far as I can recall, with a few notable exceptions. By this point we six children would certainly not have gone shopping, or anywhere else, together, except in our wildest dreams. And we had no wheels. The beater perpetually on its last legs had croaked late in the fall. I had a lot of walking and running ahead of me. We had no car for nearly a year. It was the year that father declared he was no longer a general practitioner but a specialist in bankruptcy law and the year that mother—who had been out of law school for fifteen years—at last began her career by volunteering at HELP Legal Assistance, then located on an upper floor of the Putnam Building across the street from the Davenport Bank

Building. (She swiftly earned a paid position, working in an office that she turned into a junk-cluttered extension of our living room, the new—and most influential—pulpit from which to preach her mixed-up gospel of Thurgood Marshall and Dylan Thomas, mockery and compassion in equal measure. I did not doubt that she could hold her own with the younger attorneys wearing jeans and ponytails, or with the impoverished clientele. She too had been a victim and while you did not know exactly what she understood about your suffering, her every sigh and moan made it clear that she had been hurt at least as bad, or worse. That was the bedrock unquestionable. I was at the office often in the beginning, and the place drew what was likely the roughest audience of pushovers you'd ever find—homeless men and women, addicts of every stripe—all of whom she could trust not to question her dubious contentions or suggestions, as she supplied the steam-heated place to sit, the stacks of butter cookies, and an ear eager to hear any brutal complaints. She did assist these vulnerable urban Iowans, though, she really did, fixing the paperwork so that clients received SSI disability benefits or food stamps or other aid. They got their little payments as I had always gotten mine, for sitting and listening politely and submissively to the hodge-podge sermons—change to buy a book at the Paperback Exchange, and the Big Boy burger special around midnight. They returned often to visit a character who professed to want to save the world, but was interestingly determined to exclude her own name from the salvaged-soul list.) During our carless period in a city of ninety thousand, we walked, we took the city bus or hitched rides from Aunt Julie to places we needed to go—Grandpa Stanley's house and libraries and Bishop's Buffet and National Grocery and Shannon's Cafeteria. Things proceeded much in the usual chaotic and melodramatic fashion, almost as if we did own a sputtering

Ford with a loose bumper and power windows that had lost their power to elevate, which is why I'll not excise the car. Had you questioned my family members that carless Christmas, more than one would have proudly insisted there was still a junker in the alley garage. Such was the necessity for, and influence of, fantasy at 15 Crestwood Terrace. We rode public transportation downtown and walked up to Mr. Krill's drive-up window. We did it without a thought that we might be run over. We traveled onward to see Petersen's enchanting holiday windows. Avid wishfulness allowed us Millers to tolerate an unacceptably harsh—yet inescapable—existence. It warped the most obvious facts or even briefly trumped them to create a fraught series of noir fairy tales that were intoxicatingly lived, just as sure as Mr. Hickey lived the sober life of widower and retired real estate agent. Twigmas was a perfect case in point. Less than two days after the crushing news that there would be no tree from the Wisemen lot, those knee-high branches had become towering proof that this holiday was destined to be the most special of all. The money saved on the ten-foot tree would be added to money saved on engine repairs and leaded gasoline, and money saved when father let his secretary go, and money saved on a demolition crew when Uncle Eubie ripped out rotten roach-filled cupboards for free, and money saved on new cupboards when we started storing bean cans and macaroni on the upright piano and dining room table—that fortune in savings to be spent on (what else?) presents from our wish lists. Slogan-soaked guitar-raking John Lennon solo albums for myself, the hunger striker, who had shown a mother that her "angel" was no paragon of loyalty, but a person in such need of space and privacy that he was willing to starve that beloved appropriated fat boy to death on little more than an apple a day. Blubber shelves melted away, rib racks appeared . . . but all else about me remained bloated and unwieldy: my hopes, sympathies, conflicts. Having divided myself in half to simplify things—to cut losses—I actually only doubled them! Regardless, this year of Twigmas, I was sure I would finally get the Lennon solo albums I lacked: *Mind Games*, *Rock 'n' Roll*, *Some Time in New York*, gleaming shrink-wrapped album flaps totemic as tablets. And Elizabeth, first chair flute virtuoso, would finally get a piccolo to play for her flute teacher, Mr. Pope. And Howard, the Swisher Sweets–smoking lady-killer, his trench coat. And boy-crazy Marianna, a mother-of-pearl necklace. And Nanette, a sparkly Schwinn bike; and Nathaniel, Rock 'Em Sock 'Em Robots! Little did it matter that on Christmas Eve there was but one present under Twigmas—the postal carton containing woolens from Aunt Frances, who lived in Kentucky with her miner husband, Chet. She never forgot the Iowa relatives who never sent her a thing. I titled that giftless floor "The Calm Before the Storm." The less we had, the more it must add up to. That was Miller anti-arithmetic. The red felt Christmas stockings Grandmother Rose had sewn for us older kids would be taped or nailed to the mantel of junk mail after midnight, along with ugly (but larger) store-bought stockings for the younger kids that Grandmother Rose could somehow not imagine had been added to our crowd. Her embroidered Christmas socks were artworks, reindeer and snowflakes and sleds, and like the best art, the highest art, those sequins were indefatigable. The socks would show.

MEANWHILE OUR SANTA-IN-THE-SACK-DRESS had flown the cat coop—a good sign on this night. Worn slippers protruding from the newspaper tent were ticking like a metronome, keeping time, at last, with the KRVR carol grind. "In the spire-rut, daddy?

Got pip?" asked Nanette, tugging the Travel section. "Can't say…not quite," he groaned over and over. In case we did not make it to the big day, I had already opened the last cardboard hatches of the Advent calendar given to us by pious Aunt Julie, the wife of our fellow pagan Uncle Eubie, who called Christmas "the Festival of Blights." (I came to favor the term *Festival of Slights*.) Behind the December 24 hatch: sojourning camels. Hatch December 25 revealed guess who. I then carefully pressed the hatches shut again for a reason I could not easily put into words. Superstition? What I told myself was I wanted someone else to have the honor, and it was an honor to open any door behind which you knew there was nothing that could hurt you or complicate your life. The little advent images were predictable but they were gentle and that made them something of a novelty in the house. Even the things that made you happiest—those stilts propping up your dreams: in my case the books, tapes, records—even they did you a certain violence, increasing the separation between what you actually had and what might be had. Dreaming, to be real, had to be dangerous. I flashed back to the first Christmases, when my father had set up tripod lights in the living room. We older ones had gathered on the second-floor landing and jittered and yelled: "Can we come down? Can we?" and got the wrong answer until we got the right one and screamed and rushed down into the white disaster-scene light that coated your sight like flour, the nuclear bakery light, percussion of footie pajamas on the then-new carpet and dolorous ticking of the film in the Super 8 camera and more heat of the lights and the shrill voice: "Your pile is over there! And yours, there!" and on the tree nose-like bulbs of red and green and yellow that soon went out of style with everyone but us, the pointillism of sophisticated blue and white lights causing *ah*-ing across Iowa and Illinois. Now those film canisters were buried under coats in the closet that had no rack, at the foot of the stairs leading from the living room to the second floor. "Midnight Mass!" father shouted. "The Pope on WOC!" (A week later it would be "Turn the channel! Guy Lombardo and the Royal Canadians at the Waldorf Hotel!" Violins sawing away, producing the Old World whine of "Auld Lang Syne" as one year turned into the next, and a last subtly bristled gray anchovy filet slipped from an oval can, its glistening oil the crown jewel of a humble paper plate buffet.) "Midnight Mass!" he chanted, as if he planned to stay up long enough to watch the rebroadcast. He did not mean to stay up. Enthusiasm for the sonorous ceremony was weaker than his obsessive eagerness to maintain his schedule, do what he did in the basement after the 10:30 news (smoke, use the lidless toilet) and then be upstairs before eleven, carrying on as shipwrecked men did: a castaway wedged in a single bed wedged in a room that barely had room enough for corners, his eyelids and boxers and lower lip sagging, *puff puff,* dreaming up unworkable schemes of escape. He would leave the wrapping to whom he knew not and whom he cared not.

ELIZABETH AND I AND MARIANNA AND NANETTE again went over our reasons why this Twigmas Christmas was going to be the best. We were careful to avoid mother's bed, the couch pushed against the wall splattered with Worcestershire sauce—evidence of the seasonal tradition of aiming TV-mix ingredients (the sauce plus melted margarine and three cereals and pretzels) at a Hefty bag and shaking the bag before dumping it out onto trays for baking in the gas oven. TV mix was our pemmican. It fueled my four-socks-on-each-hand sub-zero walks to the welcoming red bull's-eye of the Target store on Kimberly, and the bin of ninety-nine-cent cassette tapes where I had discovered Woody Guthrie, John Lee Hooker, Art Tatum. Was mother there now, a customer telling a clerk how much piccolos should cost? No simple scolding but a serious attempt at mesmerism, the rant about piccolo price intercut with spurious but pleasingly unruly references—her citing of Eugene O'Neill's famous actor father stuck in the same role his whole career, and the nutty marriage of F. Scott and Zelda, and Millay's candle burning at three ends, and so forth. It was mother's hope that the clerk, swaying and hypnotized, would jerk open the cash register and empty into her purse enough money to buy a bike, trench coat, piccolo, three John Lane [sic] albums, and a pearl necklace...Possible. Anything was, at least on the Christmas of Twigmas. I was not shopping with her, as I had on past holidays, munching peanut brittle fragments from the purse and scouring waxy acres of aisles on both sides of the river as we found nothing acceptable—that is, affordable. "More TV mix, Benny!" demanded father, no please, but had he used the word I might have fainted. I filled his bowl, delivered it, and stepped back quick. He was a violently expressive cruncher—another fate, I guessed, of frustrated novelists. The living room traffic was constant on Christmas Eve. Players in our drama rushed in half-dressed and away to finish the next costume change, and cats hissed, and hair was combed and teased and curled to burning. There were comic slips on magazines and paper plates on the floor. There were horrific accusations of theft and abuse. "Mitzi stole my sheet music!" "Nanny hit Nathan!" "Howard's jacking off in the bathroom!" "Elizabeth hid the broomstick cookies!" Action halted only when Twigmas exerted its mawkish but magnetic pull on a reveler. I kept looking and I kept seeing more things about the poor tree, as I still do. On the wall the branches cast the shadow of father's broken leg that had not healed right, of father's broken family tree—broken not just by him, but by his doctor brothers who ignored him, and his doctor father who before any potential visit, always called our house to ask if anyone in the family of eight had a cold, which one of us (or three) always did, and that was that: for professional reasons he must avoid our arena of infection. We were not welcome in his fancy home. Twigmas told that story, and those homely branches pointed to the larger truth of how every family, to a degree, redefines the meaning of Family in some small or large way, and the branches pointed to the smaller truth of what our particular broken family had done to our particular selves—how it had twisted the experience of time into confounding knots and tangles that a lifetime of work would be incapable of undoing. We kids were oldly young; we were closer to death than a fifty-year-old. We took our orders from the horizontal man and the woman in a thrift store shroud—ciphers who shepherded you with their smoke and mirrors. We were not being raised so much as reordered and disordered. The hour hand and the second hand seemed to trip over each other—that was not just how it felt, but how it was. A tale of the most egregious overlap, the past-tense future, the present-tense past, no beginnings, rather only ends that led to other ends, and me in 1978 checking records of old radio shows out of the library, becoming a fan of Lum and Abner rather than Bruce Springsteen, for I was an echo chamber for adult sorrow and had an esoteric need to dilute a vintage dirge with vintage humor. The backwardness of Twigmas said all this in a glimpse, and all of us that night, from time to time, bowed to the shrub limbs dressed in tinsel entrails, toward foam orbs no longer fully covered with a weave of red or gold threads, the scratched metallic balls, the merry-looking bell clusters that if shaken were astonishingly soundless—since their clappers were clotted with cat hair and dust—toward the finger-sized plastic trumpets that attic mice had nibbled, the baked clay chunks of elves and sledders. The modern light string we had arranged blinked frantically, and its colors oozed across the cracked plaster covered with the faded pastel graffiti done by us and our cousins Joyce and Janice: rainbows, suns, peace signs. These lights were America at her short-circuiting best—kinetic revelry of kitsch. The other crap—around the lights—that was too much. That was the grave crap of experiences that rewired your being, and not for the best, or rarely so. Behind Twigmas, a forensic fingerprint-smudged glass door to a built-in wooden bookcase flanked the fireplace where ashes from the artificial-scented log smoldered under a coupon-littered mantel cliff. The boughs shed their needles onto the battered box from Kentucky. Playful black kittens from Moonbeam's latest litter had partially unraveled the green garland wrapped around the tree stand and had also attacked the far end of the light string snaking across the carpet. Gazing too long at the housescape, and Twigmas lodged within it, was to have even your modest gift delusions vanquished and to face the rude reality that tomorrow morning could bring only the worst that discount barns had to offer—stuff that broke at first touch or broke in anticipation of first clutch, brand-new garbage. Country and western 45s: ten for a dollar. But a dose of soberness also granted your eyes considerable news. Finally, I saw the frail boughs for another thing that they were, the most simple and large and wondrous thing: one window into the dark of a distant man. An exotic tangle of wreckage that a crisis had lifted to the surface of his river of sadness and deposited in the humid living room for his heirs to prop up, festoon, tentatively cherish.

THE REINVENTION OF ICE

Active *dreamers — Fruit of a sprawling vision —*
Mr. Creighton's crystal poem — The labyrinth of consumption —
*Post-*Frosty *depression —Moby Purse visits the Investment Club —*
Stressful: *my newest word — Holiday on Ice times 2.3 — Big blue tarp, folded*

Mr. CREIGHTON, FATHER OF MY THIRD-GRADE CLASSMATE
Brad, invented an ice-skating rink that fit neatly into a cardboard
carton, ready for shipping across the continental United States
and Canada. Brad described kits containing bags of screws,
numerous metal strips—dyed purple, for some reason—and a
bundled tarp. After the rink's perimeter was screwed together,
cricket clips on the strips would be affixed to the unfolded tarp,
forming the big blue surprise of a circle. The direction booklet
advised covering the plastic with three inches of water but did
not address the tricky question of where the liquid would come

from during a season when outdoor spigots were ice-clogged. To create the Creightons' own backyard rink, Mr. Creighton had rigged a garden hose to the kitchen faucet, and he trusted that others would also. After all, Americans were smart customers. The patent was pending in busy Washington, DC. An accountant had been retained in the Davenport Bank Building—downtown's lone tower—and the largest PO Box had been rented to absorb the expected tides of orders from Minnesota, Wisconsin, Nebraska, Montreal. Mr. Creighton was an *active* dreamer. He followed through. This mattered an awful lot. Meant everything. A dream unfulfilled often being worse than no dream at all. I loved my own father—the failed politician, unpublished novelist, clientless lawyer—but his general inertia put dangerous pressure on the rest of us. Too many crises could be traced to a living room recliner where he sat mashing cigarette butts into a brass Dutch shoe ashtray, the blue hive of smoke on his shoulders, a man lost in reveries that were invisible shackles. (And other crises, they were due to his peculiar or bumbling actions: for example, ordering a gambling raid on a church bingo hall when he was county attorney, an act of Clouseauesque overkill which had assured his election defeat in 1967.) Mr. Creighton rarely slept, said Brad— not bragging, merely reporting. Brad had red hair and freckled chipmunk cheeks. He chattered only once a week. Otherwise he was quiet, respecting (maybe fearing?) my daily habit of depicting cataclysm with crayons—armies atop opposing cliffs, flaming stick figures falling into an abyss, goners moments after I had created them. I could not call such a picture finished unless every inch of the chasm was filled with burning people. Brad was polite always, patient to a point. At last he tapped my scribbling Angel of Death arm and calmly explained that Mr. Creighton was not going to make *a hundred grand* from the rink, but $95,786. I did not differ.

Brad smiled, the smile slow to grow, but wide, finally. He was stocky like Mr. Creighton, who wore flannel shirts and snowflake sweaters out of season. Mr. Creighton had red hair also, inspiring me to imagine what inventor Alexander Graham Bell would have looked like with crimson sideburns. (Not so hot.) Dad, said Brad, pulled *all-nighters*. Mrs. Creighton trailed right behind that action with checkered thermos, Brillo pad, and cleaners to cut through dream grease. She knew the score. Spouses of the dreamy always did. They must be there with Comet (in her case) or Chagrin (in my mother's). Some husbands offered their wives messy machinations of adoration, while other males remained distant, intent on concealing passion until—voilà—dramatically unveiling the intricate inner workings of the heart's mind, with an invention. Did Mrs. Creighton prefer the ordeal of being married to a genius because she had been betrayed by an urban Iowa Romeo? I knew only so much about her. But from the moment Brad, wearing an Aztec-patterned poncho, whispered news of the mail-order ice rink, I was smitten by the concept, its creator, and the family behind him—including older sister Brenda, who had the longest red hair at McKinley Elementary.

IT BEING THE 1970S—decade of cultural meltdown and baroque morass—I pictured no epiphany lightbulb above Mr. Creighton's head, but, rather, the globular gleam-soup of a lava lamp. I pictured his blue eyes as battery cells hot-wired to his brain. I pictured a thick wrist twisting in midair, demonstrating the physics of his inventions to bespectacled bankers seeking golf gloves in the aisles of Kunkel's Sporting Goods. Even so, from what Brad said, I gathered that previous inventions were not making money. Commercial prospects could change, however, if Mr. Creighton received patents for the electric pillow, thermostatic kite, motorized dog groomer, blade-less butter spreader, crank-powered rowboat . . . and Skid-Ender boots, which sprayed rock salt across icy sidewalks, heel-to-toe pressure flushing the crystals from multiple hollow chambers in the soles. And if patents were not awarded, well, this stuff was still necessary, or at least vital—or if not vital, without a doubt *connected*, the fruit of a sprawling American vision. In order for customers to transport a rink order form safely to the corner mailbox in January, Skid-Ender boots must be designed first. Mr. Creighton did his thinking and tinkering in the split-level ranch above Jersey Ridge Road, six winding blocks from my house and just before the asphalt slithered under the Locust Street Bridge and climbed past a tree-concealed apartment complex where our classmate David Van Camp—the touch-football star—lived. Quickly I grasped that the rink was the most ambitious Creighton project yet. It addressed deeper problems than did a motorized dog groomer. It far surpassed famous late-night-commercial standbys such as the vegetable slicer-dicer, and K-tel's Pocket Fisherman, sold to thousands of gullible boys and hale men who could afford nothing better and were courageous (i.e., stupid) enough to carry hooks near their privates. The rink was social. An event. An evening to be shared by friends and relatives during the darkest months of the year. It was a recreation that tree-concealed apartment complexes might add, and bereft middle schools, and minimum-security prisons where embezzlers could use an outlet for their creative figuring. (Prisoner #34567, plus the figure eight.) How had Mrs. Creighton reacted to the unfurling of the rink blueprint over morning coffee? I pictured her shawl sliding off, her face an agog tic-tac-toe grid filling in with *x*'s and *o*'s. *Eureka! This is it!* Financial failure did not automatically breed ennui, as it did in my home. Sometimes money trouble did the opposite, fueling a feeling that your American Dream was due to come true at any minute. *Ice Capades, Inc. letterhead! Peggy Fleming TV testimonial! Ticker symbol ICE!* Crazier than hope would be a cynicism contending that all of Mr. Creighton's stupendous ideas could disappear into the file cabinet's jaw. America treasured innovation. America, Land of the Norelco shave, Playtex bra, Shrinky Dinks, and Tang. Each month new products pounced on reality, changing how citizens lived and viewed themselves. The Ugly prettified by Revlon and—believe it or not, Ripley—beer shampoo. The Unorganized experiencing efficiency thanks to the copier collation button. And when the ice rink cometh to the urbanized Midwest? Backyards would glisten like scarf-wrapped Dick Button's chirpy outdoor Winter Olympics broadcasts, or Hans Christian Anderson fables. The dormant energy in a lethargic population would be liberated. Aprons and ties and spatulas and briefcases on ice. The flashing ice.

TO SCHOOL BRAD BROUGHT the latest issue of *Outdoor Life*, or a magazine like it. He flipped pages while silly Libby behind us bound herself to a desk with construction paper chains. "Look," Brad said, pointing out an ad nestled within a column of classifieds. LIVE THE WINTER WONDERLAND DREAM! BUILD YOUR OWN SKATING RINK! Under the words, a photograph (postage-stamp scale) of the fun behind Brad's house: skaters, benches, lanterns. Man, what could be neater. At age nine, I might not be able to skate a living inch—too clumsy, nearsighted—but no matter. In fact, my plight uniquely qualified me to appreciate *the statement* the rink made about the possibilities of yards, free time, children, adults—a nation's future. The vision in that tiny, stark ad outshone the thousand-bulb greed of a Las Vegas marquee. If just one family named Jones in the Mississippi River Valley ordered a rink, every Smith would also have to send in checks to keep up with those darn Joneses, and from Dubuque to St. Louis skate blades would churn, spin, glitter... *Want one?* Brad's blue eyes asked—always respectful Brad. I did. I wanted that rink, not some reputation-altering Izod or Adidas shirt. My subversive mother—that overread underfunded firebrand mother of mine, who chose to wear a grimy blouse and distressed tennies because she thought the outfit connected her to American female martyrs like Emma Goldman and Susan Anthony—had taught me (and not wrongly) to abhor brand-name elitism. That rink—it was what I had learned to value: the startling, unbound, uncorporate, and very organic expression. IBM would certainly want nothing to do with such a rink, which meant you should. Mr. Creighton's crystal poem. Truly I wanted multiple rinks. From the frozen back stoop, I could narrate three-rink action in the twinkling-voice style of Dick Button in Sapporo, Japan. ("Mr. Hickey, retired real estate agent and widower, wearing the red polka-dot bow tie and green sweater vest, will now try to leap a neighbor's property line...impressive! Rick, neighborhood bully, is disqualified for punching his ice dancing partner, Lucinda!") *Can you pay?* Brad's cough asked. Pay? In copper wire. Or collected park cans. Or if generous credit terms could be worked out. Say, payments starting a year from next century, no COD charge or other legal vomit that specked the screen during midnight K-tel ads. Brad sniffed twice, and said, "Installation free." I shrugged. Translation: my mother might wrest chewed-looking dollars bills from Moby Purse if she were getting something free for them. I reached for the magazine and Brad let me have it. With the ad an inch from my black plastic eye frames and butch haircut (thanks to father experimenting with a career as a barber), I looked so closely I saw fingerprints. Didn't I see fingerprints? What I thought I saw was too often what I saw. I was one of those. I saw fingerprints. Brad, Brenda, Mrs. Creighton had been touching the ad like a lucky rabbit's foot. So much was riding on this invention. Skate-factory jobs, star-spangled-costume-designer positions, water-company rate hikes, ChapStick and scarf and ear muff sales, coaching positions, commentator salaries, and—most important—the prospects of the Creighton family. If the checks didn't pour in this time, certain bad words might occur to family members as they beheld a basement full of dusty tarps and rusty strips, and felt discouraged, then fooled, set up to hurt in the way they were hurting. The word *loser*. The word *fraud*. Words I despaired at thinking myself when entering my father's law office in the Davenport Bank Building (you could hear a neuron fidget in there) or while gazing at those unpublished novels of his, leather-mummified and displayed on a basement shelf. The words *failure* and *freak*. Followed by a word never uttered by my mother (medieval expert at suffering), but a word that adept Mrs. Creighton might well hang in the spring air—the modern world's most indispensable noun: *Divorce*.

THE CLASSIFIED AD DID NOT make near the splash at show-and-tell that I had expected it to. What had I expected? Unrealistically, I'd expected classroom excitement akin to that

which always swept the country on the final night of the Olympic figure skating competition, when a new Ice Queen was anointed by pouty buzz-cut judges in thick suits resembling rhino hides. Millions of living room hearts leaping as America's darling leaped. Or falling when she took a spill, as Janet Lynn had in Japan, landing on her tutu, sitting for a second like a party guest taken down by a collapsed ceiling decoration, stunned, near tears...and the camera zooming in to record the first tear when it fell, and the tear falling, or not falling, depending on whom you talked to the next morning...How *did* the class react to Brad's unprecedented presentation? One student commented that only ants could read the ad and that ants didn't skate. Others sat behind this wiseass in silent agreement, even Libby—whose face, like the face of my sister Marianna, was lip-dominated and lush. Mrs. Davis scolded the heckler and turned to Brad, only Brad was not there to comfort. He had tucked the magazine under his arm and retreated to the back of the circle of chairs. Mrs. Davis—short hair, clean face— ended show-and-tell in a gentle voice. She never yelled or slapped erasers against the board. She understood that elementary school would make or break kids without any help—knew the pink brick building housed a foundry where a nation's destiny was being forged by the power of rules, good and bad, rules whose eerie confederate, the stale hallway air, struck at the senses in a hammer-and-tongs style. Mrs. Davis was the least obvious homeroom teacher. No blinding polyester pattern. Just sedate cotton collars, like sealed business envelopes. She could see that Brad was fine— the clear skies of his big eyes. He had exhibited the magazine not to convince people about the rink's worth, but to share the wealth. If others did not believe, well, their loss. But me—I felt snubbed for Brad. This was all to do with needing a worthy cause to get behind, instead of just opposing the mainstream and its unrelenting regulations, constrictive labels, rampant hypocrisy, celebrity escapades, and Red Dye No. 2 and other poison additives that my death-affirming mother, in her rummage-sale shroud, liked to point out on the boxes she quixotically bought by the cartful…so effective a victim of, and preacher against, "The Status Quo!" that at the end of a long night in her company the well-built Midwest, from Chicago to Kansas City, lay in splintered ruins in my brain, ripe for reconstruction at the sound of the next school buzzer. I needed a *life-affirming* crusade. And Mr. Creighton's invention became that on the winter morning the class failed to appreciate the beauty and gem-like rarity of the rink set into 1973's mishmash. The rink was a commercial product not menacingly mundane and/or chemical and/or life-cheapening, like the products satirized by Wacky Packages stickers—Killette Fright Guard Deodorant, Peter Pain Peanut Butter, Blisterine Monster Mouthwash. It was instead a product offering a way out of the labyrinth of consumption, maybe the last chance to escape. Who were these runny-nosed snots to sneer at an ice rink that could save them? They were the children of dentists, surgeons, stockbrokers, real estate agents, and the owner of Davenport Pack, a slaughterhouse. They would have sold their souls for an in-ground swimming pool useful for just two months each year. But the sensational shimmering Ice Capades rink, in service from November's first freeze to March's last frost? Nah, no appeal. *Because they wore designer sunglasses at recess*, hindering their ability to identify worthy bandwagons to jump on. And below their wraparound insect lenses: *ski lift tickets*—five or six of them bunched and dangling from the zippers of their puffy down-filled coats. There could be no clearer statement. The Ronsons, Singers, Belknaps, and Quinns believed that, to be fun, February recreation must cost plenty and happen far away at an altitude-challenged Illinois mountain with creaking backbones of lifts and a lodge serving soggy fries to chew in front of the weak lukewarm glow of a gas fireplace. And those weekends when they weren't besieging wondrous alps of the Midwest? Park sledding was too pedestrian. They might own a Finnish leather-laced toboggan and pronounce that tantalizing verb *tobogganing* a dozen times each winter, but performing the verb's action was impossible, since they had been unable to procure killin' toboggan-wear. They had protective, proactive moms who spread a religion of their own—the belief that paying big money to be cold in Galena somehow prevented the cold from causing frostbite. The Ronsons and the Singers had Maxwell skis to wax and Dimrod boots to brag to each other about (with, for no evident reason, every other word being *joker* or *ding-dong* or *turkey*) and slope-shattered ankles to heal and cable television in their bedrooms to watch. They had never experienced the feral January gloom of cat litter and bills and broken toys and more bills and tinsel in cat vomit, a disaster that was man-made and so called out for a human genius with the power to rekindle holiday excitement. *Moon-glazed rink, loudspeakers feeding* Pagliacci *to the spinning soul of grace, the next Janet Lynn from Rockford, Illinois.* Television could not enliven a doomed room—only fill it with life mimicked. Sure, I watched the tube. There was no way not to. And there were things worth watching—like the sweet last scene in each episode of *The Waltons*. Night shot of the mountain house, window lights blinking out one by one as a lumber-mill family said good night. "Night, Ma." "Night, Pa." "Night, John Boy." "Night, Mary Ellen." I could have listened to that round for hours. Voices wafting melodically into the forest shadows, love taming whatever evil lurked there. (John Boy wrote novels on red Big Chief notebooks and I asked for five for Christmas, knowing I would get at least one, and I did.) But

the rest of the television universe? *Green Acres*: canned corny
jokes and automaton laughter. *The Sonny & Cher Show*: variety
hokum emceed by the most mismatched couple since Nixon had
hosted Elvis in the Oval Office. (What chemical did Cher inject
in order to get along with Sonny for sixty minutes?) *Brian's Song*,
or terminal-disease dramas like it, which allowed the audience to
feast on a banquet of tears and relax during the commercials—
same ads as always—Charlie the Tuna, or a clueless kid on a dock,
swinging his legs, singing about how he loved to eat hot dogs all

day. But he didn't. He was thin, energetic. It was me who liked to eat hot dogs all day, and look at the result! No, I couldn't. Instead I compulsively fondled the growing flab fiasco—hip shelves, belly rolls, and lately: breasts. Cellulite (I learned the term from the *National Enquirer*) that spilled around my school desk and, each night, slid across coffee-stained couch cushions. I tried to get a grip on who exactly I was but kept losing it—a boy-blur swollen with salt and sugar. Upset. Eating and watching what I knew was bad for me. Worst of all the cartoon special *Frosty the Snowman*. Frosty was made of white stuff that fell from the heavens, right? And that divine stuff—each unique flake—what came of it? *Drip, drip, drip, drip* ... Frosty's annual dissolution while trapped in a greenhouse (murdered by fragrant, humid poinsettia breath) ended the holiday before it had started. In certain dim Nielsen households like ours, viewing was no set of choices but requisite high-dosage anesthesia, reducing sensibility to an itchy insensibility, eyes glued to the screen's lightless light, a chill cave-gleam.

ONE BIG TRICK OF CHILDHOOD is its concurrent connectedness to, and separateness from, the adult life. Our first and oldest experiences tangle relentlessly with all that follows, and in turn new becomes old, and the old, new. For decades I have been studiously revisiting the fanciful yet factual mail-order rink as if the invention counted as a major—albeit unknown—turning point in the country's history, a pivotal moment when peace might have been attained by a citizenry at a reasonable cost of no teenage lives. When January could have meant healthy outdoor serenity— fresh air and legions of ice queens—rather than debt, petrified fruit cake, post-*Frosty* depression, and Super Bowl madness. Had the rink sold big in 1973, might that sporting event never have grown from a one-blimp wonder into a month-long hyperventilating frolic of formulaic hype? Might the glimmer of millions of backyard rinks have illuminated a better path out of the night of Vietnam, recession, DC corruption? A path that would have left less of the best of us behind, carried more beauty and knowledge forward? Thinking so is fantastic, probably unnecessary, but it is authentic to me, rooted in the rink's revelatory personal meaning. For Mr. Creighton's creation materialized at a moment when I was losing my way, losing essential attachments at school and in the larger world. I knew it, but could not stop or even slow the process, only watch darkness creep nearer. The dark, say, at Middle Park, where I would be dropped off and forgotten, and then remembered, and then picked up, caught in car headlights, the front door creaking open to that voice, her voice, in which I could hear more dark, those jowls bubbling with air as if something terrible and absurd boiled in there, and something did, her enthusiastic account of the murder of the Clutter family in Kansas. Or, the moaning offer of a foot rub that I in my loneliness would be unable to refuse. Or the dark and unholy fear in doorways, after ringing the bell of a relative who might not let you in. Or the dark of a broken father's smoke-veiled gaze. Mr. Creighton's rink became an embodiment of my wish to regain the innocence already lost to family trouble and to those chasms I drew when not talking to Brad, my head leaning close to the spreading flames. The rink was no surrender to the encroaching disaster, but one way of holding it at bay, a solution to screw together in my imagination as I stood at recess and stared at the frozen gravel beneath a long sigh of January sky. It was to me all I have detailed, and one more thing, too. The camaraderie of a rink was *the help* I had needed when a babysitter's boyfriend tossed me into a blizzard at age six.

WEARING ONLY SOCKS AND PAJAMAS, I stood stunned and disbelieving amid front-porch drifts. It was like I had been sucked from the living room by a rowdy tide of escaping heat. But, in actuality, whatever his name was, Boyfriend, had lifted me over his hairy head and spun me around and tossed me out the door. Giggling Sharee, the babysitter, told him to stop—too late. He had thrown me out of my house. How could a stranger throw me out of my house? Had he been taking lessons from Grandfather Miller and those other relatives who would not admit poor Miller kids into their fancy homes? Was Sharee's boyfriend on LSD? Was he crazy? It was almost funny. Had to be a joke. I laughed, twisted the loose brass knob. The door did not open. He had locked it. I pounded. Yelled all the words. Still the door did not open. The wind blew and the porch transformed into a cramped corral of white horses. They leaped over railing rungs, tails flapping in the dark. They reared and pumped their crystal hooves in the frigid air. Side-yard evergreen boughs thrashed as if trying and failing to control herds of snow stampeding from the sky's bleak mystic meadow. A nightmare. Harder I pounded, crying: "Let me in! Open up!" Slush seeped through my socks. The whinnying wind tugged at my pajama legs and arms, numbing my cheeks. What had I done that was so bad? I had reminded Boyfriend that he had no right to order us around. It was our house and I was the oldest and must protect it. What else had I done? Couldn't remember. I pounded more, crossed my arms to keep my heart from jumping out, then reached out to twist the knob once more. Mother! Father! They were out in the storm, somewhere. At "Investment Club." He would be a crooked tree of tobacco fumes in some corner of the host's tidy and besieged home. She who applied lipstick like graffiti—vandalizing her own face—was probably giggling, stuffing party crackers and liver pâté into Moby

Purse for me, as she had promised to do. "Back at ten?" she had unsurely told Sharee when handing over the indecipherable instruction sheet clawed by ink. Frizzy Sharee had nodded and promised to take good care. Sharee, youth-council member at Aunt Julie's church. Sharee in a ten-color shirt skimpy in the middle, where there was much to cover, and wide in the arms like a super-cool tablecloth gone amok. Sharee who phoned Boyfriend as soon as my parents' car slid down the alley. He came quick and behaved like a chair. She sat on him, tickled and giggling and blurting "Duh!" and "Doy!" to make all of us cootie fearers feel stupid. It worked. Wasn't that enough revenge? I pounded and pounded now. Curly manes of snow settled onto the porch floor, while above a rodeo turmoil of incoming gusts bucked against the porch ceiling and its dark lamp globe still full of last summer's bugs. From far away came the metallic keening of tire chains, akin to numerous cash registers ceaselessly ringing up the same exorbitant price. Again I twisted the cold brass knob, loose from use like all our doorknobs. "Let me in! I'll freeze out here!" Inside: Sharee, the toasty non-nanny; belching Boyfriend; belligerent brother, Howard; and frightened sisters, Elizabeth and Marianna. Along with my Etch A Sketch, schnauzer magnets, Smith Brothers cough drops, Famous Authors card game, Burl Ives's *Jimmy Crack Corn* record, Spider-Man comics, miniature magnetic chessboard, spring-action basketball game, panda bear blanket, Erector Set in the heavy red plastic carrying case that alone gave me so much pleasure I had yet to build a thing with girders and joints. Had it all forgotten about me already? I turned, stared down at the low, unterraced side of the street—buried cars, ice-faced homes, a few lit windows whose glare filtered through the falling snow and pulsed like lighthouse beams across a violent sea. My soaked feet burned and my cheeks stiffened, far—very far—from the brothy good-bye kiss/hug that my mother, smelling of Oil of Olay, had delivered on teetering white heels. Being kissed by her dressed up was different, better, formal and fugitive in a good way. For a moment, on the storm porch, I thought I could still smell Oil of Olay, that buttery perfume, but I was wrong. This was so much worse than when I'd gotten separated from her at Kresge Department Store when I was three and the army man in the parking lot had brought me back inside, lifted me onto the counter. All the army men were now in Laos and Cambodia, tiptoeing across minefields. How long could I survive with no coat, no cap, no mother? As long as Ethan Allen in his forest hole camouflaged with leaves? As long as Harriet Tubman in a swamp, breathing through reeds to elude the barking dogs? As long as the Boxcar Children in their dank, rusty, but perfect home? Even before this night, I had sensed they all had something special to teach me. Fight when you can. Move on if winning is impossible. Suddenly, staying put was the worst possible thing. I had to go, get moving, seek or perish. The first steps away from that door were like no others I had ever taken, terrible with the weirdness of walking on air in a tunnel while feeling weight pressing down on and into my head and chest. Each step populated by a horde of thoughts too close and loud to be understood. I slipped down six stairs framed by snowcapped flowerpots balanced on the cement shoulders of the porch. The short, steep front hill was covered with dunes of snow, a sweeping and sprawling surf of changeling snow. My hold on the porch shoulder allowed me to escape a possibly fatal slide to the street below. I reached the narrow side yard at the foot of the neighboring snow-swept terrace—the higher house of Mr. Hickey, now nearly deleted by storm murk. Gone a welcoming outpost of sweater vests, polka dots, high blood pressure, boards on the bed for back trouble, bouillon cubes,

Lipton tea, prunes, nickels for naming state capitals. Our side-yard path also gone. Tractor-tire sandbox gone—dragged away, for all I knew, by draft horses from hell. There were cantering flanks of snow now. Flakes brushing my face and mixing with my tears. I could die for all Sharee cared. I could freeze like a prairie pioneer disoriented by a whiteout, found dead in front of his own cabin! Sky and Iowa—which was which? The whining gales crushed against vague cliffs, antic white spirals vanished into gorges the storm had gouged. I could die of frostbite like the Little Match Girl, feeling in my last living moment a false fairy-tale warmth spreading over my rigid limbs. Must keep moving, must move, move, keep wading through the knee-deep drifts, staying right next to the house: iron coal-chute cover, aluminum dryer vent, foundation icicles grazing my bare palms like a fortune-teller's bloodless fingers, rucked wall culminating in a corner and more terrace, and finally the back stoop caught amid a rude choreography of twisting trumpet vines wearing white tights. I stumbled up the back-stoop stairs. Twisted the icy knob. The door did not open. I pounded. "You got to let me in! You got to let me in! Got to!" Kitchen light. Boyfriend at a window visible through the chorus line of vines. He taunted. Thumbs on cheeks, hands wagging, pointy harlequin mouth, eyes of a pumpkin. He was not done scaring me. Maybe he had just started. I stood, shivering, knowing I belonged inside, and something else—that I might belong outside, too. Like Harriet. Like Ethan. Like my mother, making not friends at "Investment Club," but enemies, with her criticism of Dr. Sheppard's recent acquittal on charges of slaying his pregnant wife. But what had she to lose? After all, she had no money to invest; she searched her purse for coins in the checkout lane—digging for lost dimes, and not finding them. Father made her go. She hated it, she told me. I slid my red freezing hands under my armpits, the last warmth.

Thoughts scattered, scattering more. Even if I did get back inside, would anything be the same as it had been? Or all things familiar but not right, not mine even when touched? Sharee's "pouffy" (mother's word) hairdo appeared next to Boyfriend. She saw me. Frowned. Tugged Boyfriend. They disappeared but the door did not open immediately. They must talk first. Wiping wet hands on my sleety shirt, bawling, I looked for help nearby, then out at the yard and the garage cottage, the slope of terraces across the alley, territory trampled by hooves of snow, with more horses galloping down the dark mountains, galloping, galloping through alley spumes and squalls, past garbage cans, ledges, and gutters coated with frozen campfire ashes.

THREE YEARS AFTER THAT NIGHT—thanks to Brad and his dad, the eccentric Mr. Creighton—that nightmare swirls into a sweet dream that I can see and feel. The backyard-blizzard ruckus induces retroactive glimmers of red, green, and yellow. From the stoop I see a faint ring of light, tucked between the concrete retaining wall and the opposite edge of our narrow terrace. The glimmers grow brighter, get closer. A rink, Chinese lanterns, and benches. Figures materialize—sequined skirts, turbaned chins, fur muffs, a whirl of skaters laughing, shouting. "Way to go, Brad!" "Beautiful, Brenda!" "More hot chocolate!" "Dufus!" "Mom, put the Chipmunks on the stereo!" The wind has died, only a few fat lazy flakes drift from the sky's spent bucket. I remain on the stoop. Though the party is on my property, I am not invited. To be invited requires certain social skills, and skates—Brad perceptively understands I have neither. And I am as close to the action as I can get without being invited, and for me that is best. The least stressful. (*Stressful*: my newest word.) Observing, I am denied what? Nothing except injury. Sharee opens the door behind me, voice nicey-nice fake. "Poor baby. Come inside! Warm up!" Without turning, I suggest what she can do with her heat. The door shudders shut. Bravery has paid off: suddenly I have grown mittens, boots, a wool coat, matching burgundy scarf and cap that Dick Button would envy. I am breathing white kittens. The air has the creamy smell of refrigerated carnations. The storm that trampled the terraced neighborhood near to death—what has it done in the end? Incorporated every terrace and driveway into an alternate galaxy of a gazillion crystals. Won't my frowning parents be surprised when their arthritic Ford sedan, bristling with salt, creeps down the alley. Out on the rink Brenda, the athlete, executes a jump and lands perfectly, red ponytail swishing, swishing. Guests clap and imitate in vain. Back arched, legs crossed, down goes another Katherine on her frilled keister. Brenda offers tips to the fallen. Second attempts, third attempts, even fourth tries—no improvement. But cheers, yes. The rink is the answer to season after season of the same TV programming re-cooked to appear fresh, the answer to living rooms smelling of all the Februarys since Eisenhower, a dog biscuit–like reek, carnivorous and dull. The rink unwinds the burial stink. It is at once exotic and humble, like a unicorn eating out of a trash can. The festival of scintillating blurs as alluring, and hard to grasp, as brothers and sisters. That ice glow, the widening ripples of reflections...a nonsubstance, but also *the* substance, of the rink's reality. I see it as a glimmering time machine that does not spin people into the future or back through the past—it flings the senses into an endless and ever-evolving present that stretches tonight all the way to the desk where I sit tonight in New York City, writing about a boy of nine composing another dream that will help save part of him from the

household calamity. I see on the rink the rule-obeying jolly new babysitter hired after Sharee was fired—Thom Hart, in the red St. Ambrose College sweater—skating and making friends who will help him later. (He will be elected mayor of the city in 1986.) I see reflected on ice the headline of an article that appeared in the *New York Times* on February 10, 2010: "Rinks Become Backyard Entertainment Centers." Too late, too late, too late, I see. But Brad grabs a hockey stick anyway, because in the dream it's still too early for it to be too late for him, or for me on the snow-duned stoop. Brad smacks a puck. Goal! Brenda, the blender rotor, spins at high speed, red ponytail a control switch sticking straight out from the back of her pretty head. What makes this alchemy possible, besides Mr. Creighton's initial epiphany? Water. Gallons of water added by a rink owner. The democracy of the fact is ravishing. And the science sound. Technology need not be complex to be effective. Galileo's telescope was a runt and it discovered more than many a ponderous planetarium. My own telescope, fashioned from a paper towel tube, had reach—once I had glimpsed the ball drop in Times Square, I swear. The less you have, the more you must make of it. People—what are they made of? Water, mostly. And the earth? Water, mostly. How can a product consisting wholly of stuff vital to life fail?

AND MR. CREIGHTON LUMBERS OFF NOW to heat more cocoa, while Mrs. Creighton's eyes follow him, maybe worried, maybe not. Some bucktoothed peacoat rushes up to her. Friendliest neighbor you'd never want to meet. The paragon of palaver, answerer of his own questions. "Perfect night for it, huh? Couldn't have asked for better. Did I see you working at Jack and Jill last Thursday? Musta been you stacking apples!" Alley telephone poles thrust their upper crossbeams into the night, warding off any demons armed with blow torches who would melt this homemade paradise, warding off every unholy aspect of another Super Bowl. (Pregame interview jock-jabberwocky. Taco chips sludged with bean dip. Fifty million toilets flushing in apocalyptic unison during commercials. More than a hundred million screens choking on the emerald idiom of artificial turf and restive cheerleaders and Roger Staubach the scrambling quarterback and Bob

Hayes the aeronautic wide receiver and an illusory lip-synched halftime unspectacular starring red and blue and pink vapor and chicken feathers and fifty bikinis and rheumy neon-jacketed pancake-dusted commentators looking as shrunken and forlorn as the snowball I had once placed in the freezer, trying and failing to preserve a weapon for later.) Mr. Creighton reappears and thumbs curl around steaming mugs. A girl cries: "I wanna go home!" Already? Already. Mrs. Creighton deals with Lucinda—frowsy at ten—skates dangling from her neck like an albatross and cap dragging a purple pom-pom. Ski masks sprout frost stubble. For no reason boys begin to cry the most popular playground phrase: "Big-time!" Then they have a reason. Charmed Brenda makes skating history, carving no figure eight into the ice but a decimal number, to help Americans acclimate to the European metric system. "Big-time!" Holiday on Ice times 2.3. I spot a new arrival, the AAA tow truck driver, Mr. Lay-Off-Me-Why-Don't-You?, a surly pro who jump-starts our loathsome car when it stalls in the Eagle supermarket parking lot. He smiles at this viable engine of fun running on sugar and ice and caroling chipmunks. A minister might categorize a rink as a decadent, dangerous luxury, but some things are necessary precisely because they are unnecessary and do not fit with the schedules and routines that occasion monstrous disaffection. (Complaints with enough heads to make you wonder if carports were not actually spaceships that delivered to urban Iowans the alienation they commonly expressed about the stuff they centered their lives around and claimed to love—like relatives and the Chicago Cubs and that "almighty dollar.") Now Brad points out the Bobby Hull hockey stick autograph and, in his brave hesitant fashion, becomes talkative, informing guests about the registered letter Mr. Creighton has dispatched to Dick Button of NBC, asking if he will consider appearing in a full-page ad to be placed in *Outdoor Life*. I know just what the letter said.

Dear Mr. Button: Steady yourself. I've invented a portable ice rink...And I know just what Dick Button will write back. *Dear Mr. Creighton: What a wonderful notion. The nation has been on thin ice for too long. I'll be glad to help in any way possible.* I inhale the rich odor of cocoa, an oaky musk thick as a goalie's mask: for one fanciful second I am save-expert Tony Esposito, a teammate of Stan Mikita on the Chicago Blackhawks. Beyond the igloo humps of the retaining-wall hedges, I see my favorite lantern color: pale (almost green) blue washed into silver and illuminating a lavender angle of the garage cottage. "Watch out!" Boys crash, then proudly rub their knees as Mr. Creighton comforts them with news of the Skid-Ender boot. For the first time I wonder if the rink comes in a decorated carton. Brad has never mentioned the carton. Icicles on the carton? A photo of Brenda in midair? The rink might help people live outside the box, but still it needs good packaging. Every American product requires an impressive container to hide the mean or flimsy makings inside and thereby boost consumer confidence, making it possible to endure the problematic setup. I forget my place and yodel: "What's the rink box like? If you want, I'll design it! I've already written two poems about parks in the style of Emily Dickinson!" Nobody hears me. Mrs. Creighton is opening more Swiss Miss packets, cutting carefully along the dotted line in order not to end up covered with powder like her husband, who pulls at foil like it's a rip cord, opening a brown parachute of dust. Most of the cocoa brushed off, he stands with a boot on the rink's rim, snowflake sweater, gloves, beard, his gaze lifted skyward, toward the universe of Mars and Saturn and Jupiter, so similar to the heavens within, where galaxies of thought orbit and where feelings streak like asteroids toward unseen targets. "Dad!" calls Brad, and Dad laughs. That is his job now: salesmanship. To joke, cajole, rouse customers slumbering in their shingled groves.

REMEMBER: REALITY RESTS on the back of what isn't—what might not or cannot ever be. When, in real life, a rare rink order did arrive from Wisconsin or Michigan or Minnesota, I bet the Creighton family rushed to the basement and packed a plain carton. Brad handing the many metal strips to Mr. Creighton, who counted out loud. Brenda bending, bagging the screws and the bolts. Mrs. Creighton stapling directions and re-counting everything everyone else had counted. At last they spread out together, fanned the big blue tarp, and folded, folded, folded—not wasting one second.

A STUDY IN SEQUINS

Metabolism of a tornado — Cap'n Bernie and the bad nurse —
Shimmering path to Universal Studios — Gray bologna — "Be my friend!" —
"Frenched" by a unicyclist prodigy — Clingers and Refugees — "Let go, fatso!" —
"Where's Mitzi?" — Bad shoes, poor diet, scant sleep — Moths of more maybes —
Patio doors to Hades — The Perv at Duck Creek Plaza — "Hotcakes is here!" —
Another family's stains — Atomic retaliation — My "bod" moved against me —
Longest ride home ever — Alligator tears and three-pound lollipops —
Sunset Strip reconsidered — Pizza boxes danced jigs — Aloft in the nest
of candy-colored bulbs

BRIDGET LOMBARDO, MY SISTER MARIANNA'S BEST FRIEND
for a time, became famous at age eight, winning local talent
contests by tap dancing and twirling two batons while singing a
ballad re: a Southern belle forever searching the back streets of
Brownsville for the cad who'd left her standing at the altar. *Delta
Dawn, what's that flower you have on?* Mrs. Lombardo—a woman
not so patient, with the metabolism of a tornado—had chosen the
tune for Bridget after *Billboard* analysis (Tanya Tucker's version
#6 on the country chart) and no doubt with equal decisiveness
had dashed past the discombobulating inventory at Ute's Uniform

Store (nurse smocks, band tunics, mechanic shirts) to reach a corkboard wall appended with snazzy outfits—first seen, first snatched: blue-sequined halter, red tutu, zircon tiara. "Bill me, please." During the morning TV interview, conducted between Popeye cartoons by "Cap'n Bernie," the performer gave credit where credit was due: Mom (not allowed on the set—sending hand signals from a booth) was "super-duper!...the greatest!...a total lifesaver" who had endured engine trouble on the way to the gymnasium stage somewhere in Illinois, and had bravely applied Bridget's eyeliner and lipstick and rouge at an interstate rest stop named after Carl Sandburg, plainspoken poet of the prairie and of the Midwestern industrial cities (Chicago, St. Louis, Milwaukee) into which waves of grain were still endlessly draining, whole amber oceans disappearing daily into vats at factories producing cereals such as Cocoa Puffs and malevolent malt liquors like Colt 45. "Without Mom I'd be nowhere!" squealed Little Miss Iowa 1976 to Cap'n Bernie. Dad was not thanked, because Dad was long gone. Who cared? She was on television.

BRIDGET PULLED EVERY ANTIC out of every ligament. Nervous mother and I watched with intense interest as we gobbled salty handfuls of potato sticks from a family-size tub on the couch. This wasn't a typical Miller instance of tracking local tragedies in order to briefly evade, or displace, our own troubles. Bridget had stolen my sister Marianna's heart away—her new best friend and the first bad influence who wasn't an immediate relative. My mother in her nightgown wiggled and cushions wiggled with her, meaning I wiggled also. We agreed: to be as silly as Bridget required *something special*—serious courage. We relished

the surreal face-off between the hyperactive pint-size girl and the near-catatonic Cap'n, who winked at scripted intervals. Bridget answered his every twitch with two of her own. She did a backflip: an elastic chimera of innocence. She was being filmed. It was the first time and you don't forget your first time of being milled into a leap of light over hills and into the homes of the elderly, the unemployed, and classmates faking sore throats. Bridget somersaulted, a squeaking blaze of littleness magnified to extinction. She needed to pee, though. The host in the yachting cap announced a short commercial break ("Circa 21 Dinner Theater, *Fiddler on the Roof* now thru . . ."). I could imagine what happened when the ON AIR sign blinked off. Stiff-legged, as if his shoes were wheels, Cap'n slid closer to Bridget, now eye-level with his brass coat buttons. It was funny. Suddenly she didn't have to pee. Cap'n's dark blue gaze made her feel like she was wearing his blazer along with him. It was hot. He wasn't speaking. Could he talk only when the cameras were rolling? Was the show on only when it was on or was the show on always, whether on or not? Cap'n had run out of winks for the time being. She needed to pee, after all, but was it too late? She knocked her knees together and gave Cap'n the Kewpie-doll smile usually fired at pageant judges near the gym free throw line. Cap'n rolled backward. Bridget thumbs-upped Mom: Mom thumbs-upped Bridget. The potato-stick tub bumped my thigh: my keeper digging. Was my sister in the sound booth, too? Mysteriously, the question never came up. Mother slapped a warm hand on my forehead. There had been offers of purse pills earlier. Her thyroid medication, I suspected. She had gone to the doctor long ago for a big bottle and then hoarded it. She was a bad nurse—but a bad nurse was the best kind when you were faking strep. We waited out a portrait-studio ad. If you lived in Davenport you watched WOC, as Rock Islanders watched WHBF and Moliners watched WQAD. (Ronald Reagan got his start on the radio end of WOC in the 1930s, recreating baseball games that had already occurred, a common game of pretend in the pre-TV era.) WOC's hilltop complex was notable for its tower, whose call letters glowed like monolithic electric-stove burners. WOC = Wonders of Chiropractic. The station had long been owned by the family of that science's bearded founder, Daniel David Palmer. (His wealthy grandson and current owner, also named David, lived in Dr. Miller's condo complex.) Across the street from WOC stood Palmer College, where students studied spine manipulation as seriously as Bridget did. After the ad ended, Cap'n Bernie welcomed us back. He called Bridget "Bridge" for short, unless I heard wrong. I heard all through mother-son static, saw all through mother-son murk. Or did I hear only her static, see only the murk—nothing else? "How does it feel to be on top?" Cap'n asked her. "Fantastic!" "Mind doing that number again?" "Sure!" Tumble, twirl: *Delta Dawn, what's that flower...* "Wonderful! How long do you practice each day?" "Hours sometimes!" "Does this interfere with homework?" Her ensuing silence seemed to indicate unfamiliarity with the concept of school. Cap'n moved on—did she like her chances in Reno of winning a spot on *The Merv Griffin Show*? "Of course!" But then she recalled a lecture on modesty, adding: "We'll see!" (The Nevada showbiz scientists wore cardigans, gold chains. Those judges beheld such a wealth of equally untalented talent in the tutu blur of eight hours that picking the winner probably came down to a coin toss. "Amphetamines!" is how Mrs. Lombardo, whom I dubbed Mombardo, would later explain the triumph of the "little bitch" from Columbus, dabbing Bridget's tear-riveleted cosmetics and vowing to "even the playing field," without saying how.)

BRIDGET AND HER MOM LIVED out their noir fairy tale on Middle Road in a rented house within sight of the McKinley Elementary School grounds. Together weighing barely a hundred pounds, they each stood at a frustrating remove from any high cupboard, yet it was "no prob," in Lombardo-speak, for the diminutive pair to latch on to the conflated showbiz sphere that was then (thanks to the advent of the daytime talk show) starting to expand further, to erupt into the relentless celebrity culture existent today. All they had to do was flick on the television, and its aura painted the carpet with a shimmering path to Universal Studios. Through every American home this byway coursed, if you had the gall to see it, believe it, and they did, together. They were always together, Bridget and her mom. They bickered in a play way which deepened their bond, strengthened the positivity of their shared mission: fame and fortune for Bridget. How different from the thick mind-meld of me and my keeper. Our goals conflicted. I needed the put-together guardian that she was not, she needed the intimate companionship no son was constructed to provide. Our throats were clotted with envy, and potato stick muck. We discussed the open-and-shut case of "Bridget's exploitation" in a dungeon drone. "*What Ever Happened to Baby Jane?*—the movie," my mother said, "that'll be Bridget in five years. Sunset Strip on Middle Road!" "What about Marianna?" I asked. "Mitzi? Bridget's groupie? Can you imagine?" She sighed deeply. I sighed less deep, simply not as numb, not as despondent. I tried hard to keep pace with her in the sorrow department. But it was more my style to shadow Mr. Hickey on the terrace above, knock, knock, 7UP, man-talk about baseball and Muhammad Ali. Or if I managed to pry loose from our pretentious mother-son clench at night and was too tired to climb the little hill to make small talk in a cozy kitchen, I stood alone in our littered backyard, shadowing the cosmos. The dizzying conglomeration of neighbors and alleys fit perfectly with the vastness of time and space in the night sky. Suddenly I was less marooned. I was not stuck in a finite locality but liberated by the reach of its details. I stared up into the black interstellar lagoon and at certain wondrous moments felt that the stars were as close as fireflies.

A STAR SEEKER MYSELF, I could fathom Marianna's attachment to Bridget, her leap into the dark. Fame and fortune were the most American way out of a fix. Wanting them, you belonged to a club with millions of members. Getting them, you shook the grand order of things without doing it any harm. It wasn't even accurate to say the search for fame and fortune inevitably corrupted—though my mother, my trainer, contended this. Fame and fortune were the one sure way to level the playing field between the sexes, races, classes. Lombardo madness amounted to the familiar rags-to-riches madness, *Life* magazine madness. Whereas Miller madness labored to what end? What calling was I being trained for—being bent all out of shape to achieve? Warbling lyric drunk? Psycho killer? Three-hundred-pound (but stunted) freak who lives in the attic with Marvel comics in plastic sleeves, tears stuck to cheeks like tar? At this juncture (The Long Slide Toward Hunger Strike, let's call it) any of those outcomes was plausible. Passion's fog thickened around the couch where we munched, hunched, wished, giggled and orated. I kept discovering that my mother was none of her many different voices (the commanding lawyer, the silly-billy flapper, the laconic bag lady), but rather a vortex of continually juggled echoes. It was a rude riddle of cancellations that the younger children often fled. They saw the toll her company exacted from me—my gelatinous pallor and listless stares of misapprehension during her monologues. Was our mother-son mind-meld a suicide pact or the only death worth living for, grinding out? The only thing we could honestly offer each other was ambivalence about what we had to offer. It constituted a tribute to our love that we troubled ourselves with that difficult genuine exchange every now and then instead of living solely on illusions. "Doing my best," she mumbled, unconvinced, on the eighth day of nursing my so-called sore throat instead of treating my abject terror of rift. And I answered weakly: "I know you are," afraid to be convinced she could do no better. It was little wonder Bridget had stolen Marianna's heart away. The Lombardos were one bracing shot of all-American bravado. Disappearing into their home was picking the better debacle, the prouder game. Their chutzpah made one kernel of ability to stretch far as an eye could see (or at least to Dundee); whereas Miller malaise reduced a house full of advance degrees to the gray (going on green) bologna in a lukecold fridge. The sunniest aspect of Bridget's dream? Its extreme flexibility made it extremely executable. One week Making It Big meant Bridget and Mombardo seeing several movies at the mall cinema. The next it meant buying a new costume (Uncle Sam hat, tinsel-shagged cane) and staging a revue for sparrows in the backyard. The quest for celebrity equated to a queer practicality of training footlights on successive disappointments until they shined.

ANY MAIN ATTRACTION required an entourage. Bridget collected admirers like a wily dogcatcher. Her singing talent often excused her from attending McKinley Elementary School— what Mrs. Finch and Mrs. Savory offered not being vital to a showbiz career—but she would burst out of nowhere to capture kids meandering homeward after the final buzzer. Of particular interest were girls exhibiting symptoms of vulnerability—head itchers, nose pickers, muttering Maggies, or lost dreamers, like Marianna, staring at the pavement. Marianna wore tomboy overalls but already, as a third grader, drew honks from teenage boys and married horn dogs with a thing for blondes of all sizes, all ages. Ten times at least I had heard about the first meeting of

Marianna and Bridget, and I ruminated a lot on the portentous event, splicing Marianna's triumphant details with my observations of the Lombardo pad during the late-night rescue missions mother and I made to steal back the heart well stolen. Summaries were impossible to come by. But I got the picture—the R-rated biopic flickering in the theater of my cranium: Bridget in sultry-lisp mode, threadbare leotards, halter glitz, Betty Boop lashes, sandals; Marianna smelling cigarettes and sensing a first supplier. Bridget yelled: "Be my friend! My friend and no one else's!" She tugged Marianna across dying grass toward the bungalow and its decorative hodgepodge masonry. There was a pizza box lodged in a scrawny hedge. "What's your name again?" Bridget asked, shoving ringed fingers into the lidless stoop mailbox to check for incoming contracts and, I suppose, love letters from Brando. Finding nothing, she made the Red Skelton desolate clown face. My sister repeated her name: "Mar-ee-ann-ahhhh-roonie." "That's too long. I'm calling you Marie. Shhh." Bridget yanked the door knob—it was loose from abuse but not dislocated and drooping like the tarnished knobs in our home. "Mom's real hot. I cracked her Brenda Lee record." Forward they crept into the domestic dim, tiptoeing around tables and chairs, restraining giggles until they got upstairs and fell to pieces. They showed each other their scars. (Marianna was famous in our family for scalding her bare feet with the chicken pot pie she had removed from the oven bare-handed and dropped.) The new friends smoked until four Kool cigarettes were *history*. Marianna basked in the fumes, I imagined. She was on her way, finally. Going somewhere. Bridget being the star made Marianna at least a costar in her own life. They shared BBQ potato chips, the clay-colored flavor dust smearing fingers that they then sucked. Full of flavored smoke, Bridget's bedroom resembled a smoldering candy store: cherry-red sheets, polka-dot

pillows, Raggedy Ann wallpaper, batons, pinwheels, pom-poms, hats with star-spangled paper bands, Styrofoam top hats, paper garters, training bras with kite-string straps, inside-out period costumes: Gay '90s and Roaring '20s and Wild West. Cuds of chewed-looking spandex leggings dwelled in drawers that never got closed. There was a single dusty blown-glass Delta Dawn rose in a plastic vase. The only clear space was an area in front of the bed that Bridget called her stage. "Want me to show my stuff?" She didn't wait for an answer. With astonishing speed Bridget's clothes flew off. Revealed: skin dyed in some places by costume run-off and in others bruised by the acrobatics required to Make It Big. On flew her yellow leotards ("leotrads" in Marianna-speak) and the matching sequined vest, the honeybee Ute's getup chosen to accompany the irresistible ragtime theme of *The Sting*, starring Robert Redford and Paul Newman. Mombardo had first encountered the routine in a magazine for stage mothers. Bridget Bee, vintage 1928, spun and spun and spun her baton-stinger, which might (she hoped) also behave like a radio transmitter, emitting a sweet signal to tickle the brain of a producer lounging on a Bel Air pool deck until he couldn't stand it any longer and rushed to the airport in a tartan robe, bearing the Contract with a dotted line where Bridget's name, and no other in Iowa, belonged. (Aside to cynics: It happened to Jean Seberg of Marshalltown, a petite seventeen-year-old plucked from among thousands of hopefuls by Otto Preminger to star in *Saint Joan*.) The overplayed cassette tape struggled valiantly in its machine slot: Scott Joplin's rollicking composition mired in aeronautic buzz and fuzz. Sequins undulated and glittered. Bridget slipped and fell to her knees—a clever mistake on purpose to steal the breath of grandmothers not present. She rose, a chorus line of one, and mouthed words to a song with no words. The terrible fate of having to rhyme! She did not care. She had an audience. *Sting / Wing / Ling-Ling / Bring*. She snatched the bowler, strutted mannish like Liza Minnelli in *Cabaret*. (More? thought sister. More.) Tap shoe on stool rung, elbow across knee, Bridget imitated a wizened saloon prostitute gazing wistfully at the low ceiling over her memories. Backflip, cartwheel, and—*ta-da!*—splits that did not split her, as the chippy ragtime roar-chatter faded and a single mother could be heard downstairs on the phone, enjoying her own yelling: "Don't got the alimony, don't cut it, buster!"

MOMBARDO, IN THE MOVIE IN MY MIND, slammed down the receiver, and pulled up a shade, and spotted a handsome hunk of neighbor taking out the garbage. Inspired, she respiked her hair with styling gel from a kitchen counter jar, and grabbed the Hefty bag squatting on the floor like a serene Buddha. "Nice day, eh?" called Hunk from across the street. "April in Davenport!" yelled the lithe figure slinking down the driveway as best she could while dragging petrified pounds of fast food. Hunk faltered. He did not know the song she referred to. He knew it was October: not the weather to be wearing no shoes and blue jeans and the photo shirt depicting Bridget at the Mississippi Valley Fair. "Isn't it lovely!" Mombardo added, dropping the trash and slide-stepping in front of the stench to keep it from defiling the healthy presence of this male who had yet to do her wrong. He nodded, smiled, turned, frowned, shouting over his shoulder: "Good day!" No invite to drinks and dinner but pronounced with an *umph*! that backed her up against the damp bag. She felt licked in the worst and best senses of the word: finished, yet hardly begun. (Within a few years she would snare a mild-mannered widower on nearby Forest Road.) Back inside, she announced: "Bridget! New Friend! Let's order pizza from Happy Joe's!" The girls were for that, having not eaten in the previous hour. Bridget wanted pepperoni, Marianna sausage, Mombardo garlic, a pie with multiple personalities, then: "One Sybil special, if you please!" A solemn man taking orders in order to supplement his meager social security check warned that it would take "longer than usual," and it did: an hour longer. Mombardo spent the time waiting by repairing an orange tutu Bridget had slept in. While stitching and patching, she imagined the labor connecting her to relatives in the Old Country, stout fishermen's wives atop pier barrels, mending nets torn by swordfish. The girls retreated upstairs to smoke, talk, twist and pull and shoot garters across the bedroom like rubber bands. Marianna described how her daddy the Lawyer cooked hot dogs prehistoric style, on a fork over the burner flame, meat skin flaring and sizzling to a chalky ash with pink in the middle. Bridget thought for the first time: *Could be I'll have to ditch her.* Then Bridget described being "frenched" by a unicyclist prodigy at the preteen unisex pageant. Marianna thought: *Bridget's a baddie.* Just like this sister was a baddie, according to my mother, for running off, and Howard was a baddie for stealing bucks from her purse to buy chips and hitting people. Our parent had broken a family in two over her knee, casting me, and sometimes Elizabeth, as the only good souls. "Pizza!" shouted Mombardo. Box open on the table, steamy isles of cheese and meat. The girls had at it: ripping off hot triangles, burning tongues and screaming in delight. Mombardo expertly folded slices and airmailed them down her gullet. Nearby stood an heirloom china cabinet that had never housed a single dish—in previous decades enclosing only the dark concept that much too much had been paid for it at Montgomery Ward, these days crammed with Bridget's awards: trophies vertical like skyscrapers, ribbons culminating in red or blue or yellow buttons impacted with folds, velvety hyper-labia. "Where'd you win that?" asked Marianna. "Springfield," said Bridget, flossing with a plastic fork. "And that one?" "Oak Park, I think." "Tell the *whole* story!" implored Mombardo. And a whole story followed: something about a Sally and tissues stuffed where tissues should not be stuffed, Trini and batons stolen during an electrical outage, the pipe bursting at the Motel 6, and judges "on the take." Another epic rife with specifics yet inflicting the evocative vagueness of a Sherwood Anderson story, leaving listeners with questions that grew and drifted like storm clouds outlining inexpressible truths.

IN BRIDGET'S LIVING ROOM my sister had crossed over and become Marianna. The defining difference between us children was how we each reacted to the family trouble. There were Clingers (Elizabeth, me) and Refugees (Howard, Marianna) and the frequently baffling outcomes of those choices. Refugees stumbled over their own feet, got hurt, were forced to crawl back wounded to the pit. Clingers, by virtue of attachment to chaos, were blown far away by its incessant ill wind. Birth order had much to do with the all-important initial reaction destined to color every subsequent one. It is no accident that the youngest pair (Nanette, Nathan) turned out to be milder personalities. After the nadir of the Twigmas year, the carless year, more moolah trickled in from various sources (mother's Legal Assistance salary, father's resurrected law practice) to pay for basic necessities, along with frequent raucous trips to Ponderosa for meat with lines on it or to Country Kitchen for the "All-American Breakfast": a family's subversive angst mainstreamed for all to see at a large Day-Glo table, a tableau disrupted by arrivals of lagging Millers and exits by angry ones, and wicked insinuations re: Those Who Bothered Not to Show at All—three of us typically AWOL, since Howard could not stand my uncool blabber, Elizabeth had to study Latin or practice flute, and mother hated watching her husband—representative of bankrupt farmers—indulge a decadent appetite for extra cups of sour cream costing fifty cents. Observing the rash errors of elders taught Nathan and Nanette the danger of declaring an affinity for anything: sour cream or clinging or flight. Refugees and Clingers were obviously tormented, always at odds. Howard and Marianna had no patience for the partial and mannered escapes of Elizabeth and me, who read our way to Paris in half an hour or visited Hickey's haven. Marianna sometimes visited him, too, and played the "state capital" naming game, winning a little change, but she couldn't sleep there. It was not enough. It was no solution for a Refugee. Like Howard, she desired alternative lodging, a new family. The search often landed them in trouble. Few good options existed, yet desperation demanded that they choose shelters and extend their stays by deploying charm and guile. They perceived the fierce reality: it is easier to totally rewrite a life than to edit it, as night edited remains night, a shackle revised remains a shackle.

"I DON'T CARE! I'm going to Bridget's!" No one was stopping Marianna from leaving her family in the dust so she must stop, make it clear she was running away, doing the worst and best thing a child under ten could do: seek a situation with a better chance of working out. "I don't care what you say! Bridget's number one!" Marianna twisted her head back and forth, back and forth, and her bangs whirled like a golden helicopter propeller. She was preparing to take off once more for Lombardo pizza, Band-aids, batons. I still see her framed by the battered screen door. She stood half in and half out of the kitchen of flies and rancid butter. Faraway in the house an unpersuasive warble: "Stop...her...Benji..." I snatched my sister's hand, wet and flopping like a hooked bluegill. If she did not hate me, she hated my fingers cuffing her. "You can't stop me!" She was right. I was the meek obese guard—best at imprisoning myself. She pulled hard. She dragged two hundred pounds of me onto the back stoop entwined in trumpet vines, where the couch voice couldn't be heard. Mother couldn't get up, of course: there were game shows, and her feet ached. "Fatty! Let go! You can't make me stay." "Listen, honey. Do what I—" "You can't make me stay!" Scream-sleet in my ears and sun running under the stoop's roof like a yolk broken: our tussle in shady colloidal light. Tugs traded, cries. A little I loosened my grip on Marianna, grasping instead my uselessness. I could enclose but not soothe the panic in her warm writhing hand. I could offer no trustworthy assurances. I felt her absolute immersion in the violent current of her frustration, and understood she would be carried off, sooner rather than later. Why detain her? I could not much longer. Granny Stanley's arthritic mottled hand was better equipped to cup and calm disquieted kin. Her fingers looked weak, but the swollen joints—like magic stones—washed out of a solid place inside her, out from the deep of sheets, and you were met with the sublime honesty of her modest intention to *be there*. I could not hold my sister, nor she me. We could not hold each other. That was the problem with us: the curse of the family. "Let go, fatso!" I let go. She went. The ton of me could not reel in an ounce of her. She charged though the backyard litter—cans and cartons kicked, her hair coptering—and toward the alley's serpentine cracks. In my heart of hearts (as Granny's saying went) I knew that my survival, like Marianna's, would be contingent on luck and dramatic events at present unforeseen. Like her, I must locate and cultivate strangers or neighbors who could satisfy a hunger for nurturing attention that our legal guardians, consumed by suffering, could not reliably provide. Mr. Hickey's asking "How are you, Benny?"—softly stated but with severe concern—created in a flash a different smiling me, reflected in his bifocals. For this sister, one Lombardo Band-aid promptly applied might be revolutionary. Small acts made love's largeness real. They were what made it tick and tick and tick.

"WHERE'S MITZI?" not asked by Elizabeth or Nanette, because the upstairs room the girls shared was more livable when sleeping but two on the bunk, with the floor mattress free to absorb the overflow of Lip Smacker lip-gloss canisters, stuffed koalas, and teen-idol trading cards. "Where's Mitzi?" not asked by me: I knew the answer. "Where's Mitzi?" not asked by father because his best solution to any problem was "wait and see." It was mother who huffed the loudest good-riddance huff. Translation: *Clingers are Clingers, Refugees are Refugees, what can you do?* Then out wafted the old flea of a proverb to circle my overblown twelve-year-old carcass. Humans, mother contended, often make their worst choices before making the best ones. I guessed she was referring to Marianna and herself. I hoped to hell she was right, while knowing she was far left, and most often wrong. I coughed into my hankie. I waited, like father, to see what would happen next. The family was her show to direct, script, star in. The rest of us were peons skating on banana peels. The situation was perfectly set up so we could only do wrong by each other, "right" being an existential trick of picking the lesser wrong. Were she and I on the brink of another Kmart trip during which nothing would be bought but trouble? In an hour would we be across the river, making the next withdrawal from Grandpa's bathrobe bank, taking Granny's blood pressure, *120 over 80*? Suddenly mother sat up straight on the eating couch, swiped crumbs and poetry anthologies off her front, and knew, for certain, that a daughter had strayed from the antimaterialist, antiglitz path, and not any daughter but the one named after the overdue library book *Tell Me a Mitzi*—as Nanette was named after the Broadway hit *No, No, Nanette,* and I after the Depression-era Benny doll that had been dragged through the mud by countless Southern girls, and Elizabeth after a queen. "Your sister! Bridget's stole her again!" I agreed. "We'll save her from sleazy Bridget!" she continued. "That Mitzi camping out on the Sunset Strip!"

BUT NO RESCUE WAS EASY, naturally. We waited until it was dark, as rescues were best undertaken then. Usually a teaspoon of gas existed in the tank (she bought a dollar's worth at a time at the Mobil station) but enough gas to make it? We never knew until it was too late. Should we actually squeeze our faltering intentions into the car squeezed into its dilapidated hovel, it was a prime occasion to pause, and congratulate ourselves. The story of our lives was the herculean effort expended to get nowhere. The rescues played out pretty much identically throughout years, the only alterations were these: a thin teenager played the fat mama's boy after 1977, and Marianna's east-side havens changed over time. The Lombardo interventions were especially memorable because they were the first, setting the pattern, and because the route to Bridget's house was the route I took to school with my mother. Those three streets changed my sister's life, and mine, forever. The five-minute drive up Crestwood Terrace, down McClellan Boulevard, and up Middle Road we easily stretched into fifteen minutes, me riding shotgun in the sputtering vehicle, wanting to help, feeling helpless, seeing the truth one second, not seeing, seeing, not seeing. We were moving at least. Weren't we moving? Nothing was awry yet. We had not hit one pothole in a pothole-filled world. "Bridget will be sorry!" mother said. Our bald tires hit the curb, rode it, dropped hard off it, the chassis chiding our rears. "That Bridget…" Mother made grave predictions about the effects of baton twirling on a soul and waited for me to agree, and I shrugged nervously, agreeing as best as I could. No statistics at my disposal, as usual—statistics ran other kinds of American lives. I had only a disturbing hunch the Lombardos were superior to us despite being lesser than us in every way. We pulled up in front of their house. Mother tried to stare her next thought into my brain and did an adequate job, but to be sure, she said it, too. "Go," she said. "Go get your sister. I'll keep the car running." She referenced sore appendages, and was not fibbing. She was sore head to foot: bad shoes, poor diet, scant sleep. Still, I wanted her to knock on the door. It was her job. She could charge the big bad store manager Wolfe, taunt him and turn him into a mouse refunding ten cents. Why couldn't she go to that door and get her own daughter? The real reason was always something she would not or could not enunciate. "Go to thee door, Ben-ja-min"—her lawyer voice far from the Supreme Court and stooping now to bully a boy. "Get your sister, now!" She needn't have yelled. But she had a fondness for prodding and I, a masochistic sponge, for absorbing. I could learn a vital thing about anyone by making myself available to be hurt and seeing if the person would do it.

I STRAIGHTENED CROOKED EYEFRAMES clamped to the dark room of my mind. I exited the car slowly, one leg, two—pimpled thighs chafed by dirty pants. I felt ridiculously obliged to try to stand in for the mother who had vanished inside a mother, as I tried to stand in for the father who attended no school events— me sitting in his rightful place in the bleachers and auditoriums, cheering on softball brother, symphony sister. It was called being "the oldest," a title of nebulous comprehensiveness. There was no idiotic thing "the oldest" wouldn't think of doing, of saying yes to. I inched the creaking door shut. I feared crossing a dewy lawn to ring the bell of a hip-swinging neighbor lady not expecting company. She might have a boyfriend named Deke who packed a .45. There were other worries, of course. And deep philosophical issues (DPIs) to mull, because DPIs were reliable buddies to call on when you had no friends your own age. One thought bubble popped to reveal another bubble and that bubble to reveal still another. Supposed actions of mine amounted to a combination of 98 percent stillness and sweat and *ifs*—if I could only come up with the right ten-word sentence to unlock Truth's door, if I could only take one step in a safe or positive direction. Through a window I was promised: "We'll go to McDonald's after, Benji." I crept across the sidewalk. Slimy mash of grass underfoot. Crickets, traffic, moonglow, peaty froth of spring air, and behind me, in the driver's seat with its reek of vinegar and fuel fumes, my mother's face bronzed by streetlight, frown and furrowed brow, the portrait of a woman not proud of herself. Self-destruction had shamefully become her greatest achievement—the most ornate result of decades of expending energy. Imagine being so mixed-up that you could neither completely abandon a daughter to the night nor find it in you to personally retrieve her. Maybe mother felt Marianna was better off in the care of Mrs. Lombardo. I listened for owls, gunshots, cocktail singers, ravine trysts, poker games, writers scratching and writers tap-tap-tapping, trying to break through mental blocks—"the itch" they had—and, when it got real bad, as with my father, "unpublished manuscripts" were born, and some (I guessed) had memorable first lines like "At times I forget that I killed a man." The novels in our basement were to me most memorable for my father's habit of typing the first seven words of every chapter in caps: tall healthy stalks of letters pleasing to look at. Maybe he was meant to be a famous typesetter of the novels of Wolfe, Faulkner, Farrell. Moths of more maybes floated by. Maybe I despised the mother I appeared to love more than life. Maybe, behind love's veil, I hated. Dare I despise her for not making up her mind about how awful she was? For being crazy bad, then ordinary bad, then crazy bad again. And what was Marianna feeling behind these Sunset Strip bricks? What did she secretly wish for, secretly fear the most? Would knowing she was not forgotten after all by her toxic family be more appealing than the wriggling ordeal of wooing virtual strangers? The closest I came to Refugee status were those Saturdays when my obsession with Marvel comics trumped my obsession with Mother Queerest and I demanded to be dropped at Wayne's Comic Book Store in Moline and spent four hours flipping through the alphabetized stock in boxes on folding tables and another hour outside, after closing, shifting my tonnage from foot to foot, praying alternately to hear the primal rhythm of her honking and never to hear that racket again—to be scooped up by the police and declared an orphan so I could be officially adopted by Mr. Hickey or Thor.

SPOOKED, HALFWAY ACROSS THE LAWN, I fought my wimp's urge to look back at the car. Maybe I should slit my throat now with glass aglitter in the Lombardo driveway. Maybe I should hope for no answer to seven rings of the doorbell. "Rescuing" sister meant returning her to the place where Howard bullied her and she shared towels with slobs (the brown stains) and slept not well in the Victorian-belfry shadow of Elizabeth, who became the classics she read like I did. Maybe Marianna was better off hustling on Middle Road's Sunset Strip . . . I turned to retreat. But where would I run to? In the car waited irresistible burger bribes and domineering lawyer threats, the creepy rustling-leaves gossip voice and those heartrending strangulated girly giggles. What now? Mother released her death grip on the wheel, waved weakly. She meant . . . what? Good-bye forever? *Good luck, chum, I know ya can do it?* But she didn't know I could do it. She panted on a perch of blistered vinyl, waiting to see. In her mind the city was lined with patio doors to Hades and the hunch was correct an amazing amount of times, given how wrong she was about so much. I waved back at the vague woman snared in darkness and light in a carapace manufactured in Detroit. She had been, I guessed, about Marianna's age when . . . what? Things she half-said had convinced me—rightly or wrongly—that she had jumped from a moving car in Dixon, Illinois—the child named Tommy Lynn rolling into the ditch next to railroad tracks running along the canal. And—another guess—that she had never been the same since being taken hostage and escaping or being pushed out of the car by her kidnapper. Was such an incident the root of her compulsive habit of half abandonments, half rescues, of letting her children wander off into harm's way only to haplessly snatch us back at the last moment for a consolation trip to McDonald's? It certainly could look like history's curse cast on the present— unlucky victim twisted by trauma into an attacker, she the heavy-breathing greasy-haired abductor at the wheel, my sister and I playing her former part: jumping into one dark to escape another dark...But who was mother getting back at? Us for being born? The girl she had been, telling a stranger yes in an alley when she should have said no? Perhaps she was using us to punish herself again and again for that mistake, wanting to help us but forcing herself to endure the torment of sitting idly by as we drifted into danger. Or maybe this was her only way of showing us what it was like to be her. But the potential cost of this off-label mothering was stratospheric. There had been terrifying close calls in parking lots and parks and malls. Part of me was perishing as my faith in this parent expired in slow, murderous stages. Under her thumb I had developed the useful mentality of a modern-day serf. Without expecting pay, expecting only more crude servitude, I did what I was told eleven times out of ten. And the thing to do now was to dart, not think. I managed it. I managed robotic steps in the scripted direction, telling myself: *Rebellion is all within. Rebellion is all within. Rebellion is all within.* The heavier the yoke, the lovelier the idea of freedom.

I GLIDED ONTO THE SPOTLIT Lombardo stoop. That door is now, in memory, the entrance to a maze of east-side doors with Marianna in the center, increasingly harried and haggard, her powdered face exciting neighbor men sensing an opportunity or wealthy classmates with the right drugs, Chicago clothes, and sporty cars. To many fine houses I was driven, on many fine folks I called, and was let into the foyer—"Wait here, Dan"—or asked to wait outside while "Cutie" was fetched. Privilege and its chill draft in the wake of Lombardo kitsch. I licked my chapped lips and reached for the bell but retracted my arm before it was too late— before I played the "hero" again. Anxiety needled my neck. Was I a hero? On many nights I encouraged mother's bad-mouthing of the other kids so I could reap for myself a tasty treat that otherwise would have been shared. I convinced myself, briefly, that I was Prince Valiant for agreeing with the cruel things she said behind the backs of Howard and Marianna and Elizabeth. Should the half-mad lady have no one to say half-mad things to, she'd be worse off! Her paranoia, worse. The chip on her shoulder, bigger. And that was not good for any of us. *Got that? You betray the others because it is the best thing for them . . . it'll make their life easier after it makes their life harder.* I a hero? What a joke. When the man wearing the windbreaker and sunglasses had approached Marianna at Duck Creek Plaza I did nothing initially. We were in Waldenbooks. I had dragged her there for a helping of Beauty and Truth and she didn't care. "I want to go." It was a spooky empty store in a half-occupied mall: outlets clustered at one end. Employees slept standing up. An incredible stench of cleanliness. Marianna drifted to the front near the checkout, and the perv— trolling the vacant promenade—saw her, bored and agitated, and asked: "Will you help me pick out a dress for my daughter? It's her birthday. She's your size." Marianna, like me, fell for flattery. He led her across the tiles to So-Fro Fabrics. I took time reacting. In front of the spinning rack of popular John Jakes novels I thought for a few minutes about what the man had said, then hightailed it out of Walden into fabricworld. I couldn't see them. Patterns bore down on me from seven directions. Plaid bolts of cloth on wall dispensers. Checked bolts of cloth spread on cutting tables, and the logs of designs stretching five high down the aisles. I freaked. I ran forward, panicking, and there the perv was. Sunglass lenses glittering, gilding his vicious intent. Wearing the kind of innocuous jacket any dad might wear. He held my sister's hand. They were within steps of the door to the parking lot, and his car, and ditch death. I squeaked: "Where you taking my sister, mister?" He turned, let go of her, and melted away like he'd never been there. Marianna looked around. She cried and cussed. She was going to get a quarter for helping, and I had ruined it. I led her kicking, screaming, back to Bishop's Buffet and mother, enjoying her fifty-sixth coffee refill, and there I really let Marianna down. We told mother. Her eyes bugged, she called me a hero, and talked of another "case" that had not turned out so well. She was saying to us: It happens all the time, it happens to everyone, it's the quirk of America and will always be—so-and-so's brother, he got dragged behind Kmart and molested. "Our hero!" she then yelped, to make it more official, and squeezed my shoulder, and kept yelping and slathering praise on me the rest of that livelong day. But were I a hero I would have nagged my parents to report the incident to the Davenport police. I did not do so, when I could have fingered the perv in a lineup. I could have sent the bastard to Iowa's Sing Sing—Fort Madison State Penitentiary. I was a good nagger. Nagging was the sole sport I excelled in. I nagged full-body, full-tilt, "I want . . . I want . . ." in a chugging Rock Island Lines rhythm to beat all. So why did I let mother let the perv off scot-free? Marianna in the manicured paws of a beast dressed like half the men on the street, my sister prepared to die for a quarter, and now forced by mother into service as a pitch-perfect groupie for me, her hero! Marianna, clapping on cue. I was her hero! I saved her from the perv! I heard the mealy echo of that moment of glory as I stood on the stoop too afraid to ring the bell. I felt sorry for me being me. Why did I waste a single second pitying myself, the sham hero, or my mother, the sham guardian? Today, knowing that Marianna perished at forty-four in an Illinois institution, after two failed marriages, drug overdoses, and a decade of increasing debilitation before her death, it's clear who had it worst.

I RANG THE BELL. The door flew open. Mombardo cigarette, spiked tinted hair, Mickey Mouse tank top, jeans administer-
ing a pelvic exam. She yelled: "Hotcakes is here!" Clocked by the
greeting, I weaved on the doormat, almost went down. What kept
me upright was the hunch she'd go down with me—on me—she'd
be all for that, rolling around together. I blinked, then glared at
the unexpurgated visage of a stage mother. No mournful-sigh
apologies to me, no second-guessing of herself, she was carnal-
ity stripped to the bawdy bone. Was this what my own mother
would see if she looked in the mirror, and why she avoided them?
No. The women were different breeds of exploiters. Mombardo's
immorality was plain and crisp, devoid of pretentious frippery.
"Enter, baby!" Her eyes burned rubber over my loathsome
regalia: church-sale attire. I stated a preference to remain outside.
She smiled the smile of an undone zipper. "Nonsense! How *old*
are you now?" I hated to say it but I remained...twelve. "In some
countries they call it the age of consent!" I flushed. She'd be
happy to answer questions I had about a herpes epidemic titil-
latingly referenced by cool classmates. She'd give me herpes if
I asked, probably. Her katydid arms were spreading. "The little
ladies are upstairs! Have a bite to eat!" She moved the bungalow forward five feet. I don't know how else I could have gotten
inside. She asked what *my* talent was. Feeling that the Poet thing
would not fly on the Sunset Strip, I always lied to Mombardo. I
mentioned the new PBS show *Austin City Limits* and my hopes
of tinkling the triangle behind country rockers like Neil Young
and Emmylou Harris. "Triangle, huh!" The rescue had begun.

THE DENIM PENDULUM that Mombardo called her
"tush" pitched as it scooted across the rather bare rooms which

nonetheless felt almost as chaotic as the cluttered rooms in my home. One detail set the defilement tone: cigarette butts afloat on cola in a Styrofoam cup sitting on an exercise mat. They told the tale of a mother and daughter who had only each other and thus, by a familiar quirk of familial algebra, had less than nothing on the cruelest nights, and on others—their bright marquee goal—the Sands Hotel for Bridget. I noted splotches on chandelier shades . . . taco sauce? ketchup? soy sauce? coffee? *Another family's stains*: disgusting in a way your own never quite are. "Sit your buns down!" Mombardo said. She was a fat boy's Medusa, though I had far more tangled hair and the bigger chest: my mushy rack. But I declined the offer. No, I'd not sit under a chandelier that resembled a befouled electric napkin. I looked in vain for a comfy recliner, some dim calm corner to soothe my assaulted senses. The space was nude, light-blasted, with an around-the-clock bus-station feel. "Enchiladas in the kitchen. From Rudy's. Go to town, big boy! I'll tell that darling sister of yours you're here to pick her up. I hope Bridget agrees! Pizza on the dinette. It's newer." Exit Mombardo. Shouting upstairs! I produced the crinkled white flag of hankie that mother had stolen from father's bureau for me. I snotted my brains out—continuing the multigenerational cavalcade of congestion. I swiveled, looking around for booze. In our house there existed one bottle wearing a dusty wicker coat. It lived on the top shelf of an obscure kitchen cupboard. Long ago—the story went—my father, who did not tipple, had unfor-tunately received this fine wine from a client who could pay for his divorce no other way. Since no tragedy should go to waste, mother had filed the bottle up there to make it look lonelier and more befuddled: like a rotund understudy cursed by luck to linger forever backstage, silent. She pointed Mr. Wicker out as a notable landmark on the family's slog into poverty, and because nothing could ever be allowed to be as simple as that, she kept pointing, talking, using him to prove what he disproved—the attractiveness of the "barter system" compared to the evils of money.

I HEARD MY SISTER before I saw her. "You can't make me go!" I didn't pretend I could. I had to bribe and hope she'd agree to leave. But Marianna was no fan of burgers torn in half by mother for sharing in the car cave. I mentioned she might steal a pair of Elizabeth's clean socks when she got home. "They don't fit, stupid!" Over her tomboy outfit she'd pulled a Bridget costume, sequins flashing like galactic granules. Her voice was changing. She talked in the same strained top register as Bridget. Lolita trills of preteen girls beset by expectations that they be "sexy." Marianna's keening, combined with the family language contagion that she had caught, produced the sound of a Barbie who had written an honors thesis on Lewis Carroll. Wacky words tumbled from the unstable height of her tone like cargo jettisoned by an aircraft in trouble: "You flubus! I'm not going out that door-a-roonie!" Bridget snorted, trying to get the joke, and, when she didn't get it, added high knee action and baton work. Bridget wanted me to wink at her. I refused. I fancied myself a feminist. Bridget winked for both of us. She knew her job—to deliver "the goods" in every situation. She wailed bars from "Delta Dawn." That had to be done more often than not. I was starting to see why. The alternative to one song was no song, and the difference between owning one song and none was incalculable. Owning one song, you owned a shape into which you could always pour amorphous feelings and thoughts—a shape to lend support to the sketchiest, yet most promising, angles of being. It was the grand difference between owning a life and much less—squat. Marianna

stomped, head whipping. "I'm staying at Bridget's foroonie-ever!"
Mombardo was transfixed. "Bridget wants me to stay, fatso!"
Marianna thrashed in front of the trophies. "Flumpter-bus!" she
shouted. "You pooped your panties at arksaw practice!" Bridget,
balanced on boot toes, shrieked. Mombardo stood hushed. I
hadn't expected such atomic retaliation. Immediately I tried and
failed to convey the impression to one and all that I was a quiet,
learned flumpter-bus above addressing juvenile subjects like
pantie pooping. The correct term was *briefs*, since I was a male,
but it was true that on apocalyptic mornings when I could locate

no passably soiled briefs, I had—shameful to say—borrowed shiny too-tight peach panties from the clothes heap in the girls' room. Elizabeth knew, had talked. "Pantie poop-us!" The Big Chief notebook I might have slid behind languished outside on the car's dashboard. Even farther away, on the windowsill in my bedroom, was the solace of *Barrack-Room Ballads* by Kipling—the palm-size chapel of verse to stick my pug nose in, removing it, at least, from harm's way. Sis had me dead to blights. My eternal stint as a twelve-year-old continued. Already I had run into enough trouble to mull for the rest of my life and still most of the 365 days of 1976 awaited. Any firm rebuttal would be answered by descriptions of how bad my booty had smelled when I dragged a cello case into the house, hop-sliding, chest heaving, crying tearlessly—the doll pupils. To escape Marianna's continued onslaught and the facial wens of Mombardo's hush, I retreated deep into the bunker of me and cowered, a favored posture of reminiscence.

CELLO SECTION, LAST CHAIR, loon of nature calling on the lower shore—gently at first, a soft lowing rip-rap of pressure. I thought I could "hold it," like on a car trip. We were in the midst of evening orchestra practice. I tried different positions to quell the building pressure. I rocked forward, slid back, teetered side to side. The biggest and most troubling part of me—my middle—prepared to strike. I bowed the air in front of my cello, not touching the instrument's strings. I knew the piece being played was Bach (the stand sheet said it) and that was good enough for me—I trusted other players to make music happen. I had little idea how to play the cello. It was futile to seriously practice an instrument in our house unless you could, like Elizabeth, enter a C-sharp trance state and remain there for an hour, a thousand miles away from naughty cats and Howard burning rye toast again. At orchestra practices, and holiday concerts, I always held the horsehair bow at a safe remove from the banged-up and out-of-tune school-owned instrument. The other cellists were used to my many angles of air sawing, and thankful for no wrong notes. They sensed nothing amiss now but what was usually amiss: me producing wave after wave of quiet. But this was another kind of quiet, I knew. This was the quiet before a storm. I fidgeted with urgency, and dread. My "bod"—as McKinley gym teacher Mr. Taves called it—moved against me. Somehow getting up to find a bathroom was not an option. It sounds funny—but I did not know *how* to walk out on knobby Mr. Pope and the Bach polyphony. No clear path led out of the cello section. If I bulled through the phalanx of bowers I might well dent the fine European instrument of Greg and be responsible for a repair my family could not afford. And even if I did manage to harmlessly scramble over virtuoso Greg and his glower of executed excellence, then what? I'd be facing a pair of widely separated practice-room doors in a school not my own, Eisenhower Elementary. Which door was closest to the bathroom? How to get to it without being jabbed by Mr. Pope's baton? Cripes. I must hold it. Try to, at least. As Marianna's blond bangs coptered when she was threatened, I tended to squint behind my eyeframes like a myopic sharpshooter. Amazingly, this unconventional strategy seemed to be working. For some minutes I felt as closed as the Hoover Dam. With my eyelids clamped shut to create a throbbing retinal shawl of red, blue, silver, and orange pixilations, it was like seeing Bridget perform on the dam. It was like I was going to do it, hold it, and avert. My gritted yellow teeth. My elbows pinned to my sides. My tennies braced against the linoleum. I could do it. I could hold it. But then a number of negative factors came into play. This was a rare late practice after a long day of indiscriminate snacking on available goo and gunk. And my focus on the damming task, though intense, was not complete. It continued to rattle me, the disorientation of being in a wealthier modular school, the odor of warm wax, fruity new paint. Was I being watched? I made the mistake of opening my eyes to check. Light smacked the fading raiment of the dark's pixels. I recoiled. Mr. Pope's baton stabbed the air, and the violas responded as if seriously wounded, and I heard mother whispering at the end of the bed, rolling my toes between her palms, telling me again what I should do if a Texas drifter entered the room after she left it. "Spit, Benji, scream, urinate and…" It happened. I dropped the Load in my corduroy pants in the practice room at Eisenhower Elementary School with the tinted windows and latest A/V equipment.

THE MOST SHAMEFUL PART was that I could have held it longer, physically, but on hearing the agony of the violas I let go willfully, aggressively, as taught. I let go in protest and in terror, as on some mornings when I woke to six-octave screams of sisters fighting for the bathroom and turned over onto my belly and peed a pool to drown a day. This was worse, of course. Being in public, being not pee. Warmth oozed down my legs and all around, all around. My gaze swam toward the safe dock of a clock on the wall behind Mr. Pope. I waited for the music to stop, for someone to shout: "Look what…" The music did not stop, there was no shout, and somehow no one knowing was, in a way, as terrible as everyone pointing at the pantie pooper. One more incredible example of how secretly interwoven a family's madness could be with the status quo—how one opposing force could easily accommodate the other. Without so much as a stutter step, Bach blended with the waste of me and my waste with Bach's artistry. It was turning cold and sticky and colder and stickier. I lifted my arms at wing angles to aid the drying process below the belt loops. I restrained tears: good at it like my mother, who never could let herself weep, afraid—rightly—of being drowned by her sorrow. In slow motion I flapped my arms up and down. It helped. I felt drying occurring along the backs of my thighs, which I had elevated inches above the chair. I tilted forward and crouched in front of the chair, cello between moist legs but not touching them. The stem rested on my shoulder. It was my greatest performance ever until Mr. Pope ended practice in his quiet adenoidal voice. Walking presented a challenge. I slid, and hopped, combining both motions, exiting the band room into the hallway and trailing behind Rod, the cello player whose dad had offered to give me a ride. "Come on," urged Rod, concerned, a deep voice for his age. I felt like half of me was back in the orchestra room. I fixated on odd details as the panicked do. The spaceship of hall lights. Bulletin board daisies. There was no smell except mine, the reek I barely managed to stay ahead of—slide, hop, slide … The ride home was the longest ever and I had been on a many epic circum-ambulations with my mother. A small truck cab, three in the front, the concentrated stink of cheese and poodle and the breakdown of starch. Tensed against further flooding, seated respectfully above the upholstery and starting to chafe, I glued my silence to city sights that might save me—the lit ranch houses promising a quick clean slide into a bubble bath; corner mailboxes in which I could live a "boy of letters" life; tree shadows branched with unprecedented personal meaning. Rod was an excellent kid, no brat. He wore his belt a little too high. His sister, Regina, had been struck by a car on Locust Street and almost killed. On the playground she wore a helmet over her healing skull. Rod was by nature forbearing, a Cub Scout. But human. He giggled finally. His father held it together longer, but my faint good-bye broke his concentration. He choked on "Good night," guffawing as I departed the truck cab.

"PANTIE POOPER! I'm staying! You're not my dad-a-roonie!" I wasn't. I was, though, the oldest male within shouting distance. I half held out a hand, quailing: "Come on, Mitzi!" But my pathos couldn't stand in for my mother, who could beam, propagandize, raconteur her way through disasters whenever the ploy of first resort, martyr-in-a-shroud, failed. I had seen her brutally charm provincial grocers with sultry allusions to "my year in New York City." A crisis rarely worked to my advantage. I lived on the verge of nervous collapse, as my sisters and brothers had figured out ages ago. "Dingo!" said Marianna. "Come on," I pleaded, stepping toward her. "Make me, pooper-dooper!" Then I lost it. I did not yell, stomp. Me losing it was me silently, hatefully, thinking only of revenge. *Whatever happens, I'll get you back for what you said.* "Shut up," I said. The tension caused Bridget to cartwheel, and frown on my behalf, and cheer for Marianna. Bridget knew audiences sought inspiration and desolation in equal measure, alligator tears and three-pound lollipops. Emotion simplified: *Thaaaaaaaaat's entertainment!* I lunged at Marianna, hooked the little fish of her hand for a second before she wriggled free, ran around to the other yummy side of the pizza-party shambles. Come get me, her wagging tongue dared. I did not go get her. For one thing, I wouldn't fit back there, between the wall and dinette.

For another thing, I was pitying her again. When Marianna was seven—recent past, but long gone—she had declared a definitive ambition to be an architect. Told everyone. I had not forgotten. (Could never forget. The night before her first marriage, I stood at the rehearsal dinner in the Bettendorf Holidome, as dank as the tropics, and rambled about her architect ambition as her in-laws-to-be—an Irish Illinois farmer and his wife—blinked in bemusement.) This sister had wanted to be an architect! In second grade she did not, like me, draw gorges of burning figures. She drew dream houses for citizens to be happy in. The crayon roofs were oversupported by stilts. She sensed all homes were houses of cards and had adjusted her designs appropriately. With inglorious enterprise, she had drawn dream houses right on the walls of her own dump of a home. Mother approved of graffiti because not to would be "censorship" and she vigorously annotated her argument, citing Norman Mailer's lavish praise of "street art." But buying Marianna sheets of draft paper would have been a deeper statement about the value of expression. Dime-store pastel scrawlings on plaster were yet another example of the nightmare inhaling the best of us. Then, in a blink, the architect had made way for an insecure girl who thought her only chance to make it was being Bridget's friend. "You pee your bed, too!" Hard-news reporting now. She meant to stain and stun, and succeeded, but it wasn't about me I told myself—not really. This was about her. She was protecting her dignity in her own foul way. "Sheets on the door!" (Hung over the door to dry, yes.) My hands dangled limp below the table's plane. Were I to suffer a final collapse then and there, she'd be sorry. But I wouldn't. Most of me was out of her reach. I lived in my private orb of woe as she lived in hers. She couldn't have imagined the life I led in front of her goofy face, my private smothering motherbubble of poetry, serial killers, gossip.

Knowing little about me, she should distrust me. Distrust was the staple foodstuff of a family alienated from each other and the mores of their city. Marianna was right to be suspicious but still she would pay. I hardly had to raise a finger to exact my revenge. The momentum of the situation's wrongness would do most of the work, as it had done many times before. I only had to remain upright, go with the flow, blandly intone "It's time to go, Marianna Rose." Bridget and Mombardo looked puzzled. They did not know anyone by that solemn name. "Mother's mad," I said. Marianna did not like the sound of that. I embroidered: "And she'll come in if you don't go out." She could hear that I had for the moment conquered doubts about my legitimacy, which generally happened when the outrageousness of waiting for an adult to intercede became too much to tolerate. "Let's go," I said, and added the low growl of "Now." Marianna caught her breath, wailed: "She's driven away! She doesn't care! She never has!" Mother may have packed off but I doubted it. I guessed she was still out there, dining on Vincent Bugliosi's Manson family history and pausing periodically to glance at the Sunset Strip on Middle Road and ponder, as I did, how the Lombardos could be bolstered by their avid fantasies while our Truth and Beauty crusade made of us mincemeat.

WHY, BRIDGET AND MOMBARDO were rich with the pure desiring of fame and fortune! Just wanting it—nothing else— seemed enough for them. They raced on, released from the weight of contradictions, the misdirection of misgivings. There was no bad fame, no bad money. What was there was always there for the taking—by them. Bridget's gyrations of sadness were more faked than her gyrations of joy, I kept noting. She had hope of something in the near future. What was not to love about the countless ways fame and fortune could come to a person in America? All it took was the good audition, the right connection. You didn't even have to be worthy, thank the heavens. You could be lucky. Luck was what beat history back best. And if, once achieved, your celebrity status faded, well, it was sure to be reclaimed when you died in the kidney-shaped pool. The only sorrow on the Sunset Strip at present was an invasion of Miller sorrow. Bridget and Mombardo were pleased with their bleak, shiny existence. Logic indicated they should be suffering more. But they weren't woeful in any way, not on television and not in person. They were sassy. They were cocksure. They did not act sad and beaten, which meant…they were not sad and beaten…maybe they were even happy. Could greed be as powerful a soul nectar as poetry? (Or as powerful as poetry *usually* was—mother, for example, drank deeply of it and her soul still wilted.) The confidence in the Lombardo house kept digging at me and my assumptions. Bridget believed she could go far by following the advice of one who had not gone far—Mombardo. It was wrongheaded but tireless boldness, and, for the time being, triumphant. The Lombardos didn't waste time being "sensitive." That gig never paid. I had to be impressed by their pristine callousness: it almost amounted to insight. The more sensitive a person was, the more he suffered, and the more a person suffered, the greater threat he posed. Sensitive humans, socked again and again, could become bitter enough to attack others again and again. It was the story of many of the killers mother told me about—they were the shy ones, the artistic ones, the exotic lilies. Perry Smith, the killer of the Clutters, gently touched what was left of the farm girl he'd executed. That was only one of mother's many examples of horrifically awry sensitivity. The egomaniac driving toward definite goals would not swerve to do damage for the sake of damage. A warped sensitive soul, however, just might.

MARIANNA POUNDED THE DINETTE: pizza boxes danced blocky jigs. She radiated disgust as it is best radiated—in dreadful spits of silence. She stuffed a pizza crust into her mouth. Bridget made more happy-sad-happy faces, facsimile emotion for facsimile lives. Mombardo suggested ordering Hungry Hobo "sub sandwiches: crème de la crème!" It was amazing the sense her nonsense made—how it fit into every scene, this normal American abnormality of me me me consume consume consume. She ran off to get the menu in the kitchen. I was famished. Depleting, this rescue business. I'd make no order, though. If I did, I might be asked to "chip in." It was cheaper to fawn over the jigsaw of leftover pizza slices. There was no stinting on the amount bought or the amount wasted. Where did the funding come from? (I never found out.) Mombardo wanted girls to stuff their faces, Mombardo wanted to stuff her own narrow face. It was a far cry from my mother in full martyr mode, insisting that I—not she—order at Big Boy, and then, when the platter came, asking for "just a little bite," whereupon I would slide the burger and cottage fries across the table and say, "Take what you want," and mean it (she could look hungry as Appalachia), yet she wouldn't take the big fat bite I knew she wanted—not letting me give what I could—rather instead reluctantly choose one fry, the stubbiest soggiest cottage fry, and dunk the carbo nub into the puddle of ketchup and push the plate back my way, muttering: "Oh, honey, that's enough—finish the rest." For weeks she seemed to live on nothing but free grocery-store coffee and hard candy and the perverse satisfaction of exposing her children to the religion of compulsive self-denial. If she had had the run of the most beautiful castle—Castle Stanley in Scotland, say—she'd find the most miserable maid's room to sleep in. "No one for Hobo?" asked Mombardo. Bridget patted her waistline, sniffed a model's sniff. Marianna spit out the half-chewed crust. She noticed that Bridget had stopped declaring support of a sixth consecutive sleepover. Bridget was bored. She must do what she could with minor fame while it lasted, time was a-wasting. She had to make tracks before the road got rougher. She needed producers, directors, collaborators. Clamorous Marianna could sing no duet. Marianna only insulted, Lolita-trilled. She owned no plausible uniforms—her socks didn't match: yellow and green. The sister who would not go had pulled off the sequined halter and flung it to the floor. She was at last edging in the direction of the door, head twisting, hair elevating.

MOTHER HONKED. The sound slowed us on the wet front lawn. To get to the car was to reach the next debacle, the next interment. My sister and I got quiet. It seemed that one yell of ours out here would shatter the city to shards—the Iowa we needed to cradle us. We did not hold hands. Separately, but close together, we crept like shades in and out of arcades of shadow. I told myself a sad, but slightly hopeful, thing. In the many years of botched rescues to come, it was something I often thought to calm down: *I cannot be her parent but someone could.* If not the figure hunched behind the car's still wheel, then the man who on some nights, around this hour, lowered the newspaper and said to any daughter in the room, "Come here, Goozie," and leaned the peppery stubble of his cheek over the padded armrest to receive a sweet kiss. That was her father, surfacing, and he reappeared also when the carnival came to town, taking all his children to the midway under the Centennial Bridge. He disregarded mother's warnings about cost. He limped to the ticket window and fought with the tattooed man in it. "That's all the tickets I get for ten bucks?" he asked in his wilted tenor. Yep, it was all the tickets he got off the roll. Shoved hard out the slit, they landed in the mud. We picked them up for him. Howard and I could do what we wanted to with our tickets but father insisted on taking "his girls" up in the Ferris wheel, one at a time. This neighborhood recluse folded his stiff aching frame into the swinging basket next to beaming Marianna and her cotton candy on a stick, and she babbled with anticipation, appreciation. He called her "Muff" at such times. She liked that. She gripped the basket bar with one hand and kicked her patent leather shoes. He flicked a cigarette butt. He sang lines of a silly song made famous by Bing Crosby: *Mares eat oats and does eat oats and little lambs eat ivy . . .* Marianna clapped. When happy the man crooned like Bing and did a spectacular job, briefly. He was proving to her that he still had something in him, that the ugliest show could go on for the loveliest reason—could even reach, every so often, a few seconds of crooning: *Mares eat oats and does eat oats and little lambs eat ivy.* Then he coughed and stopped, encountering the reality of his lungs. Their basket jerked higher as the last few baskets were filled with pairs of teenagers. Then a thug in a tank top yanked a lever hard. It happened. Father and Marianna aloft in the nest of candy-colored bulbs above booths and mud and tents, borne skyward, gliding higher and then higher on the spinning wheel, like a celestial wagon bound for Venus, until, at the apex, they vanished. Their faces reappeared out of the darkness on the way down and Marianna waved at me, receiving my big wave in return.

BATTLE HYMN OF THE IOWA STATE TEACHERS COLLEGE

Mirage of the Golden Rule — Show-and-Tell Bullet — Pick a Name, Any Name — Dick and Jane and Lee and Wayne — Mrs. Savory's Last Stand — Visit Me at the IMC — The Fifty-Yard Dash — The Artillery of Melody — The Custondian — Graap Rhymes with Crap — 10 cc of Emily — Destiny's Child — The Scarecrow's Autograph — Assignment of a Lifetime — The Schwinn Fiasco — Alfred E. Neuman Goes to School — The Other Grass — Fifth-Grade Tumor Factory — Everyday Devotionals — We're Number Two! We're Number Two! — Idyll of the Thing

Mirage of the Golden Rule

ON THE WALK TO SCHOOL my mother and I measured out our steps like tippings of flour during wartime, like a ragtag infantry navigating a no-man's-land of DAV-stamped sidewalks and hedges sheltering hidden machine guns. F-bombs were flung by teenagers jerking the gearshifts of their first cars. We looked both ways for hearses when I was eight, then ten, then twelve and 215 pounds. Levee train whistles transfixed us. Clouds diapered the sky above thousands of acres of Iowa pavement. We picked dandelions and blew on their ethereal crowns and watched as the light-flecked filaments spread like luck. Scholar Elizabeth always surged ahead: didn't want to "cut it close." Howard and Marianna, who frequently lagged behind, did not need a mother to teach them how to be tardy, nor did they require her force to ward off bullies. Bullies favored Howard's bravado and the flounce of Marianna's ponytail. I needed the guard. My skirt-length XXL shirt and her soiled dress were the spectral residue of the preceding furious night of bargain hunting and runaway sister chasing and Granny nursing and burger sharing and delivering to old neighbor Hickey our panic and last living hope. The hope against hope that the next day would be unlike preceding days—a new day when at last we would figure out a thing or three. Alley cracks seeped through the thin soles of our shoes and smithereened our dialogues into half-finished sentences, half-eternal silences. "I jumped out of the car and rolled into..." she whispered, but never finished the memory. No, she would swallow and quote the first Dylan, last name of Thomas: "Rage, rage against the dying of the light!" The night was behind us, pushing. Did she stumble or did I? We lived by making simultaneous mistakes. It was difficult to sort out which one belonged to whom. We looked both ways for social diseases and rummage sales. She pointed out a garage where a woman overwhelmed by marital problems had "ended it all," car running, door closed. Then! Then there was McKinley Elementary School, standing like an illusion in the midst of our forest of grief. Chain-link fence, playground empty. No white-booted, badge-laden Ms. Commandant stalking gravel-flinging boys. No cliques of girls and their favorite Lip Smacker lip-gloss flavors. *Watermelon kicks!* Just art taped to rows of windows—autumn leaves or snowflakes or bunnies, depending on the season. Mother grabbed me as if she had seen the devil in the pink bricks and cried: "Oh, Benji!" "Don't make me go!" I answered. My trouble did not fit within school walls. My trouble fit only with her trouble, the family crisis. Years of proof existed. Our trouble never followed the Golden Rule. Elizabeth excelled, but without ever assimilating. The torque in her eyes was the torque in mine—the frustration of shuttling between the opposing nonconversant realities of school and home. She cried herself to sleep over the mean things that Heights girls said to her and how the teachers she slaved to please failed to give her enough credit. Inside McKinley we children were expected to be the sons and daughters of parents other than the sort we had, and it was impossible. We could only be us: difficult. "Please don't make me go," I repeated. "They hate me. They…" She let go of my hand to grab me better. We stood as if bolted to the concrete. Wheaties ads never said mornings could be like this. Mother, moaning, wouldn't force me to go, would she? Didn't she need me to watch *The Price Is Right* with her again for two weeks in a row while the rest of the kids were stupidly dotting *i*'s, crossing *t*'s? The fear of leaving her in her lonesome and degraded state tripled. And the other fear—of her leaving me in my decrepit state—also tripled. Parting at age twelve was more difficult than it had been at seven—a bad sign. Were we not, at last, too far down our crooked road to divert onto the straight and narrow path? In Mr. Hickey's kitchen, we caught glimpses of a Formica seam connecting all to all, lost to found, despair to dream. He showed us mercy. He made faith in country real to us—a trick that no priest or politician could pull off. He did it without teaching: he did it by being there at the table awaiting the rapping on the door, anticipating the company of our disaster, extra cookies on hand, extra 7UP, Sanka packets. Surely that generous forgiving seam must extend beyond his pristine haven, but we lost sight of its gleam when we left around midnight, creeping down his back steps and along the precarious cement retaining wall, down a second set of steps to the terrace below. What loomed ahead? The dwelling where we became more lost, more apart from neighbors and the best in ourselves, munching junk food as our widened eyes slurped up the grainy shadows of late late late movies. *The Good, the Bad, and the Ugly. The Treasure of the Sierra Madre.* That last hour of the long disassembling night could be smelled on her breath and mine now. "Can't I stay home?" She did not say. She said Mr. Jones, the principal, owned power tools rather than power. It was a joke. Jokes were a constant: our momentary cure. Vowels sloshed in her jowls. The early sun speared the taffeta of her tattered dress. Then her tone completely changed. She whispered that I had watched JFK's funeral with her in the apartment on Bridge Street: *casket soldiers flags John-John Caroline Jackie, the blanket that swaddled me enveloped by the dirge of gray ceremony, caisson, bugle taps.* She reminded me I was named for the Benny doll that Granny had ordered her to burn. This was after Granny's stroke at fifty-four. Granny loved the doll and wanted no one else to get it if she went. Mother did the job in the alley behind the Stanley home while pregnant with me, and then gave birth on November 5—a date too perfect to be fiction: Guy Fawkes Day, in England, when effigies of the traitor were burned in the streets. Mother made another attempt to part from me by getting as close as possible, hip to hip (I was nearly her height and width). She nudged—or slow-danced—me forward, saying bye in increasingly tentative tones as we passed the ravine's green lip and reached the crosswalk. She didn't have the guts to punch the PED button— yet. No child should enter a school unarmed and she told me why, again. She warned me about "tracking"—that barbarous categorizing of select students as smart on less than credible evidence—

like nice clothes. "They decide who you are and then you are that to them until you become that to you. Vicious circle! Self-fulfilling prophecy!" I gasped on cue, but also of my own volition, because it was stunning, always, to hear her prepare me for school by heightening my already ample horror of what awaited in classrooms. It was as if we were farewelling at night on a dock or at a train station, under dramatic circumstances of hurry, personal loss, social unrest. There were two stories to each of her warnings. The story of the content and the story of how the content was presented. The points she made were sometimes acute, reflecting the unfortunate conditions on the ground, but she drove each point home like a subway slasher, twisting the hilt. She warned me about mob mentality. "Don't be a joiner," she said, "promise me." I promised. The world's end, when it came, would be a group project, bet your bottom dollar. But then she warned about an American scourge illogically coexisting with the "mob mentality," the gospel of every man and woman for himself or herself, win win win at any cost. Her teeth glistened fatly like cafeteria butter pads on ice, and she warned how materialism, greed, and money had infected the bedrock institutions of democracy—public schools and federal courts and legislatures and news coverage (it wasn't "the media" yet) and more. This screed had the faint echo of a gracious gesture toward her husband, perhaps already napping on a vibrating recliner at his office, in an upholstery-induced trance. Was she lauding his lack of earning power? Not really. She wanted him to be both antimaterialist and highly paid. In this confusion of hopes, hope dissolved. Despair could consist entirely of conflicting hopes, I had learned! Yet I chanced a smile. (Seeing the evening edition spread like a surgical tent over my father's troubled head and troubled heart, I still sometimes dreamed of crawling into the recliner, curling up behind the newspaper like a

chimp curled up with a parent in a tree, his breath rocking mine, mine rocking his, the breath that could not lie or cheat or be cheap.) "Bye," my mother muttered. "I love you," I said. "I love you, too," she said. Mistakes had exhausted the magic of the word for us—but not our need to say it, and say it. What was thick about us, what was really solid, was not our love but our loneliness. She plunged her fanned fingers into my hair. Life was, she murmured familiarly, *a lonely lonely journey.* She waved at me standing right in front of her. I waved back at her, three feet away now. She commanded: "Ignore the others! Who are they? March to the beat of a different drummer!" Just like that, do it? But couldn't she see? I disliked disappointing anyone, outside or inside. I was wishy-washy. She punched the PED button. I sucked air. I shuffled, not marched, to the curb. Righteous isolation might be the closest we could come to pride, but it was keeping me almost as unsocialized as an infant. The light changed. "I'll see you soon," mother said, and waved faster, as if trying to create a gust to bear me away without my having to make the painful choice to cross. But I stood there as the light turned and she had to push the PED button once more. When the light finally changed again, we hugged. "We'll go to Granny's tonight," she promised. "We'll go to Big Boy for the Special..." She almost karate-chopped my scalp with the last of the many last waves. I ducked. I could move quick when I must—like a planet shifting on its axis. I revolved into the street, and turned, and waved at the windmill of her. From the curb she quoted Tennyson: "Sunset and evening star, / And one clear call for me! / And may there be no moaning of the bar, / When I put out to sea..." She warbled the lines like a choking nightingale, she sang them like she sang "If I Should Die Before I Wake" as her shroud receded through bedroom gloom toward the one-hinge door that had to be jerked up before it could be jerked open: then the coffin-lid thunk. I forded the few remaining crosswalk bars. Head bowed, back bent, hands burrowed in pockets. I did not turn. I made an oath not to, one of many oaths I made and broke daily. One final final final time I heard a voice faintly chiming, indiscernible mutters from her worldly corner of the dark. I moved faster, as if purposed, a last-ditch emissary whose threadbare shoelaces trailed the cement, breathless and trembling for some truce, yet all but certain of war.

Show-and-Tell Bullet

SHE COULD NOT FLY. Mrs. Finch's dresses were too heavy—triple-knit collars, anchor buttons. Her face, the marbled white of uncooked bacon. She wore spectacles over it, and on her strong wrist a silver band that I imagined was stamped with info the old Iowa State Teachers College, in Cedar Falls, would really want to know, should we arrive to find our kindergarten teacher dead on the rug—cut to ribbons by a razor-sharp pinwheel, strangled by an aberrant alphabet banner: A B V W X D H I C E F G L O P Q R S T U Y Z M J K N. It was my dream to make that emergency call, to read off her dog tag serial number—T123—to the teacher tracker, and to report on Mrs. Finch's movements, habits, skills. On the first day she had somehow known that Greg, the future cello virtuoso, dressed in three shades of chocolate, was the smartest boy in the class. He never answered a question wrong after that. He understood that Mrs. Finch had said "occident" when the rest of us were positive she had said "accident." He slept in his thinking cap, set the standard in each subject. We napped each day after sucking pinched-open beaks of Baker's milk cartons. Not wanting to miss a second of the nap, I did not sleep. I concentrated on the rug against my back and the dimness where a ceiling once was and the strange new aloneness of being in school. Unlike at home, where I was one scream in a growing family of screams, at school I felt immersed in the space of me. I hovered there, an unexplored cosmos. One day I arrived late and wet—no galoshes or slicker or umbrella. I had "roughed it," according to mother. I tried to explain as much to Mrs. Finch, with her hand over her heart. But I had interrupted the Pledge! She sent me to the walk-in coat closet. Attic dark. The dark that slams down on heads. I stepped out of my puddle on the floor, but another puddle formed. My socks squished. I wiped my glasses—at age five, my first pair. Through the door I heard Mrs. Finch's voice in another land. I was surrounded by dripping Winnie the Pooh ponchos. Mrs. Finch, let me out let me out! What if she forgot? I sucked back sobs. Things couldn't get worse, until the afternoon they did. Mrs. Finch announced to the class that my father had shot himself. She held a clipping. "Yesterday, Mr. David P. Miller—the former county attorney—dropped an evidence gun at the courthouse and it discharged. How is your father doing, Ben?" He hadn't shot a hole in one like an ordinary lawyer. He had shot himself in the thigh, but it was the best possible place to be shot, I had learned. "Ben, could you tell us…?" When able, when ready, I said, "Out of the hospital…surface wound." Then I brought the shiny copper bullet, wrapped in gauze, to show-and-tell, and Mrs. Finch shuddered.

Pick a Name, Any Name

IN FIRST GRADE, in Mrs. Cummings's class, I wrote my name for the first time, pausing often to puzzle over the block letters. I had been de-prepared for the task by a nightly parental question:

"What name are you going to pick, honey?" I thought that question had been settled at birth, but no, mother said my "school name" could be "Benjamin" or "Ben" or "Benji" or "Benny" or "Ben with two *n*'s," or other names once considered for me: "McDougal McTavish" and "Shropshire." She said my name was up to me. I didn't want it to be. She explained what an alias was. I wrote both B-E-N and B-E-N-J-A-M-I-N at the top of assignments, hedging bets.

Dick and Jane and Lee and Wayne

In the spring patient mrs. davis, our third-grade teacher, finally moved my neighbor Brad because I could not stop talking to him about his father, inventor of the patent-pending mail-order ice rink. Mrs. Davis laid down the law as soft as carpeting. "Brad, I think you should move. Ben, you stay put." I stayed put, getting fatter. In two years, at eleven, I would be a hundred pounds heavier and getting heavier still. I handed in my first story to Mrs. Davis with false feelings of achievement. It consisted primarily of repetitions of the word *then*. Mrs. Davis circled each as a mistake: easy come, easy go, then. Strangely, having two names and two desks to myself made me feel like less than one student. I spread out my drawings of burning gorges full of stick figures to compensate. I realized then—to my horror—that they were *all the same drawing of the same gorge*. I had thought spreading the pictures out would make them more satisfying, not less. It was another of what they called "slipups." But fire kept leaping from my angel of death arm. The funny thing was I only feared burning to death when I was drawing; otherwise I feared drowning in an inch of tub water, like a drunken ship captain, or electrocuting myself with a fork in the toaster, or being nabbed by one of the faces in the WANTED posters that mother lifted me up to examine at the post office, her strong hands throttling my armpits as she read aloud descriptions of neck scars and snake tattoos belonging to robbers and revolutionaries, many named Lee or Wayne. "Cobra black, left forearm, blue eyes…" Mrs. Davis, for nicer reasons, loyally followed the exploits of "Dick and Jane." *See Spot run.*

Mrs. Savory's Last Stand

May it may have been for us: December it was for Mrs. Savory, our fourth-grade homeroom teacher. The last month of the last year in a teaching career that would be no fun to contemplate in retrospect. She began to wring her hands. To bite her lip. Her dyed hair looked thick until light shot through the auburn honeycombs. Her dresses were the red that was mostly black. She wore rectangular specs and redundant makeup that matched the putty of her natural pallor. Her brooches glittered like caramelized insects. Mrs. Savory inspired me when she opened up a discussion on "current events." I was the only student who read the newspaper front to back, spread it and crinkled it. I raised my hand ten times in five minutes, commenting on the Middle East, etc. She looked pleased. Her first name was Bertha, and it was not a good time to have that name, because of Jimmy Castor's popular "Bertha Butt Boogie." The Supreme Court had banned prayer in schools so when she rang a bronze bell at the start of class, instead of saying, "Children, it's time to pray," as she had for decades, she said, "Meditation time." I had to love the deft word choice. I meditated on how wonderful it would be to attend a Chicago Cubs game. Then she cranked and cranked the pencil sharpener until

the room smelled like sawdust. It was a statement. She did not
want to stop teaching and die! The mandatory retirement was unfair! At sixty-eight she still had the desire and the skills, welcoming new challenges. The previous summer she had overhauled
her lesson plans in preparation for the arrival of the new Harcourt
Brace readers containing words like *flabbergast* and slang like *yep*
and up-to-date references to airplanes, busing, poverty, pollution,
divorce, overpopulation, and the key to ending global hunger: sea
kelp. The younger Mrs. Davis mourned suddenly departed Dick,
Jane, and Spot, but not Mrs. Savory. She was prepared to lead the
way to 1980 at least. "Bertha," Principal Jones reminded her, "you

know rules are rules." She did, and didn't. In the middle of the last day, she tore off her specs and rushed from the room clutching a hankie, and the hall monitor entered. Mr. Schwenieger was alert, friendly, prepared. He wore banana-yellow pants and lime-green cardigans and whistled an elegiac "Up, Up and Away." Elizabeth had a crush on him. "Where is Mrs. Savory?" Eric asked. "In the restroom," he said. "Keep on with your work." Fifteen minutes later Mrs. Savory reappeared, arms behind her back. She reminded us that Greenland was not as large as it looked on maps.

Visit Me at the IMC

At an "aud"—as auditorium gatherings were called by Mrs. Jenkins on the intercom—Mrs. Pharenkuchen declared the library extinct. "When you need answers," she said, "visit me in the IMC." I could do without this librarian, but not without books, and soon passed under the INFORMATION AND MATERIALS CENTER banner to find the library as I had left it after checking out *Ethan Allen and the Green Mountain Boys*. What a relief! The card catalog was not blinking. The shelves were the old wooden ones arranged in the same orderly rows. It was like entering a Bavarian clock. All that was new was the banner. "Can I help you?" Mrs. Pharenkuchen cried, and her jacket shoulder pads rotated out from behind the desk. She can't have had square eyes and a pointy, nailed-on nose. But she did. With six pounds of costume jewelry to take on and off, she should never have had the time to get rid of the library and invent the IMC. But she did. "Projector?" She was not a teacher who directed fleets of data into the harbors of minds. No, she was detail-oriented about one detail alone: slide-projector availability. She believed it was her job to refuse you a projector, so it would be available to refuse to someone else. "I'm sorry, but those projectors you see behind me"—like gray-snouted pigs in the glass storage pen—"are *reserved*." I stated my business. She cuckooed: "Biographies! *Humpf.*" Reading was not fundamental to her. Possibly it was better that way. Enough librarians were "grabbed" by books, and "blown away," and other prosecutable participles. Mrs. Pharenkuchen rotated back behind the desk. She hunched over the top and fondled the only thing on it: the date stamp with the smooth tear-shaped handle. She manipulated it absentmindedly like a gear shift, as if she were driving the day up the hill of the day, over the hump of that ever-extendable "any minute." Nowhere did the second hand of the clock sound more labored than here. The *Tick-THOCK, Tick-THOCK* of the mules of minutes lugging the preceding millennia in their packs. "Quiet!" bellowed the IMC empress—not at me, I was positive. I had not made a sound. At the clock, she cried it, or at a nightmare resounding in her noggin. I crept into the stacks, my shadow trailing me like an ill-fitting suit. Many of my experiences were too big to be worn with grace. I sought allies on the shelves where George Washington Carver was serving a ten-course dinner consisting entirely of peanut dishes; Florence Nightingale feeling the forehead of a scarlet fever victim; Benjamin Banneker drawing street plans for Washington, DC; Madame Curie heroically dying of radiation poisoning in her lab, dying for the cause of knowledge; Helen Keller inventing sign language at the pump; Amelia Earhart flying into fog. I met up with Harriet Tubman again in the swamp.

The Fifty-Yard Dash

*F*OUR EYES CLARK KENT BUDDY HOLLY *pop bottle fatty glasses dork tell us your time in the fifty-yard dash fatso tell us blubber butt tell us what you got when you ran the fifty*. I wished for gym races to start at the finish line, and when they did not, when the Phys Ed teacher, Mr. Taves, blew the whistle and I required a few seconds to get it going, seconds other racers made other uses of, when I was that busty boy left in the dust, a funny thing happened. I rejected competition without quitting. That got to Mr. Taves. I accepted last place as the best place for a fourth-grade boy who had never conquered his love for the Madeline picture books by Ludwig Bemelmans. In last place I basked in my growing distance from the sect of hyperventilating strivers nearly asphyxiated by the oxygen they gulped. A wheel of cheddar could have beaten me, head thrust back and daydreaming, boobs squirming in my shirt like kittens in a bag.

The Artillery of Melody

"MINE EYES HAVE SEEN THE GLORY of the coming of the Lord: He is trampling out the vintage where the grapes of *wrath* are stored; He hath loosed the fateful lightning of His terrible swift sword: His *truth* is marching on!" And then Mrs. Nichols rose off the bench in the mezzanine music room and stepped out from behind the upright piano, and paused a few feet from the flagpole stuck in its iron base in the corner, her gaze lengthening into a faded blue corridor that led out of the room and all the way to the unseen shaven face, carefully parted hair, and pinned pant legs of Mr. Nichols, a World War II veteran who would be in his wheelchair at their nearby home, which smelled of liniment and last night's baked beans. A warmth of fond attachment swept over the rows of chairs like the ripple of a houseboat wave, and—*forward march!*— Mrs. Nichols smacked the strident triangle or clicked the castanets. The purported "fun" began. Copper cowbells. Xylophone miasma. Her retinue of directing gestures included extending her arm and opening and closing her fist as if she were trying to milk a fleeing cow, or hugging the air faster and faster until she had not arms, but churning roller dams. School molecules were like that. We forgot how lame those old songs were and sang our hearts out. "Praise the Lord and Pass the Ammunition." "Pack Up Your Troubles in Your Old Kit-Bag and Smile, Smile, Smile." "This Land Is Your Land," giving the whole country away to each lucky singer and listener, Gulf stream waters to New York *Eye-land*. At the Teachers College Mrs. Nichols had learned how to eat a ballad with a tuning fork, defluff record-player needles, repudiate synthesizers, duct-tape cracked maracas. She had never met a Rolling Stone. Her closet contained no blue suede shoes or leopard-skin pill-box hats or mojos. She doled out gold-emblazoned "ribbons of participation" after chorus concerts in the first-floor auditorium. I prized these purple and red and green ribbons. They were my only untainted reward for being drained of youth by the vast demands of childhood. I kept them in a business-size envelope, which was the most secret place I could find in the bedroom I shared off and on with my brother Howard; his canary, Cindy; and the Lindbergh kidnapping tale told by mother as a tree outside the window creaked like a ladder a felon was climbing. Sun poured into the music room, light that vulcanized the windowsills. "You're a grand old flag, you're a high-flying flag..." Then she played Copland's *Billy the Kid* on the hi-fi that had a gray lid like a Soviet leader's square brow. I heard lassos looping, broncos kicking...and penciled a passionate letter to the composer requesting an autographed baton. (No luck.) She let us bring our own albums once a week, providing they were "clean," and she put the needle down on the wrong track of mine, *The Monty Python Matching Tie and Handkerchief* and a character in the skit "Word Association Football" droned "bastard" and I was the coolest kid for three seconds, before Mrs. Nichols deported me to the mezzanine.

The Custondian

THE LANKY CUSTODIAN wore a light gray uniform shirt with darker gray pants. On butterscotch-pudding puke he sprinkled pink granules. Instantly the mess was absorbed, the floor again producing a burgundy candlelight glow that I relished. I needed him to apply that magic potion to my pissed-on mattress. I needed him to sprinkle that potion on mother's dress of the month. His mop cleansed linoleum of sins. He was the miracle worker of my McKinley gallery of blurs and cameos, but to others—to the Atari

Hush Puppies Spalding herd—a charge, a slave, or barely human *Custondian*, with limbs paddling in back-hall sloughs, his T-shirt collar showing, there to mock. His face was a hangdog face hung upside down, every sag went up. A scourge of agreeability. The "social contract" cruelly dictated that he be joyous over his sorry station, his ancient place in the pecking order. And he did it, maintaining a rigorous cleaning schedule. I was in awe.

Graap Rhymes with Crap

MRS. GRAAP'S BUSINESS was akin to that of a tissue box—to stand still and never run low on dry metaphors to capture, and conceal, a culture's roil and spew. What she said she should have sung to upper-grade history students—it would have helped—but she did not sing. *Government system of checks and balances*, she chalked onto the blackboard. And what if the checks bounced? I wondered. At my desk I huddled around the new same old apocalypse: pencil cartoons of *The Price Is Wrong* contestants burning to win "top prizes" in the pit of a Burbank studio. I had met these lost souls when school made me sick and I stayed home to help mother analyze American foibles filtered through, and highlighted by, the game show conceit. At the top of each cartoon, I drew, in viral letters, those famous words thundered by the Zeus of offstage announcers, Johnny Olson. "Come on down, Tina Lee! Come on down, Jessie!" Each COME ON DOWN banner consisted of dozens of COME ON DOWNs wound like fishing line within the spool of a dark outline. Below there were I-want-new-Maytag-Amana-appliance slobber rivers; I-want-Acapulco-holiday gopher teeth; vertebrae culs-de-sac of posture-pee-dick-mattress bliss. Necks resumed above the faces, growing out of scalps and hairdos like hollow tree trunks and forming steaming hot tubs in which a second set of facial features floated like soft soup vegetables. My pencil lead poured so furious and fast I smelled its heat. I angled the tip sideways and applied the fattened lines in a blur, the motion of my hand like a manic fan blade spinning a half circle, retreating, spinning another half circle, over and over. I pressed hard to make the lines permanent. This was engraving. This was craftsmanship. My hand working that page as hard as mother kneaded the balls of my feet while telling me true-crime tales of the day. Manson, mansion, mayhem. When every inch of space was filled with materialist trauma—as filled as America was filled to the gills with wanting and getting and wasting—I flipped the page to admire how the images had nearly sizzled through to the other side: the whorled inferno of junkified dreams.

10 cc of Emily

I HAD MY EMILY DICKINSON READING—injections of Emily—to bring me back to my senses. "I heard a Fly buzz—when I died— / The Stillness in the Room / Was like the Stillness in the Air— / Between the Heaves of Storm—" Emily's poems were like wind rushing into a clock and pushing its hands past hours that did not matter to arrive at the only moment that did. For her, and me, and mother too, everything started and ended at cemeteries. But Emily's closedness was an openness. Her kingdoms thrived atop a petal or in the scriptural flare of a wren's wing. Her slashes were like the teeth of skeleton keys, and each word gave itself to you in a secret way, like a floorboard giving way under the insistent pressure of a boot. She was unpredictably solitary, ebulliently solitary, unlike the hiker depicted on my black-and-white march-to-a-different-beat poster: he, clearly, was searching the dreary woods for one reason only, the best branch to hang himself on. Emily had successfully published herself in her own house; the modest materials of those books lent them their integrity. She trained light on the darkness and pinpointed the darkness in the light, its simultaneous coolness and heat, its goneness and its hereness. Her fears, compiled so exactly and so musically, became a kind of wisdom. "With Blue—uncertain—stumbling Buzz— / Between the light—and me— / And then the Windows failed— and then / I could not see to see—" Hers was an organic infinity, no preservatives added.

Destiny's Child

Eᴌɪᴢᴀʙᴇᴛʜ ᴘᴀssᴇᴅ ᴍᴇ ɪɴ ᴛʜᴇ ʜᴀʟʟ, racing toward another A. I remembered when I was four and I dropped my sister out of a second-story window of the house on Scott Street—the house before 15 Crestwood Terrace. She landed in the backyard, crying but unhurt, still in my life. I recalled looking down at the white spot of infant. Father, who had been napping, ran into the room in a T-shirt and boxer shorts, waving his cigarette, and raced out to assess skull damage. I was trying either to kill Elizabeth in a jealous rage or to save her, to toss her from a smoky house ablaze with an unfortunate marriage. Father had neglected to watch us, allowing me this murder attempt, and where was mother? Wherever. Our slipping out of each other's hands started at the start. The betrayals were hardwired into cradles, playpens. I had dragged my sister from her playpen to the low sill and had nudged and nudged more, not enraged, but methodical, with a vague sense of destiny.

The Scarecrow's Autograph

MY MOTHER'S FADED DRESS FLOATED down a second-floor hallway prior to the third-period bell. She had conned her way in. She had handed the monitor a line, and gotten a pass. She was best at that. "Benny, Angel! A letter from Hollywood!" She located her son, hostage of the status quo, outside of the math teacher Mrs. Hopper's room. I was horrified, but graffitied over my horror with a grin. She might save me yet. Everyone saw her: the torn sleeve, the canvas shoe burst at the toe, the helmet hair, her rough hand held high, waving a self-addressed stamped envelope—*my postwoman my guard my bedroom besieger my ICU nurse my one and only.* The stains on her dress would lead you to believe she had been stabbed seven times on the five-block walk but was refusing to fall. I shut out spectators. It was just she and I exchanging greetings beside a stream of floor reflections. I felt needles inside as her lips formed a wedge and descended, not far, to deliver the wet kiss on my ready forehead. I loved her like a weather vane loves wind. "Look what came!" she said. I looked. After Copland in New York had neglected to answer my autograph request I had instituted a program of writing West Coast stars, lesser lights likely to reply: character actors, one-hit wonders. It had worked before. Huntz Hall, star of Bowery Boys movies in the 1940s and '50s, sent me his signature in 1972. I snatched the envelope, whose corners appeared to have endured pioneer travails on the long trip. "Open it!" she commanded. I ripped and felt what I always did when opening mail: a slight relenting of the deforming pressure of isolation. Out slid an autographed black-and-white shot of Ray Bolger, dancing Oz scarecrow lacking a brain, losing handfuls of straw . . . but being him (like being me) meant coming apart at the seams. *Best Regards, Ray.* I wet a finger. The ink did not run. Machine signature, hundreds stamped daily. *No no, you're wrong: it's fancy waterproof ink from a jar on the hay-bale desk on the MGM back lot.* "Look everyone! Look what Ben..." Everyone looked, seemingly billions of kids staring at me. I smooched the amphibian bulge of her proffered cheek. She squeezed the Charmin of my pudgy arm. It was love again. I did not dare pull away. Who was I to pull away in public, or anywhere? I took what I might get. Each next touch could be the touch I was missing. Love was all—whether you were giving it, getting it, or living in want of kisses. "Bye, Benny!" How could she depart without rescuing her little Thoreau from the herd mentality, the Capitalist hell? The dress poured down a dim staircase like storm runoff into a drain. (She was leaving empty-handed and empty-eyed after pulling off the coup, depressed as usual by a success which only reacquainted her with the fact that there existed no one in the city who could stop her from continuing to be her—that brilliance living on, squashed, like a bug's wing twitching on bathroom tiles—no one who could stop her from continuing to make scenes because the only great thing she could do now was to light the dynamite of frustration, passing up nice thrift-store dresses by choice, rarely bathing by choice, cultivating the homeless look because—why else?—our house, our family, made her feel far from home and disposed of. Country girl from Dixon, urbanite, feminist, complacent housewife, lawyer: the fragments of her personality went at each other like mad dogs. The outcome of the fight was her chop-shop mind, and the feeling, which she passed along to me, that one could trust only in distrust. Half of any experience was what it suffered in storage in the mind, mired in other experiences, until the paste of Time, word-infused but untamed, assumed the impressive, if misleading, shape of Memory.) The buzzer sounded. Barks followed me into the room. Tweedy Mrs. Hopper watched me struggle to my place. I placed the envelope from Hollywood in the center of my pink desk. Where my mother had patted me, the skin tingled. I imagined that waffles felt like this when flipped. I knew that all of my classmates were still seeing her, continuing to see the hole in her shoe and what was sticking out of it. I could have told them she was glad to have any shoes, glad to have feet, even. A number of times she had mentioned a barefoot Illinois boy attracted by the licorice gleam of hot tar. He had run onto the road just poured. The pink soles of his feet were torn right off. It could have been a tall tale, but I was convinced that her lies— being whole—revealed at least as much about her as did the truth shrapnel she fired. *Who was that grief-masked woman?* A woman who had aged with phantasmagorical fury between the births of Howard, the third child, and Marianna, the fourth. Her respiratory system then became a raspiratory system pumping out the family language contagion. Her gums began to rot and her head ached constantly. Her suffering became mine via a moral imperative: my birth had been the beginning of it all. Had she remained single, and childless, she would have been far better off. I never questioned the unfortunateness of my birth as I saw her buckle under motherhood's burden. I wanted to *explain* her to my classmates. I wanted to explain she was one of those riddles you did not solve but turned this way and the other way during sleepless nights, seeking a glimmer of the mystery's outermost edge, that edge being as close as you'd get to understanding her confounding conflux of dolor, ambition, mistakes, rotten luck, activism, despotism, depression, law books, lawlessness, and poems. She was the inversion of the American Dream. All the rising out of poverty had sunk her back into it in the end, her college degree and law degree a ticket to more dirty rooms filled with bugs and hunger. That figureless figure was now grimly drifting down Middle Road, grafting her sighs of regret to the yellow Iowa smog. "Open your books," Mrs. Hopper finally said gamely. I wet my finger, touched *Ray*.

Assignment of a Lifetime

"I WANT EACH OF YOU TO PICK A PERSON, living or dead, and write two paragraphs about what it might feel like to walk in their shoes." Miss Haack's narrow face tilted in order to dive (more than drive) the assignment home to the fifth graders assembled in this snug room on the first floor looking out on the north lawn. "This person could be an American or a foreigner such as, for example, Gandhi." I kangarooed to attention. Family trouble had trained me for little else but what Miss Haack had requested as if speaking to us each alone and not to a group. I woke in a peed-on bed, not wanting to be me, and naturally started imagining the alternatives. "Or Anne Frank," she tolled, her tone extra sober as she stood before the class in her navy jacket and cone-shaped skirt. She was definitely saying: *Here is your one-page homework for a lifetime to complete over and over until the day you die.* Sunlight strafed our desks. I shut my eyes. I had always found that closing the curtain on surfaces lifted the curtain on what swirled behind them—the most important stuff. The subject, said Miss Haack, could be alive or dead. And I assumed that meant she would also accept paragraphs about a person both alive and dead, like my mother or my father, but if I had to consider my parents first out of respect, I had to dismiss my parents first also, on account of space limitations. Miss Haack would need to mount a bicycle to reach the end of paragraphs about them. My brothers and sisters were nixed as well. They were too much like tunnels with no light at the end. One possibility was Henry, the poorest kid at McKinley. His father had beaten every word out of him except the one starting with *F* and ending with *K*. He gave the finger to cars on Middle Road and got happy when flipped off in return. His thin suspenders, circa 1932, made my old clothes look new. Another leading candidate for my empathy was the deaf boy who came in the bus full of other deaf kids after we had been shown the movie about sign language. Needing friends, I volunteered to tutor these newcomers, and was assigned a boy with a mustache. It was called "mainstreaming." Then there was Charlie and his quaint chirping laugh and pointy runny nose and his pa, who sold reference books door-to-door ... shyness the silent disfigurer. Also my heart went out to Regina, sister of my orchestra friend Rod, for her tribulations. After her near-fatal casualty on Locust Street, where she'd been struck by a car, each day she strapped a helmet onto her bumper-thumped cranium and wore three-inch safety heels on her shoes. Her stitched and powdered face looked eerily like a mannequin's. Yet true empathy was more mysterious than observed details. It was a tender current exchanged between the depths of lives, never rote or obvious, as invisible as sonar. After sitting there for a long time, taking soundings, I heard the crush of footfalls in the sugarcane, gasping, dogs growling, men shouting, splashes and gurgles. I had my subject: Harriet Tubman. The slave submerged in muddy water, breathing through hollow reeds. Harriet outsmarting her cruel pursuers, inventing an underground railroad that saved thousands of lives. She was a healer, and I wrote something to this effect: *Lovely ideals in the Constitution did not give birth to the freedom road: one woman did in the back of her mind and bottom of her heart*... "Who would like to read their story aloud?" asked Ms. Haack, and Andy, a doctor's son, stood up and began: "Were I Ben's tennis shoes, I'd be sorry. I would be buckling under the weight—" Miss Haack shrieked. The class frothed. "You apologize to Mr. Miller right now!" said Miss Haack. Andy did and was sent to the Office. Never had I been defended so swiftly. When the bell rang, Miss Haack pulled me aside with the least drama possible. An ephemeral strand connected us now. She twitched it. I stopped and felt it was my job to reassure her. "I'm all right!" I was the histrionic stoic, producing *all right*s as squid produced defensive ink clouds. I felt it better never to ask for help than to ask and get none. "That was a terrible thing that Andy did." I nodded. "There will be repercussions." I had heard the word once before. "You sure..." Miss Haack looked for tears in my eyes, wrong place. Wadded up in my pocket was the hankie I wept snot into day and night, the real jelly of the inner life—its ingestion, congestion. The rag was both gummy and crisp. It smelled of eggs, glue, chicken gravy. When bullies approached I unfolded it and they backed off as if confronted with a squid's wrinkled foreskin. "Yeah," I said for the fifth time. "I'm all right." At last Miss Haack understood that I meant "all right" all right. Or heard that I was choosing for important personal reasons to say nothing was wrong when things could hardly be more disastrous. "You are being very mature about this," she said. Certain misunderstandings were absolutely reviving. We parted on the best terms. Miss Haack had my back like a cleaver. I almost wished to be humiliated again the next day to see my ally in action, but the next day no student dared take a step in Andy's new Adidas shoes.

The Schwinn Fiasco

Ms. Commandant, playground attendant, informed Howard that only students in fourth grade could ride bikes to school, and Howard later informed father, who was sulking in the recliner, behind the evening edition. "I got a bike and I can't ride it!" Howard shouted. Father, with the new credit card, had purchased Schwinns for every family member—including his spouse. It was his most shocking investment since the weekend he had presented me with a new sickle from Sears after our neighbors called the cops about our grass. Or was it a scythe? Anyway, a crescent blade befitting apocalyptic horsemen of yore, as if we were living in 1673's rack and ruin, not 1973's. Mother's blue bike had a baby seat in back. The thing was already on its side in the basement, tires gone flat. My sisters and I kept a safe distance from our new bikes, too. They had slithered onto the scene too quick. Their brand-nameness could not overcome our suspicions about the giver. He hadn't asked any of us if we wanted bikes. The charge-card orgy was the sole result of a mistaken notion: *a family that pedals together stays together.* Sweet, but that didn't cut it with us. He took it for granted that we wanted bikes because we were kiddos, but we were no progeny of Norman Rockwell. We were his complex children: leery characters sick of being taken for granted. Winning our hearts must be a *process* taking longer than the time it took to swipe a MasterCard! Besides, we wanted a new car, a Dodge, that's what. Only Howard wanted both. "You got me a bike and—" The mummy wrap of newspaper slowly wound off belly rolls, and father—like a college megaphone of long ago—boomed: "You will get to ride your bike, me lad! I'll see to that! I will!" Nine times out of ten "I will" meant: *I won't ever, leave me alone.* But not this time. Portions of his arthritic carcass began to lift off the recliner cushion in an order that might eventually amount to verticality. He hurt all over, but the gold fillings deep in his mouth twinkled. "Let's go, Howie!" he said. "But school's over today," lisped my brother. It was 6:30 p.m. "Then tomorrow, me boy!" And it happened. The next morning they crested the hill of Middle Road—Howard teetering on training wheels on the oversize bike and father hobbling behind, frenching a Camel cigarette, funneling smoke out a corner of his mouth. Mother was hiding at Mr. Hickey's house. I had rushed ahead to school as I rarely did, and when I saw them coming I hung my paws on the chain-link fence in disbelief. Then everyone on the blacktop saw Howard's head flung back, rebellious, proud, as if he were riding a motorcycle at seventy along a sidewalk, while his lame father tried to keep pace. The game of hopscotch stopped, and the rope jumping, too. Ms. Commandant whistled for reinforcements: Principal Jones and Mr. Taves, the gym teacher. Father and Howard crossed the street. "Stop!" yelled the Commandant. They halted at the playground entrance, holding their ground. Howard snarled a nine-year-old's imitation of a Hells Angel. Father looked lost in thought. Jones and Taves arrived. Jones a brown suit and turd of a tie, Taves a pair of red sport shorts and a whistle. Three necks between the two. Tave's complexion that of canned salmon. Jones's nose a sweaty trivet. High noon at 8 a.m. Taves squirted Binaca Blast into his sour mouth and Jones grunted. All day Taves marinated his gums with that stuff. Together he and Jones approached my brother, astride the Schwinn's banana seat and waiting for father to throw a punch. Jones said: "Well, safety first, you know how…" Father merely nodded and extended his hand. They shook. Then father and Taves shook. Father barked at Howard: "You heard what the guy said. Off the bike!" My brother, death-gripping the handlebars, shook his greasy head of hair. "I said—get off that bike! I'm going to ask you one last time—" Howard belted out his new mantra: "I don't care what you say! I'm running away to California!" Jones and Taves lifted bawling Howard off the seat. And father, limping, fuming, pushed the new bike homeward, looking in the distance like an overgrown kid who had suffered a flat.

Alfred E. Neuman Goes to School

I BROUGHT MY ENTIRE FLAKING COLLECTION of *Mad* magazines to school for moral support. These issues I had bought for nickels and dimes at garage sales, thrift stores. Some I had picked out of the library free box. I took them with me from room to room and filed the stack under my desk chair. I occupied a throne of William Gaines, Don Martin, Dave Berg. Between classes, I inched along the halls like an archivist carefully transporting desiccating cakes of pulp Americana. A trail of cartoon crumbs led into the deep woods of my emotions. The *Mad*s kept me company. At recess I was that joker with *MAD MAD MAD* pressed against a chest that had started the trouble by containing my turnstile of a heart. Other kids gawked. No cry for help could be more comic, transparent, futile. I was not sent to Jones. No teacher took me aside. They saw either what they expected to see—more routine rubble—or a two-hundred-pound wingless moth best left to the *Custondian*. Or, maybe, they saw nobody at all.

The Other Grass

At the water fountain, in a soft and slightly melancholy voice, Brent described to us the centerfold of a *Playboy* he had at home. "Her blond grass," he murmured, and kept repeating the words, *blond grass, blond grass, blond grass.* His friends leaned into the words. I stood apart. I could hear that Brent was maturing and I blushed. I understood, better than before, how behind I was. I wanted Brent and the others to wait up for me *something terrible*, as Granny would drawl. But I was too far back. They wouldn't, and shouldn't, wait up for me. They had their passages and I had mine. Only I would forever be poorer for missing out on timely explorations of youth and Brent no poorer for having missed out on my rites on the roads at night with mother or in my upstairs bedroom. I had a sill radio and *Ripley's Believe It or Not* paperbacks—not *Playboy.* I had Spider-Man, Krazy Kat, and a warped Parkway Chubby Checker record. I had Whitman to gorge my eyes on, leaves of grass no neighbor complained about and which I did not have to harvest like a preteen grim reaper with the scythe from Sears. But that day at the fountain I would have traded every single brilliant line for the other grass.

The Fifth-Grade Tumor Factory

Wherever mother squeezed me at night—shoulder, knee, arm, toes—tumors sprouted by morning. In first period I detected cancer spreading to the left nipple. In second period, cancer of the ear. Third period, thigh cancer. Fourth period, stomach. My fingers spent hours underneath my loose clothing, groping blubber, examining. Wherever she touched me on the walk to school, more tumors. But I was a few more places than she could reach. And she many more places than I dared to kiss or clasp. At eleven at night we would play catch under the streetlight with a balding green tennis ball that bounded back and forth between our thrift-store togas. We would sit on the curb afterward under the orange tepee of light. For a moment things were better in the heat. I secretly considered any curb to be the pinnacle of a buried staircase. The fantasy elevated my lowness at just the right moments. Then she spoke as she could only speak, a moan within a sigh: "I can't go back in the house, let's you and I ..." and so on. Favoritism, the most common poisoner of brother and sister relations. On the terraces above, the serrations of houses resembled a sudden ridge of pagodas. Across the street curled a curb on the edge of the steep ravine where a man who burned trash lived. Cement joined troughs of darkness on either side of it. "I can't go back there," mother exhaled. "I can't. I can't." But she was rising to go back in there. She took my hand, led me out of the light into the night and the blackness like a conveyer belt reeling us up terrace stairs and front-porch stairs ... into the house to all the rest.

Everyday Devotionals

THE HEAVY WINDOWS of the art room had been jerked open to release the unavoidable stench of the artistic process. Class ended and Mrs. Costello motioned me to the front of the room, where the sinks were, and the paper cutter, and the counters lined with jars of brushes. She wore a suede vest with purple beads and moccasins with heels. She extended to me a rainbow booklet entitled *Everyday Devotionals*. "Take it," she said. I did not. I told her what I told worried teachers. "I'm all right," I said, and licked my face because if I didn't the enraged skin bracketing my lips throbbed. Each lick eased the pain for a second, then made it worse the second after that. Wasn't that the way of the world? Mrs. Costello's voice fizzed like a chaste glass of sparkling cider on New Year's Eve. "Please, take this, as a gift, from me." I reconsidered. After five more tickless ticks of forever, I took it. I needed any gifts I could get. "I carry a copy in my purse," she said, "for when I'm stuck in traffic and impatient." Owning no purse or license, I waited for direction as to how to use the verses. "I know these prayers will help you quit...licking your lips." The red circle of blisters around my lips—the front-and-center raw O like a violated anus repositioned, like Dante's and Hawthorne's nightmares—that ring had gotten to this sensitive teacher, who had once stopped class to plead with me to stop licking. She cried: "Freeze!" And then across the room of statues with pulses, she begged, "Stop it, Ben. Please." The fire of my shame leaped tables to torch her—it seemed! But I could not stop any more than creepy Howard could stop sniffing his fingers, Elizabeth stop grinding her teeth while she slept, or Marianna stop chewing her nails until they splintered, bled. We all felt the ill pull of the house darkness. The stillness where there should have been movement. The movement where things should have been still. We dug ourselves deep little holes of pain into which we could escape from the larger pit, and then filled these holes with what we could. Howard's favorite song: "Wild Thing." Elizabeth's button collection. Marianna's habit of eating black olives out of the can. We shared towels and toothbrushes and round steak, but nothing could be shared without a fight, without someone losing. My mouth was blistered as well it should be, burned by the stolen food and the gossip that had passed in and out of it, burned by the kisses planted on a mother's froggish cheek! You kissed her and she turned not into a princess but into more of a monster to adore. Mrs. Costello knew that certain students required aid the school system was in no position to provide. "When you feel the urge to lick, read a prayer instead ... for me, Marie." Her name, stripped of Costello: Marie. Though I'd have thought something like Orlundia—Orlundia of the flamboyant knotted scarf, the bent nose broken in some artsy accident at the Iowa State Teachers College. "Please try harder," she said. I promised and licked. She cooed in agony. Bestial was my shame, and Marie thought that without a missionary's intervention, alleviation was no real possibility. But, again, she did not know my true story. The hope I lost was tormentingly matched, always, by the hope I regained by many means, including dumb ones like slipping a lucky penny in my shoe. Had I no hope, I would have thrown myself out the upstairs window when I woke in a wet bed again, instead of crawling in the other direction. Much of my trouble stemmed from the immense complication of hope. I told Marie thanks. Then the lockstep hullaballoo of incoming students flushed me onto the mezzanine. There I examined the booklet—a slumping Mark hitting 2:17. Palm trees of Galilee. If God has the whole world in his hands, I thought, he's got butterfingers, keeps dropping it.

The staples impressed me most. They were brass, it looked like. They were the action of a press pumping away in the middle of the night somewhere in the urban wilderness. Presses were sacrosanct, however flawed their output. I fondled this proof of a press, then added its prayers to a crowded pocket. The next day, at the industrial sink, resurrecting brushes as was her wont, Marie fizzed: "Which prayer speaks to you the loudest?" "The lamb prayer," I said. "Which one?" she asked. Caught, I blurted: "Them all!" Her voice evaporated. She nodded to keep from shaking her head.

We're Number Two! We're Number Two!

I UTTERED MY FINAL *ALL RIGHTS* IN FIFTH GRADE. The next year, my last at McKinley, I learned I was capable of spending the quarter that Granny had given me at the Paperback Exchange, where I bought *Acapulco Rampage*, starring Mack Bolan, aka The Executioner. I learned what my mother must have long known— that being broken not only made you weak, but also granted you infected edges to threaten others with. I learned that the easiest way to get through a school day of not fitting in was to strike at your enemies first. I yelled "Puritans!" at boys who parted their hair to the right. "Sellout!" at the others. I cheered against my school at basketball games. I stood on the visitors' side of the gym waving a GO PLEASANT VALLEY! BEAT MCKINLEY! sign crafted in Mrs. Hamann's class. I chanted, "We're number two! We're number two!" as my eyeframes jogged down my nose and I jabbed them back into place. Taves was stricken.

Idyll of the Thing

M RS. HAMANN AIRILY ANNOUNCED that we were going out to play dodgeball. She was not like the other teachers. She had forsworn the Teachers College to attend the University of Iowa with a thousand men. I fell back in the line exiting the building. The Great Wall of China might have had better luck eluding that ball than I. Girls nailed me with ease. When the class reached the playground gravel, I *informed* Mrs. Hamann that I was not going to participate in dodgeball—did not have the time—I needed to finish my first book of poems on the steps over there. I pulled out the work in progress. Three inches wide, five inches long, pages cut (almost straight) from white construction paper and bound with red thread like Emily's books. Penciled in teensy block letters on the cover was the title *Dream On*, filched from an Aerosmith hit. Izod alligator shirts backed off. That book looked of another era—the era when kids walked miles to school in blizzards. No machine involvement, no corporate imprint. I had made it pretty much out of nothing but mistakes. But it was something. I cradled the book and raised it higher so Mrs. Hamann, who was tall, could see it. If no art had happened quite yet, vital things connected to art had. The pages reflected one impressive truth: I had bought the thickest paper at Ben Franklin, thinking it would better bear what I had to hit it with. And besides, from what I had seen, few artists had any art to show for their efforts. Artists had their failures and their challenge, which was to delude themselves into continuing the humanizing effort of creation without being fooled, like my father, into overestimating what they had done. "Five days I've spent on it so far," I told Mrs. Hamann. She flinched, choosing her battles. Made of flimsy new teacher stuff, she must be. She quivered like a cardboard cutout. "Are you sure?" she asked. I was sure. I nodded and then she nodded. She let me go, she was going to let me do it! Maybe she understood what I did—that doom had only one out: art. Anyway, I turned. I left them to their debacle and they left me to mine. I did not look over my shoulder to interrogate my luck. If anyone watched me they did not for long. There was nothing to watch but a fat boy putting one flat foot in front of another while clutching his misbegotten art project. I wanted to be Emily without imitating her and thought it was just possible. I had written my first poem when I was nine, and it was perfect. I wrote it while watching my mother read the *New Yorker* magazine from the library free bin. She held it more tenderly than she held children. She smoothed wrinkles inflicted by previous readers. She turned pages reluctantly. She'd had her mysterious year in New York after college, and on the couch in Iowa two decades later seemed reminded of what had been possible then. As she sighed the sigh to end all sighs, I wrote my ode's beginning: "New York, New York, I love you so." I rhymed it with "subway glow." I was not including that poem in my first book, however; that poem was too old. My first book must consist exclusively of new work, I was sure, don't ask me how. I had so far finished six new poems that combined Top 40 hits with Emily's garden in Amherst in the 1800s. I was, finally, on my way, right? Correct. I was on my way. My shoes kept proving that I had, at last, obtained social real estate of my own, with three stairs at the end, waiting. I heard no taunts. I heard no parting shots from Mrs. Hamann. Apparently no one had any intention of stopping me from writing poetry if that's what I intensely insisted on doing. Live and let live, die and let die. Had we—en masse— lost our minds? Maybe, but I liked it. Near to ruined, I was going off to the stairs to conclude my poor book, the most concerted attempt thus far to ford the darkness that had enveloped me. No

gravel pelted my back! It was quiet. Relief all around. Everyone
was better off now. I looked to those three distant stairs like others
looked to their saints. I had found my place at school at last. It
had been under my nose the whole time. For years those three
stairs had waited for my company and I for theirs. Classic poems
were not composed by a boy sitting "Indian style" on a basketball
court. Hadn't happened once in the history of the universe. The
stairs were near a sheltered bike rack where chains sheathed in
bright rubber glistened like candy-coated eels, even in shadow,
coiling around the crowded spokes, hubs, and frames of numerous ten-speeds, five-speeds, and dirt bikes. An alley of salt-and-
pepper pavement separated one side of the rack from the metal
bowl of a water fountain, which protruded from the building's
bricks. It was the only playground fountain. The outside of the
bowl was tarnished like an urn. The inside was shiny. Whenever
I drank I almost swallowed the spigot in order to examine the
bowl's gleaming surface of abrasions, delicate as facial down.
When wet, these abrasions appeared to undulate, revealing,
within each drop of water, river-channel depths. The fountain's
handle, in the shape of a gnome's nose with three bridges, was
the remainder of the magic. When fully tweaked, it produced a
Niagara that arced overhead. Ropes of crystal current landed near
the bicycles and shattered into leaping transparent toads. The
technical mechanics of this sublime display, and why students
were allowed unmitigated access to its power, were McKinley's
most fabulous mystery. The water was the temperature of the day.
The steps adjoined the fountain wall. Beyond the steps existed
blond cement where grades lined up to reenter the building.
That verandah-like space was bordered by a bank of grass and
the staff parking places. I spotted Mrs. Sly's sports car. She was
the "school counselor" who staged puppet shows that did not do

too much to protect children against drugs, matches, joyriding, or bad strangers. Sunshine shifted over fences and school bricks. It was then as if the steps were rushing forward me to greet me! We met halfway. On the top step I settled, *Dream On* on one knee, elbow on the other knee, and in that hand a sharpened pencil. With a finger I traced the stitches sewn at night in my room. They were the field surgery on a voice in pain, the best writing I had done, involving everything that writing was meant to be except the hard-to-find words. The dodgeball game continued. I heard yells like intimate whispers but the players appeared miles away. Hamann might as well have been blowing her whistle in Guam. I retraced the red spine threads dipping in and out of the paper. I opened the book to the next blank page and waited for the tumult in me to merge with the serenity there—for a roar to resolve, to release a civilized or instructive message, not a dying echo but a melodic equation, a well-configured theory, something true to my energy and contradictions without being wildly off-putting and despoiled. Outside the haven of Mr. Hickey's kitchen I had never been more imbued with silence. I felt patience reshape the breech between myself and the page, closing it a tiny vital bit. After many minutes no voice had emerged to displace the innate keen within, but as I waited for one, dunes of light drifted under the point of my poised pencil.

BOOK TWO

THE

TERRACE

ABOVE

A TALE OF TWO KITCHENS

A dapper sailor's final port — Parade of visitors — The earth did not
revolve around your misfortunes — A lesson in lessonlessness —
A poodle, dispensed with — The five-dollar bill taped to the window —
Out come the prunes — Salmon loaf of love — Extra innings —
Crimes involving maggots — The sky bucket

THE WHITE CABINETRY IN MR. HICKEY'S small kitchen snatched
the dull glow of a ceiling globe, intensifying light into a gleam beyond sourcing. Here visitors experienced what it might be like to
sit in a Magicube flashbulb as it fired, flared, died gray-bluely. The
counter was that mortal color, the speckled floor linoleum also.
Reflections zigzagged across refrigerator chrome, and the porcelain sink extended from the pale yellow wall like the lip of a giant
shell lodged in a sand dune: fitting subject for a snapshot. Or if
not the conch, then the oven next to it, livid ancestor of the microwave—caged burners and Bakelite dials inscribed with Rosetta

Stone fineness: 425°, 450°, 500°—with heat that had burned a Sphinx eye in the enamel on the side of the appliance facing the spindly table and its green gap-back chairs. The major items on the table were a five-band radio, aqua Tupperware pill counter, wrist-strengthening red plastic hand grip, and Colt pistol that Mr. Hickey's thoughtful sister, Alice, insisted was necessary to ward off burglars that preyed on housebound men whose rose bushes had grown wild, or mostly wild, because every so often Mr. Hickey did dramatically outsmart the actuarial table and on the terrace above our ramshackle house, wearing a fedora and gripping garden shears—cutting big bouquets for neighbor women. Indoors, regardless of season, this bald milk-white man sported a buttonless sweater vest and clip-on bow tie—polka-dot, striped, checked, or all three—sartorial splendor in dramatic proximity to bloodless lips, perhaps the only pair in Davenport, Iowa, that would never utter the F-word in response to news footage of village-hunting B-52 bombers and President Richard Nixon, that weary bird of prey, haunting the rose garden. Unbelievable. But Mr. Hickey was there to be believed: he existed. Words rustled dryly from his mouth and through a veil of Tiparillo smoke. With the ginger ferocity of a dapper old sailor he mopped the floor a tile at a time, buffed cabinets with a strip of an old T-shirt. The hearing aid. It behaved like a burr that had developed a cheddar cheese rind then learned to play a flute. And it was not the most novel thing about him. The most novel thing about Mr. Hickey was the divot in the back of his head where he had been conked by a swinging boom while stationed on a Coast Guard boat docked off New Orleans. It was a miracle he was not still sailing through the Gulf air. The largest thing about him was the owl-ish empathetic gaze magnified thrice its actual size by the thick bifocals. Always he perched on the chair in front of the stove, with the Sphinx staring over his shoulder, and a guest occupied the chair fronting the door to the enclosed back porch stacked with storage boxes, some mysteriously labeled "JK" or "FLH." He received neighbors throughout the day, and long into the night: people fleeing homes where not much was cooking to spend time in a kitchen perpetually smelling of food because the window was never opened—*Don't want to waste heat*—sealing in rich scents of salmon loaf and chicken soup, bland Malt-O-Meal and Epsom salt odors, branny cigar stench, minty arthritis rub vapors and the furry funk of a little wicker bed where the pug, Mikey, had once slept, God rest his drooling soul.

OH, THE ETHER OF THAT KITCHEN made a body feel secure. Like the rosy resident of a Wild West greenhouse run by an eccentric botanist determined to keep the sweet dream of decency alive. He fawned over withered human specimens with utmost reserve, bald head rolling backward while fingers crept forth to deliver a refreshment. Cynics were watered with ice-cold bottles of 7UP and steaming cups of Sanka, the uncoffee in the orange foil packet. Doubters were fertilized with factory fresh Archway cookies, Nilla Wafers, Finn Crisps, Wrigley's Spearmint gum, Old London Melba Rounds, and free pink passes to the Shriners' circus at John O'Donnell Stadium. Summer was especially busy for Mr. Hickey, with school out and days so long. More like dog years they were, the unsetting sun making a brassy mile-wide mess of the muddy Mississippi and brilliantly fuzzing smog over the art deco spear of the Davenport Bank Building. There was no appointment book. Traffic managed itself—the complex class puzzle of the old east side neighborhood fitting peacefully together in a single room, albeit because visitors rarely encountered each

other—the tightly hinged back door slamming as the front doorbell rang. In July of 1975—to pick a month—Mrs. Knickerbocker
stopped by before heading to her job at Ma Bell. A "together"
Caucasian divorcée in a tiger-print dashiki and salon Afro, she
updated Mr. Hickey on the condition of her youngest child,
Toby, born without a nose, and beautiful blue eyes on the sides
of his head. Surgeons at the St. Louis Children's Hospital were
building the boy a suitable face, many operations done, many to
go ... Next came red-haired Larry Swann, serious son of the stern
founder of Swann Inc., a cardboard-box manufacturer. Larry's
admirable but masochistic dream was to buy a used car without
taking a compromising cent from his old man, earning good clean
money by mowing neighborhood terraces that were not large but
frightfully geodetic, fraught with angles and corners—every home
situated right next to, and apart from, surrounding saltboxes,
bungalows, ranch-style dwellings. Larry always parked the green
Lawn-Boy, with its canvas lung, next to Mr. Hickey's back-porch
steps. Marianna, my only blond sister, fair as linen, entered the
kitchen after Larry. She rarely missed a visit and the opportunity
to earn nickels by naming the locations of state capitol buildings
that in Mr. Hickey's estimation were marble balloons inflated
not with the politician's hot air but democracy's lofty values: due
process for all, free speech, equal representation ... "Florida?"
he inquired. *Miami*, Marianna thought, but did not say, recalling
half a word from yesterday: "Talla..." finished by his whispered:
"...*hassee*." Chock another nickel on the ledger. His nickname for
her was Ready Money. "Illinois, Ready Money?" She tugged the
tomboy railroad cap, and sighed, and fingered bubble bumps on
the 7UP bottle ... answered "Chicago!" Mr. Hickey's neck tilted,
bow tie askew like a polka-dot plane prop. "Try again." "But Chicago's got it all." Soldier Field, she meant, Sears's new tower, the

Museum of Science and Industry, Shedd Aquarium with the great white shark. "The answer is Springfield, Ready Money." "Springfield?" "Correct." "Spring-*field*?" "Correct." Marianna peered suspiciously from behind the green bottle, not seeing how such a sleepy sounding name could anchor Illinois and its antics to the map—that state across the river where black squirrels haunted parks and squirrely men, their fine homes. Grandpa Stanley beginning to drink and wallow in the stock market reports at nine in the morning in his brass-tack-studded recliner. Dr. Miller sipping filtered cigarettes in a silk smoking jacket in the luxury apartment

overlooking Rock Island's poorest neighborhoods. Illinois had moxie and gall and swagger. Illinois was shnockered. Illinois knew things Iowa would never know, and never want to know. "It can't be Springfield," she proclaimed. The old man tapped a cigar out of a svelte white and blue box, pressed the plastic tip between his lips. He struck then dropped a burning match into the coil ashtray, and the flame slid down the stick like an orange snail with a pale blue shell. He inhaled gently. He exhaled stationery, creamy envelopes of smoke wafting over pill counter, hand grip, pistol, radio, Marianna's quivering cap brim. It could not be Springfield, not until he explained the glitter of government was a plain glitter that belonged on the prairie, with space all around, not crowded by space age neon and sparking el tracks . . . just as roses were not displayed atop a flashing television set but on a side table, allowing the eye to fully perceive the bare beauty of each individual bloom. Springfield was a monumental city precisely because it was little, just as the most humble US citizen was large, being heir to big American Dreams, which required participants to start out with nothing, and come from nowhere. "Really?" asked Marianna. The cigar cantered in the haze. "*Spring*-field," she yelped. Mr. Hickey made her see the sense of it and that was something. That was genius of a sort. The genius always is one who sees what others don't and communicates the vision in a way that makes it accessible to many. Chalk another nickel on the ledger, Ready Money.

NEWFANGLED DIGITAL WATCHES across Davenport were beeping twelve when I waddled up the short steep hill for my first daily visit to the white house. The gray midday sky, tinged lavender, resembled a dirty sink with a cloud-clogged drain. Mr. Hickey stood at the back door, having just sent Marianna off with enough change to buy a 7-Eleven Slurpee, the Marvel superhero cup, collect them all: Iron Man, Spider-Man...It was always dark on that porch. Shadows sifted from boxes behind the man, and the sweater vest undulated with each breath like a ghostly accordion. Above the bow tie was the teacup chin that somehow had survived a brief boxing career in the 1930s—how, I had yet to discover. He liked to talk about you, not himself. He believed that bragging up victories or dwelling on tragedies was presumptuous—the earth did not revolve around your misfortunes but around the sun. Principled reticence never to be confused with mother's willed amnesia regarding the Past. She was ashamed. She was fearful, hunted. Her panting silences horribly embroidered a room: in her breath you could hear wolves. And when she did get around to telling a story about being denied butter at the dinner table of a miserly farmer she worked for one summer or being sent at the age of nine to fetch her father from a tavern, count on the true tale being interrupted often by giggling or a groaning theatrical refrain of "Ahhhhhhhhhh lonely journey...Life is ahhhh loooohnely journey..." I gazed up at the thin grin and bow tie spreading its green wings like an exotic moth. I felt so lucky then to be his neighbor. I would not trade for a dozen Mr. Rogerses. I opened the door, and he said the first word that he always said to me. "Benny," he whispered, like the Elton John song "Benny and the Jets" and the pill Mrs. Sly's dragon puppet warned the sixth grade about, and Jack Benny who butchered the violin on *The Tonight Show* and the Benny doll that Granny had asked mother to destroy after the stroke—the ancient country toy a daughter hated to burn—ashes I had been named after. "Benny, come in," said Mr. Hickey, and the subject became physical fitness—all the exercises I must do to get in shape to endure the strain of the American Dream: twelve-hour work days for next to no pay. On the trip across the porch he advised "hitting the rope"—that is, jumping rope like a girl. I was seated at the kitchen table by the time he finished listing the many health benefits of rope jumping: quicker reflexes, improved circulation, stronger lungs. "Are you thirsty?" he asked. "Parched," I moaned, and then asked: "Playing with a yo-yo is about as good as jumping rope, right?" Absolutely not. He told me why—no feet or lung or heart involvement. I had seen an acrobatic Duncan Yo-Yo Pro at Kmart and knew different but it was best to get the bottle on the table quickly, and agreeing did that. "Thanks, Mr. Hickey." I took a slug of the citrusy brew containing no citrus. He settled lightly in his chair and suggested I jog around my house six times each morning. Too blind or kind he was to register the fact that our side yard was clogged with legal files that father stored outside in mock fulfillment of a law requiring lawyers to maintain an archive. String dangling from rotten rubber eyelets, reinforced box corners rusted. Folders inching through split lids like straw spilling from a cow's mouth. But it wasn't straw. It was signed affidavits, wills, stock certificates, wedding licenses…snowed and rained on…the insect-infested paperwork of a man with no faith in himself or the power of any court to address the mess people often made of their lives. What could I say? What I said: "You got it, Mr. Hickey." Just as I did the sit-ups he assigned by saying I did them. "Thirty, and ten extras." The forehead rippled: a rug my words had tripped on. Lying, however, he could not directly accuse anyone of. Yes, I got fatter and fatter: 150 pounds at ten; 215 at twelve. But those bifocals saw two guests for each one—you and who you still might become: *thinner, stronger, smarter.* He quoted crusty Angelo Dundee, Ali's rhyming trainer, and stylish bespectacled John Wooden—the Wizard of Westwood—basketball coach of the nearly unbeatable UCLA Bruins…different personalities who preached the same gospel: *Take pride in yourself*. I nodded and sipped, sipped and sweat gladly, understanding that a house without a warm kitchen was a home with no heart—a few bedroom hotel, just one more foreign place to run up bills. I listened to the story of brilliant Paul Moon—the Central High basketball coach in a class by himself, winner of seven state titles. *Here—look at this*. The clipping was very old, the team wearing high tight shorts, a gaggle of skinny limbs orbiting a coach resembling Mr. Hickey—a formal hairless man who looked like he could not have beaten an egg. "Fifty-two games in a row he won." It was true—the article mentioned that, and retirement, MOON TO CALL IT QUITS IN 1954. Mr. Hickey closed his eyes for a little rest. I watched birds fatten like opera singers at the window feeder, marveled at the sarcophagi profile of the refrigerator and that bulging oven door to daunt a safecracker: four inches thick with hinges singed blast furnace black. I tried to stay calm as the host's fingers trickled over the pistol trigger in search of the pill counter's Saturday compartment packed with capsules and tablets. His neck fluttered like awning fringe as he swallowed, and swallowed. I peered through a doorway into the dark dining room, where an oxygen tank stood on the table, and also the apparatus that mother would soon use to take Mr. Hickey's afternoon blood pressure reading—Velcro pad, stethoscope, pump bulb, needle gauge. Beyond that shadow realm was the illuminated living room and the Magnavox ruled by *Donahue*—the sensational new talk show. So friendly, that Phil, with a boyish mop of platinum hair, dorky glasses that got knocked crooked when he hugged celebs and ordinary people who had been to hell and back. He was a comfort to all those who had no real kitchen to visit and so much to say that could simply not be said in the three minutes that it took a microwave to cook a complete meal. The audience lined up in pairs outside the WGN studios to board the camera-equipped ark that could sail through any flood of tears. Sympathy oozed from the host's size-thirteen mouth, congealing around, and smoothing over, every thorny moment. He made macho rock stars so comfy that they got mushy, used vague words like *journey*, followed by unvague words like *rehab* that inspired in this viewer the dreariest form of hope: *If Alice Cooper felt suicidal, then came back to sell out a nationwide tour... maybe things will improve for me too if I start fantasizing about jumping from every bridge I see.* How stupid. But still I had put my name on the six-year ticket waiting list, for who knew how long Mr. Hickey would be around to provide the higher ground? Between dining room and kitchen existed a narrow bathroom with a deep fat-lipped toilet and mirror and a claw-foot tub where he marinated aching joints in Epsom salts. Three cigars he smoked during the visit, or four, or six, and after the last puff, darn if my seventy-year-old friend did not risk cardiac arrest by demonstrating the Dynamic-Tension muscle-building technique of Charles Atlas. He pressed his white fingertips together until they turned possum pink... and that sweater vest got redder, flexing like the chain-weave ligaments in a transparent anatomy figurine. The green bow tie sweated another orange polka dot, or had I miscounted?

MOTHER ENDED MY VISIT on medical grounds. She burst unannounced into the kitchen and had to—right away, that second—take Mr. Hickey's blood pressure. "Hello, Tommy," he muttered. "Benjamin," she snapped, hugging Moby Purse. "You go home now and watch the little ones." Already, I was on my way. Once I had stayed and watched and regretted it. He so carefully rolled up a sleeve, she slapped the Velcro pad on the tender skin—ivory bunting—and pumped the bulb, and kept pumping, and did some more pumping, then snorted "240 over 180!" and tore off the pad with such violence that Mr. Hickey swooned in the chair, tongue out. "Can't stay, John! Got to pick up Elizabeth from orchestra practice!" If Toby was between operations, he stopped by after mother, proudly pointing out where his zippered face had come from, chin tissue carved off buttocks, nostril bones shaved off the left tibia. If Toby was in Missouri having that nose tweaked, the Knickerbocker twins—Donald and Jeff—took the state-capital quiz; then Rick, the son of a piano teacher; Billy, a bulky Boy Scout who loved to say "sheesh"; Lucinda, silent dark-eyed lover of animals and proprietress of a Habitrail that wound through three rooms; Wayne Coddell Jr., only child of a stock car driver; and plump Maggie Feeney, who wept on encountering any stump marking the spot where a tree had been cut down . . . Each guest, in turn, gasped when the host's bald head briefly vanished into the gleam of the cabinetry, as if—for ease of cleaning—he had paid to have his dome enameled in the weird far reaches of the Younkers men's department. They glazed over with wonder when Mr. Hickey opened the cabinet containing low sodium doppelgangers of every boxed and canned good shelved in the adjoining cabinet. Suffering from an advanced case of generosity, he offered even kids the option of saltless crackers and sugarless cookies. "No thanks, sir." Ditto for the Carnation Instant Breakfast sample packet he had received in the mail last year and been trying to jettison ever since. "Honest, I have all the packs I need." They earned state-capital nickels and endured the crickle-crackle of the radio that needed a longer antenna and played a two-person version of solitaire invented by Mr. Hickey because he was never alone long enough to finish a regular hand. Often they carried car wash tickets, cookie order forms, Florida grapefruit sign-up sheets, but no trumpeter hurried to mention the Bandorama in sunny Pasadena since no question existed about the outcome of the solicitation. He would buy the fruit: he always did! Energy was better spent begging Mr. Hickey to talk about his fabulous boxing career, shoeshine boy days, or military service. Sometimes he added a delicious detail to what you already knew, and even if he did not, well, it was always astonishing to hear a biography reduced to little more than punctuation. "What year were you in the Coast Guard?" "Nineteen forty-five." "What was it like?" "Nineteen forty-five." "Get shot at?" Forget that, won't go there. Instead he made for the stove, *shuffle, shuffle, shuffle,* and put on the pot containing water left from the last heating and the heating before that—twice boiled water to be reboiled because pouring new might deplete the reservoir and deprive an east-side spinster of the brisk cup of Lipton that she needed to get going. After the mid-afternoon parade of children, Mrs. Moore arrived to build up her strength for the battle that would take place later with her husband, a pencil pusher on Arsenal Island, the government facility devoted to howitzer production. Mr. Moore drank and got violent—slapping, punching, whipping Richard with a belt buckle and once chasing his wife out the door, around the car in the driveway. She said: "Hasn't been much of a summer, Mr. Hickey." Or "I'm at the end of my rope." Or "Things can't go on like this." Then talked on and on, as Mr. Hickey listened, not interrupting to sugarcoat the pain like Donahue, but sitting and simmering quietly, appalled by the girth and the depth of the revealed wound. A deep blue dead place: emptiness rimmed by pain. Mrs. Moore beaten. Hurt unreal for having happened, and less understandable the more that was understood about it. A lesson in lessonlessness. He handed Mrs. Moore a pink tissue. He poured the fresh tea water that was now called for and placed the pot on the burner. Flames feathered through the black cage. A whistle. In went Lipton sachets, and onto the table went mugs—her thick fingers firmly wrapping around the handle like a parking lot tree trunk grows through a long fence spike, dividing and then rejoining, fantastic swirls of oaken lava.

THE WEIGHT OF A MAN, I tried to act the part in our hotel. Hardly a Hyatt. More a third world Ramada abandoned by the staff during a popular uprising: crayon-scrawled walls, clothes heaped on the stairs, indigo carpet cluttered with super-hero Slurpee cups and greasy paper plates, old magazines and classic water-warped paperbacks—*Borstal Boy*, *In Cold Blood*, *The Ballad of the Sad Cafe*, *To Kill a Mockingbird*, *The Pocket Book of Modern Verse*. Scratched lamp shades cast custardy light that kindly coated old couch cushions without illuminating the centipede fringe of rips. Legs crossed, I spread the sports section and read how easily Steve Renko of the Expos shut out the Chicago Cubs, ten strikeouts, two hits. Shouts outside: Nanette and Nathan chasing the blue LTD down the alley, yipping joyfully as mother slowed to turn onto Crestwood, then wailing as the loose bumper clattered away in a cloud of exhaust. That chase was beneath me now. No more grief dances for lovely Mrs. Williams to see from her hotel window. Either mother whispered wetly in my ear in the kitchen that she wanted me to come with her, naming a nearby corner where I was to wait to be picked up, or she didn't. The screen door slammed and the little ones demanded: "When

she coming back? When?" Hard to tell. A little trip often became
a long trip involving stops at Kmart and Target to check the dollar
bins, National Grocery store for free coffee, Ross's Truck Stop
to to filch ketchup packs before the drive across the river to take
Granny Stanley's blood pressure. "Tell us. When?" I suggested
they each draw a picture of a sad clock, and promised to take them
on a walk later to see the stars. I was nearly as sad of a babysitter
as Sharee had been. They melted away to play jacks. I crossed
my legs and thought: *this sucks* and *shove it*, but adultly said not
one word. I read box scores: Pittsburgh 4 St. Louis 3. I itched
my scalp, spat into my hankie, tugged at the baggy shoulders of
a peach Penguin shirt donated by some dentist's widow to the
Temple Emanuel rummage sale. By a quirk of fate I now owned
Mr. Dussellman's finery—all the pastel tents that had sheltered
his pointy nipples while he was camping out in this uncomfortable world, stuck in traffic on Interstate 80, digging for tees at the

driving range, listening to Mrs. Dussellman's cholesterol monologues that ended with the words "early grave." It had happened,
just like she said. Mr. Dussellman was dead and his expensive
tentwear in purgatory—enduring the perpetual blizzard of a fat
pagan boy's dandruff. I set the sports section aside and smoothed
the moist brown down on my upper lip while gazing at the other
lounging guest: father, the partially visible man. Some Sundays
he robotically led a disingenuous march to mass at Sacred Heart
Cathedral, but on weeknights all you saw of him were tan slacks
and stiff legs, slippers filled with the concrete of his socks, and
long fingers holding the *Times-Democrat* aloft as if it were a huge
slitless masquerade mask. Antenna-like hairs curled between his
knuckles. The sole of the left slipper was clouded with wear, the
other sole shinier because he put as little weight as possible on
the bad right leg connected to a ruined hip socket connected to
Dr. Miller, possibly. Mother kept refining her case against her
regal father-in-law, citing his record of treating relatives, a practice
against medical protocol. It was "always wrong"—except on those
many occasions she treated my ailments with french fries or the
night a hot chicken pot pie flipped onto and scalded Marianna's
bare foot and Uncle Carl, father's brother who ran a burn unit,
was just the man to phone. Compassionate Carl materialized out
of the bog of family unrest to dress sister's wound. But otherwise,
"always wrong" for doctors to doctor relatives, as H.P. Miller had.
Enraged at the shenanigans of his middle son, an impious artist,
"Your grandfather purposefully set Dave's broken leg wrong,"
she claimed. (Though she allowed it could have been a case of
accidents compiling one snowy night—Dr. Miller's tragic inability
to focus after a meal of roast cluck.) The making and spending of
big money made men cheap, she said. And not only that, honey,
Dr. Miller had been the attending physician on the night the first

Mrs. Miller died in childbirth, in Wisconsin. Oh, and one more thing, he was also the man to give the order to unplug the second Mrs. Miller—who I knew as Grandma Rose—after she had the heart attack. He gave the order when she had been in ICU only a few days. (Or minutes: each of mother's stories had many time frames.) Then? Well, then, feeling abandoned, Dr. Miller bought a poodle, but the poodle did not obey and was dispensed with after a few weeks and he married his secretary, Opal. Mother's voice would slow to get in more details about a virginal secretary of seventy deflowered by her boss. Mother always made good use of our time alone—*good* being a relative term, surely. I could have sworn she treasured the brokenness of families, and especially the ruination of her husband's strong body and his inventive spirit gone up in smoke—become bitter, self-mocking, bloated with the smallness of lowered expectations. He watched Cronkite through the gray mask, *Mannix, Ironside, Hee Haw, Masterpiece Theater, The Lawrence Welk Show.* When mother cried, "We've got to pay this, Dave," and dropped a phone bill into the chasm, it bellowed: "What for? There's no poorhouse. We're safe." Good report cards were delivered and he offered no congrats, pretending to be as dead as Mr. Dussellman, a charade repeated whenever one of us asked a hard question, such as "Can you go to my choir concert?" He was there, and not there at all. On some nebulous lifelong vacation booked by the Heart of Darkness travel agency and simply trying to survive, I knew, trying to outlive his stay at the terrible Ramada. Nonetheless, my sympathy for him warred with my disgust and outrage. What were we to do about dinner? What about gas for the car, cash for field trips and school supplies? He would be so much better for Nanette and Nathan than I could be—six feet two inches better. *They need you, I need you, mother too, why don't you ever try?* Eight fanned fingers became four as he remained out of view while switching sections or even entire newspapers (*Times-Democrat* to *Des Moines Register* to *Chicago Trib*...). Behind that wall he created politbureaus of smoke. Burrowed deep, he crunched potato sticks like a squirrel and he swigged generic root beer from a peanut butter jar. His farty belches sounded like a human variation of a truck tire blowout: *Frapurburbur*...He gurUPed, gurUPed, a combination burp, hiccup, grunt. Each cough was the tolling of his lungs, and when I just could not listen to the Father Death Suite any longer, I tried to slip away and got caught. "Going to visit Hickey again? Are you?" "Um." "A meddler, that's what he is." Such insults could be flung with confidence because he had never met the neighbor and never would in the decades they lived side by side, in separate worlds borne of the averted gaze. One man cowering behind *Marmaduke* and William Safire. The other not daring to look directly at the terrace where once the fastidious Widow Fry had lived, and now chaos reigned. Reports delivered nightly were quite enough.

UP THE HILL I ROCKETED. *Bang bang* on the door. Father's math did not add up. My having no one, how could that be a plus to him? He should be glad of the free counseling next door, take advantage of the perk himself. *Bang bang.* But he hurt too much to do anything but hurt more. He needed a comeback special like Frank Sinatra—an orange curtain wide as a sunrise...twenty-two-piece orchestra...millions cheering so hard for him to succeed that he did. "Ol' Blue Eyes is back." *Bang bang bang.* But Sinatra did not have to become someone in that hour, just sing a little like the wonder crooner he had been. Whereas since father had failed at everything from novel writing and local politics to the practice of law, he needed to prove so much more to a suspicious audience of seven that in theory wanted to clap but were sitting on their hands, fearful of being let down all over again. *Bang bang bang.* Mr. Hickey, where are you? The five-dollar bill was still taped to the kitchen door's diamond window, which meant he was not being robbed—if ever the bill was gone I was to go home, dial zero, and ask for the police. No, likely his hearing-aid battery was low and he had just pushed aside a man-of-war TV tray and reached for the pistol that would see him safely through the dining room with the little silver Christmas tree on the buffet—a craft made by the wife you forgot about until the May anniversary of her death rolled around, the only day he spent by himself. *Bang bang bang bang.* I rubbed my aching fist. Birds swept the last light out of the sky. The air turned blue. Mr. Moore was home now, threatening Mrs. Moore, as Lucinda hunched over the Habitrail, and Neil listened to *Jesus Christ Superstar* on headphones. Mrs. Knickerbocker was reviewing hospital bills. Maggie reading up on the larch. Billy looking at maps in preparation for the annual Boundary Waters canoe trip. Larry counting mowing money and Rick playing drums. The beat sounded like the neighborhood's pulse—going in so many directions at once, racing, alarmed. There was a menace to dusk unequaled by midnight, when the moon's trusty lantern shined. Now, dark voided light and light voided dark. The number on Wayne Coddell's parked stock car floated over that backyard like a phosphorescent cloud of prophetic gnats: #54. This was the time when dogs became hounds and yards turned into moors…bushes sinking into mossy grass, border garden bricks membranes of the heavy objects they had been ten minutes ago. A junker rumbled down the alley, past the little garage where Mr. Hickey's Model T sat on blocks—hood shiny because he still purchased car wash tickets from church members who then got the chance to buff a rumble seat, sit behind the wheel, smoke a cig or worse. "Better not tell Hickey, Fatso." Wouldn't think of it. Just like I would not mention this address to Charlie, whose dad sold encyclopedias door-to-door, though the idea occurred each time I saw the kid's teeth at recess. Charlie's family needed money bad. On the other hand, Mr. Hickey was in no condition to shelve twenty-four Britannica volumes, let alone those hefty quarterly supplements. *Bang bang.* The inner door opened a crack, revealing an inch of sweater vest. I waved and squealed hello. A dress shoe extended, succeeded by another shoe, slacks, polka-dot bow tie, bifocals. Mr. Hickey fording a river of shadows...hands hiked to waist level, white as the gloves of an armed butler on a daring mission: Mr. Sherlock Holmes in disguise and near to outwitting the diabolical Moriarty again.

THE COMING OF NIGHT erased the bird feeder hanging outside the kitchen window. In going, the natural light stole speckles off the floor's linoleum, and the oven Sphinx eye—earlier two blues, dark within pale—had totally blackened and appeared to be closed, pondering why a man would rinse and place on the dish rack another Low Sodium Meals-on-Wheels container when five hundred Styrofoam replicas were stacked in the cellar. Other riddles occupied me. For instance, what qualified mother to take blood pressure readings? Had she crashed a Holiday Inn seminar for nursing home aides? And where was that freaky contraption now? Cooling off in the Kelvinator after a high reading? "Sit down," said Mr. Hickey. Two hundred pounds hit the chair and it held. Overhead was an American Legion calendar which each month featured a new configuration of bloodred poppies. A line was drawn halfway through the current date box. The retiree, unsure if he had twelve hours to live, took a half day at a time, rather than adhering to the vaunted one-day formula. Either Mr. Hickey was politely experiencing the viselike pains that precede a heart attack (the symptom an episode of *Emergency!* had taught me to expect) or the old gentleman had glanced at his reflection in the refrigerator chrome. Sweater vest cut to ribbons. Brutal scene from another Hollywood saga that substituted a few sword fights and French kisses for a thousand sprawling years of history. "What can I get you?" he inquired. Two sugarless cookies, the kind most appropriate for a boy in my condition, and a 7UP, pretty please. The nod said: *You've shown resolve, young man.* More than I intended, since all the cold soda was gone, just warm left in the case on the floor. *Damn.* While Mr. Hickey cranked ice cubes from a tray, my eyes roamed the night table. The pistol, like usual, was on the far edge of the Formica—no way I could reach it and have fun shooting shredded wheat biscuits. The radio, in its perforated leather girdle, had been pulled away from the yellow wall and an Astroturf strip (a gift from Larry Swann) lay next to the speaker so we would have something to watch while listening to a novelty called "baseball under the lights." Cookie packages were arrayed end-to-end where the radio had been in the afternoon. The red hand grip had migrated to the counter under the gleaming cabinets, near a four-slot toaster with the plungered profile of a detonation device. He had emptied the coil ashtray and set out the evening's allotment of cigars—two cellophane-wrapped five-packs. Between pill counter and pistol stood a tall glass of water to wash down a nitro tablet or humanely moisten the lips of a dying burglar. Dramatic alterations to be sure, but no preparation for the prune box at table's edge—proof that elegant Mr. Hickey suffered from a most inelegant problem, first letter *c*, last letter *n*. How could it be? Bran for breakfast, melba toast for lunch, shredded wheat for a snack, meat loaf and beets for dinner...The fiber went down, the sun sank, and out came *the prunes*, wax paper tufting from box top like Count Dracula's starched cuffs. Never mind the label double-talk: DRIED PLUMS. Some nouns were Krazy Glued to their objects. "Rhu" + "barb" = gnarly rueful fiber. "Pr" + "une" = public relations doom. Photograph prunes at any angle, in the most gracious light...put them on a blanket on a Malibu beach and still they'd resemble a clump of glossy bat torsos or London scabs circa 1856. The desecration of ripe fruit. Clotted juice. Wrinkled, gummy and tarry, cancer-colored. A blessing in unholy attire: for where would Mr. Hickey be without sixteen ounces of California prunes? Bound like a mob hostage in a Key Largo cottage...instead of sweetly sighing: "I'll be back in a few minutes, Benny." He took the pistol with him and, I imagined, would get rough with his digestion system if it did not deliver. The bathroom door shut. I ditched the awful diet cookies, devoured three real ones, then a fourth, then sat back, experiencing some new intestinal issues of my own that began between the ears with the food for thought and extended from there to my ankles. Was it possible to suffer constipation and diarrhea simultaneously? I managed it. I employed the age-old control of rocking in various rhythms. My right side was a burbling river. My left side was reenacting birth pains I had experienced one morning on the basement toilet facing the green steel shelves lined with leather-bound novels father had written for New York and which New York wanted no part of. The titles—stamped in gold—I knew by heart. *Nicholson's Last Game. Osage Orange. The Red Faucet.* I could see arrogant Dr. Miller paying for the binding of those books. He would not want any of his sons to be rejected by a Ruth with an office on Fifth Avenue. He would

believe that a book should be judged by its cover and would purchase nice ones for his son David's failed books. Straining at the stool that Saturday, I felt closer to those books than ever before, though they were against the far wall at the bottom of the basement stairs. Each page was a vacant lot of words. I had again and again opened those books hoping for an outpouring of a man's thoughts...his feelings...the world as only he saw it...sounds as he heard them...decisions as he made them...the seething stuff of life and death...and instead found the "Hey, bucko" dialogue and "darling gals" and "azure vistas." His most casual barks from the recliner were more enticing: "Bring me that carton of lick-tick-stick!" (His lyrical word for milk.) One thing was certain, balmy weather had not made him the brooding creature that he was. Where in him was his dark and valiant story hiding? The tale of how the world's richness poured into him and turned thin, bitter? Were there no appropriate words for things he had experienced as the son of callous Dr. Miller and Grandma Rose in the white gloves and hat net? Had father not known how to choose among the many available words or just not cared to search hard enough for ingredients needed to make a genuine book? He could be linguistically ambitious in spates—muffus-roonie-goozie gibberish riffs proved it! But when he and mother shoved aside the status quo and its stilted language to make room for supposedly higher expression, the paralysis materialized—the spouting of inanity or not saying a living thing, the groan, the sigh, the cough. Then they wore the full import of their lives like an imprisoning jacket, not a set of fascinating truths. Then their expressions crumpled like paper torn from a machine and discarded. Then there was nothing but life's lifeless results—sourness, amorality, stasis. They had no characters. They had no plots. And spending so much time in their company did to me what bran did to Mr. Hickey—it often plugged me up.

FINALLY MY DAPPER HOST reentered the kitchen, dentures ajar with relief. His magnified eyes, like twin rudders, steered him into the port of the kitchen table. He put down the pistol he had threatened his intestines with. He turned on a game, sipped water. Would I, he wondered, like some salmon loaf that Alice had dropped off yesterday? "You bet." The pan went into the oven…out it came. Warm loaf tasting a bit like tuna fish, a little like potted ham. And covered with fingerprints. Whorl upon whorl: court-admissible proof of a sister's love for her brother, and love's nutritional value.

MY NIGHT VISIT ENDED around ten o'clock, unless the baseball game went into extra innings. If it did, and I got home at, say, eleven, an unhappy camper waited in the kitchen. Mother, elbows staked to the rickety table, eyes caramelized by the day's indignities. "Gawd, I've been waiting forever." Really just half that long, but she had a valid point. There were forevers hidden in every minute. Our two percent milk going bad a week before the official doom date proved it. "What on earth took so long, Ben-jah-men?" I could not say the Houston Astros tied the Cubs in the eighth inning, on a Bob Watson triple, and won it in the eleventh when outfielder César Cedeño hit a homer. Reentry friction precluded discussion. I bent toward her bowl-cut hair and scary gaze and varicose veneer. I could not bear to overtly reject what seemed to be my last living parent. Living to suffer, living out refusals of happiness, but living, oh my, living. She was the family don, the monster. And I, leaning, was learning anew each day that I'd twist into any shape she required. However grotesque, it became the next shape of the attachment—if only a connection to my need for attachment, no true hold on her. The wasn't-ness she was was there for the taking. When Rick, the block's bully, taunted me from Mr. Hickey's yard and I rushed up to put my Hickey boxing lessons to use and was instantly knocked down and had my hair grabbed and head pounded into the cement at the bottom of the back-porch stairs—what had I cried? I had cried in an infantile stupor: "Mama…mama…" It hadn't happened that long ago. I still had the headaches. And there, in the kitchen, I felt the fever of a sick room—hers, mine.

ON THE CHIPPED ENAMEL STOVETOP rested the personality of the pan used to fry bologna cut into squares or cooked whole but slit in the middle to prevent the pink slices from bulging like goiters when the fat ran off and shrinkage occurred. On another burner sat the preposterous coffee maker consisting of two dented aluminum orbs one atop the other à la a robot prototype from 1948. The cupboards did not have police tape across them but should have—crimes involving maggots and Ritz had taken place inside. Boxed goods were kept on the warped counter, and a swollen stick of Lady Lee butter on the table plate, drowning blue flies and reflections. Mother had been denied butter at that farm table when she was the hired hand, and now butter never left her kitchen table, even if that meant no-good butter, the sepia insect-leg-infused rancid butter. That table was a wedding present that Granny Stanley had spent all her S&H Green Stamps on. "Tell me, what took you so long…" Her sack dress a shifting weather-stained sail. Her burst tennis shoe and jagged toenail, again. I thought: *Why not wear those new blue canvas shoes Elizabeth got you at Target with her concession-stand pay? Why the worst pair—the pair that gives every step the rugged character of a death march?* I mumbled something—something I wasn't thinking—something our script allowed. Light seeped through a grime collage on the interior of the ceiling globe. Atop the fridge lurked clippings and books she could not presently cram into Moby Purse, slumped next to the screen door. Roaches made for the dishes in the sink below a splintered sill cluttered with pennies, hydrogen peroxide bottles, puckered soap slivers, a balding toothbrush flecked with baking soda (her toothpaste), and the paper-towel tube I used as a telescope to see anything on the block that I wanted to. From many places came many smells that on this night unified to create a licorice-y funk. "It's not fair of you to stay so long with John!" She proclaimed it again, substituting "Mr. Hickey" for "John." She said it a third time, substituting "right" for the word "fair." We had the same sad repetition problem borne of the same sad fear that no one was close enough to us to hear what we were saying. Though it could sound even worse than that. It could sound as if we—in our thrift-store shrouds—were Gregorian monks who had done un-Christian things at a monastery in really olden times and as punishment had been reborn to chant everything but the world's beautiful music. "It wasn't nice of you to staaaaay . . ." I agreed with four nods, staring at scorched boullion cubes lodged in the stove-burner wells along with torched spaghetti stalks and kidney bean pebbles. The surrounding enamel had a wet gray look from being sprayed by fat from the hot dogs that it was our Cro-Magnon family habit to cook on a fork over an open flame. You knew better, outside. In the old hotel, well, you did what had to be done. Lived by five-second tape delay, whenever possible, carefully editing the present to serve your needs—fulfill desires for a clean healthy mother and home turf not splashed with nitrates, insect guts, coffee tear trails. "I've had such a hard day, Benji." The thought of it lifted her up. Each hard day the same day full of identical demons/angels reorganized into invigorating new grids, a despairing melodrama to count on. "Gawd was it hard." We were the same height—she at forty-five and me at twelve—no differential to deflect the heat of disappointment forced through a flushed mesh of fluttering jowls. "Such a hard . . . night." The tongue curled back, *gurgle, gurgle,*

gurgle, uncurling to wail of "it all." That "it all" I had down, but also had no clue about. Father. Grandpa. Store managers. Neighbors. She named names her way. "That so-and-so, who does he think he..." Definitive indefinitiveness. The malaprop-mania and moronic mimicry and carnival bark and Ophelia paranoia. In a family of damaged voices, she kept taking top prize. Her voice was the most maimed by her own energy. Her voice was the absolute champion at rising to seek less and less expression, less and less order, echoing with vile accuracy her turbine of internal ambivalence, the monsoon of dilemmas re: what was what and who was who and where was where and when when. The code-blue voice

I dreamed of resuscitating with insipid gifts like bookmarks and fountain pens but which could not be repaired, only absorbed and mourned and, eventually, analyzed. Her spiels made everyone uncomfortable for a good reason—because her life was immensely uncomfortable. The life dissolved meant messages dissolved! She was being true to her agony, true to her incoherence, if to nothing and no one else. She was her own canon of wildebeest literature that Refugee children—Howard and Marianna—ran from unsuccessfully, since the same "it all" that afflicted my mother also feasted on their brains and hearts. "But you care," mother said to me, "only you." A kiss slammed me as legacies will. "Bye, honey." She dragged Moby Purse away. The screen door shuddered shut. She left to wail "it all" all over again for Hickey. I backhanded her spit off my cheeks. Why had I listened? *Leaned*...Because the longer the ugly show went on, the more you needed it to end and became capable of convincing yourself that the next kiss—*the next*—would be the tender or honest touch you longed for.

I PICKED UP THE TELESCOPE, went into the backyard to spy on mother and Mr. Hickey. His hearing-aid battery was dead but no matter. She enunciated in a way that could be lip read. "Oh boy," he muttered, hit again with the sludge of stuck people who never tried to be bigger than their terrors and thus became them, infinitely. Hickey's bald bean swiveled. He strained to tell her, like he tried to tell me: *Look away, Tommy, look outward for your own good, stop picking your wounds or they'll never heal.* But she kept picking. "Doesn't that take the cake," he sighed, and the red sweater vest buckled under the weight of the bad that still existed in Davenport despite so much good: Charla the peppy Meals-on-Wheels lady, cardinals, goldfinches, unbeaten Paul Moon, and Junior Achievement. Her lips made many *w*'s and many *h*'s—pursed and opened and pursed. *Hurt and waste, waste and hurt, always a creature out there hurting and alone, wasted—see what I'm saying, do you?* At last she fell silent, and he asked his biggest question: "What's wrong with Dave?" My titular father, her legal husband, MIA, POW. "Is he—?" She cut in. Out of her mouth scrambled a startling admission: "I don't know." Three little words summing up the situation better than a thousand complaints. She sank in the chair. Mr. Hickey peeled the cellophane off a fifth cigar, shakily struck a match. Smoke and more smoke, the window filling with smoke as if my mother's latest discontinuous epic had leveled the beautiful kitchen like a wrecking ball. It was the most dynamic room in any house, built on the delicate foundation of give-and-take, teaspoons of this and dashes of that. Its recipes were complicated. I put down the telescope and climbed the hill. Dew and bugs—the urban cricket orchestra. In Mr. Hickey's backyard, illuminated by the fanning beam of a security light, sat the sky bucket: the large corrugated tub poised to catch rain filled with hair-nourishing minerals—iron, zinc, magnesium. Neighborhood women had a standing invitation to ladle what they needed with a Chase & Sanborn coffee can. Tough water for those toughing it out. Microwave moms were revolted. "Haven't you read about that acid rain?" But Mrs. Moore sometimes gathered the rainwater to take home. Did Mrs. Knickerbocker? Mrs. Dankert, the cocktail waitress who lived below us? I knew my mother washed her hair with nothing but acid rain. Once a month she did it, on all fours, in the backyard. "Tend the bucket, Benny?" Mr. Hickey had asked earlier. And this I could do now for him and for her, plucking twigs and candy wrappers off the dark water, as inside they waited for a phone call, or thunderclap, something to break the silence too deep for words to fill.

IN HICKEY'S HAVANA

Man Gunned Down by Memories — Ali vs. Foreman —
Mr. Hickey's animal self — Contenda for the fat farm —
Nine plastic cigar tips

T HE CIGAR SMOKE WAS THICKEST in Mr. Hickey's narrow bedroom. Sometimes I peeked at that fog bank after he fell asleep on the living room recliner to the lullaby call of a Chicago Cubs baseball game, *three up, three down, three up, three down* ... Mr. Hickey never snored during the afternoon nap. He sighed, softly. He slept like an intent scholar at a research library, little white finger arching off the arm rest to flip the page of an invisible book—*Famous Bunko Artists of the Nineteenth Century*—then settling with the grace of a feather. These interludes frightened my sister Marianna: she feared he was dead and ran down the terrace wailing the bad news, igniting a commotion that ended with many Millers accepting cold green bottles of 7UP from Mr. Hickey, along with his grave apologies for taking pills that caused drowsiness. I, too, worried about our irreplaceable friend perishing, but not of an afternoon nap. The event would occur in the immaculate kitchen on the anniversary of his wife's death—Man Gunned Down by Memories—or a random night in the clouded harbor that was his bedroom. The door, always open to vent the unventable stench, faced the dining room, where Mrs. Hickey's little silver Christmas tree haunted the buffet next to a table spread with neat piles of paperwork and the ungainly medical devices an elderly citizen needed to make it from one taxing federal form to another. The table legs cast shapely shadows on the worn rug. I stepped around them, not over them, never said, "Excuse me, ma'am," but always considered doing so, and the entire way sniffed the glorious, lowdown, almost meaty odor wafting from the bedroom, so different from the mild nutlike smell of Tiparillo cigars in the living room and kitchen. That odor was the gourmet ditch canapé with hints of Indian Summer and this stink a malodorous main entree—heavy, dull, South American incinerated root and stem loaf containing the stultifying stimulants old men needed to survive wee morning hours. *Geezer grass.* At the threshold of Mr. Hickey's reeking sanctuary I stopped, toes on the right side of the doorway saddle, head in the wrong, tilting toward the bed barely bigger than a cot and barred rather brutally at both ends. Boards lay across creased sheets like three rowboat seats. Mr. Hickey believed sleeping on boards was good for the back. He suggested to visitors (even children) that they dispense with cushy Posturepedic comfort, endure spine-toughening torture. "I've some boards in the basement you can have, Mitzi." And if she answered, "Thanks, Mr. Hickey, but I hear mommy honking; we're going to the grocery store," he considered that a yes and had an older kid like me run down and scrawl *For Mitzi* across a plank. More lumber was on hold for neighbors in the basement than books on reserve at the Davenport Public Library, all the boards stacked in the corner and dusted during Mr. Hickey's weekly trip to check for fire hazards like rags, inspect the mousetraps, and inventory supplies of snow salt, bird seed, security bulbs. Up in the bedroom, the rowboat was defensively wedged between a permanently pulled shade and the gaunt bureau with tarnished brass knobs. A tiny bedside table—barely big enough for a hearing aid and ashtray—stood under the windowsill. On the bureau was a square wind-up clock in a tortoise shell traveling case, a fifty-count box of Tiparillo cigars, bowl of matchbooks, bottle of nitroglycerine pills, and a nifty plastic toothpick dispenser, always full, because he had no real teeth left to pick. Top drawers housed what must be the world's greatest collection of clip-on resplendent bow ties—each tucked in its own thin box. And bottom drawers, they held unmentionables, including a device that disturbingly distended the sweater vest on days when he was having trouble with his hernia. Five feet separated the bed bars from a closet containing the rest of the makings of a gentleman: starched dress shirts, creased black referee-type slacks, chaste racks of belts, shoe tree, felt hats on hooks. I could not have imagined Mr. Hickey separated from these trappings if I had not checked on him the night of the August blackout, banging on the door and ringing the bell till he appeared, holding a kerosene lantern and wearing nothing but skivvies and a V-neck T-shirt. My first thought was telling. I did not think the man had undressed due to the heat—not Mr. Hickey, not before nine o'clock in the evening— I believed that the vest, shirt, bow tie, and slacks had evaporated off his ethereal skin ... The bedroom walls were bare and stained a gravy hue from nicotine. It was not a boy's bedroom or at least not my bedroom, where snot crusted the walls like buttercream frosting, and propped up on the loogie-spattered bedroom sill was a postcard of Wrigley Field's grassy infield, ivy-covered walls, the giant brick bowl overflowing with sky. I had mailed three dimes to Chicago to get it. The card edge was scalloped, a detail that endlessly fascinated me. It made the image of the field appear more alive, as if it might, at any moment, secrete more seats, or more sky, or more Cubs—good ones. The man's bedroom was serious. In a man's bedroom there were hankies enough, all folded. The spare ceiling globe hovered over the spare furniture like a prison searchlight. Feeling for and finding the switch, I flicked it on, then off, as the emaciated beam only made the room seem dark in a different, more unseemly way. This was not a place to spend the entire day like Granny Stanley's bedroom, with its candy bowls, humidifier, window view of neighbor Paul's bird feeders, year's supply of bobby pins and Dippity-do styling gel, teacups and Constant Comment sachets, stethoscope, calming rain recording, a three-mattress bed of quilts, and towering teak posts etching the outline of a monsoon-proof Tahitian hut. Her bedroom was a safe house within a house: a refuge that might have been put together by savvy Red Cross volunteers—which was sort of what mother and Uncle Eubie were, rushing around the convoluted bi-state area from family disaster to family disaster. On the other hand, should Mr. Hickey spend even half a day in his cigar-befouled chamber, he might suffocate or go mad in the perpetual dusk and ineradicable smoke. A decaying exotic resort, that's what his bedroom was, the last seedy port of call tinged with the greasy ether of shoe polish and the briny tang of Epsom salts—*that old Havana* to which he quickly repaired during the day when he needed to peel off a sour shirt, and where he went late at night for a harsh little rest from the feminine realities of existence, the hours he spent gallantly hosting neighbor ladies in the kitchen, listening to their troubles with wild children and wilder husbands, providing wise if odd advice ("Why not try washing your hair with rain from my backyard bucket?") and generously realistic reassurance ("Tomorrow is another day, I think"). He slipped the *The Pennysaver* over the pistol so as not to alarm Mrs. Feeney. He changed the radio station to please country music lover Mrs. Moore or easy-listening fan Gloria Knickerbocker. At the end of the evening he whispered a last good-bye, usually to mother around midnight—"Take care, Tommy"—placed those dentures in the aqua bathroom cup, tugged on pilly cotton pajamas, and climbed onto the bed planks, drifting away to Cuba and points south.

MR. HICKEY WORE A BLACK BOW TIE and *no sweater vest* on the October night we gathered in his kitchen to follow radio reports of the boxing match in Zaire, Africa, between former champ Muhammad Ali and the young reigning king, George Foreman. "Turn on the radio," I squealed. "Soon, Benny." I stared at his dress shirt that looked so undressed without the sweater— the sweater my heart clung to like mega-lint. "The undercard must be over by now, Mr. Hickey. It's gotta be." "At eleven," he whispered. "*Eleven.*" Downtown at Masonic Auditorium a rowdy crowd watched preliminary bouts on a big screen, booing whenever the closed-circuit feed powdered or went wavy-granular. Jerry Bernaur, the sweetheart across the street who deboned hams at the Oscar Mayer plant, told me everything the next day—beer thrown, ushers pushed, posters ripped off lobby walls. And I told him all about my big fight night, starting with the shocking appearance of vestless Mr. Hickey on the back porch, answering the bell like a ghost-referee with four opaque eyes. The kitchen light revealed a shirt with white sleeves, yellow pocket, yellower shoulders, brownish buttons. Was cotton root rot to blame or the weird fashion of 1937? I tried to think of a delicate way to ask the question as Mr. Hickey's pink lips pinched the plastic cigar tip like an addicted bivalve shell. *During the Great Depression did the Arrow Shirt Company recycle cloth?* No. *Did Chicago's Aragon Ballroom host ornithological masquerade parties, requiring that men come yellow-breasted like finches?* No, no. "Ali's going to whip Foreman!" I finally gasped, needing to say something and locate by sound my friend all but lost in the Tiparillo haze. Mr. Hickey softly agreed—"Hope so"—and more smoke spumed over ashtray coils, leather-girdled Panasonic radio, aqua Tupperware pill counter, prune box…reaching the far corner of the Formica table and lending the pistol a Wild West aura of shoot-outs past. "Foreman will be done in one," I predicted and took another slug from the warm 7UP bottle, bubbles foaming tepid over my teeth and prickling tongue, provoking such a wince that I was again offered a highball glass of ice cubes but again refused because tonight we were beyond the reach of quaint Midwestern niceties like aluminum ice trays with handy-dandy cube ejection cranks, far beyond checkered tin bread boxes, four-slot toasters, quilted pot holders, even though all these items were in plain sight, just a few feet away. Mr. Hickey and I were fight fans in a sweltering Havana cabana, snacking on spotted bananas, swampy lime potions, stale cookies, and cigar smoke. We were part of a gregarious global congregation hunched around five-band radios—buzzing Philcos—whistling short-wave jobs—bent and foil-wrapped antennas connecting rich and poor, the humblest locales with the snazziest venues such as Rio and Monte Carlo. Factory workers and viscounts, prostitutes and beauty queens, grand prix drivers and garbage truck drivers, winking reactionaries in tuxedos and unblinking revolutionaries with coconut leaves stapled to helmets, double-chinned me in the XXL rummage-sale Penguin shirt and Mr. Hickey wearing that Arrow tunic of two yellows—all of us in the thrall of a poetic brawl that promoter Don King called "The Rumble in the Jungle." Since being stripped of the heavyweight title in 1967 for refusing to participate in the Vietnam War, Ali had been imprisoned, released, defeated by Joe Frazier in a fifteen-round bout at Madison Square Garden, and then? He had beaten Joltin' Joe in an instantly historic brutal rematch (they were each other's last name's now; Ali Frazier / Frazier Ali: say one, think the other), and after that? Ali got his jaw broken by Ken Norton. But on this steamilicious night in 1974—the real champ would show. Floating, stinging, singing about it afterward to Howard Cosell and George Plimpton and Norman Mailer, too—the literary gorilla who'd stabbed his wife not once but twice, as mother always liked to say. "How's Tommy?" the old gentleman asked, interrupting my reverie. He was the only one who pro-nounced mother's rough country name like it was the name of a delicate woman, softening and stretching the syllables so they sounded warm and mushy, almost rhyming with *hominy*. "She's all right, I guess." His magnified oystery eyes quivered wetly. He wanted specifics about events since her morning visit. Not many details: the exact right few. He wanted me to speak clearly and as efficiently as Hemingway or a Triscuit box, to isolate the day's vital ingredients: important places visited, people met, errands accomplished, weather endured. "She's all right?" he asked, pressing for the perfect five-word sentence. "She..." I muttered. "She's..." *Main events whirled through my mind—her knockdown drag-out with the Woolworths manager over the price of a*

duct-taped bag of root-beer-barrel hard candies; she and I carting
off the entire Bettendorf Public Library free-magazine box (the
New Yorker, Forbes, Ladies' Home Journal ...); Moby Purse
gulping handfuls of ketchup, mayo, and mustard packets from the
McDonald's condiment bar (10 Million Stolen by Ben's Mother So
Far); our rolling Dumpster nearly smacking a polka-dot cement
mixer; buying a dollar of gas at the Shell station on River Drive,
another dollar of gas at the Gulf station on Brady, finally arriving
to fetch Elizabeth from orchestra practice at Eisenhower school and
finding her playing violin in the pitch-black lot to subdue any
lurking Frankensteins, and after my sister hurtled into the backseat, why, Mr. Hickey, she nearly stabbed mother to death with a
horsehair bow, crying, "Where in the H-E-double-toothpicks were
you?" and then screeching much worse after being handed the same
old excuse: "I'm doing the best that I can, Betsy," backed up by my
earnest testimony to the effect that the LTD had been racing toward
the lot for hours, only not in a straight line. "Mother's ..." I
muttered. "Mother, she ..." sat in the smelly LTD in the crooked
spiderwebbed garage after we arrived home, not wanting to squeeze
out a door that only opened halfway, scraping you—not wanting to
face the bean-caked dishes, Nathan's juicy diapers, verbal abuse
from Elizabeth, Howard's infernal eternal requests for a buck, and
father, belly heavily bandaged by the metro section, yelling that he
needed some kippers. King Edward kippers! Won't someone bring a
dead man some salty greasy kippers! Mother, she sat in the front
seat sighing those wet, gale-force sighs indicating tortuous knowledge of what could be accomplished with that brilliant mind of hers
and how little was getting done—less than nothing—another day
squandered on bargain hunting and a long long night to go,
siiiiiiiiiighing and sucking root beer barrels, itching a scabrous
scalp, reciting beloved snippets of Emily Dickinson ("Mine—by the

Right of the White Election!"), Dylan Thomas ("Do not go gently into the night!"), Vachel Lindsay ("General Booth is coming, coming to Heaven, beat the drum, O beat, O beat, O beat ..."), and most every line of "The Circus Animal's Desertion" by W. B. Yeats, ending "... rag and bone shop of the heart," digging for cold french fries in the seat folds and not finding any and finally letting the car door have its evil way with her pelvis and slouching across the backyard toward the porch and the rotten kitchen where a bunch of bananas purchased earlier for Mr. Hickey had since turned leopardy—groaning at the sight of the spots and reacting very badly to the news that I HAD BEEN INVITED to listen to the fight and would be tagging along on her nightly visit next door, so badly that she teetered on her tattered tennis shoes, accusing me of "neighbor hogging," and then stomped back to the garage and steered the LTD, her Ship of Sorrow, down the alley—rumble, wheeze, rattle, putt-putt. "She ...," I muttered. "She's ..." How to sum it all up?—the paralysis, the unending energy, the intelligence, the stupidity, the greediness, the selflessness, the poetry, the little-girl talk, the cruel gossip (agony felt and agony inflicted), the thousand-and-one emotional shell games and never a winner? That was a life's work for an Einstein of an editor, and William Einstein Shawn I was not. I was the grunt of La Mancha with the spiked stick, stabbing ridiculously the windmilling litter of each minute. There was so much in a minute—the secret life of it inside you, the official life of it outside you—the big tangle of facts that lied in little ways and the lies that told truths facts could not. That was a minute, and each one was just too precious to discard because who knew how many more there would be, with the LTD bearing down on cement mixers and dump trucks as if they were full of goose down, not two tons of fill. Mr. Hickey, he so elegantly distilled the biggest adventures into a few nouns and verbs. The three-year

career as a boxer became: "Flyweight. Fought in barns. Beat a
heavyweight once by staying behind him." There was much to learn
from that precision, only what I learned was to be more precisely
comprehensive. To gather with ever more girthly care the slippery
swirling muck of reality that somehow was forming—molding—
me, my family members, and neighbors, into hard and fast indi-
viduals, dull or interesting, accomplished or failed, criminal or
decent. In my mind I enlarged small events like forensic photo-
graphs, examining all perplexing beautifully ugly details when
stranded at a swimming pool or library parking lot, kicking pebbles
or rusty cans while mulling every filament in mother's mustache or
Elizabeth's despair or a store clerk's toupee, searching searching
searching for the Meaning of our trouble and the trouble of those
around us. Because I wanted—God, I wanted—to be released from
the lurid mysteries of American chaos, the rich but deadly wreckage
of the fallen sky we were caught in and tripping over. And Mr.
Hickey, I suddenly realized, gazing at his patient porcelain fea-
tures, which had been petrified since the first of the seventeen times
and counting that I had said "She's . . ."—Mr. Hickey, the polite
soul, he just needed to know whether to put the teapot on for
momster, and I better not delay answering any longer—the old
man had a weak heart and only one tank of oxygen in the dining
room, every cubic gulp of which would be needed during the bout to
be broadcast in a nerve-wracking War of the Worlds *special-report*
format—three-minute rounds lasting ten or more minutes, however
long it took the WBBM sports director to edit and deliver the AP
wire report from Zaire. "Mother, she . . . went over to Rock
Island . . . ," I guessed, not lied—important difference—". . . to
take Granny's blood pressure . . . and won't be stopping up
tonight."

MR. HICKEY'S CHIN QUAVERED like a teacup enduring a passing train. I assured him it was no emergency—nothing to worry about, no turn for the worse: Mary Ellen was doing just fine with her sugar diabetes, kidney problems, lingering stroke symptoms, and that drunken lout Grandpa. Nod...nod. "Be sure and tell *hominy* hello for me." I said I would. He took a long slow drag on the cigar, smoke not shooting from the mouth but dribbling down the shirt front, then I knew. I knew a thing I very much wished I did not know. I knew that Mr. Hickey, subsisting on a fixed income (Social Security plus a meager Coast Guard pension), bleached only his shirtsleeves to conserve Clorox and save dimes to put toward the purchase of treats for his many daily visitors. (Each sleeve in a bowl, held down by stacks of quarters, I imagined, the shirt front dangling between.) The shirt front nobody would ever see because of the red sweater vest—no one but me, on this evening, and it was no accident. He wanted me to see the tobacco-stained seams. He wanted to present fresh proof of what an ignoble struggle life was for even the most well-intentioned of males. It was fight night: the right night to let your animal self loose—the sweat stains and nicotine stains and stale primal thirsts that might be tamed but never extinguished. Forget all the fatuous *Sports Illustrated* copy about boxing being "the sweet science," every right cross a rogue thing of divine beauty, *blabber, blabber, blabber*. The beauty of a knockdown punch was its pure beautylessness—the teeth of the struck man sticking through the lower lip like boar tusks. Fans cheered broken noses, detached retinas, cauliflower ears. They rose at ringside, in front of closed-circuit screens, next to radios at taverns, bistros, casinos, piers, international airports, prisons without running water. They saw the blood-mask and pumped their hairy fists, waving rivulets their way, desiring to be sprinkled, baptized by violence, released from the stifling bonds of civilization. Weekly Mr. Hickey admitted the awful (to him) truth that he had run a gambling game as a young man, confessed with forceful sorrow, and I nodded, nodded, but seeing this shirt was something else—the active stain on his existence, deepening a little each day, despite generous deeds done and so many temptations resisted. He was human, that was all—and that was everything. Everything. It meant courage and fear, strength and weakness, generosity and selfishness. Contrary traits linked in the most amazing ways—illogically inter-reliant.

For instance, the nakedness of boxers—their very vulnerability—required them to be more vicious than athletes in protective gear. It was Ali's savagery in the ring that gave such beguiling legitimate power to his pretty press-conference smile, the lyrical utterances, and the long fluttering eyelashes.

THE RADIO RECEIVER CRACKLED as Mr. Hickey caressed the tuning knob and adjusted the antenna. He looked like an expert safecracker subduing a giant cricket atop a little Zaire safe full of Mobutu diamonds—right, left, right, left: *krehkkkkrzzkrkrezzhkkk WBBM, news radio ssseventy-eight.* It was raining in downtown Chicago, wind off Lake Michigan gusting to ten knots. Sixteen elevator inspectors were under arrest for taking kickbacks, with more arrests expected soon. A Lincoln Park man had shot his girlfriend three times and then turned the gun on her German shepherd. Or something like that. And the office of Alderman Eddie Vrdolyak had no comment on the South Side waste-disposal contract scandal. "In Zaire..." the far off land of Zaire zebras, Zaire sky, Zaire sun, Zaire moon, Zaire jungle, Zaire villages, Zaire kalimbas—handheld teak pianos with metal strips of various lengths to pluck (mother's sister, Deena, the globe-trotting chemistry professor, had sent us one)—amid tinkling Zaire music and Zaire dances, Zaire zoot suits and robes and dresses, Zaire limos and Zaire pushcarts, Zaire creation fables and Zaire camera cables. "The bell sounded and..." neither boxer did damage, trading just a few hard punches. "Ali'll get him in the second round. Foreman will be through in two." "Cassius," Mr. Hickey whispered—using the former champ's birth name out of habit. "Cassius Clay better be careful. This kid can punch." Right, I acceded with a nod of the 7UP bottle poised under my sticky lips, Foreman *had* won Olympic gold at Mexico City in 1968—it was in the *World Almanac* on my bedroom windowsill. "Cassius has to play it smart." Down went the Tiparillo and up went the delicate pugilist's two little fists. Aggressive sugar bowls they looked like, hovering in front of the bigger bowl of Mr. Hickey's enamel-white noggin. "Protect the head with the right," he murmured. "Jab with the left, jab and dance, jab, jab, dance." Hands in my lap, I agreed—yes, for certain, no doubt, that was how to win a heavyweight fight. Then Mr. Hickey reminded this 210-pound, four-feet-ten-and-a-half-inch contenda for the fat farm to "hit the rope and stay clean," and I promised to jump rope to improve my agility and also to keep away from the mob wiseguys and gamblers who ruined many palookas, including "Two Ton" Tony Galento and Primo Carnera, the ex-champ Mr. Hickey had met in a flea-ridden Iowa hotel lobby in the 1930s. Even Joe Louis—the Brown Bomber—had ended up a "greeter" for a Las Vegas casino, his wheelchair flung like shrapnel under the throbbing spectacle of a neon sign, shaking hands with whomever. "I won't wager any of my snow-shoveling money this winter, Mr. Hickey. I'll save *it all* for college." He smiled mildly, reinserted the cigar tip between his lips, and smoke genied out of nostrils as fragile as china thimbles—belts of smoke, ropes of smoke, smoke towels and smoke fedoras floating across nicotine-stained Havana walls and crawling like lazy fronds of a ceiling fan. *WBBM, news radio sssseventy-eight*, hissed John Madigan, night news announcer. It was still drizzling in Chicago, expected low of sixty degrees. Investigators were removing evidence of Medicaid fraud from a South Side podiatry clinic. Avoid the Pulaski Skyway due to a five-car pileup—take Roosevelt Road, the Cermak, hop the L, rent a fishing boat, anything but get on the Pulaski. Now, an update from Zaire... "The bell sounded and Ali retreated to the ropes, covered his face, took a left from Foreman, a right, another hard left…" Mr. Hickey choked on the smoke like it was milk that had gone down wrong. The Greatest retreat so early? Ali who had done the bravest thing a male could do—call himself pretty in public. "Another body blow by Foreman, another right, then a left, and the bell sounded." *Cuh-cuh,* coughed my host, *cuh-cuh-cuh.* Over his cringing shoulder peered the oval blue eye in the oven enamel, and I had no answer for the Amana Sphinx—no friggin' idea why Ali had willingly cowered, dancing no jig, hiding his face with both Everlast gloves. Both gloves. It just was not him. It could not be. All week he had traveled Zaire winning over the populace with his openness. That was Ali. He lived not behind castle walls but generously in front of TV cameras—prancing, preening, singing, predicting, taunting, scolding, philosophizing, proclaiming what he believed, what he would and would not fight for. In a world of phony celebrities and carefully worded press releases, Ali was the Real Deal, unmanaged by his entourage and leading them (Dundee, Pacheco, Boudini) around the globe, cutting a wide swath of excitement through every country entered. Ali = All Intelligence, All Inspiration. He was the best thing America had going for her after the debacles of Saigon and Watergate. He could not be tired after one round. He was ageless. He was the freshness a country needed, the immense energy and hope that always had been required to prop up the sprawling notion of America—and without which there would be a sea-to-shining-sea collapse, Ohio sliding into the Pacific right behind California, an avalanche of cars, blenders, blow dryers, televisions, microwaves, and millions of other consumer goods that made life so much easier but were no replacement for belief in oneself. Ali was faith in the moment of his being—faith in the power of heart, brawn, ideas—faith in free expression and faith that America was strong enough to withstand the harshest shot of any honest critic.

And Ali—our one and only Ali—was crumpled on the ropes, taking an awful beating from Foreman? Yes, and it happened again in the third round, and the fourth, too, the fifth, and the sixth as well. "Another body blow by Foreman, two lefts, a right, two lefts, and the bell sounded." Mr. Hickey dunked the host of the cookie into the wine of Sanka. It might help, but of course it would not. He crept into the bathroom off the kitchen and unscrewed the lids of tubes and jars of muscle cream arrayed on the toilet tank, hoping I guess that the fumes would reach Zaire and revive Cassius's failing clay. But Mr. Hickey neglected to lift the glazed window. I went in and did, and the wind was blowing the wrong direction. Minty vapor pushed into the kitchen, commingling with Tiparillo smoke to create the vintage stench of a locker room before the advent of Right Guard and Dr. Scholl's: air bugless yet bug-heavy, astringent and stinging my nostrils. I should have gotten up and shut the thing then, but dared not approach the commode again—the swarthy specter of wrestler Gorgeous George might be sitting on it; or Jock Semple, Boston Garden trainer; or Paul Moon, Central High basketball coach, wearing only spats. I glanced at the sarcophagi profile of the Kelvinator, dismissing the notion of sticking my head inside for a draught of fresh air—the temptation to crawl in with the salmon loaf would be irresistible. I breathed and spoke through a finger mask. "Ali'll get him in the seventh. Foreman will be…"—what in seven?—"…will be…" Leavened? No, I was all rhymed out after "driven to a knee in three," "hit the floor in four," "take a dive in five," "out of the mix in six."

IN CHICAGO THE BAROMETRIC PRESSURE was still dropping. Authorities had identified the Lincoln Park shooter as a thirty-year-old Jack in the Box employee: unregistered gun, five

prior convictions, and the neighbors can't believe it—such a nice man murder a girl and a dog? The elevator-inspector kickback scandal had alarmingly widened to include eleven forklift operators, eight welfare caseworkers, five meter maids, and three high school principals, but no partridge in a pear tree, not yet. The mayor had no comment on that oversight or on Alderman Vrdolyak's not commenting on the waste-disposal contract scandal. Now, an update from Zaire. "The seventh round began with Ali again retreating to the ropes. Foreman delivered a right to the ribs, another right to the chest, a left almost too low, warning issued. Then Foreman went back to work on the ribs, a right, left, right…" Mr. Hickey leaned toward the radio as if trying to take the ferocious blows himself and spare the old champ further punishment. "A left to the gut, a right," and Foreman leaned on Ali, the fighters exchanged words and the ref stepped in, round over. Back soon with more action. That is, if Ali answered the bell. It was a massacre. The Greatest had not landed a hard punch since last week. Foreman had done him in—and Mr. Hickey, too. "Goodness," my old friend moaned, sinking in the chair. "Gracious." I suggested taking some oxygen. He inched his way into the dining room and emptied the slender green tank on the doily table—bow tie inhaling, safety shoes inhaling, slacks inhaling and straining the belt circling the waist like a glossy licorice whip. Fatter, he returned and immediately deflated like a handsome balloon—chest withering, waist shrinking, shoulders slumping, lending the shirt little more bulk than a hanger. "Oh boy," he sighed, grasping for the pill counter. Outside, wind fingered the fallen leaves, but in here the steam heat had curled the corners of the VFW wall calendar, and the wooden pistol handle glistened through the haze as if it had broken into a nervous sweat—worried more about Ali than burglars crawling in basement windows or stoned Weathermen bombers taking the wrong interstate exit on the way to Berkeley or the mere existence of nude John and Yoko in New York City. Only the sixteen-ounce prune box had no fears or concerns whatsoever. Atop the counter the oatmeal cylinder loomed like a totem-pole stump, and the garish expressions of the cows on the Carnation cans made me wonder by what Medici means milk was condensed. I shivered. I dampened. My eyeframes slid down my nose and through the very top of the lenses I saw Havana helicopers circling, pulsing like fireflies over the closed-circuit extravaganza squatting in its own chimerical mire. I bit my fingernails. I swigged the last of the 7UP, now a flat liquid the consistency of spit, supremely swishable but absolutely unswallowable: if only Hickey's cabana had a dirt floor. I requested a highball glass. He gestured to the cupboard—*Get it yourself, I'm tuckered*—and I got the glass, and behind Mr. Hickey's back did what had to be done: *speeeeew*, just like Ali on the corner stool in Zaire, cup under bloody mouth. Ali being worked on by Angelo Dundee, a doctor who operated without instruments, closing gashes with whispers and Vaseline. Ali glaring and biting his bottom lip as he did during interviews, mocking the rubes who believed they could destroy him. Ali aching, angry, not through— "He'll answer the bell. Right, Mr. Hickey? Won't he?" The old man said nothing, peeling cellophane from a Tiparillo box with the needy tenderness of a tobacco fiend—undressed the box, really, tugging a red strip, lifting off the flimsy blouse above it and sliding down the skirt below and placing both garments next to the ashtray. In the ashtray already were nine plastic cigar tips, each with a dark shag of ash protruding from the fat end like rotten incisor roots. The sucked narrow end shined like bone, hollow and faintly smudged by Mr. Hickey's kisses. "Ali will answer the bell," I mumbled. Mr. Hickey lifted an open hand and turned it over twice, as if to say—*ech, that might not be so good, a kidney punch can cripple, saw it once at the Muscatine County Fair, Sugar Stevens laid out flat.* He inhaled. He exhaled. The smoke twisted into awful midair faces—contorted mouths and noses and ears not unlike those of the foam-rubber store mascots mother often pointed out to me as role models. Her fondest wish was that I become a penniless unwashed and/or deranged poet like those bleary angels pictured on the wanted-poster cover of *A Little Treasury of*

American Poetry (mug shots of Walt Whitman and gang), but epic poems like "Song of Myself" did not come easy, and if I failed to produce such a masterpiece by age eighteen, then, well, then I should do the next best thing: don a cheese-wedge costume and wave at passing cars. "Wouldn't it be fun to be Mr. Swiss?" she chirped. "Sure," I said to her, and promised myself: *Never never never, I'd rather feed myself to the rollers of Lock and Dam No. 13.* I wanted to be fancy-free like Ali. Stable and reliable and as well-provisioned as Hickey. Safely free—if such a thing was possible—orbiting absolutely untethered around a Kelvinator loaded with dimpled 7UP bottles and salmon loaf. "Heavens," whispered my host, without a following "to Betsy." His oyster eyes disappeared into their deep shells, the bald head fell forward so it was possible to see the dent marking the spot where he had been dealt that knockout blow by a swinging boom on a Coast Guard ship. Dead-tired, my neighbor, not dead—his yellowed Arrow shirt undulated with shallow yet intent breath. I left that old sea lion sleeping, made my way to the window, rubbing a peephole in the steam. The moon glowed down on our backyard trash—the boxes of all sizes, the bags, the cans, the bottles, the circulars, the *Pennysaver*s, the junk mail, the paperbacks, the newspapers and slick magazines stripped of valuable Chas Addams cartoons or sex-advice columns or sage quotes for businessmen and nincompoops like us to memorize and flaunt. The light was the hue of adhesive: it made me want some glue. Glue enough to put the tons of garbage together, build a Watts tower of trash that would cast a long shadow toward the Mississippi River like a phantom tributary. I had to find a way to make use of the stuff of our existence—low as it was. Though it appeared worthless, it was not without value. How could we be nothing if our lives were woven entirely of the tatters and shreds of America, the undeniably beautiful? We were...something. We belonged, somehow. The nation was not just the best in its people but the worst in them, too. It was about clinging to ideals like Mr. Hickey did and losing them like we did each day, and Mr. Dankert, also, with his jokes about Polacks, and Mr. Moore with his wife-beating—every generation figuring out its own new way to squander, or utilize, the tremendous gift of freedom. The pane turned glossy with my breath, then paler...*white as the translucent leaves of a Cuban jungle closing in, bringing Sanka birds and Lipton lizards and Folgers instant insects, and in my chest suddenly there was a*

rustling that was not breath, it was a cabana patron in a frayed
tuxedo, flipping through movie stills—photos of Errol Flynn and
Greta Garbo and Glenn Ford and Leo Gorcey and Abbott and
Costello and the bride of Frankenstein with the four-foot hairdo.
She was the love of his life, really. He had dressed like a groom to see
that movie and then cried when the lights had gone up. He had run
out of the theater and past the harmonica-playing beggar, past the
legless fortune teller, climbing the glittering ridge to reach the night
behind Havana casinos, and there he blew the fetid kisses of last
resort, blew kisses to the rats, the bats, the gamblers, the prostitutes,
the sportswriters—Robert Markus, Dave Condon, Jerome
Holtzman—and more kisses to the poppy sellers, the Siamese cats,
the dogs, the dead fish, the ace of spades and the piano players and
the palm trees, and... "Benny, come here." Mr. Hickey had risen,
was waving me over. On the floor burned a Tiparillo. I rushed to
him—no heart attack and no dream, better: the five-band radio.
News crackling over the receiver. "TKO by Ali. In the eighth
round. Foreman came out tired, hands low. Ali went at him,
swinging—a right, a left, five blows, and the champ fell. Hit the
canvas. Whipped. Ali fooled the kid into punching himself out.
Calls it 'rope-a-dope.' A minute ago, in the press room. Rope-a-
dope, rope-a-dope. Again, here in Zaire, it's Ali! *Ali.* Ali, everyone! Ali wins! Ali's done it again!"

MRS. HICKEY

One form of tenderness — Dare to be different! — *To save
the birds from starving* — *Banana mission* — A late
and terrifying hour — *Vapor of thought and feeling*

Sometime in the 1950s Mr. Hickey wed a woman at the Scott
County courthouse, softly answering the questions asked by the
justice of the peace. It was a late first marriage for both partners
and ended soon after, when Mrs. Hickey succumbed to pneumonia. Come 1973, in a child's curious and confounding way,
I pictured the late wife of our next-door neighbor with ringlets
of white hair, a minor nose, intense green eyes, and a plump
wrinkled face, as if the dead kept aging as long as those who
loved them remained on earth. Roses grown by the widower once
won top honors at the Mississippi Valley Fair, I had been told.

Throughout the summer gorgeous blooms engulfed the skeletal trellis, casting color up the side of the white house to a point just below the tin gutter. Then, in September, the bush was ruthlessly pruned. On the terrace above, Mr. Hickey teetered like a legendary football coach pacing a stadium sideline during the final season—fedora, raincoat unbuttoned. His body might have been weakened by pulmonary disease but his will remained strong— that zest for action. *Snip... Snip... Snip...* The bow tie bobbed and the coat hem fluttered as thorny branches toppled. Flowers the consistency of crepe paper draped the polished uppers of his black shoes. Branches landed on scruffy orange marigolds and battered border-garden bricks that had once paved a Davenport street. I watched the American Beauty massacre from the kitchen where I was supposed to be doing dishes. Scouring that cheap china was futile, however. Dirty plates had lingered too long in the open air, their arabesque patterns permanently appended with crusty condiments. As on many other evenings, I had constructed a showy mountain of suds over the intractable mess. A peaked Everest of froth, now slowly compacting. Teeny bubbles whispered as they burst by the hundreds. The bush, too, kept getting smaller. A thorn caught Mr. Hickey's tan coat and he delicately tugged the branch free with the tip of the long-handled shears. That was one form of tenderness. The love attuned to the presence of each precious millimeter of the beloved. Yet admiration was not enough. Simply appreciated and never pruned, the bush would soon stop producing blooms. It needed a gardener with the courage to do the hard work of nurturing. Close the blade on what had been, so something else might be. *Snip... Snip... Snip* ... I shifted my weight from one leg to the other, pressing the bulk of my belly against the damp rim of the sink as a startling streak of light struck the gutter on Mr. Hickey's house. The scalloped metal turned a straw hue, dark yellow, bright orange. Then the fiery gate lifted and dusk's first shadows swept across the steeply pitched roof. Brown grass became browner. Garden bricks lengthened, resembling shoe boxes laid end-to-end in a closet. Three starlings veered around the chimney, then dived lawnward, under the back-yard wire to which Mikey's leash used to be attached, until cancer carried the pug off to Pet Heaven. The starlings rose, paperclips sliding across the purple stationery of the sky and tucking into a nest that bearded the little garage off the alley. Inside lurked the Model T on cinder blocks. Mr. Hickey offered to let us borrow the vehicle whenever our old blue LTD broke down. He had also been kind enough to install five concrete stairs leading down to our backyard—this after mother slipped while attempting to bring him groceries on a rainy night, rolling down the hill like a log in a sack dress. The black fedora swiveled. The bifocals scanned the horizon for last-minute sellers of raffle tickets or grapefruit. From past experience hawking melon-scented candles, I knew that money to support good causes was secluded in the right pocket of the slacks, bills enfolded by a tarnished brass clip. Along with each donation came a brief personal parable with big meaning. I had been alternately dazzled and puzzled by these tales during fund-raising visits to Mr. Hickey's tropical kitchen, torpid with teapot steam. Somehow he had been able to reduce seventy messy years of experience into a series of crisp five-second stories that neatly promoted the value of hard work and ingenuity. The one about Shoeshine Boy Hickey, shirt stuffed with crumpled news-paper that kept out the winter cold while he stood on a curb in Tipton, Iowa, shouting: *Shine! Five pennies! A nickel! A half dime!* (Stored on the back porch was proof: a "shine" box with a wood wedge on the lid and, inside, black stiff rags with an oily cocoa stink—the last breath of 1912.) The one about Boxer Hickey, lightweight conqueror of a heavyweight in a barn outside Cedar

Rapids, spending the entire match behind the blond behemoth who flailed away at his invisible opponent until collapsing of heat exhaustion in the fifth round. The one about Salesman Hickey, a store clerk who cleverly placed a SALE sign on a rack of hot-pink shirts and then watched them all disappear in less than an hour, snapped up by shoppers too eager to believe it was their lucky day. And my favorite—the one about Real Estate Agent Hickey, who did not curse or cry when a big deal fell through, but took a box camera from a desk drawer, walked to the window, and snapped a panoramic photo of the Centennial Bridge, the glittering span over the clouded water of the Mississippi that lent scale to every sorrow. Finding adjoining yards bare of fund-raising band members, the old man turned back toward the hacked bush. His pale lips parted as if urging the few remaining petals to make an end run around autumn: *You can do it—the evergreen does.* No tips need be offered about how to avoid flower pickers, because his passion for those roses had apparently created a force field around the branches that repelled thieves. (Years later, even after he sold the house and entered the Masonic Home, the bush remained off-limits, untouched by the young couple who moved in, and blooming improbably, as if rooted not in dry, unwatered soil but the rich spirit of the far-flung gardener, still very much alive, brightening the days of nurses and other residents on the good floor.) Huddling close to a last petal-bannered branch, his lungs filled with September's antic aroma. The raincoat swayed. Shears closed, his job done. (Tomorrow Larry Swann, Mr. Hickey's lawn boy, would bag branches for a fine fee.) I squirted more Lady Lee Detergent onto plates poking out of suds, and twisted the water tap. Another froth-tufted Everest quickly resulted, while on the hill, shoe leather inched toward the glassed-in back porch. I thought of the items he was returning to in the house, the Tupperware pill counter on the kitchen table next to the pistol, the oxygen tank on the dining room table, the buffet occupied by Mrs. Hickey's miniature Christmas tree. The kingly decoration she created from dime store materials, covering conical cardboard with silver ribbons, each folded over and secured with a staple.

MR. HICKEY NEVER MENTIONED his wife. Nor was a single photograph of Mrs. Hickey displayed in the house. That mysterious art project had been chosen to represent her there. And often I passed close to it while following him through the dining room that connected the kitchen and the living room, where there was a marvelous device called a "Cox cable box" that allowed even nearsighted people to see as far as Chicago and the friendly confines of Wrigley Field. Ivy-covered outfield walls. Baby-blue dugout with a red *C* painted on it. Pudgy players who finished last with good cheer and stands full of philosophical fans who understood that a losing streak could astound as deliciously as any winning streak, disrupting a life of surprises with a miracle dose of the one sure thing. Pirates 6, Cubs 3. Cardinals 3, Cubs 0. Giants 5, Cubs 4. The first pitch was at 1:15 p.m., but we would not arrive in time in this memory. Too much dim dining room remained to cross. Five of my guide's bony fingers searched for surfaces, any edge to trail and use as a rail. Cradled in his other hand was the varnished handle of the pistol that would be the end of any burglar lurking in the shadow of the china cabinet. In the middle of the floor, beyond the slant of kitchen light, Mr. Hickey's dark slacks vanished and the white shirt wafted forward: a stringless kite. Just a harmless optical illusion, I reminded myself. The kite halted, hunched, sank a few inches. Long gone were the days of backyard push-ups at dawn and jumping rope in the office on the tenth floor of the Kahl Building, vigorous routines inspired by Mr. Hickey's hero, Martin "Farmer" Burns, a turn-of-the-century wrestler who had worn overalls into the ring more than six thousand times and lost only six matches. Mr. Hickey had visited the gymnasium owned by "Farmer" in Rock Island, and had taken a correspondence course that the straight-laced he-man used to spread his wholesome ideas about nutrition (drink a lot of milk, eat only two meals a day) and fitness (calisthenics, calisthenics, calisthenics). These secrets had been passed on to me, along with a frayed jump rope which I promptly hid under my bed, fearing it could give a fat boy a heart attack just like an old man. (In the same cowardly spirit I prayed for blizzards, flash floods, sore throats to spare me from the humiliating rigor of outdoor gym class and the social hell of recess. O wonderful storm diverting attention from the Disaster of Me and My Family. Snow obscuring basketball hoops, jungle gyms, bike racks. Water lashing windows behind which star athletes and pretty girls stood, bereft and pouting. On these soggy days I waddled with confidence, double chin stuck out, creepy smile creasing my face. *Welcome to oblivion. Uno is the way to kill the time. Today, at least, we're all in this together.*) Quick little breaths lifted the kite. When enough air gathered under the cloth, progress would resume, but enough hadn't. So I turned and gazed at the Christmas tree on the walnut buffet. From a distance this craft resembled a frilly fairy dress or alchemist's hat covered with moths. Why dull silver ribbons? The Ben Franklin could not have been out of every bright festive color when Mrs. Hickey stopped in, cow bell above the door clanging, high heels clacking past the salmon doctor's scale placed like a health warning next to squat jars of hard candy and cream caramels. No, she had purposely plucked a silver spool off the pegboard hook. Ribbon the hue of bad holiday weather: fog rising off snow in the ditch…mist in the wide wet eyes of carolers singing "Silent Night" to the closed doors lining a hospital corridor. Maybe an avant-garde craft columnist made her do it: *Homemaker! Dare to be different!* Maybe she went to the store on the wrong morning, while feeling sad like many people did during the Christmas season, for real but often inexplicable reasons. Still another explanation was offered by mother, fan of "Walter Scott's Personality Parade" gossip column and herself an accomplished trader in secrets about neighbors and celebrities. From her I learned of cabaret singer Rosemary smearing *fecal matter* on an asylum wall after suffering a nervous breakdown. Of Clark's hair transplants, Welch's foam-filled breasts, elderly Dinah taking young buck Burt as a lover, President Nixon drowning cottage cheese in ketchup (as if the bloodshed in Vietnam weren't enough) and the hotel infidelities of JFK, RFK, and Martin Luther King, Jr. Mrs. Hickey? She was another "hopeless alkie"—like TV doctor Marcus Welby, MD, and Dorothy from Kansas—a poor addicted wretch Mr. Hickey tried and failed to save from "the bottle." Yet this revelation didn't sting as much as she intended it to. Even if true—and her sources always were suspect—millions had not pinned their hopes on Mrs. Hickey, just one man. And awful as it must have been when Mrs. Hickey died, her husband had not been debilitated by misfortune. That had happened to others I knew. Mr. Hickey, he cultivated new commitments in the wake of that devastating blow. He had risen from the low point to succeed as a real estate broker and insurance seller, to grow bouquets of prize-winning roses, and each December place an electric Santa head in the kitchen window facing our backyard, the blinking red nose a beacon in the winter night, spreading an unambivalent message of hope and joy over the snow and litter.

IT WAS MY JOB to bring our neighbor the bag of bird-seed for the feeder in the window next to the Santa window. Mr. Hickey, though often homebound, never forgot that he shared the winter months with sparrows. He gave my mother the money for the seed and she got it and said: "Benji, take Mr. Hickey that seed before the birds starve to death." She knew the stale crusts she threw out the back door were no solution to ornithological famine. The plastic bag of seed was the answer. It bore the image of a cardinal. It was heavy. I dragged it down our icy stoop and then up the slushy steps built into the side of Mr. Hickey's hill and along the edge of the terrace retaining wall. If I slipped and fell, I would go over the edge and be impaled by our hedges. This almost, but not quite, happened each time. Like desert sand the pearly brown flax seeds and dusky sunflower hulls sifted against my thighs and forearms. The load thumped up Mr. Hickey's porch stairs, and panting, I rang with the insistence of one with a mission to save the birds from starving to death. When at last he made it to the door I flashed my cola-brown smile, dragged the bag onto the porch and was informed that there was plenty of seed in the feeder at present.

MR. HICKEY DID HIS OWN LAUNDRY and cleaned like the former sailor that he was, albeit one tile or square foot of carpet at a time. The mop forever marinating in a bucket of soapy water. The dust broom poised for action in the middle of the living room floor. He scrubbed the claw-foot tub with Comet, reamed the toilet bowl with a brush, and continually reordered the realm of bottles and tubes atop the tank: Polident, Milk of Magnesia, Pepto-Bismol, salves with ominous instructions. *When the itching starts*...Certainly he would have arranged for delivery of groceries had mother not phoned each day to demand the privilege of doing him a favor. "There's got to be something you need at National! Milk? Grits? Ritz? Tiparillos, John?" But neither can it be said that coercion was involved, for with the late-night delivery of these items came the safety of company—a compatriot to dial zero should the dreaded heart attack occur. "Bananas, then. Epsom salts, too." She scrawled the list on a yellow legal pad jutting from Moby Purse. Then I was dispatched to retrieve an envelope containing cash to pay for the necessities, as Mr. Hickey would not hear of a friend extending him credit for even half an hour, let alone the time it took mother to meander to and from the store on Kimberly Road. "Darling! Run up the hill, again, will you?" Run, no. Waddle, yes. The screen door bounced behind the flab shelving my hips. I labored up the steep hillside stairs— one…two…three…four…five. Many more knocks than that were required to lure Mr. Hickey onto his back porch. Though he knew a neighborly visit was imminent, safety precautions had to be followed to the letter. First, an energizing gulp of oxygen from the dining room tank, in case a cutthroat ventriloquist had set him up and the knocking on the aluminum door with Plexiglas panes was the rattling prelude to a boxing comeback at age seventy. *Bang bang* on the door. Then, on reentering the kitchen, a squinting pause to ascertain if his five-dollar bill was still taped to the window in the door. *Bang bang bang bang.* "It's just Benny!" I screamed, using his nickname for me. "Benny for the envelope!" Oh yes, the envelope. Almost forgot. He located the last box of professional stationery: *John Hickey, Real Estate and Insurance.* He slipped into an envelope twice as much money as Epsom salts and bananas had cost just a few days ago, in case the rate of inflation was worse than kindly Walter Cronkite dared to report. Then, on the outside of the envelope, he printed mother's name, *TOMMY*, so there would be no confusion whom the money belonged to, and I would not be tempted to flee to Havana with it. Finally, the five-dollar-bill door opened and he shuffled into the valley between the boxes stacked on the porch. A man who had lived a life so different from the one he had planned on living when he left the courthouse, guiding the arm of his bride. No children save for strays who became all the needier for all we were given. No family vacations or boisterous holiday dinners. The AM radio a replacement for breakfast conversation, and, until his demise, only warty Mikey to kiss. Reaching the back door, he paused one last time, looking down at me, Benny. His eyes were the size of large marbles. The mild smile unflecked by emphasis. Sweater vest stretched over the angular frame like moss over some knobby forest bough. All his feelings—whatever they might be— concealed in the hollow.

AROUND 10 P.M. CAME mother's farewell: "Be back in a few minutes." She said it casually, yet somehow in a dire tone. Those minutes—I knew—were another name for eternity. And off she flew, clutching the National Grocery bag and smoothing her tangled hair. It took two hours to deliver the fruit and Epsom salts, and no amount of my jealous pounding on the back door could cut the visit short, because she always convinced the old gentleman to turn his hearing aid off, I suppose by telling him the ringing bothered her. Unethical behavior, in my view, but no surprise given her desperation. If she was totally unequal to the demands of motherhood—lacking the patience, feeling, and practical skills to care for one child, let alone six—there was no need to fake it in the abode of self-sufficient Mr. Hickey. The two sat in the tropical kitchen heat, he suckling the plastic tip of a cigar, she dunking Archway sugar cookies in a crumb-scummed cup of tea. *How wonderful to have company at such a late and terrifying hour.* Hanging on the wall, in addition to the large VFW calendar, was an even bigger yarn replica of the US Coast Guard seal—the rope-entwined anchor knitted by Alice, who lived upriver in tiny Le Claire with her husband, Eddie, a retired tugboat captain. Mr. Hickey treasured his military service, which had ended when his hat size was changed by an errant swinging boom on a ship

moored off New Orleans. Often I pictured the drastic incident.
Out went the lights. Across the deck flew a canvas stretcher. An
hour later the bandaged sailor recited his name, rank, and serial
number with the aplomb of Mr. Magoo, but severely concussed
individuals could not be trusted to read a compass or navigational
map. Off he went with a medical discharge. The chief long-term
effects of the accident were vision problems and headaches
that no Bayer product could soothe. Migraines that lasted for
days, winces warping his head until it resembled an ivory gourd

puckered by the sweltering kitchen atmosphere. The windows were always closed, creating a savings bank of warmth. The equatorial atmosphere could turn green bananas to spotted in hours. Lipton and Sanka often remained too hot to drink for an unnatural duration. Wrinkles vanished from clothing, a miracle that prompted my three sisters to pop up the hill and visit the Hickey Dry Cleaner before choir concerts. How come our slender neighbor didn't melt, sitting all day and night at the Club Cubana, dressed in a button-down shirt and clip-on bow tie? I surmised then, and still do, that the silver Christmas tree frequently exuded an icy breeze—the draft finding Mr. Hickey wherever he was. That would also explain why he did not sweat even when pumping a red hand grip—the only exercise that the sufferer of an advanced pulmonary disease could safely engage in. No, it was *I* who sweat just watching those pale gnarly fingers ply the grooved grips, the coils between them quivering with one man's determination to remain strong enough to grab (and hold) what life still had to offer.

THE CARPET IN MR. HICKEY'S LIVING ROOM was the chalky hue of sunbaked dog turds. The furniture spare and not soft: pea-green couch with skeletal cushions and narrow easy chair that looked like an upholstered medieval rack when tilted back. There was a side table next to the uneasy chair and on it a can containing the dregs of the daily beer that had been prescribed by the cardiologist at St. Luke's Hospital. To ensure that imbibing alcohol did not impair his ability to function as a role model for neighborhood children, Mr. Hickey favored a distasteful brand—Pabst Blue Ribbon—and drank the brew warm, and very slowly, like the medicine it was supposed to be. Two swallows to wash down a lunch of tuna salad spread (never heaped) on Melba Toast. A foamy slug along with a snack of prunes. The remaining piss water sipped with a supper of salmon loaf and Ry Krisp Crackers. That is, after he picked a TV tray. It was never an easy choice. Many illustrated models were stacked in one corner of the living room and each night he flipped through the entire collection. The Battle of Waterloo, Gettysburg too. Paris boulevards lined with cafés, berets, parasols, and random pastel splashes of paint designed to evoke everything else in that great city which did not fit into the picture. Hounds chasing a fox. Twelve fishermen (I counted them once) in a rowboat balanced on a ridge of ocean foam, harpoons drawn and ready to fly at a whale's thrashing tail. All these images covered with dents, as if the hunters and soldiers had long been hammering the thin metal with their fists, trying to escape the macho cliché in which they were trapped. Never would one break free to whine about sore feet and swollen glands and low self-esteem, debunking the romantic claims of the watercolorist. But annually Mr. Hickey's tight grip on his autobiography did briefly loosen, allowing neighbors to know how much he still missed Mrs. Hickey. Shocking news rang out on the anniversary of her death: "Don't anyone knock on John's door today." There was always anger in mother's voice—for she (like we children) had been fooled by 364 straight days of courtly generosity into believing there would surely be a 365th round of tea and 7UP and Archway cookies. *Say it ain't so, John.* But the drawn curtains said it was so. The newspaper lying unread on the porch step echoed the message. Early in the evening mother grabbed a few children—whoever had been "good"—and drove from Kmart to Target and back to Kmart. One year I was not "good." What I had done wrong I conveniently can't remember. However, I do clearly recall being stranded in the backyard after sundown, standing at the bottom of the hillside stairs. To my left were the molting boxes of father's legal files. (Foolish legislators! They hadn't thought to add the word *indoors* to the law dictating that client paperwork be kept ten years.) My gaze lifted, shifting to the prim white house where our old neighbor was mourning. Locked out of that house, I was locked into my own, and that meant . . . sailing rough seas . . . for if pain did not sink you for good, it was wind in your sails . . . taking you to more pain—the same lame song over and over and over, "Smoke on the Water." A floodlight clamped to the eaves shed white light on the sky bucket. I studied it, itched my calves, pimpled from my dirty sheets. Had Mrs. Hickey introduced Mr. Hickey to the tradition of washing hair in rainwater? Had she washed her hair with water from that very bucket? I thought so. My eyes walked through a back-porch window and felt its chill, the stale chill atmosphere of the glassed-in back porches of the Midwest, where summer sun cooked the dust, winter cold burned it again, in a different way, a smell of ashes in there and that cool—the coolness of neither outdoors nor indoor—still and fermented, vinegary and metallic and empty of holidays, the temperature of a netherworld shifting in and out of the nostrils. The back-porch door was dented by the pounding it had taken from we Millers trying to escape the prison of illusions. Another light clamped to the garage poured light over the rest of the backyard. Hot transparent arid brightness, not like the cold wet kind I had stood knee-deep in last winter while breathing on a frosty garage window. Through the pane I could see Mr. Hickey's Model T. It looked like a tent pitched in a Siberian cave. This car a happily married couple had once gone places in: Tipton, to see the Hickey homestead, and the shoe-shine boy's corner; Dubuque, to ride the fanciful funicular up the

bluff abutting the seedy downtown area; Muscatine, to purchase
the famous melons grown there, dark orange on the inside, green
on the outside—husband and wife hugging ridged rinds coated
with dry mud, melons landing in the backseat and rocking like
impatient children while the car's skinny tires bumped along the
so-called scenic route paralleling the river erased from view by
tall earthen levees. I imagined the dress Mrs. Hickey wore that
day was carefully folded and stored in a labeled box on the back
porch, along with other dresses, high-heeled shoes, Sunday hats,
white gloves with decorative seams, recipe-stuffed cookbooks, and

a file folder containing the Christmas tree instructions—the paper still spotted with grease from the star-shaped cookies Mrs. Hickey had nibbled while the work was done. I could see it all, and also that her death had not only altered Mr. Hickey's life but the fate of my family, too, creating a safe haven so precious that losing it for a mere twenty-four hours was nearly unbearable. What would happen if Mr. Hickey died of a heart attack while watching a rare come-from-behind Cubs victory, Billy Williams smacking a grand slam with two outs in the ninth? And what would become of the little tree? Alice might throw it away, at Eddie's urging. He was the practical one. Quiet Alice was such an expert at speculation that she had spooked herself into believing Mr. Hickey needed to pack a pistol, and then sold him on the idea, saying: *You're a mark, alone in the house. If anything happened, I wouldn't forgive myself.* Eddie, the tug captain, only dealt with the visible—years ago it had been narrow river channels viewed from a wheelhouse and now it was the waxed aisle down which he steered a grocery cart. He would consider the tree to be brittle junk and tell Alice that until she agreed, neither of them comprehending that those frail loops of ribbon were far more valuable than any hard information chiseled on a tombstone. The tree was a silver net capturing the vapor of thought and feeling, those invisibilities that form the core of a human being. Well-meaning but ignorant relatives could in an hour obliterate all vital evidence of a life, when what remained were bones and belongings. Funeral homes swept up the former and the Salvation Army the latter, special outfits placed on racks with the outfits of other citizens, vivid colors canceling each other out, creating a mundane morass of indecipherable gestures. So little left of so much. Yellow light glazed the kitchen window. At a table sat Mr. Hickey, his proud eyes producing tough glittering tears like watch crystals, the tears pouring, hitting the Formica, trickling between the aqua pill counter, the varnished gun handle. Unless he was pressing the barrel to his forehead. No time to run up the hill or call the police or do anything but send a telepathic message, so I closed my eyes, thinking, *The box camera. Get the old office camera out of the desk. Walk to the window* ... and from the terrace above came the clicking of thorns as wind pressed rose branches against the all-weather siding.

THE BUTTERMINT GUN

An infusion of sugar and manners — "Why light half a yard?" —
Paranoia in aisle six — The idea of arming a brother — For Nearest
Dearest John — Yippies, Black Panthers, and bra-burning Berthas —
Watergate Coloring Book — A tire-strung church with a pug-nosed minister —
The latest Eighth Wonder of the World — Squeezing out good-byes —
Checking on a friend

After the kmart midnight madness sale and shared crumble burger at Ross's Truck Stop, over which mother and I calculated that somewhere between two and twenty dollars had been saved on stationary, Paper Mate pens, canned ham, and other items vital to our way of life—that is to say, after all of our neon shopping options were exhausted, the LTD headed homeward on River Drive. It sounded like there were a hundred maracas under the hood, or a three-foot cricket. Mother pointed out the towel-strung balconies of prostitute motels with innocent names like Shady Grove, and again she drew my attention to the turreted mansion where "the writer named Alice French once lived" before moving to New York City and changing her name to Octave Thanet at the suggestion of a famous novelist—"that beast William Dean Howells." I took mental notes, it being too dark to scrawl anything on the Mead narrow-ruled notebook spread across my lap. Beyond the railroad tracks the Mississippi glistened like a greasy skillet and the howitzer factories on Arsenal Island were busy producing America's gift to Latin America. The car climbed Middle Road and plunged down the alley, pushing through darkness and pushed by darkness, behind which flowed still more darkness, inky tides of night filling the trench formed by cottage-style garages and spilling over back terraces, save for the one above our own, lit by bulbs which cut the murk in the manner of police-boat beams. The best thing about arrival was this brightness, which promised safety and Mr. Hickey, insomniac pilot of the terrace above ours. He would be sporting his pistol, loaded with butter mints that would turn sweet whomever they shot. The worst thing about arriving home was home: the ragged trash-strewn hedges along the retaining wall, the splintery back stoop with its love seat webbed by trumpet vines, the screen-door mesh curling off its frame like the frayed outfit of a pirate skeleton. "Let's go see Mr. Hickey," I said. "Good idea, Benji." *Blomp!* The bumper hit the frame of the doorless garage. It tilted more to the right—walls listing like a Charlie Chaplain shack. Mother squeezed out the passenger's side since her door was wedged against the wall. She wore her customary sack dress, I my XXL rummage-sale Penguin shirt—much cloth floating through the glare that interrogated every ketchup mustard gravy stain . . . but always let us pass. We flogged the aluminum door to the glassed-in porch. Call it our next iffy mission. Homebound Mr. Hickey must need something at a store that was closed—milk, bananas, cigars. Finally the inner, diamond-windowed door opened and the dapper man shuffled out, pistol pointed at our chests. A special moment. The moment when I felt like I was only heart— a two-hundred-pound vigilante valentine with legs and arms, absolutely unmissable. How much nicer things would have been if he had drilled us with butter mints. Oh, how we needed an infusion of sugar and manners, a blessed break from the whirling carnival of gossip, coupons, condiments, oaths, giggles, freak-selves. Mother did her best to draw fire. She waved like he was miles away, crying, "Hello, John!" She weaved across the top step: making a dance floor of it, forcing me onto a lower step. When Mr. Hickey reached the door, her dress fluttered against the Plexiglas like a giant june bug wing. Mr. Hickey kept his cool, though. Maybe the dent on the back of his head made him dream of weirder specimens. If not, then surely he had heard about the truly terrifying Red Brigades antics from Alice, the worrier, the most loyal and loving sister a brother could have.

I HOPED THAT AT LEAST ONE of my three mean sisters would turn into an Alice. They just did not come any sweeter. Pantsuits covered her slopes like lemon frosting. She had hair the consistency of blue cotton candy, bun-like cheeks, and an upper lip that formed a wrinkled awning over every hushed word of concern about her frail brother's safety. Riotous 1973. John paid taxes to the city of Davenport, where there was a crime rate. She and pug-nosed Eddie lived in Le Claire, which had different problems: the Buffalo Bill birthplace to maintain on an insufficient budget that funded just Saturday hours, a Main Street of faltering businesses that looked a mile longer when another window was soaped. (Only respectable carpeted taverns thrived, on the

sale of old-fashioneds and vodka gimlets.) And worst of all for Le Claire—an eggy smell that wafted from the river or the Alcoa plant, depending on whom you spoke to. Alice did Eddie's smelling for him, since he could not smell anything odd. In November, she ritually commented that the stink had "mercifully mellowed" and, come April, when rising water scummed the levee, warned Eddie that mud was back in town. He trusted she was correct— just like he trusted that her oil paintings of crying clowns were better decorations than framed river charts, and that it was more sanitary not to strip the plastic off the album sleeves of the Mantovani records that served as a soothing background to worries chanted nightly in the neat living room. "John needs a security light in the front, too." The words came out gentle and steady, serious and collected. "He really does." Eddie smiled. Alice worried with such earnestness that the spiel was in the key of a bubbling brook. "Why light half a yard?" Eddie shrugged. Alice rose and looked out the bungalow window at the tree stump with the profile of a crouching tiger. She shuddered, recalling yesterday's rainstorm, when water had careened out of the gutters, hovering like big chunks of plaster tossed by an earthquake. "Why doesn't he light the front hill?" she asked. "He doesn't think he needs to do that, Alice." "But burglars don't just come from the east, do they?" Eddie crossed his thick arms, sighed. Alice bit her lipstick: *How could someone you knew so darn well continue to be a real mystery?* "If he needs a light in the back, why wouldn't he need one in the front?" The stereo needle scratched the label; Eddie lifted the stylus, and pinging strings went back to work on "Claire de Lune." Alice settled onto the couch next to the table with the reading lamp and flowered tissue box. "I'm worried about the front, Eddie. I…" can't help it. She had done all things possible to put her mind at ease. She called to check in with her older brother each night. She visited weekly, bringing salmon loaf and groceries. She had endured a pawn shop to pick out the prettiest pistol with a wood handle. And still she worried about him and worried, too, that she was worrying too much for a person with hypertension. Her throat tightened to cut off the litany, which only forced it out faster—syllables breathy yet graceful. "He listens to me about an extra light, then, next month, there's no light, I don't understand, what with the headlines…" Dentist's Wife Mulched, Says IL Coroner—Manson Stare Casts Spell on CA Jury—Cary Grant Admits LSD Use—Watergate Scandal Widens as McCord Implicates Dean, Magruder—

IF THERE WAS A WORD for Alice's affliction, it was a noun other than *paranoia*. Paranoia was not lightly powdered like her plump cheeks, nor did it smell of lavender and frequent a cedar chest. Paranoia deflated or twisted a face, streaking eyes darkly. Paranoia was my mother in aisle six of Kmart, rising onto the toes of her tattered shoes, wailing with jubilant righteousness of clerks who switched prices, of Mr. Oliphant who *must have* reported our overgrown lawn to the police, of some husband who had driven his wife to commit monoxide suicide in a green garage, of wife-swapping orgies at Mr. and Mrs. Williams's, of the spiritual death that came from buying Keebler cookies and Levi's jeans, of corrupt doctors and principals and judges and other men who had attained respectability. The paranoid person played many parts to best her demons: sashaying Gypsy Rose Lee, then Ahab tussling with Moby Purse, then Ida Tarbell spitting into toll baskets, then Clarence Darrow arguing for a dime discount on a crushed (by her) Bit-O-Honey candy bar. The paranoid person tailored reality so that it perfectly matched fears too cherished to release. This process involved the drab and laborious manipulation of everyday circumstances, not delicious visions like a gold-gift-boxed gun on a bed of Easter grass. The paranoid person never had new ideas—just old ones recycled. Of all the males she could have married, mother had chosen David P. Miller, who limped because, she said, Dr. Miller had set his son's broken leg crooked to teach him a lesson: *You won't again meddle in the affairs of others like that, pushing a friend's car stuck in the snow!* How cozy and convenient to wed proof of your every crazed criticism of professional men, and males in general, and patriarchs of any aged stripe. Alice took no comfort from her dreads. She truly lamented the high crime rate and spent a good deal of every day shaking her head at the stories read in newspapers, seen on television. Fear did not drive the concern, but sweet love. And so the weekend visit always included a few rounds of buttermint ammunition, as well as a list of songbirds that had landed in her yard of late. Oh, deep affection could lead to deep places—some dangerous, some delicious, some outright bizarre. Consider all of the musty library basements and dusty stores that mother and I frequented to feed our passion for literature, pawing through box after box until one of us found a classic and squealed, "*A Son of the Middle Border* by Hamlin Garland!" The cover might be water-stained, the pages flaking, but our attachment to Garland was pristine—a glorious glow reflecting off the faded volume. Art. Real live art. Magic art that soothed suffering as no medicine could, and reached spirits otherwise unreachable. Like me, mother always calmed down a little when there was a book in her hand, even if you couldn't tell from the way I jittered and she recited. My blank notebooks were just as beloved, because the white void contained our untold stories of anger, confusion, restlessness, wonder, and despair. I always calmed down when there was a good old Mead notebook in front of me, even if you couldn't tell from what I wrote. The spiral was my lyre and on it I had strumming to do. Writing was hardly writing yet, but it was a certain posture—a hunch, a clench, an excuse to dive right at and into blank pages like those that had once siphoned the hopes and complete attention of my father. Possibly—if I spent enough time around blank pages—the man would mistake me for one, jerk the recliner forward, stick his head through the cigarette smoke, and finally bequeath his secrets— thoughts about what it was really like to be Dr. Miller's son, or, even better, some deep swirling fatherly feeling re: some aspect of *my* existence. The notion did not seem odd. Love demanded what love demanded. It could make any behavior acceptable and transform the most unthinkable act into the next logical step.

THE IDEA OF ARMING HER BROTHER had formed like an exotic dessert in the oven of Alice's kindly consciousness, baked by incendiary headlines, speeches, film footage—until served one evening for Eddie to choke on. "I wouldn't worry so much about John if he had a way of protecting himself in case of…trouble. His birthday is coming up. Let's surprise him with a gun." Alice had artillery in her bonnet, not a bee. I imagined her entering a Dubuque pawnshop and charging the glass case full of old weapons, behind which stood a man wearing taped glasses and a greasy brown suit. He snarled quite a few things that went right over her blue hairdo. She considered a darling derringer, admired switchblades, pointed at the jeweled handle of a saber on the wall, asked if it was from "Arabia," got no answer, inquired about "the chained black sticks," was told, "Nunchucks. I don't have all day, lady, make up your mind." Then she spotted a respectable Colt (wooden handle varnished, barrel black as a charcoal pencil) and asked Eddie's opinion. Eddie thought: *Alice has the look of someone who will not be denied.* "That'll about do it," he said. ($59.95.) Next stop: Allen's card store. Eddie knew better than to go in there. Under the crepe Hallmark turkey, Alice produced the gun, asked the clerk for a silver box (in homage to that Lone Ranger fellow). "Holdup!" the clerk yelled. Alice explained that the gun was a present for her homebound brother in Davenport, apologized, asked again where the gift boxes were, and was answered by a fat manager who had waddled over, trailing smock strings. "Aisle three," he squeaked. "And keep the gift in your purse." She found a box the right size, but gold, so she picked out silver wrapping paper and three bows—red, blue, and white. John would love that—he was a patriotic bow tie man. On the way to the checkout counter a buttermint display caught her creative eye. The candies were the size of bullets but much prettier: pink, yellow,

The Buttermint Gun 273

blue. She snatched three rounds. "I'm winging it," she admitted
with a chuckle to the gulping clerk. Back at home she told Eddie,
"I think I'll wrap the gun right now so I don't have to do it in
the morning." Eddie retreated to the garage and paced, smoked,
prayed to God in heaven that Alice did not tickle the trigger out
of curiosity or clumsiness. She was plush with flesh, not all of it in
control. She often stubbed her toe at night and wondered aloud
if such a thing as steel-toed terrycloth slippers existed. A car
down the block backfired. Eddie nearly jumped out of his black

shoes. Breathing deeply, he went inside, found Alice at the dining room table, arranging Easter grass around the Colt. If he did not cover his eyes, he wanted to. "Almost finished," she chirped, picking green strands off the chamber and handle. Over it all she sprinkled butter mints. "That's enough, don't you think?" asked Eddie. She agreed—it was enough. On went the lid, the wrapping paper, and the satin bows. Next morning Alice insisted on carrying the gun to the car; Eddie was stuck with the salmon loaf and driving. His eyes went back and forth between the highway and the silver box on Alice's lap. Back and forth, back and forth. Alice was frosted with polyester, capped with cotton-candy curls, and thinking her unique brand of thoughts: *John needs a gun as sure as he needs that little green oxygen tank on his dining room table. He is the rarest of rare men: a high-profile neighborhood figure never seen in the neighborhood, always the first on the block with a shoveled walk and a mowed lawn, thanks to his army of helpers. He's a recluse; wall-safe rumors are apt to abound. With the buttermint gun he can reform any robber, sugarcoat the darkest heart, implant niceness so deep that stealing gems and cussing will no longer be an option. Blam. Blam. Then they have tea.*

MR. HICKEY REMAINED SHOCKED by the gesture to the end of his life. Often, as I sat in that warm, cigar-scented kitchen, he related in an awe-choked voice that his brother-in-law had nothing to do with the pistol lying between us on the Formica table. "Alice," he said, blushing in the way he blushed—turning red around the ears only. "Alice. She insisted . . ." because she would never forgive herself if John was murdered by a kid who heard a devil message after playing the Rolling Stones backward, or a convict escaped from a Flannery O'Connor story. "Eddie had nothing to do with the deal, Benny. He told me so, and...and...that she wrapped the pistol...with the safety off." I nodded, seeing it all. His bare, smoke-veiled head bucked under the weight of the mystery. His little sister with jump rope and jacks, Alice of the hair curlers and wedding ring and apricot pantsuits—quiet, nonviolent, religious Alice had arrived one afternoon with a gold box containing a weapon worthy of John Wayne. Yes, it was the right thing to do because Alice—who could do no wrong—had done it. But nonetheless, Mr. Hickey had to wonder, whatever had inspired her to enter a pawnshop? Had the scary Law and Order speeches of President Nixon contributed? Had she been hypnotized by the July Fourth fireworks display over Buffalo Bill Cody park, those explosions forming great glittering roses that trickled so beautifully into the river bend night? Mr. Hickey looked to me for an answer. It was another special moment. He hardly ever looked at me that way, seeking assistance—only when many inches of snow were predicted. I could not shrug him off. I could not help him, either, since ten plows could not have parted the befuddlement drifting across his brain. Instead, I did the next best thing—looked across at my elderly best friend wearing the polka-dot bow tie, bifocals, dentures, and considered him as seriously as he considered me in my dirty, ill-fitting clothing. His magnified eyes shone like over-easy egg yolks. Shocked, yes, but not in a totally bad way. What sister worth her title could not send a brother reeling backward? For a relationship to be vital and alive the participants must retain the ability to shock and puzzle each other—not fall into roles too ironclad and predictable. Alice knew Mr. Hickey would find a way to accept whatever she did, and he did, though the work had to be repeated again and again, in the company of a twelve-year-old whose idea of support was gawking. Still, I *was there* for Mr. Hickey in his moment of need, as Phil Donahue *was there* for rocker Alice Cooper (purple eye shadow, goofy teeth) and the ex-wife of Mac Davis and Truman Capote, genius writer metamorphosing into a pink and hideously scarfed gossip. I stood by my mentor when he was stripped of optimistic clichés, knock-knock jokes, and exercise advice, and nakedly faced the fact that his dignified, powdered sister had armed him. He carried the pistol from room to room, barrel pointed at the carpet and quivering, ticking, palpitating as Alice's heart must have under the plaid quilt, as she dreamed of Angela Davis, John Lennon, Abbie Hoffman, armed and arm-in-arm, skipping down the river road to Davenport. "Would you like to see the silver gift tag?" His bony but strong fingers crawled through the maze of cigar boxes on the table and plucked the tag from a Lipton tea box that was too sturdy to throw away and had become an archive of important small items such as paper clips, pennies, and pushpins. *For Nearest Dearest John*, Alice had printed. He was dear to anybody who got to know him. I still believe he could not have fired that pistol even if he had suddenly been transported back in time to the Alamo. Placed on a parapet with Davy Crockett, Mr. Hickey would have played the medic's role. He could carry the gun in deference to Alice's judgment, and wish the gun on gray squirrels that attacked the bird feeder affixed outside the kitchen window, and (in theory) point the gun at crooks, but he was not born with a trigger finger. He had stripped the silver paper off the box that day, lifted the lid, and stared at a weapon lying on a bed of grass sprinkled with pastel candies. Alice said: "For your protection, John. I worry so about you being here alone." And then: "It was the nicest one at the pawnshop. I browsed them all." And John looked at Eddie in the gap-back chair, and Eddie looked at John in the gap-back chair. No banana bread. A gun. No fruitcake, but a gun with a hammer, trigger, and butter mints sprinkled around it. Dear dear me.

WHILE TALKING, Mr. Hickey was apt to pat the pistol handle as if it were Alice's hand—as if he were returning her stunning gesture of concern. There was one thing I could have said to him, but never did, not wanting to complicate things. I could have pushed the 7UP aside, leaned over the table, and proclaimed: "Alice is as confused by your security lighting as you are by the buttermint gun." Every week, after Eddie and Alice dropped off the groceries, she asked me, watching the excitement from the dusty terrace below, "Burglars don't just come from the east, do they, Ben?" I did not know. I was not a burglar yet. But I agreed, 17 Crestwood Terrace was a dramatic sight at night—totally dark in front, totally light in back. An Up with People / Dale Carnegie feeling spectacularly joined with an FBI / CIA vibe. Faith in America warring with suspicion over her tendencies, and always winning big—since the front hill was so much larger than the slender strip of turf attaching the house to the garage. Masked crooks might come from alleys—in Mr. Hickey's old-fashioned mind—but darned if that would make him scare off all the denizens of the moon's jade light, which inspired songwriters and brave volunteers like Charla, the Meals-on-Wheels lady, who parked her station wagon on Crestwood and climbed the stairs carrying a Styrofoam tray harboring much hot starch. Sometimes her curious daughter tagged along. Sometimes doorbell dings died on a front porch weatherized in a cocoon of plastic—and she had to walk around to the back, but a nice walk it was, past rose bushes that bowed toward her like long coachman's coats, until she turned the corner and got snared by the interrogative glare of eave bulbs. Those Hickeys, they were simply brilliant at covering every 1973 angle. They looked vulnerable, but the Strategic Air Command in Omaha would likely be more caught off guard by a Russian nuke attack than they. And should Iowa be overrun by a ground force of Yippies, Black Panthers, and bra-burning Berthas, Alice only needed to tape lead to the next birthday card and bring a few more two-hundred-watt bulbs ... On the other hand, if the nation pulled out of its economic, social, and political funk, they could honestly say—unlike many citizens—that they had never lost faith in "the American experiment." Theirs was a strong faith, because it dared to grapple with newspaper accounts and sometimes doubt them. A hope not dumb and dashable like my own (a dud sparkler could shake me) but complex and durable, a fine weaving together of the light and dark that had entered their lives over decades of depression and boom, war and peace. Taped to the two-pound telephone in Mr. Hickey's living room was the business card of the electrician who'd installed the fearsome security bulbs, and, too, the number of Mr. Lytle, the president of the local chapter of Junior Achievement, which offered teen vandals the chance to see how businesses were run— unfettered access to back rooms and cash registers. In the kitchen drawer were American-flag toothpicks to hand out when IBM colonized Mars and enough peanuts to placate an angry elephant, if one should escape from the yellow circus train. The dresser in the smoky bedroom was a repository for Frank Lloyd Wright stamps—as the post office famously planned to keep delivering right through the nuclear war and Mr. Hickey would want to keep up with bill payments. Atop the dining room table was a box of stationery emblazoned: JOHN HICKEY, PROPRIETOR OF BLUEBERRY HILL and an order form for a gas mask to wear over his oxygen mask, which he wore on very bad days. The form was filled out, but not completely. Exercising the sort of discipline that made him Mr. Hickey and not Alice, he allowed himself to add only one letter to the grid on harrowing evenings when another rubber-bullet ruckus prompted the glum thirty-seventh president (his suit tight as a safecracker's glove) to take the stage at a war academy, inflict a menacing refrain: "My fellow Americans...my fell..."

PRESIDENT NIXON HAD ACCESS to everyone and everything...except goodwill. He and his henchmen were the stars of the last coloring book I ever received—the Watergate Coloring Book from Kmart. Mother got it for me when I was twelve. It was on sale for a quarter. I owned no black crayons so I never filled in those images of wire-tapping, etc. I kept the coloring book on my desk as the most authoritative proof of what childhood boiled down to in that era of disenchantment. It came down to Nixon BC (Before Cover-up) and Nixon AD (After Destruction). Hearing his war-academy speeches, I wondered if Pat might not see one as an opportunity to sneak across the Mexican border wearing a straw hat and chinos. Who could blame her for running from a man so gloomy that he could make the name Henry sound ominous when alluding to the Secretary of State, who also needed a shave and big attitude adjustment. Honestly, how could we be subjects of that alien king? His baggy face and hoarse voice referenced eons of travel from a dark planet to a slender podium in Annapolis, Maryland. On a stage lit like a back alley, he hunched and pointed, splicing the grim-reaper specifics of law enforcement with vague references to millions of new jobs to keep "those types" (the poor) out of trouble. American Dream this, that, and

the other. It was confusing. It was discouraging. He was not a
walrus named Taft or Bull Moose Teddy, not a bookish Coolidge
or regal FDR, not a heroic Eisenhower or suave John Kennedy
or folksy LBJ. He was always, only—Nixon. It was best, however,
that he keep speaking in his gruff way and thus delay the standing ovation and his obscene response to it: the moment when
he thrust his arms into the air and splayed two hairy fingers on
each hand—the double-victory V, supposedly, but those twitching digits resembled the shears of a maniac intent on cutting the
country into a string of faceless paper dolls with names such as

Pinko, Fairy, Kike, Spic, and Wop. (The truth came out on the White House tapes, *bleep, bleep, bleep*.) Our leader, the menacing Quaker. Who, giggled mother, *hee hee hee*...squirted ketchup into his cottage cheese. It was not trivia. Trivia was never trivia. Trivia was philosophy: All the world was a blender and the men and women and children in it merely ingredients meant to be added by politicians to ongoing wars and economic plans. It was a perverse and surreal experience for quailing patriots like us, viewing the fuzzy feed from an academy of war, the president blackly flapping above a blizzard of cadet blue. His irresponsible rhetoric excused our own. He was—in fact—giving us a gift. He gave Mr. Hickey and Alice only stomachaches. Being decent citizens, they didn't have the option of laughing at him. No, they had to find a way to support the president, and the more unsteady he became, the more they had to prop him up, lest he and the country topple. That meant listening carefully to each dissonant paragraph, especially the passage right before the standing ovation and the lofting of the victory shears. By then, terrified Alice and Mr. Hickey could really have used a lullaby. (Sadly, there had been no president since Lincoln who could hold a tune.) Even a simple "Sweet dreams, Americans," would have helped. But a Cold War president didn't dare say "sweet dreams," even to his wife. It was not leaderly—a weakling concession speech that might be picked up by a headboard bug and precipitate an atomic strike on Milwaukee. No, if Nixon whispered anything to Pat before her sedatives took effect, it was: "The B-52s are circling Hanoi, honey." For the only way this president could allay fears was by stoking them with a recitation of the soulless acronyms of bombs, missiles, ships, subs, and planes available to defend democracy from her enemies in Moscow and New York City. He paused, up to something, and grinned for the first time in the entire speech—grinned like the proprietor of a twenty-four-hour candy shop—and the darnedest thing happened behind that enamel curtain, involving salivary glands and glottal stops. The name of each tool of absolute destruction came out sounding like a mouthwatering treat. *M-3 frappé. F-14 chew. ICBM bonbons.* Million-dollar dainties suitable for preteen soldiers and any old lady from Le Claire. *Napalm drops. Chinook helicopter crunch. AK-47 nougat.* Alice squeezed a needlepoint hankie. Alice—who dusted while listening to optimistic easy-listening epics like "Sunny" and "Tangerine"—worried the president was not sleeping enough, not eating well, drinking *Hen-er-eee* under the negotiating table. She worried Eddie might get drafted at age sixty-six. And pictured herself seeing him off at the train station that no longer existed, blowing kisses to a car of bemused elderly inductees. She understood that she was not without responsibility in the grave global situation—that she had a small part to play in the arms race. *Tomorrow: get more mint ammo.* And the day after, who knew? She might box up a bazooka, order a tasty M1 rifle for John. Buy all the gold-angel Hallmark paper in Iowa and work for weeks wrapping an F-something fighter jet (hanging a deodorizer in the cockpit, tying red bows on the wings)—anything. Whatever it took to keep from getting a phone call at 3 a.m. from the Davenport Police Department: *I'm sorry to disturb you ma'am, but...*

JUST AS ALICE—without ever raising her voice—radically defied convention, so Eddie dismantled my preconceptions of what a river captain was like. He had no tattoos, did not curse. He wore a wool derby rather than the requisite anchor cap. His voice was soft like Alice's, though deeper. The crew must have

gotten bad backs leaning over to hear commands, smarted from
not being screamed at, and, rubbing carbuncles late at night, wondered how in hell they'd ended up on a tire-strung church with a
pug-nosed minister at the wheel, shepherding a big flock of coal
barges. The only clues to Eddie's occupation were his forearms,
which bulged dramatically under the plaid flannel shirts he wore
in winter and, in summer, protruded from short sleeves like buoys
weathered by currents of Alice's concerns. Those buoys smashed
flies that she had not the heart to kill. They mowed the lawn and
waved to other retired captains, for the town had the highest

percentage of such men in the state, maybe the country. It was not an accident. A treacherous stretch of river just to the south made Le Claire a natural place to tie up for good, and smell the...mud. Eddie's main piloting job now was the drive to Davenport. He and Alice would begin by stopping at the Hy-Vee to purchase the staples of Mr. Hickey's homebound life. Already in the trunk was the wax-papered salmon loaf. Alice—on purpose—had worn an outfit that matched the Impala: a powder-blue dress appended with a dragonfly broach. Turquoise pebbled her neck. She watched to make sure Eddie did not trip while carrying groceries to the car. He did not. But his buoy arms turned the wheel a most scary direction: *south*—away from the old homes of Le Claire, none of which featured a widow's walk. (Those were to be found on dwellings farther down the highway, belonging to the ancestors of captains who had unwisely tried to sail another twenty miles before retiring.) Eddie drove with enough speed to arrive before noon. Their car rolled into the small driveway and inched forward and crawled backward until not an ounce of metal protruded into the alley. Certainly Eddie drew on his experience with tight river locks to get the job done. Nearly fifteen minutes it took to place the car perpendicular to the nailed-shut door of the garage, with its late great Model T. Alice did not get out. She had to be there in case something happened. When it was all over, she felt again how lucky she was to be with Eddie, and told him this by saying nothing. They emerged smiling: derby and skirt. Eddie was barely taller than the car. He cracked the trunk but could not reach the goods, so Alice loaded his arms with bags, the salmon loaf, and, yes, the world's largest cylinder of oatmeal. From our terrace, I watched. They did not see me. They had eyes only for the door to the enclosed porch neatly stacked with storage boxes. The forty pounds of fiber listed, and Eddie weaved, as Alice debated whether ringing or knocking was more likely to induce infarction in a man wearing a large visiting-day bow tie—the kind that looked like it might fly away.

THE VISIT LASTED at least three hours, sometimes four. Groceries were stowed in gleaming cupboards. They discussed songbirds and weather, while reusing Lipton tea bags and listening to a radio that was in clear contact with Chicago, 175 miles away. They did not play gin rummy. The only safe card game in Mr. Hickey's mind was solitaire—other games reminded him he had run a gambling game at a cigar-store counter four decades ago and fleeced men, taken food out of the mouths of their children. The topic of crime would not come up, either, it being too much on Alice's mind. But the side effects of blood pressure pills were discussed. Plus the high price of gasoline, an outrage known as the thirteen-cent stamp, the income-tax filing deadline right around the corner (ten months away), strategies for removing age spots from mirrors, and my mother, the highly educated neighbor lady raising six children without much aid from her husband, who each evening was held hostage by the newspaper and at dawn limped off to the Davenport Bank Building and hid there, fielding few calls from clients. Alice shuddered to hear that tale of woe. The nautical shadow of Eddie's forearm cruised across the wall: the host's head instinctively veered behind a monolithic bran box—the Coast Guard boat boom had afflicted him with Sudden Ducking Syndrome. Alice smiled and dearly thanked her brother for not smoking. Eddie suggested slicing the salmon loaf. And Mr. Hickey's manicured fingers went to work: setting out plastic plates, fetching tin forks, a knife, and a spatula. Tea water was also heated, this action being the necessary end result of all other actions. The reused bags produced a brew the ochre color of hard water. Eddie and Mr. Hickey complimented Alice on the hand-formed salmon loaf, and she reminded them that the recipe was on each golden can of Bumble Bee salmon. They nodded, savoring anew the salty tang and complex texture. Baked dry and pinkly yellow on top. Moist and flaky and almost white in the middle. The bottom browned, with a toasted flavor, crunchy oil-soaked threads melting on the tip of the tongue. Eddie had a second slice despite Alice's disapproving glare—she was already worried that there would not be enough. Mr. Hickey guided the radio dial away from Wife Mulched, Students Riot, Politician Indicted...toward baseball: the other American pastime. Cubs vs. Giants in "the friendly confines of Wrigley Field." Announcer Jack Brickhouse had a plain but shapely voice that fit in the ear as pleasingly as a dowel fits in the palm. He did not say much about the long, unsuccessful road trip. (They were all long, even two-day trips.) Instead he described what a lovely day it was on Wave-land Avenue—the sun shining and Lake Michigan wind whipping flags above the ivy-laced outfield walls. Then the stretch, the pitch, ball four, "José Cardenal takes a big lead at first. Kessinger takes a lead off second. With only one out, it could be a double steal..." Alice frowned even to hear of a crime against the San Francisco Giants, who were paid nice salaries to endure stolen bases, plus the meal allowance, which, more than any other thing, made me want to be a star outfielder. A hundred dollars a day for candy and crumble burgers. Mr. Hickey, however, grinned, his lips parted like pale corn husks to reveal a double row of false-teeth kernels. Baseball records were meant to be broken, he whispered. (Unlike bay windows, Halloween pumpkins, the oath of office.) Sitting next to the table radio was a six-inch strip of artificial grass

that would never produce a dandelion. Alice stroked the Astroturf to calm her jittery nerves. "Isn't that turf something," Eddie
exclaimed. Mr. Hickey told them—as he did every visit—that
the sample was a present from Larry, the lawn boy, and that this
space-age grass already covered the ball field at the Astrodome,
the latest Eighth Wonder of the World. (Quite quickly mankind
had produced seven long-lasting wonders, but the eighth kept
turning to scrap.) The Cubs allowed two more runs in the fifth
inning to fall behind 4-0. They all shook their heads. It was—in
Eddie's words—"getting late." Mr. Hickey and Alice never had
the heart to say that, but did always have the presence of mind to
agree—goodness, it was after four and the drive to Le Claire was
best completed long before dusk wrapped its druid robes around
hedges, the air filled with the urban incense of turf and cement,
tree stumps turned to crouching tigers, libraries closed, and
LIQUOR store neon clicked on, the apple-red letters burning in the
dimness that thickened to a tarry black on respectable side streets,
where alarm-system decals had lately begun sprouting like poppies on living room windows—ovals zagged with Zeus's lightning
or depicting Arthurian riot gear: shield, sword, slotted mask.

MR. HICKEY OFFERED ALICE HALF the Hy-Vee groceries
that had been put away. When she politely refused, he offered
them to Eddie. When Eddie said thanks, but no thanks, they all
stepped onto the glassed-in back porch and said farewell. This
feat took a while, since neither Mr. Hickey nor Alice nor Eddie
could be told good-bye without replying in kind. It was like a
round. "Bye, Alice." "Bye, John." "Bye, Alice." "Bye, John." For
me the scene was framed by ragged pine trees spaced between the

retaining-wall hedges. That wall was only seven feet high, but the figures above seemed to occupy a Swiss chalet in the Alps. "Bye, Eddie." "Bye, John." "Bye-bye, Eddie." "Bye-bye, John." The world might have ended before they finished. And possibly that was the plan, their grand strategy—to stand whispering until the A-bomb fell or the Yippies invaded and put them out of the misery of parting one more time. The sky, though, did not flash red, then mushroom brownly. It just grayed in a way that bayed in your eyes. Mr. Hickey asked Alice to call as soon as she and Eddie made it safely back to Le Claire, though she would never have forgotten, this call being an event as jubilant as their arrival in Davenport. "First thing, John, I'll ring you." Eddie bumped the door open and exited, followed by Alice, both still whispering, "Good-bye, John, take care." I held my breath, fearing an avalanche of hernia belts, girdles, polyester lapels, bifocals, turquoise jewelry, safety shoes, hosiery…but neither Eddie nor Alice plunged into our trash-cluttered hedges, and fragile Mr. Hickey remained on the back porch. His neck winged with polka dots, he observed the departing visitors like a myopic dove. At the bottom of the gray stairs, Alice turned. Because Alice turned, Eddie did too. The three exchanged waves, Alice's hand caressing the air as if it were a crying child's head, Eddie saluting bravely, Mr. Hickey's white hand squeezing out good-byes—open close open close open close. From an upstairs window of our house came screams, Elizabeth trying to shame Howard out of the bathroom. "Bastard! Let me in! I've got an orchestra concert! It's not fair! You've been in there *an hour*! I've got to shower and—" Eddie swiveled, made for the Impala, his gait a bit bowlegged and a bit meandering: what might be called a thoughtful strut. He disappeared behind a scraggly pine. Alice vanished next. I paced the dirt below, nearly beside myself with excitement: after visits we sometimes exchanged pleasantries. Me and the inventor of the buttermint gun, me and the retired tugboat captain who'd seen his share of whirlpools and mermaids, port cities and dams, coal and alfalfa and corn. A cigarette butt flew out the torn screen window. Howard called Elizabeth everything she had called him and more, much more. I did not worry that Eddie and Alice would understand what was being said. Only a family member could have translated that warp-speed exchange of sibling Chinese. What I worried about—when the derby did not reappear after a minute— was that Alice and Eddie were snared in the tree, our tree, that reached over Mr. Hickey's property in a way it should not, just as our trash collected against the fence surrounding the Dankerts' terrace below. Should I dial zero? Ask the operator for a pine pruner, a lumberjack? Things did not look good. On the porch Mr. Hickey kept squeezing invisible fruit, *bye bye bye bye.* H: "You bitch! Make me leave! Kick the door open! I dare you! Do it!" *Crash!* E: "Come out or I'll plug in the curling iron and—" Eddie coasted into view on the other side of the pine. Whew. I cheered. And Eddie looked down, seeing not a hopeless two-hundred-pound twelve-year-old boy with chapped clown lips and a stained rummage-sale shirt dress, but rather the Future of America in need of a firm push in the right direction, some attention and respect, a concentrated dose of decency to stave off a robbery conviction and inspire Junior Achievement membership. Eddie stepped close, too close, to the edge of the retaining wall. He pinched the derby brim … and next came the most special of all special moments, when an heir to Twain tipped his cap as if I were one of his nautical colleagues in embryonic form. The gesture was momentarily blinding—I saw myself at the helm of a Mississippi tug pushing literature-heaped barges: Sinclair Lewis, Hamlin Garland, Sherwood Anderson, Zona Gale, Octave

Thanet. Then, as the fantasy's glare subsided, I noticed again how much Eddie looked like Mr. Hickey. Not just sort of—*a lot*. An alarming *a lot* that I somehow forgot when I wasn't directly confronted by the bald reality. Both men were short, hairless, and dapper in a cost-efficient 1930s way involving black shoes. They had—of all things—identical nostrils. Pug noses with flared, egg-cup nostrils. This improbable concordance overrode the fact that Mr. Hickey had the elegant frame of an actor playing a U-boat captain and Eddie the profile of a pier piling—thighs splintering off a thick torso. The nostril match made them twins in my mind, which meant Alice...Not far did I delve into that tricky issue, just far enough to realize that I should not speculate further and— also—to conclude that great worry about her older brother's welfare had far predated the 1968 riots and Nixon's Law and Order speeches, extending back to the days of *Captain Midnight* on the cathedral-shaped radio, when she was a young woman. Of all suitors, she had picked *the man most likely to dispel her fears*, as opposed to my mother choosing a haunted husband. Yes, Alice had wisely found herself a brother look-alike who was sturdier than the real thing but nearly as soft-spoken and snappy, filling closets with trench coats and natty hats that she could behold any afternoon for a little peace of mind, even if her concern about John would never really be dispelled. "Good luck," said Eddie in a manly whisper that finely mussed each syllable. Blue frosted slopes floated from behind the tree. Alice. "Burglars don't just come from the east, do they?" I shrugged. "John needs a light in front. I really think he does. Just like in the back." The tent of her upper lip extended. "He promised me that he'd look into getting one more light this month. Will you remind him, Ben?" I said I would. "It only makes sense to have a light in the front, if you've got one in the back." I agreed: it only made sense. "How is your mother?" She asked this with such tenderness I felt ashamed for not worrying about my mother more, though I worried about her constantly, especially when she murmered, "I can't take it anymore. I'm going to go right out of my mind." But I did not worry in Alice's fashion, as if each word weighed a sweet ton. I did not worry with her human care. I worried like a gaudy machine light flicking on, flicking off. I worried like a child. "How is your mother getting along?" I named the store she had run off to with Marianna—the rare Marianna outing being a ploy to avoid Elizabeth's preconcert grooming frenzy. Marianna would expect to get something, a new shirt or darts, and didn't know mother's shopping trips rarely involved shopping—my sister would return in tears, dartless. I might have warned her, but there wasn't time. "Say hello to your mother for me, will you?" I said I would. "Say hello from me, too," said Eddie. I promised. Then he wished me good day, and Alice had to ask one last time: "Burglars don't just come from the east, do they?" I shrugged. She turned to wave again at Mr. Hickey, still pumping ten fingers, making gallons of invisible orange juice."Drive safely!" I cried, and immediately regretted it as Alice paled, imagining tornados and robbers who preyed on US 61 travelers, and detour arrows, and those red pylons arrayed like Mao disciples along the shoulder. "Let's go, Alice," said Eddie, derby reclamped on his bean. They disappeared behind our shed of a garage. I made the cracked driveway in time to see them settle into the sky-blue car. The bumper inched forward and backward in deference to property lines and nonexistent traffic, forward and backward, forward and backward...until it slid into the alley. Standing on the edge of the terrace, next to overturned garbage cans, I waved as the Impala rolled away, and saw Eddie's head leaning to hear Alice's initial hushed expressions of post-visit concern about her brother. "John always listens to me about that light, and next week, there's no light. It makes no sense, lighting only the back, leaving the front dark. I hope Ben remembers to tell him. He's ... a good boy." And when all that loyalty and love and memory and American fear and American hope disappeared down the hill, heading *north*—the next scary direction—I lumbered up the hill to get my first savory slice of salmon loaf and hear Mr. Hickey whisper: "Alice—she insisted..." while he reached for the glossy grainy handle of the buttermint gun, and patted it, and patted it.

IT WAS ALICE who made sure I received two plastic baggies containing Mr. Hickey's clip-on bow ties after he passed away at the Masonic home, in 1987. A few years later she and Eddie were struck by a falling tree limb when they went to check on a Le Claire neighbor during a summer storm. They were seriously injured and never recovered. They had to check on their neighbor, no question. They couldn't live with themselves had they not tried to make it across the soaked lawns. They were the same age as that shut-in, and prey to the same fears. I see them creeping out into the rain and the wind, night sky flashing above. They could not sit inside, warm and wondering if a friend was all right.

BOOK THREE

THE
CONCRETE
GARDEN

TIME AND TEMPERATURE

The irrefutable gospel of TIME and TEMP — Perverse philosophical discussions — Nonfrastructure — The family octopus — "Way killin'! Dy-noooo-mite!" — Offing the fat boy — Sesame seed bun = satanic manna — This hunger strike — Before and After snapshots — Angles of architectural angst — Mr. Minard's humanity — No holes in the soles — Baldness of every degree — The stabbing of dark by art — Hallelujah! — Plastic flowers — Top poets — Nothing adds up — My only hometown

A FEW MILES FROM EAST DAVENPORT, on the billboard run of River Drive, blinked the irrefutable gospel of TIME and TEMP—2:34, 78°, 2:35. The rows of bulbs pressed their news against the atmosphere. At times the numerals branded themselves onto snow squalls, at others they lent their golden incandescent edges to clear fall afternoons or bored throbbing grottos into the ochre of a downpour. Filtered through a paste of dispatched summer bugs, the pulsing bulbs possessed an addled heraldry that honeyed the air. Whenever a bulb failed, some cousin of a cloud in white overalls would replace the dim, rigid light. One wire-stitched panel faced upriver, the other down.

The twin panels formed an open triangle atop a windowless brick building across from the Clayton House Hotel parking lot, a stone's throw from the hornet hum of traffic on the grating of Government Bridge. The sign's banner initially advertised the *Davenport Times-Democrat,* which became the *Quad-City Times* in 1974. The low levee (and often "snaggers" fishing for channel cats) lurked behind TIME and TEMP. In front of the building snaked train tracks and around it all, during rainy seasons, thrived a density of vegetation, weeds like bushes breaking up through the pavement and grass as thick as bunches of lettuce. I imagined that nutrients locked under downtown pavement had rushed to this spot. The colliding greens transfixed me. Iowa grew the world's food and yet urban Iowans often ate out of boxes, bags. We heated up icy blocks of spinach. The riverside growth put me in mind of the spicy pine woods around Dr. Miller's Wisconsin cottage, where my family spent by far the best week of our year—though it was inevitably the week that none of the other relatives wanted, and had left for us. Uncut and spirited greens! This was before bike trails lassoed such limbos and neutralized them with sod strips, asphalt ribbons, and mile markers. The sign blinked right where Thomas Wolfe would have placed it if he had been a city planner, the minutes of any given day trickling their disposable meanings parallel to the Mississippi's white-capped and urgent infinity.

UNMISTAKABLE FOR OUR FAMILY was the sorry news TIME and TEMP invariably delivered. 2:36 not 2:00! In slow motion we raced toward the already-done performance of Mr. Spoons on Rock Island's spooky pedestrian mall. Couldn't time ever revolve around hours-late people who ignored street-fair-entertainment schedules, needed battery jumps, rode brakes, and lost keys to the yawning maw of Moby Purse beached on the kitchen table? Cars zipped past us, kicking up plastic and paper litter. It waltzed on the hood, then was sucked under a creaking chassis or hopped the roof and paged across our trunk, dented in a way suggesting the contents of a time capsule had erupted in there. (One comfort was a AAA card peeking out from the dashboard anthology, marking the place of our other comfort: Dylan Thomas. "The Force That Through the Green Fuse Drives the Flower." "A Refusal to Mourn the Death, by Fire, of a Child in London.") We raged upon missing the best parts of weddings and funerals. The bigger the gala, the more anxieties it provoked. Anxieties made invalids of teenagers. "Ben won't come out of his room and we have to go!" Incontinence prevailed at departure. "Wait! I got to pee!" Other siblings got hung up on picking the right shirt or blouse from a floor pile containing no right clothing. It could take as many as four trips to the car to get in the car. "The tickets! Where . . . ?" Once we did finally settle in the car, every bleary Miller could be found stuck to the condiment-yucked seats, wiping portholes in window grease, as we passed the sign, to check if southbound TIME matched northbound TIME, which it always did, fuck. "We wouldn't be late if the kitchen clock hadn't said we were early!" The kitchen, the last room between commuters and a bumper-bashed alley garage, rarely cooperated. We missed the first pitch of softball games, the first crack at reception blue cheese. Daily we were twelve or more hours late to the Stanley house, essentially my grandfather's six-room saloon affixed to the space where Granny slept holed up with her doilies and humidifier. (At dawn this unassuming Kentucky lady began waiting to learn whether or not she still had a pulse—only her daughter, Tommy Lynn, or her son, my uncle Eubie, would be able to tell her, after they had donned the stethoscope that lay on the bureau next to the Dippity-do jar.) Or late, say, to another reading by elegant Julie Jensen McDonald, author of *Amalie's Story* and *Petra*, novels about Danish farmer ancestors. But my mother and I thoughtfully made amends by rudely lingering. In toto we were at the event longer than any other attendee. "Thank you for coming," gushed a threatened hostess as we pillaged cookie trays and drained the dregs of the punch bowl. Mother and I were worst at comings and goings. Perverse philosophical discussions often detained us. She would ask the questions she had been asking me since I was little: "Which of the five senses would you give up if you had to give up one?" She spoke of the senses as if they were addictions, curses. I told her: "Smell." She asked: "Which limb would you sacrifice if you had to sacrifice one?" I told her: "Left arm." (I was right-handed.) Howard and Marianna suffered least—they had the fewest places to be on time to. Elizabeth and Nanette suffered worst. A half hour tardy to a half-hour music lesson, either upset sister was capable of executing ballet-caliber kicks in the teacher's driveway. Lateness stirred their blood like sugar overdoses. Then, after furious disappointment, came the next nail-biting bout of anticipation. For the same TIME blinks that broadcast our doom also, importantly, nudged the ruined day closer to a new day and its opportunities, which perhaps we would not pounce on and mutilate.

AGAIN BENDING AN EAR TO THE PAST, I hear wind wheezing in the door cracks of our puttering car and feel my fourteen-year-old skeleton mashed against uncushy upholstery and see, out my porthole, the Mississippi, half tamed by current-bracketing dams and the channels dredged by the Corps of

Engineers. Its chocolate PCB-tainted water teeters and melts into grays and silvers, dotted with commodity-heaped barges, the commas and dashes of scrub islands—one of which a fifth grade classmate, Milne, reached in a Huck-esque raft made from milk cartons lashed to cedar deck boards. A host of haunting urban junk appears along the levee. Shuttered snack shacks and vegetable stands and doorless appliances. Conoco stations run dry and vaguer ruins angling out of an industrial oblivion, the residue of the Santa Fe Railway, sewage plants, flood-monitoring posts. Sheds here and there; construction trailers spaced out like chess stratagems. The tin chimney salted with crow shit. A windowpane—a switchman's former worldview—now half crossed out with boards. Is this the past clinging to the present or vice versa? The first rail crossing of the Mississippi took place here. An engine rolled over a bridge standing where the Government Bridge still stood, and East was joined to West by clouds of steam and

a motor's keen. Connections are hidden out in the open. It is the mystery of humble perseverance. The glitter of broken glass differs from the gleam of corporate towers only in scale. The bricks marinated in acid rain appear more solid than the pale virgin masonry of an I-80 Wendy's. I deem it all "nonfrastructure." The trudge of days, apparently one like the other, deceptively leads to competing ages that are unlike each other—that dismantle each other—the little that's left of 1923 or 1856 there before your eyes, like the outstretched branches of time's otherwise invisible orchard.

WHEN ABLE TO BREAK AWAY from the responsibility of cheering up my depressed mother or shouting "Go Nate!" or "Go Nan!" at a softball or soccer game—that is, when I wrestled free from the tentacles of the family octopus—I explored down there where the air was bready with mud and intense stillness reigned: the hush of the continuum on the edge of River Drive rush. Until blackbirds. From mulberry bushes they exploded, red-dotted, to harry my cranium, shaved to the slickness of a seal, and my frame with all the angularity of an easel. The birds dove at the Hawaiian shirt draping it. I darted, swore, ducked, swatted in vain at the diving timpani of beating feathers, their militant *ack-acks*. Sometimes those spawns of Alfred Hitchcock drove me into a crouch, head between knees, but I did not care. I kind of liked being safe. After spending many years failing to rescue days—to make wrong right—a temporary respite from the role of the ill-fated hero was welcomed. Rubble spawned rubble. And that rubble attracted other rubble, endlessly. As I wandered through it I wondered how reality ever managed to appear locked down, stable, preordained, so tick-tock-tick, when that obviously wasn't the case, since even the same choice made again and again by a person or group could have different implications. I walked along collecting railroad spikes and rocks—the smooth, the jagged, the quartz-veined. I had a soft spot for the hardness of survivors. I squinted at grains of rust on smoky-smelling doors. It was like looking into a snow globe, only the snow was atomic sand. The drag of personal grief lessened when immersed in a gone era's glory laid up and burned out, pissed away, beyond repair and goddamn looking like it liked it. That truck tire lounging in the grass—would it choose to roll down a hard road again? American endings, involving no pyramids or falling temple pillars, did not weigh too much. They were airy. They could assume the look of luck on a besotted vacation from luck. American endings lacked solidity because often American beginnings lacked solidity. It was *Gatsby*, over and over and over. It was *Huck*, over and over and over. Fog and water, the fertile ashes and chiding dust. My breakdown, at age fourteen, had delivered me back to myself, just as a city's wreckage delivered the low from which the community would surely derive its next high. Nothing inspired developers like a brownfield or a toxic swamp. Let's build a casino there! Cookie-cutter loft apartments with a Mississippi view: half a mil! Any city, like any identity, existed to be claimed, abandoned, reclaimed. Mutations were always allowed. The final assembly of me was a disassembly, the sliver and his double shadow hiking the vacant lots or stuffed together in the front seat or the back, late as usual.

MY GHOST, THE FAT BOY, always trailing close behind, whispered: *How can half of you be more viable than the whole? How* ... I had no definitive answer for him. I had details.

There were many surprising details: they kept stampeding in my brain, raising questions. The abyss that had pruned a child to his bones was not flame-filled like the one my red and yellow crayons conjured in Mrs. Davis's class, when the family trouble was intensifying and my mother and I targeting each other as the best thing going. My real abyss was weirdly endearing. It was my own room. It was full of what I adored. Marvel comics and rock records and Emily D. and spiral notebooks (the blue lines stretched like high wires that my words walked at their peril). It was Mr. Hickey's gentle voice mistaking, in the beginning, illness for discipline: "You're looking better, Benny." Instead of flames, the abyss was occupied by handfuls of puffed wheat (20 calories) and the Granny Smith apple (75 calories) that burned a tongue which had forgotten sugar, that landed in a shrunken stomach like a cinder block. My descent began one day after I ritualistically ate my last bag of Fritos in the kitchen, dragging each corn chip across the pliant bar of generic cream cheese, creating salty furrows like some crazy farmer tilling the snow. In these furrows I planted a crop of fears. I had had a vision in our car, blocks from the house where Grandpa Stanley would curse us for being late to take his abuse. I saw me as a heart attack victim in a year if I did not "slim down." All of the death that followed was me trying to live. I plucked a calorie-counting booklet from the checkout-line rack at the grocery store, just as many fat ladies before me had. Then things got, in a most difficult way, easier. At last I had a plan. It was a graph I made: since I was in charge, it could be executed. I counted the Easter-morning Communion wafer as 9 calories toward the daily total of 587. (A self-sacrificing Christian for a day.) I kept a log, recording the different ways I reached the same calorie figure and the number of comics I read. (My eyes ingested the exploits of Spiderman, the Fantastic Four, and Howard the

Duck, gluttonous consumption without clogging arteries.) The scale needle swept like a harrow across numerical wheat...I shed the first fifty pounds with amazing speed—as if I had been bloated with that volume of cola and the dam had broken. "Please eat," pled the parent who had fattened me up for this slaughter. She did not ask why I had gone on a hunger strike. She did not dare. At Bishop's Buffet she plied me with pecan pie slices during our family literary salons. I responded, in a dry, faraway voice, "I'm going on a walk on Duck Creek Plaza." That felt productive. Finally I was placing my trouble on a pedestal as high as hers. Each day I strove to make her feel my anguish as she had made me feel hers. The results were mixed. Her attention span was short. But each step away from any table of temptation was an assertion of my right to my own lonely journey, one as time-twisting as hers. My refusals warned her: whatever happens now is as much about my difficult past as yours. And I made the threat stick. After losing the first fifty pounds, I shrank further, from 165 to 145. I was told: "Soon you won't fit into anything but clothes for little boys! Do you want to go around wearing checkers, polka dots, and purple stripes?" I shrugged. She couldn't discourage me. I was no longer an oar for her to row to fairy-tale lands. I was no longer luggage for her to stuff with her baggage. I was my own baggage extracted from that maternal heap. And my father? I played the song "Old Man" on Neil Young's album *Harvest* many times daily—a son's reedy voice beseeching OM to "look" at him now. In our living room a newspaper rustled, grumped, "Don't yell at your mother! You're nuts! Fat? You looked fine to me, ate like a bird..." You looked fine to me? The man had not lowered the paper. At a thrift store I unearthed a white dress shirt and white pants and I wore that outfit every day to Sudlow Junior High in dated homage to John and Yoko's Montreal bed-in to protest war. The outfit remained perfectly white in my mind for months as it soaked up my stinky, nervous sweat. I fixated on the Kansas song "Carry On Wayward Son"—a sappy rallying cry for beleaguered sons to lay down heads and rest. Mr. Furstenberg—the junior high math teacher who wore strong cologne—caught me inking POWER TO THE PEOPLE on my arms and hands. "You're a very handsome boy," he said. "Don't." Another case of mistaken identity. I dropped further, to 140 and 135, then 130, 125 . . . My shirt sprouted ribs and some students were complimentary. "Way killin'! Dy-noooo-mite!" Junior high gym teachers who had once tormented me with extra laps around the playground flagpole now took credit for my emergent skeleton. It was the strangest adulation, yet adulation all the same, and rather easily borne. I was dying for attention of any kind. I could make people shriek with wonder when I pulled two inches of skin off my wrist and more off my upper arm. Foxes followed me down the halls, asking for the name of the diet pill. I blushed. No foxes other than my sisters had willingly talked to me before. I said there wasn't any pill—the trick was abstinence. They did not know the word. "Tell us!" they cried, disbelieving. Kiki. Reesa. Bonita. Hunger imprinted the parentheses around my mouth. At night the pellets of saliva formed.

MOTHER, IN THE VOICE OF A NURSE losing her beloved patient, threatened a trip to a public clinic. We were in the old car, leaving the house and clattering toward the bottom of the alley. She had meant it only as a bluff. "Just promise to eat," she said, "and I'll turn right around!" But she had no way of sensing my excitement about being examined by neutral parties. Her power was always contingent on you mistaking her energy for power. I was finally onto the trick. I shook my head: no promises. At the public clinic the Doctor of the People (DOP) greeted my emaciated visage with two jokes told one after the other, and both indecipherable. I could still be baited into conversation, being a natural loudmouth, and I made the mistake of mentioning that I liked basketball. He spoke at length about Bob Cousy, the famous Celtics guard, as I stood withering in front of him. He was offering me a role model. His smock was covered with animal pins and smiley buttons to cheer up neglected slum children. DOP pointed to the scale. I got on. The weights were adjusted. He produced a height and weight chart, found me lacking, and suggested weekly weigh-ins. I was all for that. My mother protested in vain. Her usual strategy of aggressive haplessness, which steamrollered fifteen-year-old clerks, was no help with DOP, who routinely dealt with gangrene and infant mortality. The weekly visits were on. It was a splendorous development: my crazy routine had forced itself onto her. Each Tuesday the skeleton exited the English class taught by three-hundred-pound Ms. Moore (to die of diabetes before age thirty) and entered the car rumbling at the curb, and was pleaded with, offered money to eat, and shook his skull, rubbed his ribs, and mother and son arrived in a waiting room of fifty coughs and no copies of *Harper's*, no *New Yorker*s. I dropped to 118, 117, 116 ... DOP warned me again that my body was consuming itself for sustenance. I nodded, it was nothing new: we were a family that ate our dead instead of burying them. I had spasms in bed—the dehydration. Icicle fingers. Temperature of a Slurpee. I went almost a week without defecating. I could have reassured my mother—a family that fails together stays together—but the time was never right. I would chew a finger in aisle nine of Kmart and feel fed for the time being. I guessed few people escaped their origins alive. At the beginning of this self-starvation, there had been a tremendous flash of hate, rage at myself for the years of say-ing *yes yes yes yes* to my mother's *will you carry? will you guard? will you give?* and rage at my mother for missing no opportunity to perforate my identity. But the fire died quick. That rage, as if by magic, migrated to some of the vinyl I spun, albums of outrage by the MC5, The Last Poets, Phil Ochs, Country Joe McDonald, and Lennon. Their red-hot voices fried the stale bedroom air alive, while inside me existed something else: exhaustion's metal-lic chill, a tone and rhythm similar to a Miles Davis solo, sound weary of its own avid timbre—fading in the middle of a statement or even at the song's start—notes continually bending toward an inward, unfathomable dark. I was, after all, engaged in a mercy killing. I was methodically killing the fat boy in his own car seat, in his own favorite discount stores, at Sudlow Junior High, and in his own bed, especially there. Most of my starving I did alone in the bedroom, sprawled atop a mattress archive of nocturnal accidents. I offed the fat boy. I took him down. The act was as premeditated as that of Perry Smith, the murderer (and bed wet-ter) immortalized by Truman Capote, the one who might count as mother's favorite of all the killers she spoke of at night when I was eleven and twelve, sitting on the edge of my stained mattress, before she exited slow, wailing the bedtime song "If I Should Die Before I Wake." Perry, *evil lonely Perry*, who had limped from room to room in a farmhouse, shooting a family dead ...

SEEING MORE RIBS, and extra-bluish fingers, DOP arranged for me to visit the Shrink of the People (SOP). The pipe smoke and potted plants were thick in there. I told SOP I could not leave my bedroom unless I counted random accumulations of items on the floor and then, a few steps outside the door, turned and went back to do another count—worried I might have missed an apple core hidden under a sock. The confession caused SOP to request a meeting with my parents. They went to the appointment, but they did not stay long. My mother said my father "stormed out" of the office when asked a question. She did not say what question. I could hear she was both mad at him and proud of him. His storming out allowed her to leave without taking blame. When picturing their exit I pictured a short clothesline threading into a hallway—billowing empty dress, slacks, undershorts, shirt. DOP then arranged a free mental-health evaluation for me at the university hospital in Iowa City. My mother and Uncle Eubie, the restive elementary school teacher, and Eubie's quiet wife, Julie, took me. They stopped at a local McDonald's before the appointment and tried to feed me burgers. Everything, they said, would be all right, fixed, if only I ate a burger. Oh? Sharing burgers with a despairing parent had ruined a good part of me. I had a hold on that element of my convoluted story, at least. Sesame seed bun = satanic manna. I was gratified to behold their confusion when I again declined. At the hospital, praise God, I was led away from them and calorie-free stuff happened, including a written test. I was left with it in a room the size of a phone booth plus twelve inches: beige carpet, a desk with pine knots (all-seeing, all-knowing knots). Then we stopped at another McDonald's on the way out of Iowa City and I refused to break bread with these hedonists once more and they forgot about me and ate well at the window with a view of one of those I-80 exit ramps involved in the genius-importing business of the Iowa Writers' Workshop. I sucked ice at my own table, gazing, as the befuddled artist must, into my own blight. Where else would grams of light be hiding? The ordeal of being weighed like dead meat and questioned like a criminal I found satisfying, but I shivered in the fine franchise air-conditioning on that sweltering unforgettable day.

THE MINNESOTA MULTIPHASIC PERSONALITY Inventory I took that day, combined with an interview at the hospital, eventually resulted in a diagnosis still rare in 1977, especially for a male: anorexia nervosa. (Marianna later suffered dangerous bouts of bulimia.) DOP had penciled the dread words onto the pink slip of paper that he handed my mother. Standing beside her, and seeing those neat block letters, I had a strange thought typical of my malnourished state of mind. I thought: *Now I can't run for public office.* The newspapers would find this out once I declared a candidacy, and it would be a scandal. Mother acted concerned and thanked DOP and he told a joke to break the tension and we never went back. Clinics, then, were what ailed me. Yes! It was all discoveries—this hunger strike—discoveries beginning to end. I had discovered I had it in me to erase me. I had discovered that my parents were hapless in the face of that wish. I had discovered that institutions were equally hapless, and helpless. At the clinic it was one trouble after the next: too many to track and follow up on. I had now to discover how things would turn out. Decades later there would be the psychological ramification of feeling like I had been left for dead in my own home by the state, and my parents, but there would be no proving that. I just felt that way, at times, when remembering how a big bad diagnosis had prompted no treatment whatsoever. My mother's mental state was such that she may not have even known she was not still taking me to the clinic. I did not demand to go back, either. In a way it was nothing new. The stakes were higher, but in every other way it was like being again in a dark parking lot waiting for a ride home that was not coming. When that happened I did not scream like my sisters. I thought of things. I looked at the stars. I was infernally determined to be self-reliant, because I never did trust that help would come from anyone but myself and my own efforts. The summer between seventh and eighth grade. At dawn I would hear the bugler playing morning reverie to the barracks at the Rock Island Arsenal. I had been hearing those notes ever since I was a small boy. Many different buglers. The river could be seen from the corner window in winter, when the trees were bare, but not then. Our maple, balanced like a gargantuan gymnast on the terrace edge, was leafed out. Most of the day I stayed in bed, reading comic books, starving, sleeping, starving, waking, playing records. I reached off the mattress and flipped the Plastic Ono Band record to side one. Bell tolling, Lennon screeching "Mother!" like a mad English owl. The noise was the next best thing to hearing a siren coming to my rescue. I picked at my loose skin: the fat boy's body bag clinging to my arms and legs and stomach. I had stretch marks like a woman who had given birth. Going below a hundred pounds would invite organ failure, according to DOP. I wondered if Howard had noticed I was about to die again. Howard did not act like he noticed the family, but much later he would say to me at the McClellan Stockade, a bar in the Village of East Davenport, "I had a brother and then I didn't, you weren't there." We siblings, though riddles to each other, also had a knack for guessing the truth. When a disc finished playing I did not always turn it over right away. The forbearing ministrations of the now very worried Mr. Hickey swirled in my addled head on the dirty pillow ticking—"Have some water, then, Benny"—and Leon Russell's gravel pit of a voice singing of strangers in strange lands and wisecracks from Broadway goons in the Damon Runyon paperback on my sill and Emerson's "Build, therefore, your own world!" exhortation and Granny Stanley murmuring my name in her mud-road way, the *e* sounding like an *a*: "Now, Ban." And under all that, or audible over it, my own jaded whisper: *What's the use of dying again after you've already died?*

NO SINGLE VOICE INTERCEDED to steer me away from the final edge, but from all the spectral hands on deck came something—strength? care?—that allowed me to drag a skeleton down the stairs and to the kitchen and the can opener and the fork and tuna fish and Miracle Whip on the Ritz cracker. I lifted the cracker with an unsteady hand. I had not eaten anything like that in many months. It came down to cracker or no cracker. If I did not eat the cracker, what was left of me would die. (Forgive the melodrama: I was fourteen. That's the truth as I saw it.) It was full circle, Fritos to Ritz—or rest in peace. I had no illusion that eating again could fix what had broken inside me, however. My mother was wrong about that. Healing would be a matter not of curing the brokenness but tending it, heeding its many messages. I would have to learn to live with my elimination of a child who deserved much better—if indeed I decided to bite down, and go on. I hesitated more. Then I took the bite. The richness of the oil set off sensations. My taste buds exploded. The roof of my mouth sparked and my tongue sizzled and flaming wooly bullies crawled up and down my cheeks, trying to bore their way out. I shoved the rest of the cracker in. More Independence Day fireworks. I was—I knew then, I knew it!—I was going to do what Mr. Hickey had long encouraged: regular exercise. Sit-ups.

Push-ups. Jumping rope. As the rancid stick of butter on the table plate was my witness, I was. I had ended my end just short of the end. And the certitude of that moment of the bite had removed it seemingly by centuries from the previous moment of ennui and death wish. It was as if the moments of moments ago were already under glass somewhere, scratched on pots. The hollows of my eyes were bursting with the flavor of Chicken of the Sea. I would live to do calisthenics, on the one hand, and on the other, well, I would live to see what happened, just to see, that's what, and that was enough—for now. Moving heaven and earth was out of the question. They would stay right where they were. One of my first acts of recovery was to send Before and After snapshots, and the tale of the tape, to the *National Enquirer*. I got back a form with a dot matrix personalized salutation. *Dear Mrs. Miller, We regret to inform you . . .* Disappointing, but worth a try. Putting those snapshots together in an envelope was my next attempt to do emergency field surgery on a self—to narrow the wound. To this day, when I visit a new doctor and my medical history is taken, there is surprise at my not having soon after gained the weight back. But there was no one left to hang the blubber on. That boy really was gone. I never suffered another bout with an eating disorder either. That year it was as if a violent drifter had passed through the terra of my body, done a heinous thing, and moved on . . . though it was not so. I am the fat boy and the thin forever, yet can never be both simultaneously—in a living sense. I was never, for a moment, that. One cannot exist without the other but each is a strident denial of the other—each is the death of the other. They exist on opposing sides of a schism functioning as glue, as the river that divides Iowa cities from Illinois cities also brought them together to form the Quad Cities, a label with a deceptive sound of solid manufacturing.

 SLIVERS—LIKE SEEDS—can be borne on the wind, and after my pruning, if I really wanted to get somewhere on time, I had a way to do it. I could walk, run, or ride the Fuji bicycle I sold my comic book collection to buy. (The Schwinn that father got for me had long ago rusted to death in the basement.) I decorated the Fuji frame with daisy-patterned contact paper—which more commonly lined cottage cupboards. It stuck good. It gave bike thieves doubts. Dreams and demons, nipping at my wheels and heels, kept me on track. Two miles, four, six, distance didn't daunt

me. Or when it did, I hitched a ride to literary events with Norm Ross of Writers' Studio, the retired Rock Island Lines employee, prompt as a train schedule. To be on time could be as easy as calling him or leaving plenty early. No one expected me home by a certain hour and on the return trips I luxuriated in my dramatic journeys, picking between bridges for variety. I wore no watch. I trusted time to hunt me down, and it did. My watches were the public time displays along the route, bulbs or neon or sundial-like clocks facing the chlorinated fountains of bank plazas. The thing was to be no more a victim of the family's vehicular vortex. I forced Nathan—younger by a decade—to walk places with me. I believed I was teaching the kid freedom, but on those walks he learned to resent me, I think. We walked to Target on Kimberly, and to story hour at the Davenport Public Library, sometimes passing interesting people, people who had changed their names to decimal numbers or who believed the government was secretly producing mechanical bald eagles in Arizona in case the real birds died out. I tried, in so many awkward words, to convey to trudging "Nate"—in his Ocean Pacific shirt—that inhabiting a desolate crud-caked sidewalk next to River Drive was akin to entering a secret kingdom that we—and Mr. 2.31—could call our own, an urban Midwest never featured in movies. Sidewalks would, eventually, return us to the house hysteria, but it would take long—quite long. In the meantime we had the warm open road, and each other. Never mind the Mazda owners speeding by! Nathan had no idea what the hell had happened to me. I sensed he might never guess the right guesses. How would he know unless I told him the whole story, and what wise sentences could possibly straddle its idiotic girth? Nathan was outwardly the most normal and calm brother. Inwardly—who could guess? He did not say much at any age. On walks he clearly informed me that he was upset by walking slower and slower, frowning. I tried to convince him that in the gutter things were happier. In the gutter was a family reunion of litter that brought to mind missing brothers and sisters—a popcorn bag (Elizabeth's first job was at a ballpark concession stand), a Moosehead bottle (Howard's brew of choice), a lipstick vial (Marianna all over), green tinsel (Nanette). There were many awful walks—from Nathan's viewpoint—but the worst was certainly that Saturday I convinced him to accompany me to Grandpa Stanley's house in another state. River Drive to Government Bridge, over the Mississippi to Arsenal Island and a second bridge over the Rock River to that edge of downtown Rock Island where Jim's Rib Haven was, and the house with chickens out back. We climbed past hillside duplexes set at extreme angles of architectural angst (an urban renewal project since torn down) to reach the ridge where investors lived. It was another two miles to the Stanley home. We were coming to mow Grandpa's lawn, that's what I kept telling my brother. We'd split the money and it would be a lot. When Grandpa answered the door, drunk, he accused me of being late. The strings of obscenities. The bathrobe belt drooping. It was noon. He slammed the door. I rang again. The door did not open. I felt as upset as I had when I was tossed out of my own house by the babysitter's boyfriend when I was six. But I was not alone now. I had led my little freckled brother into this nightmare. He refused to cry. He kept it in, and I strived to also. Nathan and I sat silently on the steps, then started back.

I WALKED, OR RAN, all the time. I would run to Writers' Studio meetings on the west side of Davenport. Very late one night I ran home four miles from the Mississippi Valley Writing

Conference—across the river at Augustana College—after helping Cozie put away folding chairs following the reading given by chipper Max Allan Collins from his latest detective novel. Another day, in the morning, when I was walking to Central High in a thunderstorm (no umbrella), my favorite teacher, Mr. Minard, saw me and pulled up to the curb. He taught a one-of-a-kind course called, simply, Humanities, in which issues like abortion and capital punishment were discussed frankly. He let me do the final paper on Capability Brown, the famous eighteenth-century landscape architect. (It ended with a hallucinatory reimagining of my trampled yard—swans, a pond, arborvitae. I attached a drawing. There was a little bridge over the pond which was roughly the size of the rink that I once dreamed might exist on the same accursed mud, if Mr. Creighton ever got his patent.) His sedan was quite new. I was soaked. It said everything about Mr. Minard's humanity that he did not care. He was at this time a city councilman also, Davenport's Renaissance man. "Get in," he urged in his soft airy voice. It said much about me that I did not instantly take him up on the offer. I hated to relinquish my hard-won liberty, even when that meant walking through a storm. I did, though, this once. Mr. Minard and I had a nice talk about literature. This was around the time when my father began yipping: "Benny doesn't know when to come out of the rain!" (A comment he would include in one of the few letters that he wrote me after I left Davenport for good—maybe three in twenty years.) To him, one who walked in the rain was a fool, and uncivilized. To me, though, sweating was the long cry I had long needed, and the rain was a parent washing away tears from my eyes, forehead, and cheeks. What I had seen happen under roofs did not give me any trust in them as shelters. Each mile walked or run or biked was a major miracle for being under my full jurisdiction.

IN DECEMBER OF MY SOPHOMORE YEAR, I jogged three miles to the Masonic Auditorium, overlooking downtown Davenport, to sing Handel's *Messiah* with the Central High choir. At home, over the performance outfit—dark, wrinkled rummage-sale slacks and button-down shirt—I pulled on a sweatshirt, a green mohair sweater, and doughy sweats. Mr. Anderson, the strict white-haired director in his last year, demanded that every singer wear dress shoes. I owned a pair of thrift-store wing tips I was proud of: no holes in the soles. I shined their uppers with tissues and Vaseline. The laces, striped with eyelet grit and resembling uprooted roots, had been scavenged from another pair of shoes. I triple-knotted them. I was used to running in street shoes. (Early in the next year, when I answered the call for track-team members, Coach Ira Dunsworth tenderly took me aside and explained about running shoes.) My bones were holding up. I pounded down the alley to Jersey Ridge Road where it met Kirkwood Boulevard. The temperature was in the single digits. Snow crusting trashcan lids glowed indigo. The modest dwellings along the city's last brick boulevard had small yards but an optical illusion of snow and the night made it appear at a glance that the yards were estate-sized, the houses distant mansions. Worried about slipping, falling, breaking my hip, I looked ahead for glints of ice under streetlights. There were many. I zigzagged around what looked like shards of broken mirrors. I knew those shards. When no escape existed there was that one last escape of altering the way you looked at a dire situation—the smashing of the mirror reflecting a hopeless reality into little bits that you could more easily live with, that almost shimmered like a path out. I ran in the plowed street, and against the traffic, as was my safety habit. I never went on a walk or run without first picturing dying on it, a hit-and-run fatality, a drive-by shooting. The fat boy kept warning: *You'll never*

make it without me, even if I was nearly the death of you. Crystals sprouted on my Buddy Holly eyeframes, strapped into place. My cap was pulled down to the glasses. Under the cap was the hood. Various scarves and collars had reduced my face to the size of a pink grapefruit. Freezing shots of air burned nicely in the lungs, celebratory zings. I got an adrenaline boost from knowing that no one else in the choir was running to reach a spot on the rickety risers, and, furthermore, that most members would not even consider such a thing possible, though it was as easy as dressing until you resembled a bear and putting one elderly dress shoe in front of the other. I was not a fast runner. I was a plodder. But my plodding felt fast to me at times. Laurels of breath and rhythmic strides spread warmth beneath my clothes. My face was numb but within that improvised pelt I was cozy and—I thought—a fit heir to the pioneer legacy I had encountered in Hamlin Garland's *Main-Traveled Roads* and elsewhere. I was toughing it out, trying not to tumble. I was American nuts and bolts of movement. I was, as always, also writing in my head. I was writing an instant history of my present-day Davenport. Miles behind, miles ahead, the frozen plains of parked cars; the eaves blinking red green red; there the saltbox abode of the *Wiiiiiiiiiiiilber*ing wife who won the husband-calling contest each year at the East Village of Davenport Festival; there the hovel where Tod Harding had lived until he murdered his cousin and was sent to the penitentiary; there the blue bungalow where the mother of Nanette's friend Lavonne heard a window open one night and grabbed a shotgun from under the bed and shot Lavonne's father, who had misplaced his front-door key; there a maple tree bare that went up and up and up against the clear night's glaze until finally powdering into the intense purple pointilism of galaxies ... Kirkwood to Brady. I passed Palmer College of Chiropractic on the right and the WOC studios on the left, veered onto a side street, stopped, composed myself a bit, and entered a soupy-smelling lobby where down vests and snowflake sweaters milled.

THE RESTROOM WAS A TILED PONDEROSA. Urinals with the hip-hugging partitions. To piss was to feel loved. I felt the devotion of marble and porcelain. My gaze followed geographical cracks to no conclusions. Then I peeled off my soaked layers in a stall, rolled them into a single ball that could be easily stowed backstage, and exited the stall. I mopped my face with paper towels, then used different towel wads to wipe the grit from the lubricant-slathered leather of my shoes. The pair shone once more. I had no hair problem. The hair problem I had solved by finding people to shave my head for free. (There were more of them out there than you'd imagine.) This was me, the fragment that time had grown. Me as equipped as I would be until I reached my thirties. Come hell or high water winging it, splicing it, every finger crossed. Body humidity had ironed out the wrinkles in my shirt. I straightened the collar. I didn't worry that my classmates, or Anderson, would notice the armpit stains stretching nearly from hips to shoulders. I could not worry about junk like that or I'd never exit the restroom—never go anywhere again. With the clothes ball tucked under one arm, I dodged familiar lobby loiterers. The lonely, it turns out, reap almost as many hellos as popular folks, and after the merry automaton greeting, the sad usual questions: "How's mother?"—and after that—"Father?" Who? I climbed the stairs to a stage where choir members milled around risers. I stowed my clothes behind a curtain and when the stage lights blinked I joined the tenors. Up there I could better see the empty balconies and the decay of the ceiling: blistered paint, desiccated plaster—what?—angels, were they? Other spots of no paint, no plaster. The auditorium was rotting from the top down—as institutions did. Orchestra seats were filled. Baldness of every degree. The place looked as if it dated to the city's last certified heyday: when trains from Chicago pulled into the station, boats arrived from New Orleans, and there were flappers and Bix horn solos. The audience seriously rustled as the old maestro—tux jacket, white hair, baton—assumed his place in front of us at the music stand. He shuffled, head down, like a grumpy baseball coach going to the mound to change pitchers after a home run has given the other team a big lead. He looked up. He sniffed. The thin grin hardly concealed a foul mood which had recently caused him to fling his briefcase out of a classroom into the hallway. It had slammed a wall and cracked open: a black egg spilling old scores. Mr. Anderson did not want to retire anymore than McKinley's Mrs. Savory had upon reaching the mandatory age. He turned his daunting head, glared at the sopranos. He glared at the basses. He was short and had deep-set eyes. He cared about classical music to the extent that everything else in the world disappointed him. He scared me, but I admired him. He lifted the baton. Performers and the audience braced for what was to come. Blunt oratorio trauma. Anderson twirled the baton slow, a last second of silence. Then he lunged forward, stabbing, stabbing. I was ready, and not.

STABS IN THE DARK—the stabbing of dark by art—as in the corner bedroom where my mother delivered true-crime stories and Dylan Thomas lyrics with equal bobbing enthusiasm; as in a dim living room where a cigarette butt jabbed the brass ashtray beside the recliner, showering it with embers; as in the school practice room when I had fouled myself to the tune of Bach and Mr. Pope's slashing baton; as in the hunger artist at work in the night of days counted in calories; as in the Writers' Studio pens unsheathed and jotting, the pencils out and erasing, revising, revising.

WAVES OF SOUND BEGAN TO BUILD. Like many traumas, this one was peaceful at the start. The air did not instantly gleam with saliva droplets. But there were, immediately, wrong notes. School choirs were minefields. They gathered together twenty or more kids with no natural artistic predilections. Clear voices, maybe. Strong voices. Yet that hardly made art inevitable. It made very loud, and very clear, the failures. Mr. Anderson was already scowling. He was not pleased, not pleased yet. He forced the tempo, brilliant parlay. The *Messiah* sang itself after building up speed; the chant of the lyrics and the chordal polyphony suppressed everything but magnificence. It was impossible to ruin. It was the larger-than-life work that would not exist were there not, around the globe, in every human century, multitudes of little voices ready and available to wail wrongly. I did, after swallowing my initial terror, and then I loved being the tenth tenor. I loved the immense sacredness of this work—and I was godless. The *Messiah* had far more layers than I wore. There was no evading the work's work. Off-key notes tumbled together, weathered a storm of their own making, then landed ashore on Hallelujah! Hallelujah! Hallelujah! It was the ruination of sound in the name of a higher cause: musical expression. Handel's spiritual *On the Road* composed in a few weeks and acting like it. A marathon incantation. The length was the worst, and best, thing about the concert. The length allowed singers who lost their place in the score time to find it again. Some perpetrated with their torsos what they could not accomplish with their voices. Gyrations worthy of *Soul Train* in the alto section. Others squealed like someone in the shower discovering the hot water heater is busted. Wonderful! Counselor! The Mighty God! The Everlasting Father! The Prince of Peace! The ocean foam of Anderson's hair licked the air. In the audience comb-overs stirred, hand muffs held in laps shifted, knees were gripped. From row to row there spread a disorientation not unpleasant. It was the feeling of being unhinged from the gamut of mundane details that made a life understandable and catapulted into a sphere where the trivial was no longer available

to shield a mind and a heart from the magnitude of life's uniqueness upon this rock in a void. Wonderful! Counselor! The Mighty
God! The Everlasting Father! The Prince of Peace! Out rolled
prayers from my irreligious mouth—out they stumbled. It was
one welcome break from trying to fathom the world in terms of its
fathomable elements, which were no help in fathoming what most
needed to be fathomed: the mysterious insistent interplay of light
with dark. I was no liar of a singer, no hypocrite. I was a believer
that the earth's story spoke of the touch of a force outside the
human realm which might be communicated with only through
the complex codes of Art or Scripture and the primal screams of
love and loss. Hallelujah! Hallelujah! Hallelujah! Refrain crashed
into protean refrain. Mr. Anderson bent double, his frame a
battened-down hatch that then sprang open and up, the baton a
weaving cutlass. We were pirating eternity in singing this song of
hourful minutes. If we were angels, our halos were short-circuiting. Would Anderson refuse to shake hands with us afterward?
Would he run over a parking lot pylon, smash the tinted windows
of a van? His end as a conductor was infuriating to him. You
could see it in each spasm of his baton. Without any choir to direct, he would no longer be Mr. Anderson. And we kids—without
the *Messiah* to sing—what would we be? We would be no more,
and no less, than our hunger, which frequently perceived opportunities where there were none; we would be desirous faces and
reaching arms that embraced any lame job or discounted object,
whatever was nearest to be had. We were—despite our keyed-up
bluster—weaklings. Music could shoulder the burden of those
daily execrable errors like nothing else. Music lent the scheme
of survival a bluesy dignity, a universal echo, while daring of you
more. The *Messiah* did. But our ascensions ended with the last
note. Anderson turned toward an audience wanting cookies and

automatic garage-door openers. He bowed like a kicked-over trash can. The ovation found its legs, finally. (In days to come students whispered that Anderson had "cried," a tasty detail savored by his detractors and supporters alike.) The risers emptied. Backstage I redonned my layers. I skirted the yawning throngs of folks jingling keys in the lobby. In front of the auditorium I paused on the sidewalk, considering what route to take, and then I took it, striding into the glassy winter gale. I was in a defiant mood after singing myself raw. I headed downtown. I made my choice. The long way home. Where did shortcuts lead? I had seen exactly where, writ on the faces of my parents.

I STREAKED PAST HILLSIDE DUPLEXES at San Francisco angles. I stuffed loaves of air into my lungs and pushed them out, angling my mismatched layers of clothing across the frost-scalded intersections. *How could half of me be more viable than the whole?* Running, I could control the burn of unanswerable questions. Life is short and life goes on. Time careens forward, crawling. Gone today, here tomorrow. *That fat boy's with me, I know it! No, he's gone. It's like he was never here.* I was dealing with what any other widow dealt with on this evening and all that would follow. Issues of commemoration, continuity, transition. Very soon I would quit choir and devote myself to the demands of track and cross-country workouts, which inserted hours of momentum into days and nights otherwise consisting of disruptions. Running, I might keep a boy blown apart from flying further apart and reproducing, finally, his mother's giggle, the sound of one who has given up trying to make sense of things, surrendered to a contagion of doubts. But I did sing once more onstage—at the

Central High variety show, when I was a senior. I carried out the fake guitar cut from a cardboard box in my bedroom, where every big art project had started since I was five. My classmates cheered: they thrilled to see me wearing the loudest Hawaiian shirt in my collection. Feverish, keeping a time of my own, I delivered a silly song written in all seriousness. *Plastic flowers, plastic flowers, / all I want at my funeral is plastic flowers / they last for hours, plastic flowers // When I'm in my coffin, put one between my teeth! // Plastic flowers...*

THE SLOW WHITE FIRE OF STREETLIGHTS encircled and engulfed my wool cap, Buddy Holly glasses, the pink grapefruit of my exposed skin: nose lips cheeks. Along the way, plowed acres of cement appeared to boil with pebbles, like a gruel that could sustain urban Iowans through the hardest of hard times. Far behind me already were the vehicles double-parked outside the auditorium. Underneath my clothing I was a steamy greenhouse. At the bottom of Brady I chugged into the gorge of downtown after closing time—vacant parking lots, locked lobbies, traffic lights winking yellow. Dumpsters stood in the alleys like carriages awaiting bowler-clad ghosts. I veered around a snow-covered hubcap or a migrating arctic turtle. The spotlights of the Davenport Bank Building glowed like a campfire on the gorge's rim. The wind hacked in vain at my rounded edges. I was getting warmer. There was more life to the death of a downtown than many natives could imagine. Howard and Marianna fled into these desolate streets to leave them behind, to reach some place completely different, far away and balmy. I fled the house to go deeper into the city. What one drab corner stole or destroyed, another corner could return to you—if you looked hard enough for the richness and were ready to receive it. Sidewalks and streets which seemed unforgiving or fallow had actually watched over me—guided me—as a family that had lost its way could not. Oh, there were good reasons to hope, and good reasons to be hopeless, as I ran. While I couldn't sing or run well, just months earlier a headline had appeared in the *Quad-City Times*: TOP POETS: BOY, 15, WOMAN, 97. My poem had been chosen from over 750 entries—even Elizabeth's. She had received honorable mention in the junior high school category for her poem "Gravestone Gray." Something happened with that poem of mine. It had the word *cut* in the first line, maybe an honest word: "A TV movie cut the 1970s in half…" Any honest word counted as an attempt to reacquaint myself with the humanity I had not yet squandered or lost to the family dystopia. I would always be the child of a certain illusory couple, but I was my own person too. Now my weekly grocery store treat was a green bottle of effervescent mineral water that I poured into one of our best repurposed jars and used to wash down the snack mix. Again I was taking the informative way back, the hardest way, the long way.

I GLIDED THROUGH A POTION of street glare and moonlight. Disaffection made me run but affection still made me tick. Affection for peach neon that read TENSION ENVELOPES. Affection for snow-traced trestles, and just about any sign. They all seemed to be there at this hour exclusively to keep me company. P.J.'S TAVERN: MUD WRESTLING SATURDAYS. MUSICIAN'S UNION #67. KAHL APARTMENTS. NATIONAL BISCUIT CO. FRENCH AND HECHT. Frozen heaps of sand in the dump truck lot. Robin

Hood Flour silos. Out on the Mississippi were lunar-glazed tablets of buckled ice, and Government Bridge poised like a jaw ready to take a bite out of the big river. TIME and TEMP: 10:14, 8°, 10:14. I jogged in place, watching the sign's electricity chew on the night. Blinking bulbs dashed a minute like a bottle of bubbly against history's dark hull. The numerals flashed, then a blackout. Nothing added up. Wind whistled around the sign's stanchions and I thought of the gaps in autobiographical stories my mother tried, and failed, to tell. "The man in the bus station asked me to be in a movie…" "In the library carrel I found a sandwich and it tasted better than any sandwich I ever…" Another flash—10:15 flaring like the tender petals of a bloom spread in glacial space.

AT OR NEAR THIS TIME and TEMP sign my family's biggest turns were taken. The turn back in time to the Depression-era holdout where we often ate: Shannon's Cafeteria. Mother turning onto the bridge with me in the front passenger's seat—the rest of the family abandoned back at the roach-infested address. Over the river and through the slum to Granny's house we went. Father turning off River Drive each weekday morning to reach an air-conditioned maid-cleaned office where we weren't allowed to visit without an appointment. Mother turning here to resume her madcap career as an attorney at the Legal Assistance office in the Putnam Building. Father turning here to take my dog Pinkerton to be terminated at the Humane Society after the peanut-headed postman had complained and me in the backseat stroking that dear goofy mutt's head—the mutt wagging his tail in anticipation of a tremendous treat. Sunday turns to Walgreens drugstore and the Chicago newspapers. Turns to thrift stores that clothed us.

Turns to the library that fed us Edward Gorey and Julie Jensen McDonald and port wine cheese. The turn to minor-league base-ball games at John O'Donnell Stadium and to the Royal American Shows encampment under Centennial Bridge, where father had taken his daughters up in the Ferris wheel one by one. I was sure there would be more great turns—be they sweet or cataclysmic—as I started running again into the icy wind of Davenport. My only hometown. My immeasurable Dublin, my heartland Venice, my cornpone Athenian theater. This city was my early grave, and the debarkation point of a future's bones.

THE DARK ART OF RHUBARB

Cookbook overbite — "Climb, my hero, climb!" — A vegetable
surreal with realness — The opposite of magic —
Many things too many — Davenport adrift

In the beginning ninety-one-year-old Mr. Rush farmed the terrace below my family's narrow slice of the neighborhood geography. Dawn and there he would be, staining the knees of his faded overalls, collarbone pitching with such energy that his shirt looked like a red-checked tent in a storm, poles stressed to the limit. Dandelions came up, and jagged inches of crabgrass. The rusty trowel shoveled pricklies. Milkweed fluffs were plucked off the soil's dark lapel. To combat sharpening light he donned a terry cloth visor. Sick plants were drizzled with botanic syrup from a bulbed funnel. After the doctoring came the harvesting of silky fistfuls of lettuce leaves and plump tomatoes. With a rake he pried speckled potatoes from a dirt mound. Gloveless, he yanked root-bearded onions, then slowly approached rhubarb stalks arrayed along the house foundation like the rungs of a martian ladder a spaceship had left behind. His wrinkled eyelids fluttered. He scratched that chin sugared with tiny white hairs. Every garden has a star and rhubarb stole this plot. Each stalk a cunning arc from the ground, green blushing ruby-red and culminating in a heart-shaped poison leaf. The charm of rhubarb was deadly, as all charm is—to the vulnerable. And not just Mr. Rush was spell susceptible, but my mother also. She went wild over rhubarb the way wolves went crazy over the full moon. Grabbed the twine-tied bundle from my arms and tossed back her head, bowl-cut bangs fraying as she groaned: "How nice of Mr. Rush to share." The dormant kitchen then came fantastically to life—a Fanny Farmer cookbook with cover overbite hit the yellow folding table like a cinder block, and cobwebbed cupboards burst open. Baking pans appeared, antique ingredients, too—dented tins and rumpled sacks stamped with images of Indians, hammers, residents of Sherwood Forest. She sighed at the sight of Robin Hood's feather. There were extra books on the table. I wondered if she was going to add poetry to her pie. She reached for a tome, read a poem out of it, but put it back where it belonged, on top of the five other books. She sniffed a yeast rock. She greased pans with the soft butter that had been sitting out for days. Something began to happen that resembled baking. The air filled with puffs of flour that appeared to be ghosting from her ears like powdered memories. Hers came in funny forms—not genealogy, or snapshots. There was, for instance, not a single photo of her wedding. We children guessed father was there . . . but who else? And what flowers had she carried down the aisle as the organ whined? (Thinking

she needed an album like any other bride—if not Kodak, then
Crayola—my sister Elizabeth and I had drawn a big church with
a ding-dong bell. Happy relatives we had never met, gathered on
the steps. Father standing tall in a new blue Sears suit, because
a man on his wedding day could not have a bad leg. And tearful
mother wearing a sack dress with a lacy train, cradling a rhubarb
bouquet. We later found out she was married not in a church
but in the gloom of Grandpa Stanley's living room.) Mr. Rush's
response to the grotesque charisma of this vegetable was quieter
but no less intense. Like a savvy Hollywood producer at a casting
call, he lingered in the wings of the roof's shadow while deciding
which high-kicking stalks were ripe to star in a low-budget production called *Rhubarb Sauce*. Sometimes none had what it takes.
But other days he strolled to the garage off the alley, fetched a
chipped machete and came out swinging. Tall tomato plants were
inadvertently decapitated. Siding suffered major damage. Fiber
flew, pounds piled up. And he must wrap the entire harvest in
newspaper and give it to me to give away because his freezer was
packed with rhubarb sauce, some containers dated prior to 1963,
the year I was born. "Aye! Fay-vor! Kin?" Hunting without ear-
plugs had destroyed his hearing, and the deafness oddly could be
heard from afar—spooking cats two houses away and halting me
on the dusty terrace above. "Yow! Kin! Yow!" He honked like the
pintail ducks he had used to pick off with a Remington rifle while
crouching in a branchy blind sticking out of a Mississippi River
slough. "Aye! Fay-vor! Please!" Cruel justice it sounded like—
ironic comic-book doom—only this infirmity was a blessing in
disguise. For it both prevented the racket of modern machines like
Datsuns and 747s from disturbing his tilling and made it impossible for him to hear the word *no*. The only way to refuse this deaf
man was to scram, which many boys did, but never me because I

relished the chance to dazzle my uncouth mother, or alarm some-one else's fancy microwave mom with a load of "What? On the welcome mat?" Latin name: *Rheum rhabarbarum.* I asked Miss Murray at the Davenport Public Library to look it up. *Buckwheat family. Native of Siberia. Perennial, herbaceous. Prized for its petioles*—"another word for stalk," she added onto the reference note, so I didn't get nasty ideas about petioles. Ecological Mr. Rush—a cousin in my mind of Mr. Green Jeans on Captain Kangaroo's TV show—could have taped a similar explanation to each gift. He possessed the knowledge. He could write too—I had seen him signing for a package with a ballpoint pen that the postman had to wipe off afterward. It would have been simple to jot a few calming words: *Dear Mrs. Microwave, Take a deep breath. Put water on to boil*...But Mr. Rush did not jot a note because he was mesmer-ized, or hypnotized, or whatever the word was for someone who believed rhubarb would be received with the same enthusiasm as the American Beauty roses clipped each June by a much younger old neighbor, Mr. Hickey, who rubber-banded paper towels around thorny stems so the courier did not end up at St. Luke's Hospital.

WAKE UP AND SMELL THE BEAUTY! Rival Hickey might sweat over his rose bush like you sweat over your vegetables but those blooms bore no proof of that labor. There was a lazy lusciousness about the unfurled petals, an intoxicating perfume that could cause even a sensible microwave mom to swoon and fall for son-ny's outlandish cultivation claim. "I made 'em all for you." Why argue? Such was the innocent magic of roses. They really did appear to have grown in the giving hand, nourished by feelings

alone. The heart's spontaneous sprawling flourish. Each bloom a blown crimson sprocket or ever-expanding military decoration, opening and opening before withering elegantly in the vase, perfect crisp picture of its former resplendent self. In fact, the fading of the rose only enchantingly clarified its dear message, creating subtle hues to press in a book, heap in a bowl, float on water. So much for the Age of New and Improved. Blooms from the same old Hickey bush continued to please even the most demanding consumers like Mrs. Wright and Mrs. Patterson. They didn't care that the glory came attached to a complementary crown of thorns, or that each bud was initially imprisoned by wiry tendrils: the organic equivalent of a medieval chastity belt. No, the break-out was always astounding. It did not matter if the petals were dwarfish due to drought, droopy from monsoon weather or long past their prime and peeled to a comma of color. A clamor arose around imperfect roses that could not be matched by perfect specimens of petunias, marigolds, pansies, tulips, daisies, and the pink carnation pinned like a deodorizing puck to the prom gown of a girl about to experience something nasty. Those other flowers had no reliable track record for safely transporting the heart's delicate cargo. They lacked the layered dreaminess. They lacked the sweet ether of a magnificent idea. The lavish notion that You Who Received the Rose were the equal of all the other human beings who had ever received roses—queens, first ladies, Liz Taylor, Marilyn Monroe, Princess Grace. And that You Who Gave the Rose were the most generous—and deserving—individual in the world. I knew this from experience. With a fragrant bouquet of Mr. Hickey's roses in my arms, I was no longer a dawdling fat boy but a prancing prince in corduroy tights who might any moment be beckoned by a third-grade damsel with two-story blond tresses. "Climb, my hero, climb, don't waste that beautiful bunch on your messy mom. She'll cut the stems short, stuff them in a jam jar already full of dead lilacs. Climb! Before it's too . . ." If such a capable vehicle for finer emotions had not existed, Leonardo da Vinci surely would have designed one—sketching a contraption with petal wings and a thorny cockpit.

ONLY A BAD POET or drunken mechanic would have invented the ungainly bundle of rhubarb Mr. Rush proudly handed over. "Got it? Thonks!" The newspaper crackled. From the stalks wafted the exotically plain odors of celery, nutmeg, mud...A vegetable surreal with realness. Its smells summoning the word microwave moms despised more than any other: *Raw*. Rhubarb looked raw. Felt raw. Rude. Rooty. Unyielding. Fibrous and unready for digestion. In need of soaking, boiling, baking. All three, in that order, over a course of many hours, to tease forth a minor trove of vitamins and a sour flavor that not even all the Domino Sugar in the kitchen of Bishop's Buffet could douse. All yours, I thought, as I dumped the gnarly bundle on a swept back stoop, and then, just like Sherlock Holmes, *retired* to the musty drawing room that was our doorless one-car garage, to watch my nemesis snare herself. Into the driveway across the alley eased a pastel sedan with a trunk containing the one box Mrs. Microwave would tonight be popping into her namesake appliance. Frozen Southern-style drumsticks retrieved, she crossed the emerald ChemLawn, ponytail tick-tocking, tight jeans causing her to walk like she had chopsticks for legs that the rest of her body did not know how to use. *Swoosh, swoosh, swoosh,* oh no. Disgust. Confusion. Looking down at Mr. Rush's gift, she appeared to be asking herself if a dog could have done it. One knee lifted very high, then the other knee, and with the grace of a hurdler in traction, she vaulted the rhubarb, and called Mr. Microwave at work. Evidently he advised donning Isotoner gloves and dumping the crap in the trash. Only, rhubarb was not easily dumped: the stalks prepared to fight for the respect due any charter member of the illustrious four food groups. She slammed down the lid and the lid bounced off, repelled by flexing *petioles*. She repeated the procedure, with the same result. She bared her teeth. She grabbed a brick off another can. I closed my eyes...The next day, however, there was no avoiding the sorrowful sight of five limp stalks trailing down the side of the can like the wilted horns of unicorns caught in a trap. I lifted one with a stick: dead and heavy. A weight on the mind. I had abetted the horrific waste, not believing in the power of rhubarb like mother and Mr. Rush did—treating that bundle like a cheap prankster prop rather than like the hale stuff of cafeteria pies that in their sourness expressed everything the rose dare not. *Had I believed* . . . And it must be possible to respect both messages, mustn't it? Why be picky? The more life you could find a way to accept, the more life there was for you. *Had I believed in horticulture hocus-pocus* . . . The brick might have popped off the lid in the middle of the night . . . the rhubarb perking up and the longest muddiest stalk floating over the lawn, through an open window and into the room where Mrs. Microwave was sleeping in skintight jeans because she could not get them off. Three waves of the dirty wand and the denim curse was broken. Mrs. Microwave was free, loose and expanding to knock Mr. Microwave out of bed. "Wha wrong?" he asked. "I feel like I haven't eaten in years!" she shouted, and snatched the mid-air stalk to make a nice fresh rhubarb sauce . . . only nothing nice and fresh existed to ladle it over.

MR. RUSH DID NOT TAKE any rhubarb dumping wrong. Why, an alley lined with stalk-stuffed cans was no cause to pout; rather, it was irrefutable proof that homemakers were so stocked up on the rustic delight that waste had become a blessed necessity. In the same undaunted spirit he remunerated delivery boys with liberty dimes (worn faceless by all the fingers passed through since 1923) as if spending freshly engraved Eisenhower coins would bring him catastrophically up-to-date, clearing the mental loan of age-old deposits a fertile present depended on. Arbor Day too he celebrated—planting a sapling in nearby Lindsay

Park. And on Armistice Day he kept an eye out for veterans with red poppies pinned to starched uniforms. *Had the parade taken a wrong turn? Were the floats, marching bands, and doughboys lost on a country road, crunching gravel and spooking pheasants?* Those holidays were trusty—albeit rusty—keys to comprehending the passage of time, and damned if he was going to give them up. And damned if his enthusiasm for May Day didn't infect my family and inspire us to weave and fill construction paper baskets with plastic grass and jelly beans and other fertility symbols

from Ben Franklin's candy department. Elizabeth hung a green basket on Mr. Hickey's door, knocked, then ran. I hung a yellow one on Mr. Rush's door, knocked, then ran. Neither hearing aid registered the banging. But by noon the baskets were off those door knobs and the celebration in full freaky swing. Lunch was yellow—7UP dyed bright yellow with the same food coloring my pregnant mother dribbled into the chicken soup to give its color a matching brilliant glow that every cracker then also assumed when dunked. Yellow, she explained, because May Day was the "Main Street Pagan Easter." What did that mean? Yellow for chickadees. Yellow for the sun. Poor Mrs. Nichol's face when I proclaimed it May Day. She flushed and snapped: "Young man. That's a communist affair!" *Not the red holiday the yellow holiday*, I pointed out and for her error received another demerit—bringing my total nearer the amount that triggered a visit to Mr. Jones, a principal who had sacrificed a big toe for his country in Korea and wore a wooden shoe plug. What a relief, then, what a joy to get home and find the maypole mother had made by taping crepe streamers to the tetherball pole sticking out of a bucket of cement. Oh, did Mr. Rush start when he saw our wild dance! (The rhubarb stalks, too, appeared to stand up straighter—eager to get in on the action.) The shovel dropped right out of Mr. Rush's hands. "Hoo-aye!" he honked. "Hoo-aye!" gummily grinning. Me skipping. Elizabeth skipping. Howard skipping. Big-bellied mother skipping, flush with the hope that a fourth child would bring her the happiness we others had not. (And why any children? What was magic about children? We were the opposite of magic. We were a mob ransacking rooms. We pulled and pushed her, and we bent her out of shape.) She shouted her favorite line from *A Child's Garden of Verses* by Robert Louis Stevenson: "The world is so full of a number of things! / I'm sure we should all be as happy as kings!"

MY MOTHER, I BRAGGED to any kid who would listen, took me to intersections—the dangerous kind. There her face turned the color of rhubarb. She squeezed my hand like it was the big one, the adult one. The world then was full of many things too many. The world then might kill us. We went most to the spot at the bottom of the alley where Jersey Road was met by Kirkwood Boulevard and Fulton Street and Bridge Street. When she did not stand there squeezing my hand to death she stood there in her old dress, arms up-flung, revealing the blue moon under each arm where she violently shaved with father's Gillette razor. She was trying to stop the cars with her waves, I thought, and she was failing. Traffic thundered by, buzzing the sheen of her shins. The engine roar worked on her. Soon enough, in the aggrieved voice of a seven-year-old, she would spit bits of memories. It was here—beside a rushing river of chrome and exhaust—that she first told me about being sent by her mother to get her father at the tavern in Dixon. And also of jumping out of a car and rolling into a ditch and being caught between the road and the railroad tracks and the canal. I connected these two bits eventually. I connected them because I needed the bits to add up to some larger story that would explain her pain. Each little bit of telling changed her face—carved it into a pear, a bellows, a punctured globe, a dented pillow. I pictured a hairy hand grabbing her in a tavern. Sometimes the hand was Grandpa's and other times it was a stranger's. I pictured a hand grabbing a pinafore in a dark doorway, another covering a little mouth, and a girl stuffed legs-first into the car that she jumped from either in the nick of time or after the worst had happened in the backseat. The car speeding out of town? Back into town? I never dared ask. Mother forgot to breathe. She buzzed with stymied haste. Her skin smudged as if she had been born and grown old at this intersection.

MR. RUSH NEVER TOSSED out a tool, no matter how splintered the handle, toothless the blade. Corroded buckets were kicked in an attempt to knock orange crusties off the virgin metal that surely existed below—or they were until the day he put his foot through a bucket, hopped into the garage, and did not come out for a long time. Blushing in the dark, like mother, like the ripe rhubarb. When the roof's shadow had drifted over the entirety of the backyard, he watered the garden a second time, unreeling hose from a squeaky wheel affixed to the side of the house. Too much hose. Unneeded yards of hose piled around scuffed boots dampened black by the shimmering halos of mist hovering in the wake of the swift foamy stream. Rhubarb bucked wildly when hit, drooling on pansies that bobbed like fleeing extras in a Godzilla flick. Releasing the trigger, Mr. Rush hiked the tinted visor brim and noted the temperature of the air, wind speed, the hue of the sinking sun. He looked to the north, where the cold came from. He looked to the south and its warmth. He looked east, in the direction of the Mississippi River, so close but secluded behind a montage of roofs. From my bedroom window I could see its brown welding Iowa to Illinois. The river stank. It contained mercury and killed fish. It mucked showboat paddle wheels with sewage. The news was all over the paper that father hid behind each evening rather than watch mother vanish in another cloud of car exhaust, destination Kmart or the sickbed of Granny Stanley. In many different and astonishing ways nature could enter your life to do you a bad turn or great favor. So wary and expectant was the expression on Mr. Rush's wrinkled face as he gauged the weather over his garden. And on my soft face, also, whenever I stretched out on the dirt to watch much bigger clouds than mother float free through the unponderable blue. Schooners, dragons, skulls, taffeta train engines . . . *tickle-tickle* on the bottom of my bare foot.

Who? The ancient man gripping a broom and laughing, proud of himself for having brought a boy back to bountiful Iowa, and the good work waiting to be done. *But, Mr. Rush*, I wanted to ask, looking down at the string beans, the tomatoes, the rhubarb—that splendorous but small window on what had been—*Where is the rest of the garden?* The sun and rain alluded continually to its existence, only to be shunted aside at ground level by umbrellas, streets, garages, air-conditioning. The city's hold on the land had been in the finger-whitening grip of the gardener on a trowel during a scuffle with an unruly rutabaga. And most all those Methuselahs of mulch were buried now or worse: enduring nursing home sing-a-longs and whipped potatoes. Mr. Rush's living dirt was not the dry kind in my yard. Our terrace existed only to archive dog urine and Stingray treads, time's endless skid and trudge. Good-bye, clock-stopping explosions of color. Spring and fall reduced to a tree here, a bush there, with white siding in between. *And good riddance*, roared a car rocketing up the steep alley. Who among the ninety thousand citizens corralled inside the curl of Interstate 80 had a spare hour to tend the paradise they had been granted? The Vietnam War had not spawned verdant victory gardens but angry rows of protesters, bushels of hair and a general frantic awareness that "time was short." Better to subsist on California lettuce and Mexican tomatoes, fitting cardboard accompaniments to any entrée out of a box. The hours and energy saved could then be spent shopping for a perfect little something that briefly returned to a life the wealth—or hearty flavor—it had lost. My family was as guilty of this futile pursuit as any microwave clan, the difference being that we heated our frozen pizzas and egg rolls in a gas oven, after shooing out the roaches. And bought with our eyes what we could not afford, methodically weaving a sanitary new existence around a cool shirt or toy, visited weekly

in aisle eight, until another sleek object took its place on the shelf and in the empty heart. Such dreamless dreaming was too often the only alternative. How could any of us—rich or poor—do better, given that our natural inheritance had unaccountably vanished? Gone like mother's wedding snapshots (if there had ever been any) and our wedding drawings, too, ornate but no replacement for the homely truth and therefore torn up by the ashamed artists. It was embarrassing to be out of touch with what you should know best. It made you want to shelter behind the thick dull shield of a brand name or cover up the source of your shame, as the city tried to do by paving its fallow territory—every acre, every mile. *Davenport adrift.* Residents floating on sidewalk slabs, asphalt, thin Sakrete, and those higher grades of cement slopping like manure out of the revolving polka-dot behinds of municipal trucks. The concrete pitted with rocks and shells. The concrete smooth and white as a hospital sheet. I cataloged the types while walking to and from McKinley Elementary—it was something to do while humming "Raindrops Keep Fallin' on My Head." And one day saw frantic workers unrolling a long sod gown to cover a strip of nude ground. And another afternoon—remember that?—rode with Mr. Rush and mother to Walgreens drugstore. She drove. We sat in back. The buckles of his overalls clicked as he attempted to show me the places along the route where he had shot ducks. "Right thore!" He pointed to a Henry's Hamburger outlet—seeing the the water, the reeds, perhaps the green sheen of feathers in the Remington's sight. "Thore too!" he honked and pointed at the glass garage door of a muffler shop, forested with opaque reflections of passing traffic.

ROMANCING THE DANKERTS

Sir Galakeg — A sad little something inside everyone —
Yawn behind the spatula — The disease called Swagger —
Pompeii biscuits — The loudest laughter — Landfill duty —
Whiffle ball rescue — Runge funeral home — A braver Ben

W HEN THE NONAGENARIAN SPORTSMAN Mr. Rush died of what the doctor termed "a major stroke" and what I'll call an attack of common sense (i.e., the epiphany it was best to depart now that Duck Creek Plaza—a strip mall—covered the slough where he had once kneeled in a camouflaged blind, picking off pintail ducks), a childless couple by the name of Dankert purchased the white house with cherry trim and erected chain-link fencing to keep their dear habitat clear of the flotsam and jetsam of Miller family life. This backyard barrier stood at the bottom of the short steep hill separating the two terraces, frail aluminum veil of privacy amending the little provided by latitude. To say the dwellings were on top of one another is not far from the truth. Had I preadolescent life insurance, I might have tied a magnet to my Zebco fishing rod and, with a short downward cast out the dining room window, trolled the Dankerts' roof gutter for treasure. Being unindemnified, I didn't dare risk leaving my younger brothers and sisters without a shoulder to cry on, as Mr. Dankert was the huge man who delivered Budweiser beer for a living. He battered open tack-studded tavern doors with the keg-loaded dolly—the "old man" taprooms where poker was played, and the new saloons where there were arm-wrestling contests and wet T-shirt contests and Attack the Mouth Night (the Mouth being the nickname of Howard Cosell, *Monday Night Football* host, and the Attack taking the form of abuse of an old TV with blunt instruments whenever Cosell's visage appeared). Mr. Dankert also lugged twenty-four-can "suitcases" into stinky urban Iowa markets sporting nursery rhyme names like Jack 'n' Jill and stale dry goods that likely had been shelved when the besmocked teenage employees were in nursery school. This fascinating new neighbor of ours drove home for lunch, wedging his large truck into the teeny driveway at an aggressive diagonal angle so that it blocked a mere three-quarters of the alley, allowing motorists the option of parking, continuing on foot. Airbrushed on the trailer was a charging team of Clydesdale horses with tasseled hooves and cape-like manes, above which hovered the ornate Anheuser-Busch *A*—quixotic scarlet letter promoting the converse of abstinence: *This Bud's for You!* (Hawthorne, roll over in your grave. Or not? Just as Lucifer purportedly owned a controlling share in Procter and Gamble for the purpose of promoting paganism via crescent moon logos on baking powder boxes, had a Puritan God co-opted the St. Louis beer company in order to systematically

brand the Midwest as punishment for a legion of secret sins?
Anheuser *A*'s blazing in bar windows tinted purple to conceal the
frolic fueled by hops and hormones. *A*'s basting on sunlit stadium
walls, highway billboards, block-party banners. *A*'s stamped
across T-shirts, duffel bags, ceramic collector steins, foam-rubber
can caddies raised high by college kids tubing down Wisconsin's
Apple River, laughter melting into forest fringe...) Boulder-girth
gut dropping to the driveway, Mr. Dankert resembled a dismount-
ing crusader back from an unholy Holy War. He slammed the cab
door hard, and I noted a flash of wedding band—a gold liquidity

of vows always altering to accommodate new circumstances. In fall and spring he wore a masterpiece of art known as the Teamster Jacket Patch. This thread sculpture of a wagon wheel—almost 3-D in density—rivaled any work by Picasso I had ogled, and I had ogled *Blue Boy*. In the summer his blue shirt gaped open like a battle wound to reveal a swatch of sunburned skin. Old tattoos misting muscular forearms. Wide perforated weight belt that could easily have supported an Arthurian sword. And the hair, the hair. Macaroni ringlets of "permed" locks slathered with salon butter, gleaming brownly. When the most popular, most unfortunate hairdo of 1976 swiveled in the direction of our sprawling lilac bush, trampled yard, house slung with tongues of peeling paint, an ejaculation of indignation resulted, whether or not any wild whirling child of Tommy Lynn was outdoors to hear it. "Pick that shit up!" commanded Sir Galakeg. *That shit* being the litter heaped against the fence, a dense moat of crap that in other years had been neatly dispersed across Mr. Rush's unfenced lawn. "Clean it up now! Or else I'll …" go inside the hovel helmeted with metal awnings and scarf a ham sandwich, because that's what he always did, having many more Piggly Wigglys to visit and little time to spare.

AT THIS TIME OF DAY Mrs. Dankert would just be up and putting herself back together with the aid of Avon cosmetics and a small magnifying mirror on a deftly extending hinge. That glass revealed no more of her face than she wanted to see. The slender mineral seam of an eyebrow arching over a tiny dark cave in which a dilated pupil floated. Lips that did not look so slack and uneven when glimpsed apart from the powdered pug nose.

Three unsprung coils of auburn hair that were an unsightly—but acceptable—anomaly when quarantined inside the steel arc of the mirror rim, safely tucked away from other coils shot to hell by hot curlers. Sixteen nights a week—at least it seemed that way sometimes—she tended bar and waited on tan booths at Lindsay Park Lounge, a staid establishment catering to those who did not like rock-and-roll jukeboxes and the riots that loud music triggered in the imagination, if nowhere else. What did she remember about last evening? Bending to take an order and the reward of three whiffs of a newcomer who had the waxy creamy scent of candles just blown out? Often Freddy Fender's romantic tenor quavered from the rainbow rental machine in this joint, seeping through speakers with the pigmentation of scaled trout. "Before the next teardrop falls..." he crooned to patrons watching and not watching *The Tonight Show* (then *Tomorrow* hosted by the sallow Tom Snyder darting like a five-foot angular gray-breasted swallow on the gabfest couch) on a Quasar television clamped above a bar with elbow-friendly padding. Turtle eyes of bored patrons crawled over the homey skyline of bottles: Smirnoff, Gordon's, Jim Beam, Mr. Boston...climbed to a bulging screen where impish Nebraska native Johnny Carson wagged pencils, feigned golf swings, traded jibes with Doc Severinsen the peacock and jocular slob Ed McMahon, when Ed was not holding an open can of Alpo dog food in one hand and a large orange dish in the other. Then a barking Irish setter bounded into the picture, teeth bared, tongue dangling, yet looking and sounding more civilized than Ed in white loafers and wide pink tie, laughing for no reason while disgorging gooey beef chunks into the bowl. (It actually looked pretty tasty.) Baritone ad-babble commingled with another delicate chorus of "Before the Next Teardrop Falls"—the first song in *Billboard* history to simultaneously top the country and pop charts, for reasons music executives are certainly still studying. "Mary!" a beehive hairdo buzzed. "This jerk of mine is full of the beans." "Oh yeah," the Jerk retorted. "If you can't beat 'em, join 'em." The waitress had no genuine smile to offer, substituting a mock expression of intense irritation that caused rumps to wiggle with pleasure on duct-taped booth cushions. She kept shaking a metal martini mixer streaked by bright taffy-like reflections of the dull scene. Another mixer, etched with a volume ladder, held swizzle sticks of many colors. Next to that was a condiment trolly containing Spanish olives, pickled pearl onions, green cherries. Displayed on the wall behind her—on all walls—were needlepoint-font placards, souvenir license plates, whittled signboards, each bearing a cliché that would be of much use later in the evening when patrons were deep in their cups and, like TV comedians, needed cue cards to be funny. LIFE BEGINS AT 70. I'M WITH STUPID. PENNIES SELDOM FALL FROM HEAVEN SO PLEASE TIP! ALL OF OUR GUESTS BRING HAPPINESS, SOME BY COMING, OTHERS BY GOING. IF I WAS AS SMART AS MY HUSBAND, I'D BE IN PRISON TOO. "What's goin' on out there?" the fuddy-duddy chorus chanted at the waitress, now at the window and gazing through a gold maze of hand-painted letters (L I N D S A Y P A R K   L O U N G E) that filtered dullness from an ordinary view the way colander comets cosomologized plain old water. Finger planked under nose to keep from sneezing, Mary thought: *Somewhere something is happening, I can feel it. I can feel it.* Across Eleventh Street stood the Turner Hall, where German immigrants in tank tops once romped on pommel horses before retreating to the basement to quaff beer brewed on the premises in copper vats. The Hall starred in the annual tour of "The Old Village of East Davenport," led by an amateur historian in blue stretch pants, Mrs. Manhardt. Near the brick building were basketball hoops with chain nets that rattled in the wind, scaring the bejesus out of Mary whenever she locked up, nerves frayed, feet aching. Behind the hoops, asphalt tennis courts, half-lit, attracted reddish yellow moths that floated like ashes from a phantasmagorical fire. And beyond Lindsay Park—the crayon scrawl of taillights on River Drive, a corroded subdivision of unhitched Old Milwaukee Road boxcars and the Davenport yachting club, where professional men gathered on weekends to get "plowed," sipping gin under a scalloped dock tent while admiring their sleek sailboats designed for Great Lakes action, not the marauding Mississippi. On the river flowed, bending past cities that echoed channel turbulence, nothing straight or simple about them, neon gnarls of bluffs, One Ways, hulking bridges. On and on the brownish or gray-green water churned, according to one fairy tale, bearing away a sad little something inside everyone looking toward the swirling current. In reality, slapping levees leaky, clawing trees off exposed shoreline, dragging summer swimmers to their deaths, and winnowing ice cover so fishermen fell through and drowned in their Ford pickups. "Another round of gimlets, Mary. Quarters for the jukebox too." Five songs for a buck. Titles printed on serrated strips of paper tucked into little rectangular frames—double red line separating A side from B side. Big ivory buttons that wiggled like loose walrus incisors, clicking when depressed, popping up when every important choice had been made. Songs that cured a poisoned attitude or tainted merriment with the tang of melancholy, melodic transfusions. The automatic arm swiveled, vinyl discs shuffled. "Tie a yellow ribbon round the ole oak tree..." chirped Tony Orlando. Then came Tony Bennett's terse version of "Send in the Clowns." "My Melody of Love," sung by Bobby Vinton, the so-called Polish prince. One more Ray Conniff chart-topper that sounded like everything Ray Conniff—strings vibrating in a jam jar.

TO WORK MARY DANKERT WORE CLOTHING more suited to a branch librarian than a barmaid, starched beige blouses, wool skirts. This organic gift for neutrality must have been part of what attracted Mr. Dankert to her. In this woman he had an implacable listener who considered loathsome oaths and slurs to be nothing more than a spate of bad weather passing through the kitchen on its way to another location. And in him she had a reliable mate who saw no reason to be bigger than his worst fears and so became them—thunder that amply explained itself, leaving nothing to mystery. On many a hot Saturday afternoon the delivery man planted a cooler atop the backyard picnic table and fired up the gas grill occupying a spot near where Mr. Rush's rhubarb plants once grew to a height of three feet. Hidden by the big lilac bush, I cataloged the clichés. Little that they shouted was not stale but the staleness boiled with life, you betcha. The shallow waters of clichés had the deep power to return to the lonely a semblance of community. *For my money talking turkey it takes all kinds on the barrelhead in the long haul naked as a jaybird this must be the place between a rock and a get a load of that toeing the line in the swing without a pot to piss in hair of the dog two wrongs don't make a right.* I noted the nearness of forking blue flames to Mr. Dankert's hairdo, weighing the proper course of action if the thinkable unthinkable happened and mousse ignited. *Grab the hose? But wasn't he beyond saving? Doomed by the tragicomic dream of upward mobility—a fantasy that gouged the heart with a deforming desire to reference the good life not yet being lived via the adaptation of a preposterous diamond pinkie ring from Zales or salon non sequitur embarrassing as a donkey's tail pinned in the wrong place? Douse those burning bangs and like as not he'd buy a blond wig in the same yearning style and be stomped to death at a truck stop by a fellow teamster.* Out came

Mary cradling a platter of hamburger patties neatly formed and marinated all night in Löwenbräu. Smoke thickened and darkened: peppery fumes so deliciously rich that smelling them was an act involving teeth. Parting leafy lilac branches, I covertly feasted on the turfy scent of searing beef—chewsniff, sniffswallow. The Dankerts had no idea how generous they were. Across the cracked alley strutted the usual guests—Mr. Neville, owner of The Mound Tap, wearing a tan safari suit, and his rotund wife in a silky purple V-necked poncho dress befitting a supervisor of go-go girls. Perspiring long-necked bottles of Bud were pried from cooler ice, cigarettes lit with opalescent Bic lighters. Steak sauce spattered the grill tray. Mrs. Dankert grabbed a rag. She didn't look irritated but captivated by the latest cleaning job. Like she was trying hard to erase the tray, reach whatever was underneath. Spanking widely parted knees, Mr. Dankert related the latest jokes learned on his winding route from winking bartenders and tavern regulars with facial features faded in the deep fashion of stone engravings. Somehow they always had a new one, those fog-shrouded mile markers sitting crooked in front of tin ashtrays, warm soapy drafts. Another tired bulletin about foreigners unable to screw lightbulbs and a pornographic tale re: a blind lawyer or absentminded prostitute or painfully confused newlywed or mole with the memory of an elephant or elephant with a prick the size of a pea. Laughter coursed from a cavern inside the men, sounding like pneumonia in July. It was almost—no it was—it was as obscene as the afternoon the Irish setter and a poodle got stuck while humping on Mr. Hickey's hillside. The table radio could barely be heard above the lung-clatter and all the better, since Jack Brickhouse was gently breaking more bad news to a dispersed universe of Cubs fans: *Bases loaded, no outs, Cardinals slugger Ted Simmons at the plate.* Mrs. Dankert hid a yawn with the spatula, staring at the greasy tray as if pondering its unerasableness. Mrs. Neville, strap sandals off and piggy feet awiggle under the table, poured beer into a glass she had requested, sun-struck liquid flowing like hourglass sand. She swigged, dabbed lips with a napkin folded into the perfect tricorner lip-dabbing shape, ever the proper go-go girl manager. She worried out loud about a dancer named Trudi ("Takes fifteen minutes to strip off what the others drop in one."), then lamented the state of her own expanding waistline as Mrs. Dankert sleepily tended smoldering patties, pressing, turning, easing down the vented grill hood and excusing herself: "That cooler's getting low on beer."

ONE SUNDAY MR. DANKERT'S SCRAWNY FATHER arrived with a twelve-pack, ending the party by joining it. Obviously the son had not inherited his sense of humor from this dour individual, who had the malicious air of a friendless bounty hunter—a man able to do without everything but the cash reward received for each severed head. A bucking bronco belt buckle capped the spot where his stomach should have been. Stubble lined the knife edge of the Adam's apple, and ten-gallon cowboy boots ricocheted off stick legs like fancy medical braces for males afflicted with the disease called Swagger. Suddenly Mr. and Mrs. Neville needed to be at the Mound Tap for an interview with lazy Trudi's potential replacement. *Ever been arrested, Miss Randi Handy? Willing to work on holidays?* Mary, she had dirty dishes to do and Mr. Dankert had a date with his old man—to drink, to grunt, to stare through the chain-link fence at Millercrap surrounding the little backyard. That pair might talk a bunch of garbage, but clearly did not approve of our kind—a trash tsunami confirming the fear which inspired their dirty jokes and bowlegged bravado, that Dankert terror of being the butt of ridicule, disrespected in the extreme. "Hey, four eyes!" the geezer shouted at me, waddling down the alley, finger probing a small yellow bag, ever hopeful the computerized machine at the Chicago junk food factory was prey to boredom and capable of every now and again whimsically inserting four fat corn chips instead of the regulation three. "I'm talking to *you, punk.*" I knew who he was talking to. No other punk was around. But I looked in the opposite direction, at Mr. Hickey's prim house on the terrace above our dump, safely upwind. What a geographical blessing. For had our litter collected in his treasured rose bushes, even that generous man might have erected a tall fence, denying us refuge in his warm tidy kitchen, with its many practical pleasures. Hot air on the back of my neck ended the reverie. Dankert Sr.! He was breathless from galloping through the gate. Toothless too. "Cart away that shit now or yubber-dubber-yubber-duyub." He kept yubbering until the message came through: "...or get a midnight visit from Sheriff Blackie Stroud's posse." *Sticks and stones can break my bones but threats can never hurt me.* Unless accompanied by bad breath and his was putrid, reeking of sour cottage cheese, peanut butter, JELL-O, and Anheuser yeast. Smelling and seeing those nude gray gums yapping above sagging zigzag seams of a Kmart western shirt caused me to realize for the first time precisely why so many galoots his age took pleasure in cigars with plastic tips. Sticking that white filter into your maw was akin to sprouting a new molar, being six years old again, with a whole unwholesome life ahead of you. "What's it gonna be, turkey? Cleanup or the posse?" I now looked to my second, that crazy house of ours, covered with curling curdled tongues of paint, and I prayed that one—*just one old tongue*—would come to my defense—flinging fierce dizzying

sentences. *Tell him, House. Tell him you put forth your mean-
est face in order to frighten off the same enemies as those on the
Dankert hit list. Haughty Rotarians. Sleazy loan officers. Naive
UNICEF volunteers. Shout, House, that we share a battle strategy
with the Dankerts. Our best defense being to give great offense—to
live the unprintable life!* No way could I get all that out. I had
been scared speechless by the word "posse." Disturbingly near in
sound to "pussy," the term nonetheless referred—I knew from late
night westerns like *The Good, the Bad and the Ugly*—to scarred
men carrying sawed-off shotguns, riding mangy horses, wearing flaring chaps that may well have been designed to conceal a
mutant genital called the "posse"—snail horns and gristle mounds
a-swirl in a foaming pubic pool. "What's it gonna be?" Hours of
filling bags while unhappy men finished the twelve-pack, glaring to make sure the job got done right. Another spectator was
the weeping willow sapling Elizabeth had obtained through the
mail and planted near the alley at the far end of the toxic clutter.
It was her birthday present. It was going to live, mother said, but
Elizabeth had big doubts. As I waded into the mess we had made,
the single by the funk-rock band War hit the turntable in my mind
and began to spin. Lyrics asked repeatedly why people could not
be friends. Why can't we? Why? The beat was my kind of beat,
up front and driving. The song sounded best when blaring out of
speakers at a public pool at noon in August, the air a roux of heat
and chlorine. My mental turntable struggled to replicate the inspiring effect. I bent over, slowly. I did not want a back injury or a
tetanus infection or a cardiac event. I filled my arms with litter and
then got a better idea. I pulled out the front of my Penguin shirt
and filled it like a bag. I could carry more that way—not much
more—but some. I made trips—alley to yard, yard to alley. It was
as if a matchmaker of a tornado had strived and failed to join all

that was Dankert to all that was Miller. Another marriage doomed from the start.

DURING THE EXCAVATION I discovered no Dankert crap. It was all our crap. Would I uncover the lost pinafore of waif Tommy Lynn, who had rolled into a ditch after jumping from her attacker's Buick in my imagination? Would I unearth a bent splint or other proof that Dr. Miller had set his son's broken leg wrong to punish him for wanting to be an airy-fairy artist instead of a doctor like his other two sons? No such luck. I found Pillsbury biscuits that had petrified Pompeii-style (jibing with my feeling that one year in our diffuse family saga counted for decades or centuries), the geology of a fruit cake, Totino's pizza slices maggots considered inedible, freezer bags coated with tater tot crumbs, a Hefty bag containing the mildewed dregs from snack mix that had been dinner for a week in April (mother, improvising domestic mobster—her, the momster—combining boxes of Chex cereal with broken pretzel sticks, Cheez-It crackers, Spanish peanut husks, cashew pieces, and smothering the salty fodder in melted Lady Lee margarine, and sealing the bag not well, and rolling it across the living room carpet clutter, a Christmas treat originally and now a year-round staple). Under the garbage bag of momster manna lurked molten cuds of the crepe paper that traditionally played a major part in birthday celebrations, webbing the living room, dining room, sun porch. And the ink had run, dying Dankert grass nuclear orange, urine yellow. Nonchalantly I toed the technicolor patches until the colors dulled, much as Cub pitcher Milt Pappas raked raked raked mound dirt with his cleats when the next batter was the Pirates' slugger Willie Stargell, best faced by a reliever warming in the bullpen. Then I had a vision of tinsel streaming out of our chimney: an eruption of overheated attic Christmas decorations foretold in some Bible somewhere. Then I serenaded myself with "Eleanor Rigby"—that saddest line of all their sad lines—Paul singing of Eleanor's funeral: "nobody came." It occurred to me that worse than dying would be to attend the funeral of a mother or a father and not cry, not be able to cry, dead to loss. I believed Elizabeth worried about the same issue. We had a special way of tormenting ourselves with ifs. But the not being able to cry was a natural concern when you had a mother who giggled when she should have wept, who kept gargling a tear too large to be released, stuck behind the dilated pupils, walled-in and sloshing. I made important eye contact with the dehydrated weeping willow—it was thin-limbed like Elizabeth and not so much weeping but moping as she moped, rigidly. Then I gathered fragments of the Beatles' 45 "Baby, You're a Rich Man" from the copse a fence formed. I picked up a dog-chewed superball, a cracked whiffle ball, a purple freebee Frisbee with fatal aerodynamic flaws that had been given out by a used car dealership on Kimberly Road, ant-corpse-covered Dreamsicle sticks, a plastic brown bottle of hydrogen peroxide that momster had emptied to subdue tooth pain—swishing spitting swishing spitting, crumpled cans of Shasta cream soda and grape soda and other unpopular flavors on perpetual sale at Target—*4 for $1*, slender L&M candy cigarette boxes, butterscotch wrappers that when slickened with saliva and slapped on the lenses of my eyeframes made present-day civilization appear congealed in amber, *whoa*.

I WISHED IT WAS 10:30, when reruns of the BBC *Monty Python* episodes on Iowa Public Television brought our family together like nothing else could. For a half hour, almost all of us were there—minus two or three—and laughing our guts out at twits struggling to step over matchboxes and tennis-player limbs flying off during matches and cross-dressing lumberjacks and the two-hundred-pound weight that dropped out of nowhere and crushed tiresome royalty. The loudest laughter came from the one who laughed the least under regular circumstances: our father interred on the recliner. He lost it, to put it kindly, as Cleese and Palin cavorted. The rumble in the deepest quadrants of his cig-charred lungs built and built until cathartic gasps resulted, the chins and tits heaving and the nose releasing a smoke-tinged violet mist as his legs bounced on the padded rest. But it was not Python Time. It was Central Standard Dankert Time.

I GATHERED READ CRUSTS—portions of paperback poetry anthologies that had not made it through the night intact—and bread crusts too, those crusts singing birds had gladly passed over. Spinach cans; tamale cans; chile con carne cans; the box formerly full of Bugles; the Kotex box; the cardboard tabs to who-knew-what urban Iowa boxes of sustenance; tatters of a red balloon once squeakily bent into a giraffe shape by the Pier 1 Grand Opening clown Mr. Honks; a heavy urban folk shawl woven of Blatz can segments and vomit-colored yarn; maps of Wisconsin, Ohio, Georgia, Illinois, Missouri, Utah, North Carolina, Nebraska, and South Dakota (it being the habit of we children to denude the Road Guide rack in the Gulf station office each time a dollar of gas was purchased and then pack the glove compartment with travel info, a ploy designed to encourage the old car to *please finally go somewhere rather than merely hinting at escape with every creak and cough while carrying us nowhere*

but deeper into family trouble); worthless utility infielder baseball
cards; inartistic Richie Rich and Sad Sack and Archie comic
published by Gold Key; Wacky Pack stickers I had quadruples of
(*Liptorn Molten Lava Soup, Plastered Whiskey Flavored Peanuts, Slopicana Orangutan Juice—100% peels, Head & Boulders
Shampoo—For people with rocks in their heads*); a water-swollen
paperback edition of *The Collector* by John Fowles about to birth
a sequel (*a novel about a collector of men who collect girls like but-
terflies?*); pale-blue pamphlets on subjects such as horse-raising,
crop-tending, rural electricity, Arizona geology, meteorology that
I had ordered from the gray Government Printing Agency catalog
because they cost a quarter or nothing but fifteen cents "postage
and handling"; the indestructible white dust jacket of *All Creatures Great and Small* by James Herriot, the English veterinarian
who had made millions with uplifting stories about bloody lamb
births and stuck horse fetuses; loads of unopened Miller Residence mail (I see/hear my father picking up the phone as a last
resort, eight rings, no one else around, his voice an icicle hanging
in the air: "Miller Residence"); loads and loads of antique mail
including many invoices from Book of the Month for popular
novels that had been mistakenly sent to us, as well as bills from
MasterCard, Mobil Oil, Sears, Roebuck and Co., Montgomery
Ward, J. C. Penney, Blue Cross Blue Shield; three toilet seat covers one of my hygiene-minded sisters had stolen from Bishop's
Buffet as a Christmas present for Aunt Julie so she wouldn't have
to stand over our black commode and risk injury as she had the
night Marianna peeked through a crack in the battered bathroom
door; will copies (*I, Barney Johansen, being of sound mind and
body . . .*) and other sensitive documents from the moldering side-
yard heap of Attorney David P. Miller's office files; an aquatic box
once home to a school of fish sticks; a La Choy carton formerly

containing a cure for a strep throat (according to momster, who after placing a sticky hand on the forehead of a feverish child often prescribed egg rolls or in severe cases an exotic frozen hors d'oeuvre called crab rangoon); Nathan's plastic Pamper washed magically clean of the horror that once lurked in it; a stained sheet from a bed I had wet at an unmentionably old age (gravy-lines of dried piss); pillowcase ticking Nanette had curiously sucked and sweetly referred to as her "lickee"; a pinstriped railroad cap from Marianna's tomboy stage; nothing at all belonging to Elizabeth— the family's sole neat nut; Swisher Sweet butts (Howard's); and

a BaskinRobbins Birthday Club postcard worth an ice cream cone that had been sent last year to Him Too Cool to Redeem It and which I had pocketed, in case the offer might still be valid, not considering until a few seconds later how wickedly the drunk Dankerts might interpret such scavenging. Immediately I pivoted, looking straight at those men to prove I had nothing to hide and thus convince them that they had not seen what they had seen—a trick learned from momster, who daily employed the stare-down to intimidate cashiers, librarians, clerks, and meter maids. Father and son ignored me, however. The beer and the humidity had finally stunned them insensible. *Quitting time.* I exited the trash moat, lugging a last shirt full of crap past the willow sapling. Branches cast no shade. The pattern on the ground that of a filleted shadow, darkness cut away to reveal trampled dust. Such an ache I felt looking down at the crossed tread marks of our negligent mob. Pain not just in my back, from the bending and squatting to retrieve trash, but all over a withering sense that this was no childhood, that too soon I had been assigned landfill duty—the responsibility for managing the waste that often came of human potential. A spirit flatlines, a dream shatters, and fragments rain down on relatives and neighbors and strangers, no matter how young, how culpable, how disinterested. You pick slivers out of your tennis shoes. You pick slivers out of your hair. *And still they keep coming!* Can't sit, might get buried alive by mother crap, father crap, brother crap, sister crap, uncle crap, aunt crap, grandpa crap, granny crap, and foulest of all—your own crap, reeking of ammonia and monosodium glutamate.

IT WAS ALSO MY LOT—being the oldest—to retrieve any ball that ignorantly sailed over the Dankert fence, rolling under the picnic table. During the morning hours—with Mrs.

Dankert asleep and the randy team of Clydesdales out of the stable, dashing from watering trough to watering trough—I could unlatch the gate without *too much* fear of being captured, although the grass felt disturbingly aware of the security breach, damp turf recording each step for a court trial. It was another story after Mr. Dankert whipped the house to life with nasty noontime quips ("So the bastard says to me, Mary. He says...") and stormed back to the truck, shifting into a reckless gear that caused the trailer to rattle, buck, shoot backwards down the alley, pulverizing trash cans and once nearly killing the postman with the peanut head. Then I had to rap on the door and request permission to enter the yard from Mrs. Dankert in the most charming tone I could muster: "Very sorry to disturb you, m'am, but, well..." The face in the dim foyer was a peach hue, grainy with makeup. Not even Avon could enliven those slack lips or brighten the eye caves anymore. The house coat. "My ball...it..." She nodded slowly, wordlessly like before, but it always seemed a major miracle. Why not berate me? Too tired from the long night's journey into day? Or was Mrs. Dankert—of all the neighbors—wise enough to *surmise* the message on the tip of each tongue of paint appending our decrepit house? Did she rightly guess that the noisy, dirty, violent, intellectually insatiable Millers were a self-reviling tribe rather than courageous crusaders, damned by our faithlessness, despair, distrust, and mocking cynicism, the inability to believe not only in the American Dream of upward mobility but any other path or ladder offering a legitimate grain of hope to the Have-Not? Did she guess that at the bottom of our brash behavior—the status quo taunting, the celebration of rebellion and invention—was the knowledge that we stank worse than our unimaginative enemies, worse than any carp-eyed Rotarian, because we perversely gilded bestial behavior with a shine of High Art, That Quote again from Dylan Thomas ("*Do not go gentle* into the fine morning, Benji.

Rage, rage, against whomever you see.") and Emerson ("No, I won't copy what's on the board, Mrs. Hopper. *Imitation is suicide.*") and Sophocles too ("The carpet is filthy, Elizabeth, but be patient: *we must wait until evening to see how splendid the day has been.*") And furthermore, consciously (or unconsciously) comprehending the atrociousness of our hypocrisy, crafted each of our insults so it eventually came back on us like a shit-covered boomerang? Whatever Mrs. Dankert thought or did not think, her merciful nod—*go get your ball*—was a fascinating first encounter with unilateral truce and the serenity that follows the breaking of a cycle of recrimination. Joyfully I skipped through the fence gate, across a lawn innocently yielding to my weight like an outdoor roadside trampoline at a North Woods tourist trap.

MY GRATITUDE FOR THESE FLEETING RELEASES from tit-for-tat reality was such that when Mrs. Dankert died years later of cirrhosis of the liver, I attended the wake at Runge funeral home, located on River Drive. A jet plane roared overhead as I crossed a car-packed parking lot, the sound of heaven's fabric ripping. I had on my latest custodial uniform, tweed jacket and unmatching dress pants from the Rummage Closet, battered cordovan shoes given new life with Vaseline, my old two-bit gangster trick. Ahead stood a mini plantation mansion, first floor windows softly glowing like a line of jukeboxes that had come to pay their last respects to the barmaid who had so faithfully plugged them. The windows above were ominously dark. Removable letters on the slotted foyer sign indicated: MARY DANKERT, ROOM THREE. To get there it was necessary to wade through a hysterical crowd of teenagers mourning a high school girl who had choked to death on an ice cube. For a minute or so, in the middle of the warm lobby, I got stuck—trapped by sobbing swollen faces, girls leaning on boys, boys clutching girls. I did not know the part about the ice cube yet—wouldn't until I got home, read the minuscule obituary in *The Quad City Times*—but it was horrifically clear that one of their own had improbably perished, left them clueless about what would happen next. Not wanting to push forward, I waited for the damp swaying wall of grief to dissolve, bowing my head to avoid eye contact with mourners, intimate unearned connection with this calamity. I had never known their beloved friend, relative, classmate. I did know what dying young was like, though. I knew more about it than just the famous poem about the athlete gone too soon. I knew that dead child in my mother's eyes. I knew the dead child in me. The fat boy erased but not forgotten. The fact of his death pulled me back always, just as dreams pulled me forward to college and the notion of taking creative writing classes with Robert Dana, whose encouragement I still remembered from the night at the Butterworth mansion. "I saw her three days ago!" someone cried. It was wrong—*so wrong*—tragedies should randomly tangle like this, the meaning of each defacing the other, but it happened constantly in the bottleneck of funeral homes and public clinics and emergency rooms. Like the night at St. Luke's when mother and I were waiting to hear if Grandpa Stanley had survived the latest emphysema attack induced by Salem cigarettes. A siren. Doors flew open, a gurney blew by. On it lay a nineteen-year-old who had been so intent on winning the hundred-dollar first prize in an arm-wrestling contest at a strip mall disco that he had snorted too much performance-enhancing cocaine beforehand and died of a heart attack on the tinsel-girdled stage under the spinning mirrorball. A wailing girlfriend followed the cold body wearing paisley polyester: *I can't call them! I can't tell them!*

I can't! I can't! Meaning the boy's parents, sound asleep on Maple Street. Meaning someone else would have to make that call—doctor, priest, or policeman—but certainly none of us in the waiting room, hunkering, numb, assaulted by ignorance of who exactly had been lost to the world, what smile, what voice. The ferocious tangle of crises at that moment—and this—asked human beings to pick up the slack of gods.

AROUND MARY DANKERT'S OPEN CASKET stood a sober semicircle of Lindsay Park Lounge regulars: drab dresses and tight suits. They were not sassy or full of the beans now. They stared thoughtfully at their favorite barmaid, recalling how quick she mixed an Old Fashioned and the counter-clockwise twist of her thin wrist as she wiped up a spill. Or I imagined they were recalling that. In the corner of the room were roses that would never open. The cards said the same thing: *In memory of Mary.* Mr. Dankert, sealed in a Sears suit, placed a hand on the casket rim, where the raised lacy lid would soon rest. He looked like an orator behind a long mahogany rostrum, letting silence speak for him. Moored blimp of a gut. A brush had subdued his bad hair. Nearby, the stiff pleated shade of a table lamp shined dully beneath plastic glistening with a whiter light. Mourners dabbing tears. Mine were frozen inside. I was a suspicious advance for another Ben—the braver one who would cry rivers. I folded my arms and thought: *You shouldn't have come.* But had I not, the regret would have been sharper. For I may not have known what Mary's song was, if she put cream in her afternoon coffee or displayed uncooked spaghetti in a tall jar on the kitchen counter, but her major choices—like most people's—were out in the open, available for examination, and quite worthy of it. Fact: she had endured

suffering with patience and dignity—politely waiting tables during the alcoholic ordeal, never allowing herself to stagger in public or curse at neighbors. Looking down at the small painted face which had once looked mercifully upon a misbegotten child, a sensation of respect swept over me, admiration for how she had managed the illness, resisted the temptation to try and drag others down with her. Dankert Sr., wearing a turquoise bolo tie, cupping a Stetson, approached me from another area of the room. The old man's shaved cheeks sucked in, then out. He said hello. He wanted to talk.

MR. AND MRS. ROSE

Midwestern sensualists — *Prairie-poet mystery solved* — *Oogly-googly pity* —
Last Supper, 1972 — *Lured into the attic* — *Passing the bar* —
Car trunk full of Dubuque dentures — *An afterlife lived on earth* —
[snort] — *Patent leather leviathan in my grasp* — Ire-onic —
To buff an RV — *"Remember me?"*

MR. ROSE WAS AS RED AS HIS NAME, and shaped like a barrel. I
was told he had been a foreman on the Rock Island Line, super-
vising a crew that laid ties and repaired rails. Unhappily retired,
easy to anger, this gnarly bloom, and meek wife, and sons, Elvin
and Mack, lived across the street in a gloomy white house with
a slender porch a few feet from the sidewalk. Pin the gloom on
dim bay windows and a steep green roof. It appeared the home
was half attic—a more fitting place for trunks to live than humans.
Next door was a taupe Victorian owned by Mr. James, operator
of a tavern on the far west side sporting no neon sign, no name

at all, just a black entrance across from railroad tracks. (Mother drove me past that dive one night *hee hee hee*.) On the other side of Mr. Rose's lair existed a compact ravine that would have been the perfect place to conduct an eighty-round bare-knuckle boxing match if it was 1890, not 1972. I had seen drawings of such events in a library book—double-chin tweed-clad spectators waving programs, spitting, elbowing. Lucky John L. Sullivan in the ring had only to contend with Jersey Joe Walcott. Our Mr. Rose needed no watch chain or bowler to be an old time lout. Put a garden hose in his crimson claw and he sprayed cats. Pass him a Schlitz and it crumpled like a doily as he swore with the spittle-y flagrance of one who had done so for a living, combining the worst of French, Italian, Chinese. *Fellatiochinkadunkcunnilingafruck.* A tri-lingual bully of a Rose emitting none of the sweet cool fragrance of the American Beauty bushes that flourished on the little terrace above our two-story dump, thanks—I theorized—to wholesome voodoo practiced by Mr. Hickey. *Out of a cigar box comes a* Better Homes and Gardens *article by C. L. Witcheepoo titled: "Fertilizing Methods for the Feeble." 1. Light a kitchen candle. 2. Sprinkle brown sugar on a pile of junk mail. 3. Chant: do-do woo woo do-do.* Given the fact raucous Mr. Rose was about, it was a good thing my frail idol rarely mulched or pruned in the Christian fashion. There could be a fatal misunderstanding—fatal for Mr. Hickey. For when Mr. Rose poked his head out the door on Saturday morning, he was looking for a fight—not the postman. Or a fight with the postman, a namby-pamby pinochle-playing letter carrier to *pound pound pound* like a rusty spike. Mr. Rose had not combed his hair since the day he was married and for that reason had lost not one strand to any drain. Clumps that fell out stayed put, piling up to form a macho sun-bleached montage. Gray eyes, crooked nose, chewed lips were tucked in the cavity between jutting brow and jaw. Did he naturally have receding senses or did he place an anvil on his face at night to ward off kisses that would make him into a gentler Rose? Under the abruption of the chin was a sunbaked neck block tinged with gold down. Under the neck was more ruddiness, seen when he exited the dreary house and quickly found an excuse to rip off a checked work shirt. One scowling glance at the cartoon goose thermometer or old dusty station wagon and—*rip*—buttons flew and out rolled the rib-slatted belly topped by tough-titty spigots. Nothing like the sagging knocker pudding of my pale father, the inveterate recliner jockey, or my flaccid boobs that were bigger than those of any fifth-grade girl, inspiring anxiety about breast cancer and spontaneous prepubescent lactation. And below the whiskey-barrel belly, jeans snug as half a wet suit. Oh, he was a hard living, hard-to-fathom botanical. Fit only for a place in Cleopatra's harem or a ghoul's caravan. At times he made Grandpa Stanley, our tufted family brute, seem like a shrinking daisy, and he out-roughed Dankert, too. Each canvas shoe looked like it had smoked an exploding cigar—even more tattered than my mother's tragic tennies. Mr. Rose, you knew, never sat down at a table without getting "stuffed to the gills" and emptying a ceramic stein as large as a liver—three feet tall with Prussian helmet flip lid. *Midwestern sensualist*, mother labeled this garden variety, including in it Rose's rude buddy, Mr. Moore, a government bureaucrat who lived on the other side of the ravine in a pea-green bungalow with a pea-green breezeway leading to a pea-green garage containing the lighter green Volkswagen bug. (Was pea-green not available at the dealership?) His wife was half Cherokee, people said. When Mr. Moore was really drunk, he chased Mrs. Moore around the yard, and the Volkswagen too, if it was in the driveway. She in a robe, he in boxers. Inside, their beleagured sons, Richard and Victor, and stoic, animal-loving daughter, Lucinda. Usually I thought mother was too hard on men, because it was true—she almost always was. But I had stood next to her, at the screen window, listening to the cries of whipped Richard echo up and down the block. I had witnessed Mr. Rose attack his station wagon with a chamois rag and no mercy. And I agreed with her hanging judge verdit in this case: stamp these lugs Midwestern sensualists.

ROSE HIPS THRUST AGAINST CAR DOORS as bare bulging arms buffed metal. The chassis rocked. He strangulated the hood ornament with that trusty rag, and I thought it explained why I never heard Elvin and Mack pleading for mercy. He gagged them. He lashed the rearview mirror with wax, his mouth and eyes sealed in a violent fit of dreaminess. What was he recalling? A powwow with Paul Bunyan? Raping Babe the Blue Ox? The murder of the FTD florist who had rung the bell in 1965? July 4, 1939, when he had jumped from a caboose and ripped apart the sissy music gazebo in a town sqaure? This long-lived Rose might well be the answer to a nagging Midwestern mystery—at least nagging to mother and me. The mystery of why no prairie boys, returned from World War I, had produced great poetry like that written by Englishmen Rupert Brooke, Siegfried Sassoon, Wilfred Owen. Why? Because Mr. Rose in his youth decimated youth, finishing a job mustard gas started, throttling wheezing Alberts and Karls and Petes as they sat in wicker chairs, wrapped in blankets from which protruded notebooks. *That's what ya get for picking up a pencil instead of becoming a pile driving man.* Done torturing the mirror, he bent over, roaring, and what a frightful trellis that back was. Dozens of ligaments quivering. Taut deepest fiber of a malevolent Rose stretching toward the bucket in a neck-to-waist flutter that seemed designed to shake sunburn off as if it were a boxer's prefight velvet robe. Such a combustible bloom of avarice and cruelty and lust for parking spaces! He looked hammered together—the product of an insane sparking smithy who had lost the love of his life to tuberculosis and responded by concocting a 220-pound industrial blossom that did not thrive on tender sentiments—but on the noxious octane of disdain. Gas-powered coal-eyed bower-rending anti-Rose. Big-bottomed bottomless pit of rancorous fumes. A Rose all canker, all astoke and afire and loving it awl thee livelong day. A rambling Rose wreck from Santa Fe Tech that really should be shelved at the Railroad Salvage store along with mean dented bean cans that survived train derailments. Head over sudsy bucket, he vented snot, unleashed the fierce foamy joyfully agonized grunt of a slave driver. He spat. He sloshed the rag around. There was a big plaid patch on the seat of the frayed jeans that had had almost all the blue washed out. Spine segments protruded like frets from the back's crude harp. Sweat dribbled off tit taps, barrel belly slats bulged: one two three four. Built-in boy whipping rods. Mr. Moore could only wish he was so lucky. "Old buddy old pal..." was slug-soft, and prone to porcine flip-floppancies and jigglations not even a Woolworths girdle could stabilize. His teeth looked drawn into his mouth by dentist R. Crumb. Whereas Mr. Rose had iron for teeth, a bear trap. It opened when he straightened. O monstrous blossoming. O flesh-petaled panorama of earthly evil. Between the lips flapped a gray tongue, or shoe of a swallowed neighbor.

ELVIN ROSE WALKED THE WALK of his father, and could cuss almost as adeptly. He smiled while threatening me with his fists. Mack, on the other hand, was scarily soft-spoken. Police blotter terms like *vandalism* and *indecent exposure* seeped to mind when they were near, and that chased me back to my yard fast. Both boys fell into the rarest category of early 1970s youth. Elvin and Mack were *glippies*, having received but a glancing blow from the monumental hippie movement: 99 percent unlovely sons of a coolie taunter and 1 percent flower children. Only Mack's upper lip was hippie—home to a shaggy Civil War mustache similar to that worn by the lead singer of Country Joe and the Fish. Elvin—a serial wearer of overalls—had the sensitive hippie ears that dug whatever pabulum the Columbia Record Club dispatched: *crash bang bong-a-lop-slop Peace Now Pretty Please.*

Mr. Rose, of course, did not give his sons any credit for their peculiar nastiness. He saw only Elvin's record collection and Mack's suspect five-tooth facial hair comb. Pansies, pickerels, pussies, pixies, queens, muff divers. He had brought those boys up to be A-one warriors like him! Racks of rifles he had provided. The bullets. Buck knives. Fishing rods. Punching bags. Barbells and tool boxes, hatchets and French postcards and the Foreman's *Golden Glossary of Threats* written in tobacco juice. "Get over here Elvin, or I'll," "Do it again Mack, and I'll," "If supper ain't ready I'll." Ill with *I'll's* the Rose household was. Threat Island, and in the fridge—vomit-colored Thousand Island dressing. After Saturday afternoon car lashing, Mr. Rose and Mr. Moore and their mousey wives sat on the porch across the street from our over-grown slice of neighborhood geography, guffawing unhumorously and slugging booze from dice glasses. I watched through parted branches of a pine rooted to the north edge of the front terrace, a tree that joined with the expansive maple to form a forgiving canopy over our degradation. (And might those trees, often overlooked in memory—so high above the trouble—be a key to my survival of it all? Lush trees gamely scrubbing the foul air emanating from 15 Crestwood Terrace, making it more breath-able? When I remember their coolness and profound foliage, I think they must be part of why I am here today in New York City, well fed, not dead. Sour season after sour season, the pine needles and leaves pointed the way out like a shifting shadowy cotillion of compasses.) Branches made a fine frame for the front-porch drama I observed: city couples entering the Northwoods of their minds to cool off after another insufferable day of BO and BS and Doomsday Clock updates. Mr. Rose wore suspenders to keep a heavy crotch from hitting the ground. Mr. Moore, *the Richard tamer*, wore a short sleeved shirt open to reveal a grungy

T-shirt V. An ex-marine who had molted like a corn snake, shedding medals and muscles, retaining only the buzz cut and zest to kill. The screen-door gray of him made Mr. Rose appear even redder, the vibrant hue of the Kentucky clay that dazzled me when we visited Aunt Frances, Granny Stanley's half sister, who sent us socks at Christmas that were so profoundly wrapped in crepe paper they had the aura of Sphinx paws to pose riddles to. *Why blue socks for me, orange for Mitzi?* Mrs. Rose wore a yellow sweater that hung off her figureless figure like flaps of chicken fat. Even when it was eighty degrees she still must contend with the chilly eyes of Mr. Rose. Mrs. Moore was tucked into a white pantsuit that well fitted her role as asylum attendant in the pea-green bungalow, tending to whipping boy Richard, who wore his soul on his eyeframes in the form of tape, and unclean Victor, wearer of headbands and ponytails, who got on his ten-speed and disappeared for weeks, nobody knew where, and each time he returned his eyes were more distant. Elvin and Mack Rose could only arrange for two and three day escapes from their hell. They had no bikes. They had no cars. They hitchhiked. Where were they now? Thumbing on US 61 and frightening Mr. Hickey's sister Alice, pastel-tiered like a wedding cake at the wheel? Mr. Moore slapped Mr. Rose on the back and Mr. Rose quaked, a bloom that drew sustenance from a family's doom. Mrs. Rose did not laugh and rock quite as much as the others. She licked her teeth. Sprouted worry wrinkles. Supper was always in danger of being late, even if lunch had just been served. And maybe too she had art on her mind: the latest paint-by-number rendition of *The Last Supper*. Or, I should say, *ignore-thy-number* because she was locally famous for altering the staid template to include guests like Sinatra, LBJ, Judy Garland, Mickey Mantle, Neil Armstrong in his Apollo bubble helmet. She had painted many celebrity last suppers as presents for friends and dentists. It was the one part of her life that bully of a husband had nothing to do with. Just as big bad giants avoid mice, Mr. Rose was terrified of craft kits. Mrs. Rose complimented Mrs. Moore on her cork wedgie shoes. Mrs. Moore tittered, swigged. Mr. Rose slapped Mr. Moore. Mr. Moore coughed. Mrs. Microwave, dressed in designer shrink-wrap, rounded the corner, fluffy white poodle on a leash. "Nice day, ain't it?" bellowed Mr. Rose, vowels swinging from the roof of his mouth like gallows bodies. Mrs. Microwave smiled coyly, teethlessly, and then—surprise surprise—did exactly the right thing: winked. Mr. Moore elbowed Mr. Rose, *frickin' horn dog haw haw old bastard old pal you.* In silent hunger they watched the well-packaged ass recede, *wiggle wiggle wiggle*…Necks cowled with cigarette smoke, bloodshot eyes dunked indecently into the crevices of each passing girl, dog, cat. They were oblivious to the ten-inch grass covering our hill—unlike Mr. Oliphant, Senior VP of Foil, who called in complaints. Or if not oblivious, thrilled the neighborhood was turning into a jungle. Mrs. Rose whispered a secret to Mrs. Moore: *My hair isn't mine. It's not a wig, either. It's steel-wool pads woven together by a great salon on Elm—go there, ask for Bluto.* Mr. Moore and Mr. Rose arm wrestled. Mrs. Moore and Mrs. Rose talked *Last Supper* recipes, *Last Supper* seating arrangements, fizzy *Last Supper* indigestion and hangover cures, very careful never to mention the sons their husbands were so unhappy with. It could only bring blame back on them—for babying coddling spoiling—since Mr. Rose and Mr. Moore had been without a doubt the best kind of father any boy could have. The men wished to play poker but lacked the focus to fetch the four deck card trolly. The silly goose thermometer in an apron looked down at them with oogly-googly pity. Posted on the other side of the door was a dark slab of wood in which ROSE had been carved by Elvin in shop class at Central High School. The men said "helluva lot" a helluva lot—no use saying "helluva little," was there? A whale of a time they had, with Moby Dick overtones, hairy hands disappearing often into their pants in an obsessive futile effort to grasp just what it meant to be a white man. Dice glasses clinked. *Cheers! Mud in your eye! Bottoms up!* Thick wet lips opened, closed, opened, closed, opened, closed...like mouths of asphyxiating fish packed in a Chinese restaurant pick-your-fillet tank. I smelled pork ribs, burgers, chicken. It was a double-party Saturday. Mr. Dankert with curly shellacked hairdo cooking out in his fenced backyard...grill urn spitting, spattering, flaring bluely as if feeding off the methane of dirty jokes...Mr. Neville, owner of The Mound Tap, pounding the picnic table and dribbling sauce on his belted bell-bottom Elvis suit...Mrs. Neville, obese ex–exotic dancer, vainly trying to adhere to the latest powder diet, while Mrs. Dankert dabbed the corners of her lipstick with a paper napkin, and dabbed, and dabbed, out out damned spot! What would happen if a cantankerous pyroheatri-arch Rose met a rambunctious sizzling Dankert? A fistfight or ho-ho-hoedown? But they did not meet. So close neighbors were to each other, and so far away that they might as well be living on other planets. Planet Backyard, a place to curse alley cats, burn meat and toss the cookies. Planet Front Porch, a place to have cocktails, but no meal, just nuts and smoke. Mr. Moore swore with cigarette in mouth, it a bobbing Patton baton. Mr. Rose appeared to be puffing the hand that cupped his Pall Mall. Every so often the men peered into the ravine at acrid blue smoke spiraling out of charred oil cans filled with ashes soft as black dove down. They looked across at Lucinda Moore catatonically petting a calico tabby. Lucinda was fifteen going on twenty-three: a Peace Corps volunteer in her own front yard. She had thick stark eyebrows and long black hair. Her face bore an amazing resemblance to that of the fur-hatted Native American figure standing to the right of Bob Dylan on the cover of the album *John Wesley Harding*. Like him, she never blinked. Her big sheep dog was named Sheba. She had parrots too, and a rabbit, three turtles, goldfish, a guinea pig, and hamsters. She did not smell like piss—a miracle. I loved her for her silent poise. She scared me, but that was all right—no hindrance to our marrying. I was used to scary females, and she to untrained creatures. My bedwetting would bring out the best in her. Every time she looked at me, part of her mouth smiled while the rest frowned. I preferred to admire Lucinda from afar. When I had been in her house I was introduced to a voluminous living room Habitrail constructed not just for hamsters but also as a defense, I thought, against a father. (The Habitrail circled and circled a room full of flimsy cigarette-burned furniture. Only she was agile enough to circumambulate the entirety of tubing web. There she stood, glowering at me, another male unworthy of the high title of Animal.) Seeing Lucinda in the yard—alien eyes averse to colonization—Mr. Moore began insulting his vulnerable boys, and when he did, Mr. Rose was reminded of the many awful things he'd yet to shout about his own wretched progeny. The next meeting of Lambast Thy Son Club. Mack shot no bucks. Elvin caught no muskies. Richard ran for no touchdowns. Mack the wimp. Elvin the woman. Richard the wastrel. Long hairs, they joined record clubs—the next best thing to a commune—and got twenty free albums and a rotten deal if ever there was one, because none of the discs featured music by Lawrence Welk or Connie Francis, Boots Randolph or Boxcar Willie. Goddamn right they must have their hides tanned and balls broken because they wore bandanas minstrel-style while listening to the queer sounds of Canned Heat, Melanie, Moby Grape, Steppenwolf, Vanilla Fudge.

What about Bill Bailey? Anyone knew the only tune worth singing was the good old good one that brought down the house by referring to "Bill Bailey" ten dozen times. "Won't you come home, Bill Bailey, won't you come home?... Bill Bailey won't you please... come on home?" Wives nodded as the next generation hid out, biding their time.

MRS. ROSE ASKED ME IN to see a *Last Supper* masterpiece in a movie produced and directed by my mind. Mr. Rose was away hunting deer or teenagers with Mr. Moore. Spotting her alone on the porch swing, wearing a baggy yellow sweater and knitting another, I had been unwisely emboldened to inquire about her chosen art form. "Missus Rose...I hear you're a painter." (A nice way to put it—really mother accused her of creating "salacious, blasphemous" pictures that could get a lady beheaded in Rome.) "You do, huh?" I noticed the nearly empty dice glass and cigarette purse on the rail. Her voice was ginny, and feisty too—as if Mr. Rose had given her a shooting lesson before leaving so she could protect herself from the advances of Mr. Moore and also bag any elk that appeared on the doorstep, fleeing fields where the he-men stumbled. "I hear you painted last, a last—" "Supper!" she cried, rustling proud on the swing. "Give that boy a...a see-gar. Come on and look at my las' supper. Best yet." She stood and the swing rode upward so technically she remained sitting while erect. Onto the rail she dumped the sweater-in-progress. Off the rail fell the half sweater and cigarette purse, both landing on the three-foot patch of turf separating the under-porch latticework and the sidewalk. "Damn it!" She reminded me I had not heard that. She slugged dice-glass nectar.

She smacked her lips, clucking a thing I couldn't make out. Her fingers were remarkably clean for a painter. She was marble-white: not a stroke of makeup, with the lover of it gone. *Rose of Carrion. The rose is not a rose is not a rose.* I stared down at the unfinished sweater—a perfect fit for a Laos land mine victim—and the feminine leather nicotine pouch, lacking the experience and authority required to touch either. She gave it. "Grab that crap. Come up. I'll showyadalassupper." The weave smelled of alcohol, perfume, fried food. Intimate texture of the cigarette pouch made me drop the pouch. I was *too young, too young.* I felt instantly sick: *my fingers had eaten too big a meal.* I looked to my left, at the Roses' long side yard—which functioned as a front yard in the dizzying east-side way. A Frisbee lay in the grass under ye olde gas lamp: tin shaft, flickering gaseous flame. "Whatcha waitin' for, Bean!" Divine intervention to keep me from viewing indecent Americana I suddenly had less interest in—given what went along with it—my name twisted by her tongue into a fart-producing legume. "Supper's dry, Bean. Finnish it yesserday." Elbows on the railing, she was more than halfway over it. She had slimy rabbit choppers. Was she the sufferer of a rare form of buckteeth that came and went like arthritis? "The best Supper yet if I say so myself." Out a window of the James's house flew peanut shells and can lids, Gramps preparing a dinner of bar snacks for that urchin Eddie who stole crusts of bread from our backyard bird buffet. "This Supper's got LBJ sitting next to Hepburn." Heart thumping, I carried the Laos sweater and cigarette vulva up steps. She grabbed both and led me past Goofy Goose thermom-eter...into a dark dark dark hall unfurling like a polluted penin-sula past rooms full of heavy polished furniture that had to be producing their own light, as all shades were drawn. Lonely bright glints on table corners. Creamy gleams on claw feet, lion legs, armrests, chair backs. None of it looked used or even like it could be. Mr. Rose hoarded woodwork like Grandpa Stanley. They worshiped mahogany grain as wolves did the moon. They banned their families from family rooms, and the quiet was that of a morgue for Tiffany lamps and chandeliers and furniture that did not look like it had been bought but snared with clever traps laid in the Black Forest of the Midwest. Mounted here and there were antlers and mallards paralyzed in midair. On shelves stood helmeted steins depicting merry scenes of Viking debauchery. Oh, it was creepy. Under any rug could be a trapdoor to Bavaria, Minnesota. Mrs. Rose, on little pointy feet, wobbled forward. "Loover's in here." Louvre, she meant. Across an Oriental hall carpet I tip-toed, the design intricate as bomb innards, and making me more nervous than when I passed Mrs. Hickey's Christmas tree in widower Hickey's dining room. Quarter-hour chimes sounded and I jumped. *Mring, mring, mring.* "Look at this Supper, Bean. Ain't it the cat's more?" Cat's meow. Mrs. Rose—wings of wool trailing from each arm—stood in a pantry converted into a *Last Supper* production facility: paints on a steel-rimmed table, water jars, brushes, a novel by Jacqueline Susann and inspiring piles of magazines: *Life, Time.* Next to the table was a professional easel graced with a painting of bleary coloration and disappointing size but truly fantabulous content. *Last Supper, 1972.* "That there is . . ." John Wayne as Jesus, Nixon as Judas, LBJ next to Hepburn just like she said, Liz Taylor sexpot apostle, Mr. Rose leering at Carol Channing, Bardot and Zsa Zsa Gabor on the lap of Vince Lombardi, Mickey Mantle, Walter Cronkite, Buzz Aldrin, Xaviar Cugat, Princess Grace, J. P. Morgan, Bobby Kennedy, Elvis. Far far out. She had it over the local Picasso, Orton Hall, often featured in the newspaper. Hall of the bland watercolors depicting barges, bridges et al. His wimpy strokes erased the weirdness of America from the picture, leaving disinfected diarrhea of culture. How did she come up with this

Mr. and Mrs. Rose 381

antic guest list? This particular digestion of icons? "Easy! I'm a natural born hostess." I pictured her lying in bed, awakened by the snoring of Mr. Rose, teeth bucking above covers as she disinvited JFK—*he's been so often*—and added to the guest list George Wallace and his wheelchair—*poor man could use a break after getting shot.* "The hard part is finding photos to use as models." Why? She showed me different *Time* magazine photos of Dean Martin in which he was smiling expressionlessly, not in the interesting way required of a *Last Supper* guest. "There's that blank look again." I nodded: good point. Being famous—the fetish object of millions of needy people like Mrs. Rose and my mother—meant keeping your face in the public eye at all times— and spirit hidden in a Bel Air catacomb—existence being the faint echo in-between. "Twenty pictures of Dino…" Her left wing gestured at a magazine pile. "And nary a good one to be had." The teeth bucked again: horrible affliction, so fleeting, never allowing a dentist the time to do a repair. What an unfair impression it gave of her, along with that cluck-clucking voice, rabbit-hen hybrid. Imagine living in the shadow of a volcanic Rose, enduring all the desperate visions that came of nearness to annihilation and getting credit only for being a *dumb cluck* when she was an artistic cluck, political cluck, dreamy cluck in short sleeves, cluck-up-in-arms, yes. She slurred more details of her experience as Davenport's La De Da Vinci. She had burned supper a few times, so caught up in painting it. She had decided to give Sinatra—*Ol' Blue Eyes*—green eyes to better portray his Judasness. "See how green they are?" She was not, she said, worried about copyright infringement. If she had it to do all over again, she would name Elvin "Parsifal" and not give birth to Mack. Once Mack lit a finished painting on fire…she smelled the smoke just in time, smothered the blaze with yarn…repainted the ruined part and taped it to the good half, a work now hanging in the office of a State Farm insurance man. Expensive brushes were always vanishing, another crime she suspected Mack was behind. She bought ignore-thy-number kits at Major Art and Hobby, the same downtown store where I spent snow shoveling money each spring, buying regiments of Scottish soldiers that tripped on their kilts during battles and, by Memorial Day, were buried in the cemetery next to our back stoop. She claimed a "religious brown" resulted from combining pink and blue and orange, and pointed out a splotch of it—a color even sadder than fecal Day-Glo hues concocted by Mrs. Costello, the McKinley Elementary art teacher. "See that there?" I saw. Her right wing flapped free of that oil spill of a canvas, coasted overhead. I nodded. Hard situations allowed you to discover great capabilities at the moment they were most in danger of obliteration. One day on the waddle to school I discovered I could hum a complete symphony of my own composition, the final drum crashing just as I reached the playground where thirty alligator shirts waited to eat me alive. "Mr. Moore owns three of my suppers and he wants another with Babe Ruth eating a hot dog and Pol Pot on Zsa Zsa's lap—wants it for his office on Arsenal Island." *Flap, flap, flap* ... but no more did she wear a D. Cluck nameplate at all. Gone with Mr. Rose was the insidious meekness. She had possession of her language, the language of *Last Supper* painting. "To get the halo glow you add a tad of red and three tots of green to old gold." She had chewed her way out of her grotesque shell! And the day her husband was due home, she would wander from room to room, picking glossy shards of light off the furniture so she could reconstruct the whole egg, crawl back in for safety reasons. "Would you like some coffee?" she said, aristocratically rhyming the word with *toffee.*

"ROSE," PANTED TEN-YEAR-OLD ELIZABETH—tan as teak. "Elvin Rose, he...tried something." She shouted it. Her accusation sent a charge through the house. For a few days, as I recall, there were semi-hysterical scenes like this one in the kitchen, Elizabeth crying "Elvin! Elvin!" at mother and me, caught in the act of sneaking out the back door as usual to elude house difficulties. We froze, we turned. This was no noir fairy tale. This was sister's faded dress, worn leotards, patent leather shoes framed between the grease-spattered stove and the loose refrigerator handle. "You read about Ike and his automatic ant dryer?" mother gurgled, reconfirming her reputation as America's worst listener. "Elvin took me into *his attic*." "Oh," she sighed, not hiding her disappointment that we had been delayed on the way to the haven of Marc's Big Boy. Mother strangely hummed the word *Rose*, sampling in her amateur-scholar way echoes—*Rose* the middle name of troubled Marianna—*Rose* the name of her husband's mother, Dr. Miller's wife—*Rose* the flowers that Mr. Hickey grew—War of the Roses and the derby Run for the Roses and Rosie the Riveter and...then, at long last, she languidly asked:"What happened?" Details trembled within Elizabeth for a few seconds before spilling, the confession itself brutalization, the truth did hurt. She twisted an April birthstone ring. The left shoe climbed the right. I felt wetness in my tattered tennies, looked down and saw that I had stepped in the plastic bowl of skim milk and dissolved bread crusts cats refused to eat, possibly because father called the concoction "graveyard stew." Mother had one old shoe on the stoop, the other on buckled linoleum. A tissuey mess issued from dropped Moby Purse. "Elvin, he..." waved Elizabeth into his yard, asked if she wanted to *pet his new cat*. "Sure you don't mean Mack?" I interrupted, recalling his Sherman mustache. "No, Elvin—Elvin in the overalls" led her past the side yard

gas lamp and up precarious stairs to the back screen porch.
Private, but not private enough. He said the pretty cat was inside.
What kind of cat? she asked. Siamese! Her favorite! She followed
him into a hallway with an aquarium, hats on hooks, spotted
mirror as in Mr. Hickey's bathroom—*gateway in time to the epoch
of smallpox?*—and pencil sharpener casting the shadow of an
organ-grinder's instrument. She listened for dancing monkeys:
heard no screeching. She smelled a cat, but was taking no
chances. Where did you get the kitty? she asked. Elvin answered
quick. *Why honey I heard meowing in a thunderstorm and ran
outside, found her shivering on the curb.* Her. A mother cat—the
dearest of felines. But still Elizabeth hesitated, having been taught
that males—except courtly Mr. Hickey—were devious to the
marrow. What's her name? she asked next. Whiskers. Elizabeth
smiled—having also been taught by our contradictory mother that
males were the only ones who could give you what you needed—a

discount! a prescription! a diploma!—though you often had to endure torture to get it. *So be deathly afraid of strangers Benji Betsy Howie Mitzi and also willing to take them for all they are worth, and—as she reminded me at bedtime—if a drifter climbs on top of you scream spit pee simultaneously—to fend off the attack.* If Elizabeth had done that stuff, she had done it cleanly: dress and leotards unstained. It was her eyes that puked electricity. "Elvin Rose! Elvin, he opened…" the door to the dark and narrow attic stairs, I imagined. At the very top no meowing or cat bed basket. But the fur smell was strong, an itch in her nostrils. Spread around were pelts. An ark-full of stacked and hanging pelts Mr. Rose had shot: deer, raccoon, possum, squirrel. Elvin stood in the middle of the stench, consoling: "Don't be afraid, I'll take care of you." He was flat, she said, ironed by dimness into a pancake of a Elvin Rose. "Don't be afraid," he repeated—more afraid than her. Not slick like the soft-spoken pervert who tried to steal Marianna from Duck Creek Plaza. Elvin had no hold on Elizabeth. She ran down the attic stairs, past pencil sharpener and smallpox mirror, down the porch stairs, crying what she was crying now: "Elvin's a mole-esther!" She rent those syllables in frustration, in anger, and glared at mother by the screen door. I glared at mother. If we didn't stand up for Elizabeth's rights, who would? Mother looked frightened. Scared for sister? Scared of Elvin and Mr. Rose? I could not tell or say. When mother looked most scared the top of her face expanded as the bottom contracted. It was the opposite of her talking, her way of gaining control. She stared into a distance not there. She was obliged to doubt we children, I knew; we were the offspring of her fog, children of the fog. But, come on, this situation demanded an immediate and authoritative response, even forty-eight hours too late. Help out! Mother blinked in confusion as she had on the Christmas morning she opened a box to find bared teeth inside, a fox stole father had bought on credit. Then she yawned "What, honey?" I could vanish into the haze quick too, but I thought I snapped back into action faster. I gave myself credit for that. "Aren't you going to do something about Elvin?" Elizabeth asked her, and me too. "Aren't you..." Then mother grinned in the mocking way she did at night, reminding everyone in the infested house: *Don't let the bed bugs bite!* She swished stale warm air and spit out: "Do what, dear? I'm quite sure Mrs. Rose already knows about Elvin. Mr. Rose too." "But...Elvin, he..." Exhausted, she could scream no more. It was my job to press the case. Addicted to compliance (and its sugary rewards), I rarely challenged my mighty mother, the law school graduate, disperser of quarters for comic books, but right then I did speak up—I did my best (my sorry best) to protect the honor of the brilliant Brontë sister with whom I had made a blood pact: *we both will become writers or perish of faithlessness to the ultimate cause of beauty and truth.* I couldn't let her die of anything else but noncompliance with the holy contract sealed with a needle's prick, two drops of plasma. Our fate was to be destroyed by our Shakespearean choices: not a high school dork. I cried: "But the police don't know about Elvin!" Mother giggled as she always did when some fool stood up for order (Good) in a disorderly (Evil) world. "And tell them what *hee hee* honey?" "Tell them he took her up to his attic!" "Nothing happened, did it?" Her eyes zoomed in on Elizabeth, hair impressively combed and shimmering, despite the travail. Sister whimpered: "It might have—might if..." She burst into tears. Made to feel like a failure for not getting fondled or worse by Elvin. "You gotta call the police," I pleaded. "Gotta!" "Police need hard evidence, *Ben-ger-man.* Just wanting to commit a crime is not a crime. If so, we'd all *hee hee hee* be in jail. Elvin didn't, in the end, do anything wrong." Elizabeth

wailed: "I'll swear on the Holy Bible Elvin is a *mole-esther*." I
offered to swear also. Mother was not impressed. "And Elvin will
say he isn't a molester *hee hee*, and that will be that. Case dismissed." She had us beat. She had everyone beat, though constantly losing the bigger battle. She could walk into any room and
unleash the static and lecture and joke and shimmy and conquer
the counterman or the librarian without gaining any dominion
over herself and the violence within. Her gaze bled all over us.
There wouldn't, but should, be an extra public service announce-
ment at midnight. *Do you know where your children are? And
children, where on earth are your parents?* Elizabeth leaned
against the fridge for support, groaned: "It's not fair, not fair."
Right, our mother found crime accounts endlessly interesting and
yet now she was refusing to take any serious interest in the
attempted attack on her own brilliant daughter. "It wasn't my
fault, not…" Prepared I was to lunge forward, catch Elizabeth,
should she collapse. Much I had to make up for—fleeing her pleas
for aid earlier, as well as the ancient crime of pushing Elizabeth
out a window of the house on Scott Street, when she was two. I
kept lambasting myself for it. What a loss if she had landed on her
imagination, on the mind that now spilled buckets of delicate
script and inked mazes of branches enduring sub-zero tempera-
tures. But Elizabeth did not swoon toward the floor covered with
husks of dead roaches, horseflies. It was I who swooned like an
heiress, every flab roll, every sweat stain, every thread of a being
frayed by agreeability: the making of right out of wrong. The reek
of my shoes propped me up quick. Mother chirped: "Nothing
happened, so there's not a thing the men in blue can do!" But she
could have hugged her terrified daughter—at least she could have
done that. I stared at the rancid stick of butter on the table plate,
swollen from heat, chaffed into glistening peaks. Stared at the

dishes piled above the sink lip like encrusted fronds of a loathsome swamp lily. And on top the fridge, that morass of paperbacks
catsup packets jelly containers coupons penny shoppers, a thick
nest where Moby Purse slept each night. Below hovered the sharp
shocked face of my sister. Her chin was pointy in a pretty way.
Her ears especially complex. Her petite mouth and nose and eyes
made a perfect fit in that tight space between high cheekbones. I
could see that no more chances should be taken with such
preciousness, but I could not see, as I can now, at a distance of
decades, that my mother was most likely afraid of involving the
police because she herself might be charged with child neglect.
Why else not report the incident? In any case, way back then I
could only know that her reaction was unwholesome, not acceptable, and yet to be excused, explained away. She hadn't heard
right or she was tired, I could always tell myself. Screen door
slipped off her back, and she stepped farther into the kitchen.
There was one more loose end to tie up, and she tied it. The sack
dress folded in half. "Don't worry about a thing, honey bunch.
You handled the situation purr-fectly. From now on we'll just have
to be on *extra special guard* against *those big nasty Roses*." My
sister scowled. It was too complex. It was so mixed-up. Our
mother knew better—she must mustn't she?—and she saved us
while sinking us—saved us from an empty fridge by conning
dumb clerks, by sweet-talking Grandpa Stanley to reap bathrobe
bank withdrawals. Elizabeth looked at me. I looked at her. We
shrugged.

WE HOPED THAT MOTHER'S BEING A LAWYER some-
how "balanced things out." It certainly intrigued us. Could a

woman who stuffed scribbled-on yellow legal pads in her purse be as lawless as she sometimes seemed to be? Or did she know for sure that we couldn't win cases against Elvin and the perv who had tried to abduct Marianna at the mall? Maybe her own trying life had taught her that there could be no justice for people of our ilk. Elizabeth and I kept our own counsel, got out of her way whenever possible, which gave us some relief. But we became as ashamed of our own failings as we were of hers. Self-blame excused a parent's mistakes better than lame alibis. In time, Elizabeth and I would be the ones who saw mother off at the Greyhound station in downtown Davenport on the snowy night she left to take the bar exam in Iowa City. It was a step that father did not want her to take, although he later lived off the proceeds of her work at Legal Assistance. Elizabeth and I wanted the bizarre and discouraging first act of her life to be followed by a fabulous second act. That night in the bus station our hopes were highest. She had spent countless hours paging through study guides on the couch and at food courts. She had enough money for the bus ticket. She boarded. The bus pulled away into the blizzard. The rest of the story we heard when she came back, and to my ears it was another sad song. She told us about how she had slept in a hallway when she arrived in Iowa City, because the person she was supposed to stay with did not answer the knock. Her tone gave the tale a nuance of braggadocio. But it was nothing to brag about—bad planning or bad luck, whichever it was. There would have been no bathroom in that hallway. She would have washed up in a public restroom on the morning of the test—if she washed up. Anyway, she arrived at the test site in a rumpled dress, with her shoes slushed, coat buttons missing, a threadbare wool cap, the Purse. That didn't sound like a second act, but rather like the same old black comedy playing out.

AT WRITERS' STUDIO I MET the opposite of Mr. Rose. Norman Ross. Norm, for short. Norm the milk-imbibing church-going railroad man who once pounded Rock Island Lines paperwork with a rubber stamp. He was friar-girth, neckless, flour-pale. Teensy hairs sugared the sides of the bald head, shimmering in the glare of the bare bulb above the wobbly conference table spread with a menagerie of stationery—onion skin, double bond, Motel 6, narrow and wide ruled tablet effluvia—sheets plenty worried by the pens, pencils, and erasers of members seeking to create inspirational verse for *Reader's Digest* or an instructional canoe story for *Boys' Life* or, in the instance of the most formidable member, Blanche Redman, a fourteen-line sonnet that Wordsworth would not laugh at. Norm frequently sat next to Blanche (and her long cigarette) because few others dared to. Plastic eye frames were strapped in the center of his pale muffin face. A hearing aid infested one ear like a swollen peach tick. His eyes were all brown iris, nose quite flat, mouth an insouciant O. Muted asthmatic snorts regularly issued from all this pasty apparatus, which teetered and tipped with literary realization, seemingly held in place only by a stiff polyester collar of aqua honeycomb design. Thanks to the invention of the plastic bone that kept the fabric erect, Norm's head never rolled off its funky pedestal. Rather, it rolled way way to the left while the friar belly thrust way way to the right as he battled a tan folding chair that irritated the back injury that had resulted from spending decades hunched over a rolltop desk in a roundhouse office. Chiropractory had failed to ease the chronic pain. Osteopathic medicine was Norm's last hope. He often said as much during the mid-meeting coffee break, drawing out the first syllables in a fashion that caused Blanche's make-up to realign and cigarette lighter to flare. "There's something to that *osteo*-pathic approach..." Puff, puff, puff. "According to *osteo*-pathy, a body benefits..." Puff, puff, puff, puff. "...er, from, uh uh [snort] simultaneous therapies coordinated by an *oste-opath*-trained..." He spoke like he was a century older than sixty, which irritated some club-goers but not me; though just sixteen I felt like I was 160 myself sometimes. An epic torque accompanies defining moments of a life. Eras can, and do, span seconds. When Fat Ben's time on earth ended, it was like he had died in a battle long ago. The event amounted to centuries of calories cut. And when I ended the hunger strike, biting a Ritz cracker heaped with tuna fish, the famine epoch concluded, and another challenge dawned. By breaking in half I broke one pact with Time and sealed another. Time that healed all wounds traded for Time of loose ends bunched with the thickness of a fabric whose authenticity was irrefutable but forever askew. The thing that alarmed me about Norm was...were...those frightful moments when his fidgety search for a comfy sitting position produced a snuffling two-column man across the table—muffin head and belly filed in different latitudes. I admired Norm for a number of reasons. Like most members, he had been somewhat uncomfortably overcome by the writing obsession, which gave him a distracted and modest demeanor. He knew he probably should be doing something better with his retirement...and seemed always to be trying to recall what task that was...and failing. Oddly, there just wasn't anything else to do but be a poet. In short chiming verse, he—a railroad desk worker—dully (but brilliantly) surmounted the obstacle of isolation from the romantic rails, producing lines packed with sledge-swinging work gangs, rip-roaring locomotives, gory sunsets, spidery coal bins, cute cabooses, oily trestles, divine depots, tragic derailments...never once mentioning the window he saw it from. Maudlin genius. Norm had a great rusty subject different from that of any other member, blessedly never involving a lace doily or hoop skirt or the rhyming of "steeple" with "people."

He also had a part-time job ferrying denture molds from local dentist offices to a tooth fabricating factory in Dubuque, a down-at-the-heels industrial city located upriver. Norm's white-haired wife, Henrietta, cleaned Washington Elementary School in the evenings, especially the office of Mr. McCue, a grim personage with an oversized puppet jaw, steely totalitarian eyes. Childless, the earnest couple owned a small sagging house in a neighbor-hood of them behind the robber baron mansions lining the bluff overlooking US 61. When Norm found out I lived just two miles to the east and down the hill, he assured me in twelve snorts that it was no problem to swing by in *the compact* and give me a lift so I did not have to walk, ride, or take the bus to meetings. It was nice of him, and—it turned out—very courageous. For he kept the appointment even after he found out that Mr. Rose lived across the street—a rascal he knew from "the yard" and still feared. Around 6:30 p.m. came the honk. Down the front terrace steps I flew, wearing my Hawaiian shirt, a hothouse flower for sure—one *Genus Benjamina.* But who, really?

MY BODY STRIPPED OF BLUBBER felt like a neon tux I was trying and failing to break in before a big event. I was the sliver on the terrace stairs. I was an afterlife that can be lived on earth. But whose afterlife? Who made it out of 1977 alive? I would still be trying to answer the question thirty-five years later as I walked cosmopolitan streets in the disguise of a New Yorker. A folder in my office labeled PERIOD OF STARVATION contains con-jectures. "The Writer" is no answer. "The Writer" is the asker of the questions. Different possibilities, in turn, seem true. The part of me that lived was the part who loved death least—i.e., more a hummer of Aerosmith tunes than a groupie of Emily's buzzing fly.

Or the part that listened closest to Mr. Hickey's gentle sermons re: the creed of paying dues, doing the hardest of hard work, and earning unique results. Or the part that was most insubstantial and thus most immune to the crushing weight of crisis: a fragrant whiff of that dreamy child of five who predated the trouble, lying on the grass and watching clouds float by. Or some nameless curio—the one valuable that the thief, in her hurry, had left behind in the otherwise denuded cabinet of an identity.

REACHING THE CAR, I became, thankfully, only what Norm saw, the kid who wrote stuff. Norm quaveringly inquired: "How is Rose [snort] getting [snort] along?" He asked this of the windshield since he was wedged so tight behind the wheel that he could not swivel. The dashboard in front of me was scratched where I had dug in my nails while he made blind left turns in the same petrified posture. The metal milk box packed with dentures (he brought back the finished product too) was locked in the trunk, thank God. The engine not running because Norm had taken President Carter's dire words about the energy crisis a bit too seriously and at every opportunity turned the car off so as to be a part of the solution and not the problem. "How is [snort-snort] old Devon [snort] Rose?" There was a telltale tentativeness in the voice. He wanted news he knew he should not want, being a Christian. Notification that the foreman was in the hospital with throat cancer. The best I could ever do was say: "Florida—Mr. Rose is in Florida," and this only in January and February. Other-wise, I said: "Keeping his new RV clean, scrub-a-dub-dub." The cumbersome vehicle was parked on the other side of the street, white with crimson trim, a square capsule on eight wheels. Mr. Rose was as obsessed with new RV maintenance as he once

had been with harassing his two sons. They were totally out of
the neighborhood picture by 1981—melted into the river valley
smog. It summoned an image of headbands and cut-off jeans and
Frisbees and records being sucked down sewer drains. "RVs get
no miles to the gallon," snorted Norm, feeling around for the igni-
tion key. "To the left," I said, eager to hear the motor rumble, the
emergency break release, *thunk*. Club meetings were the highlight
of my week. I must be patient, though. The entire operation was
destined to take at least five minutes, given the bad back and bad
eyes and nervousness over the nearness of that big nasty Rose.
"More to the left," I said. The plump hand snagged the key
and turned it. Vinyl seats shook nicely. Norm's pencil protector
gleamed like a medal on a middle divided in equatorial fashion by
a slender belt that had never inflicted pain and ignominy on any
innocent. "Have a good [snort] week?" "Great," I chirped, meaning I got more Ds, again proving I would rather be a product of my
own Dreams than those the System handed me for its own greedy
benefit. I would not let any teacher or administrator turn me into
corned brain hash. Though I never cut classes, never. Schools
had one great and enduring use—shelter from our dump and its
chaos—a bunker where every so often, out of the shadows, appeared a teacher like Mr. Minard, Renaissance man, who assigned
students to read the novels of Thomas Hardy—cool, strange, real.
"I wrote a six-page story, Norm!" instead of doing homework
like my dutiful sister, Elizabeth. "What's the story called?" Norm
asked. "It's called 'The Last Sea'!" He liked the title.

HE LIKED EVERY TITLE and always shuddered when
Blanche, the group's only critic, tore her own poems to shreds
before anyone could get in a compliment edgewise: "I don't know

if it's good. It's probably not much good. Surely, a failure. Let's go on." "What [snort] is the story about [snort]?" "It's about the evaporation of all the world's oceans into a puddle on the edge of a forest—a muddy puddle a hermit can easily step over." "Say [snort] again?" I did, louder. He got it all the second time, symphonically snorted approval and then changed the subject to "*Ooosteoo*pathy." I reminded him about the emergency break. His hand plunged, searching for the handle. "To the right. You passed it. Up. Down some. There." He pulled and the car jerked. Good progress. I patted the green Mead notebook in my lap. Sticking out was the frill of my manuscript, another mythic tale inspired wholly by reality: the intense drought I now experienced—sighs of a mother blockaded from within by a tear too big to cry—dry wholesome crushes on sixteen different girls, none of whom I could look in the eye. Even in dreams the object of my affection remained decently clothed or safely disguised as a spoonful of sugar. How odd it turned out. Elvin and Mack—trained to be tough men—blossomed into guys who requested sprinkles on ice-cream cones and sat on the bench licking while staring strangley at children. And me, whose preteen nights often ended with mother rubbing and breathing on my feet, calves, neck…turned out to be a surreal straight arrow—the kind that would appear in a book written by Horatio Alger on LSD—Ragged Hawaiian Shirt Ben. Was it all due to "reverse psychology"? Classic hunting and fishing vacations causing Elvin and Mack to dream of Barbara Streisand, kittens, cuticle tweezers. And many bizarre unbound nights with a despairing brilliant mother causing me to covet solitude with pen and paper and books and blues records or the sweet courtly formalities involved in a visit to old Mr. Hickey's home? Too much mother wanted me to become a front-page headline involving a hatchet. A hundred times she had shoved

Moby Purse—castrating patent leather leviathan—into my arms, warbling: "Carry it for me, angel. I'm too tired. I can hardly go on!" And even more often than that had left me stranded after dark in a library or mall parking lot—an hour late, two hours. Oh, she baited the predators, and granted me with the insidious smoldering anger…but I just was not tempted to hurt another helpless being, well knowing how they would feel. What I wanted to do post starvation—what I strived to do—was to dispel the horror or childhood by hurting no one, betraying no one, judging no one. Take the best of what she taught me about family tragedy and world literature and institutional politics and gender complexity and add that to plain good lessons learned in the glowing kitchen of Mr. Hickey. Dress with a sense of humor. Think of others before yourself—if at all possible. Save pennies or give them away, but never just spend them at 7-Eleven. Prize discipline, patience, silence, warm beverages. Keep cheering for the Chicago Cubs even if they lose ten games in a row. Be private and social—keeping most of your story to yourself so it does not hinder your listening to the stories of others, which is a big key to understanding that you are not as bad off as you think. Feed the sparrows Mixed Seed #12. Wear an overcoat indoors every once and awhile. Light a cigar with your bald head bent forward. Use Kiwi shoe polish. Do sit-ups and push-ups. Jump rope because it's the best exercise ever invented. And above all, never give up, never give up, never give up, not even when you have diabetes and heart trouble and maybe a week to live. Take a blast of oxygen from the tank like he did—the old boxer—and raise a brittle fist in front of your bow tie and chant: *Protect with the left, Benny. Jab with the right. Jab.* Gently. So fortunate I was to learn about manhood from a pale frail man relying on mind and spirit for power—forces that could fight in many more ways than muscles. And very lucky never to be taken on a fishing trip by Mr. Rose or Grandpa Stanley. Admittedly I sniffed and envied the decaying gear in his Rock Island garage—reels, lures, rods, nets—but I should not. The stench was that of weeds clinging to stunted walleyes pulled out of Lake Belittleyerson.

THE CAR JERKED ALL RIGHT but not enough, not nearly enough. We had yet to really move. "Went up [snort] to Dubuque [snort] with dentures on [snort-snort] Tuesday." "You did?" "Will again tomorrow." "Pays good?" It was the only question I ever dared to ask about the chattering choppers in the trunk. "Gas-oh-lean and a little stipend." Norm's bald head was yellower than Mr. Hickey's bare bean—a waxen moon. His aqua shirt shimmered like the answer to the mystery of haloes. *On earth they took the form of polyester collars that grew a little more neon and aloft with each good deed done.* I reminded him about the stick shift. "Old Rose, I saw…" Norm did not dare complete the recollection, giving me the liberty to. *Old Rose, I saw Rose knock the teeth out of the heads of many a men, and here I am today, helping to fill those mouth blanks with dentures. It's whatchamacallit…Ire-onic.* Norm reached for the shift. "Hand just went over it…back a little more, now up UP…" "Don't tell Rose I asked about him." Was he imagining Rose leaping on the hood, swinging a pickax? "I won't tell," I promised, twice. Norm patted his wallet for comfort. In that wallet was an amazing card. It gave him the right to take Amtrak anywhere in America for free. (But though he talked much about a trip to New Mexico, he never did go—fearing, I think, that the sunsets would not quite equal those in his poems, and that he'd run into an ailing Casey Jones or unimpressive John Henry.) His hand jerked the stick. The compact rolled down Crestwood Terrace as I looked back at the new RV that Mr. Rose cleaned so regularly, with such desperation.

SHIRTLESS, MR. ROSE GRIMACED while polishing small window frames with the chamois cloth. Darker cloths were used on the metal plating. He tossed ruined rags into the ravine, and spent green canisters of Turtle Wax, and a baby doll pulled out of the gutter. Sweat soaked the loose bandana noose around the creased red neck. The harp cords of his bare back twanged every time he leaned over the water bucket, and his crepey skin crinkled, and the slats on the belly keg shuddered. It was still a hard belly at sixty-nine. Sweat dripped off the tit taps. Tight jeans became tighter, especially in the crotch and buttocks. Outlined were a two-foot crack, balls, hose. The plaid patch on the knee was faded. Old canvas shoes were spotted with oil, tobacco juice. Sweat poured out the sun-bleached hair beanie, over a bulging crimson brow, into the canyons of senses, across the jut of the chin. Legs bowed as he stalked other points of interest on the RV's big shell. He yanked the trunk antenna, let it go, *boing, boing*. He pulled a handle and chromed stairs accordioned out of a cove. Treads glittered, but not enough. Rose went to work with a wire brush, *grind, grind*. He spat chowder on the street. He ruined the brush, came back with another, ruined that. Every five minutes he looked at the pea-green bungalow up the street, hoping Mr. Moore had awakened from his hangover. Mr. Moore hadn't. Mr. Rose cursed the high humidity, the price of gas, the lack of anybody nearby to cuss-out. Then Mrs. Rose came out on the porch and he swore at her royally. She apologized in the usual loud and unconvincing way about the burned meat loaf of the previous night and the lost electricity bill and the purple spot of paint on the hardwood floor two rooms removed from the one place where she was allowed to portray Mickey Mouse as Jesus Christ and Bugs Bunny as Apostle Paul. Mrs. Rose had no time or pity for her husband now. She was not tender Mrs. Dankert, who bowed her head when being verbally abused, knowing that her spouse could do much better than cuss and tell dirty jokes. Mrs. Rose handed Mr. Rose a beer and then she sat down on the porch swing, a figureless figure deep-dipped in the yarn aspic of a white sweater. She swigged a gin fizz. He crushed the Schlitz can while drinking from it—*gulp, squeeze, gulp, squeeze, gulp.* Into the ravine went the shrapnel of an unquenchable thirst. He ripped a fresh bandana from a back pocket and the ligaments strung between the wrist's fret and the elbow quivered as he scoured his damp neck and face. He barked at a dog barking at him; the pooch ran off. He shouted a hangover cure in the direction of the pea-green bunga-low, some fogey potion involving limes and a raw egg. A teen-age girl rode by on a bike and Mr. Rose did not miss a delicious second of her pumping knees, arced back and butt marshmal-lowed across the banana seat. Feral teeth nibbled a fingernail. He put the other hand on his belt, tugged, tugged. The chin dipped and he inhaled his late-life musk—*ah.* He greeted Jerry Bernaur, ham deboner at Oscar Mayer, with the current temperature in Fort Lauderdale. "Eighty-two down there. What are we doing up here?" Jerry shrugged, and turned back to little Heidi and smaller Jerry—the kids that had run out to meet the pickup, a family he had to raise. Mr. Rose yelled the Florida temperature to everyone who passed. No matter that it was eight-two degrees in Daven-port, too. It was not the eighty-two of Fort Lauderdale. In June he was looking forward to January and leaving Davenport behind

for ocean, sand, sun, and nicer barometric pressure and jumbo
shrimp and a flamingo RV court where every man was a son of
a gun, every woman a hotsy-totsy gal—where neighbors had the
same hobbies, drinking habits, disappointing children, and terminal diseases. He climbed into the RV after tossing dirty rags and
brushes aside. He shuffled cards, I imagined. He admired clever
appliances, narrow cabinetry, miniscule faucets, suspended cots.
A gilled window needed to be tested—*open, shut, open.* At first he
ignored rapping on the aluminum door—Mrs. Rose, a bit drunk,
more worried, picking at sweater fuzz. When the noise didn't stop,
he yelled: "Go away for Chrissakes, can't you see I'm busy!" She
saw what? What there was to see—window fluttering uselessly,
capturing no light, inviting no fresh air—and shook her head.

MR. ROSE IN HIS INCUBATOR of Florida escape dreams,
and me, across the street, in the humid upstairs bedroom, craned
over the extendable tongue of an old desk—that board above
the top drawer of not just any desk. It was the desk from my
father's first law office. He had sat there the year that he made
only twenty-five dollars, according to family legend. At this desk
I earned my 1.8 grade point average and from this desk I wrote a
letter to the poet Robert Dana, who had told me to let him know
when I was ready to attend college. I had taken him seriously. I
wrote to the poet my senior year of high school saying: "Remember me?" If he answered that letter two years after our first meeting—with no meetings in between—I would be able to say my life
had been saved in miraculous fashion. And I had to go forward
on the premise that miracles happened—what else? I prepared
myself for college by writing what I thought mattered. Writing for

me. Writing for Writers' Studio. Writing informed by O'Neill and Chandler and Runyon and Hans Christian Andersen—I foundered myself on diffuse influences. On the desk tongue rested a narrow-ruled notebook and words wanting to be what I wanted (noir lyrical) or, barring that, what club members would consider a fine "story"—no hex of existence inflicted on a page, but an exceptional gift for readers expecting nothing less than a wreck of years tidied by an art culling from shattering circumstances a story that felt right, what some called "plot," others "narrative." I kept on failing but kept on trying. For if certain lives, early or late, are plagued by the sensation that wrongness has set in too deep to ever be remedied...wrongness walked with, lived out, becomes the story and truth's furnace. That tale must be told, somehow, though it was impossible to tame or train. It must be told in refraction or in evolving moods. And that year one attempt was: "The Tiger in the Rose Garden." It began: *Pepnit looked out of his window and saw a tiger in the rose garden. "Father—come here and look!"* It turns out the tiger's eyes are "big and green." He is a good tiger and standing still. He doesn't want to crush the blooms. The boy realizes it. The gardener runs off, hearing a roar, but the sensitive child, he understands what is at stake—he hears no menacing threat but a serious cry for help—and, very foolishly, picks the beast a path of escape through the thicket.

EPILOGUE

DEATHS
IN THE
FAMILY

DEATHS IN THE FAMILY

As it happens, Robert Dana did remember me, and he answered the letter I sent. After four rollercoaster years at Cornell College in Mount Vernon, Iowa, where he taught, I bounced straight to the graduate writing program at NYU, starring teachers like E. L. Doctorow and Galway Kinnell. It was September 1986, and within days of arriving in New York I became convinced my father was going to die. My good fortune had never been healthy for him. There was a tragic look on his face the day he stood on the platform at the Amtrak station as I boarded the econo-liner. It was the look of a man saying more than one good-bye. I imagined that when the news came from home, I would go to the Triumph Diner a few blocks away on Bleecker Street, order the greasiest possible meal, and eat it slowly in the orange booth, reading William Faulkner and smoking Dad's last favorite brand of cigarettes, Philip Morris Commanders. (The lowercase father in life would finally be Dad once he was dead.) I'd erratically flick ashes like he did and crush butts with a jab and twist. The call never came. I was vaguely disappointed. A great city flowed around me, poured into me, without dislodging any demon. I worked hard at shining, but the darkness—like an adaptive bacteria—kept infecting the light. One day I was sure I had spotted my mother on the A&S department store steps. Same old dress. Same hair beanie, discontented hunch. When I got closer a stranger held out her hand. I placed one of my dimes in it, hurried away.

M<small>Y FATHER'S DESK</small> I had left behind in Iowa, but I found a little white one on Lafayette Street and with the help of a new friend, Vince, dragged it back to my half of the studio apartment in the candy-colored NYU Washington Square complex. I shared the room with an arts administration graduate student who decorated his wall with paintings purchased from Soho galleries. I slept on the floor on a length of foam rubber that I had asked a clerk to cut to my dimensions. I had no typewriter, let alone any computer, but something better, I thought, a scholarship. I was a student of John A. Williams, the poetic political novelist well known for *The Man Who Cried I Am*. I collected beer cans in nearby Washington Square Park and redeemed them for the change required to rent time on a Selectric typewriter at the student center, where I started "Buried Moon," a story about townspeople unearthing a lunar presence glowing through the soil. But even this mysterious fragment of mythos was the purest autobiography, another try at depicting my family's "fable of confusion," to borrow a most lovely phrase from Joan Didion's *Where I Was From.*

I<small>F I WAS AS HAUNTED</small>, and romantic, as ever, I also performed such practical tasks as appearing at a bulletproof window on lower Broadway to pay the first month's phone bill. I subsisted on oatmeal. Classes were held at night, and by the second month I procured a thirty-hour-a-week data-entry job at, of all places, the New York Stock Exchange. (And soon thereafter the Crash of '87 occurred, naturally.) I rode the elevator with the chairman of Merrill Lynch. Every day I wore the same jacket and tie from the Salvation Army, until someone complained about the smell and I returned to the Salvation Army for a new jacket and a new tie. I did not meet celebrities; rather, I met the right people. Dean, a fiction writer from Virginia, loaned me socks. Keith, South African poet in exile, took me to hear Abdullah Ibrahim's band at Town Hall for free. Ofer, of Tel Aviv, made me a salad on a night when I was hungry. I had never had a salad that good. With luck, and pluck, I stumbled through the first semester, and on Christmas Eve pushed onto a Greyhound Bus at the Port Authority station and made it home for the holiday. The sight that greeted me when I walked in the door was something. My mother had asked me to write her a letter each week and I had, and these pages detailing New York City enchantments were scattered on the floor, some speckled with cat crap. Recovering myself, I asked for a typewriter, and I got it—a discounted Sears display model—and, more determined, headed back East.

My move away interested my brothers and sisters at the start. They came to see what it was all about during those first few years. Their visits were frantic, disjunctive, cash-starved, and, in retrospect, especially memorable, being the last intimate looks we would have into each other's lives, since my holiday trips home were mostly gyres of illusion, missing persons, and Chex mix. Howard came to see me by not staying with me. He stayed with his film-school friend Erik, and the two of them bought drugs uptown with Erik's money, and then invited me to the Jersey Shore for a cookout at Erik's family's summer house, where the Emmy awards that Erik's father had earned were on display. Nathan came out and I took him to see the Chinatown chicken that played tic-tac-toe, and, developing the theme, we shared the $6.95 dinner for two at the barbecue-chicken place near Washington Square. He was not so little anymore. When he saw my gaze follow a lovely woman across the avenue, he yelped: "I'm looking, too!" Nanette passed through with the Central High choir and I left the stock exchange to meet her at South Street Seaport for a rushed lunch. She was the cheeriest conversationalist of any Miller. Around the table swirled the chatter of her friends. The next year she was elected homecoming queen. Elizabeth arrived, eye bags and anxiety. We attended the Thanksgiving Day parade, sitting in the reviewing stand, thanks to the generosity of a Macy's executive who was the father of the tall, talented classmate I had fallen in love with. Elizabeth was then attending Hampshire College in Massachusetts after transferring from Carleton—the competitive Minnesota school where she had excelled, but at great cost to her health. Hampshire was a place of no grades but much genius. She described her professor's three-thousand-page, and still unfinished, opus on Engels. He was a man we could both relate to. Turning our attention to the parade, we cheered hard for those giant bobbing balloons we had been seeing on TV since we were little—especially Underdog. It was the most memorable visit—save one.

Two years earlier Marianna had come out for Thanksgiving and a man had tried to buy her from me. We were sitting at a table at the Blue and Gold Tavern, a basement place, down the street from the Ukrainian diner where we had eaten the holiday meal. A rough-looking old guy sat down, looked at my sister, winked at me, and started putting money on the table. I did not get what he was after at first. Then I did, and told her we had to "go now— right now!" We fled into the night like in the past. Standing on the sidewalk, we tried to laugh off our brush with the warty lech and his money, his winks. Marianna, at that moment, was getting herself together again after the chaos of her high school partying days. Like me, she was forever losing it, getting it together, losing it again. For her getting it together came to mean, in the years ahead, a new school or a new marriage. Her voice had lost its Lolita trill and assumed a Janis Joplin edge, ball and chain, piece of my heart. She would soon marry Joe—only son of a farmer who had seven or eight daughters. She would soon be attending Marycrest College, in Davenport, where she took creative writing classes and won a prize for a short story she sent me. It concerned a bag woman who called herself "Miss America" and bore a tender, if crushing, resemblance to our mother. The impressiveness of Marianna's empathy was to me heightened by its having occurred after the big thing she said during her second visit to New York, two months before I was married. She came to spend her birthday with us. She did not say the thing to me, though. She said it to Anne, my wife-to-be, and Anne's mother, at the pub in the Cellar at Macy's: "You know, there was violence in our family." And then, Anne told me, Marianna talked about being "so old." She was twenty-one, sipping her free drink. That image, and her confession, lingered in my mind. I guessed Marianna was referring to being thrown through our plate-glass front door by Howard when she was a girl, an event I witnessed. They were fighting on the porch as they did often. I was eating chips and watching reruns in the living room. Suddenly a tremendous crash! Glass shards showering the carpet and Marianna lying there, stunned. She was too heavy for him to have picked up. He must have grabbed her arm, swung her, and let go. She'd hit the door with such speed the glass accompanied her inside the house like a crystal jet stream. She had been lucky—hardly cut, no broken bones— some of us said. I said it and mother said it and even Lonnie, the red-haired son of a minister, who heard the noise and rushed over. Marianna lucked out, but Howard had run off without knowing whether his sister was alive or dead, and likely feeling terribly guilty—he had a heart also. The pane was not replaced. For years a ragged length of pegboard nailed over that hole greeted our visitors. Had Marianna been referring to that incident, or something worse I didn't know about? I was too afraid to ask. As teens floating around a city in search of sustenance, Marianna and Howard were seen by outsiders as a charismatic pair of partying nomads, well fit to each other. They shared the same rich friends. They got invited to the same pool parties, stayed overnight at the same mansions. They partied especially hard after what they had been through—and that, too, was part of the violence.

I WAS VISITED IN NEW YORK by my parents exactly one time, the week of my marriage. They stayed with my Brooklyn in-laws and broke the toaster oven. They withdrew my wedding present from the ATM on Court Street as I watched, wondering if cash would shuffle out—it did. My father went with us to obtain the marriage certificate and at the municipal building advised me that I should not have put down "Writer" as my profession. He shook his head sadly, and we let the subject drop. At the time of the wedding I was employed as a proofreader of patent applications in a law office, having meandered into that situation following a stint at a Brooklyn bakery and a monthlong run as Santa Claus at the flagship Macy's store on Herald Square. Nothing was sure but the commitment I was prepared to make to Anne. My brothers and sisters drove out in a junker and stayed with my in-laws and friends of in-laws. It was one of the last times the family was ever together. We talked over each other about big plans, rarely stopping to listen. We talked as we always had—our arms thrashing like people who cannot swim. At Elizabeth's insistence my mother wore new shoes rather than a battered pair of canvas tennies. The short ceremony was held in the catering space of Gage & Tollner, a century-old restaurant. Anne wore a dress sewn from green velvet she and her mother had chosen together at Beckenstein Fabrics & Interiors on the Lower East Side. I wore an absurdly large and ebullient white calla lily on the lapel of a smart green Austrian jacket I had found at a vintage store called Andy's Chee-Pees. After we exchanged vows and rings, Nathan handed me a green velvet bag. From the bag I took a four-foot length of nylon nautical rope, white and shiny. I gave one end of the rope to my wife and we stood, holding the rope, as the officiant read an account of the ancient wedding ritual of the garments of the betrothed being tied together. This was the root of the cliché "tying the knot" and the act that came next. We didn't want our big day to be too full of itself, too stodgy and too prefab. We wanted it to end thus—with our tying a simple knot in a simple rope. And we knew, already, that on each anniversary we were going to tighten it, Anne on one end and me on the other, pulling. We knew we'd love each other until the day we died. We placed the knot in the green bag and for the first time in my life I wept with joy. I knew how blessed I was on that December day in 1989. A year and a half earlier, on her first visit to 15 Crestwood Terrace, a cockroach had crawled into my love's water glass and it did not daunt her. She simply asked for another glass. She slept in the upstairs bedroom with me, and we cuddled there, listening to the wind in the tree. I took her on long walks on the east side, pointing out what I had loved about my childhood—the sights that were the light I leavened my dark with: the yard of the late Mrs. Handler, who often stopped me to inquire how I was—whether fat or thin; the lovely mansions facing the river, with their porticos and verandahs and widow's walk railings. She asked no hard questions about my family. She filed the strangeness of 15 Crestwood Terrace under the safe heading of "Eccentricity" and left it at that. She kissed me on McClellan Boulevard. One of our walks led us to the City Center Motel on River Drive. There we made love five times in the space of three hours and then walked to Ross's Truck Stop and ordered their famous Volcano, the plates heaped with cheese-slathered hash browns and ground beef and chili beans and onions.

THE SUMMER AFTER WE WERE MARRIED we moved to rural Vermont to housesit for the parents of a college friend of my wife's who were moving to Arizona. We planned to work on our writing. I was going down fast, but I didn't know it at first. I knew I had what felt like two hearts in my chest, one throbbing against the other. I knew the days were getting shorter, the nights longer. I knew I was producing pages but I did not know what I was writing exactly, except that it involved the building of pyramids by enslaved citizens in a western state. I knew that it terrified me to read the letters my mother wrote to me, with their large antic script red-streaked by the geranium petals she would sprinkle on pages before sealing the envelope. The withering beauty of the winter New England landscape got to me. The erasures of the snow on the hills and the fields. The tendrils of chimney smoke suspended in the subzero sky over the Connecticut River Valley. Shortly after we arrived, the librarian in the nearest town had had a stroke, and I had assumed the part-time position, the first male librarian in the long history of the storefront institution. But not even this work steadied me. My wife of one year could see I was near a breakdown and together we went to the nearest public mental-health clinic, an hour away. My treatment consisted of talking it all out, although often I was only able to weakly mumble, "But my mother, she does good for people at Legal..." I refused anxiety-muting medication. The answers I needed were entombed in the very stuff of the worry, and the pain. I wanted access to every particle and had it. For the next two decades the cracking open of the past continued. At the start of the process my chest blistered over my heart of hearts, as if the grief had burned through to the surface like a flame. I hung in at the library as long as I could, which was not much longer. We moved to vibrant Burlington, where my wife got a job at an insurance company and the only work I could find was as a long-term temp at a sprawling IBM plant. I had been told to pound a pillow daily, and that I did—before Anne came home. I pounded pillows and I listened to the music of Bill Frisell, a novelist of a guitarist, his narrative riffs looping slowly, lyrically, into my troubled spaces of static and peril, love and loss.

I was soothed and inspired by Frisell's approach on his album *Have a Little Faith*, which included covers of songs by composers including Sousa, Copland, Dylan, and Madonna.

IN 1993, NOT LONG BEFORE I TURNED THIRTY, I called my parents and said what I had wanted to say for a long time, but been unable to. I did not, of course, use the best words. I still did not know the right words to use. I spit, distraught at the thought of things continuing on like normal between us when things had never been normal. I roared like a tiger: "Get help or I can't see you again!" My mother handed the phone to my father, who told me not to scream at the mother who had been keening at me since I was a child. I screamed "Get help!" at him, too, and I hung up. I was never called or seen by either of my parents again. And yet I did not feel orphaned. I felt I had already lived a lifetime with them. I did not feel the same about my brothers or sisters. I felt we had not begun, really. But when, and how, to begin to be to each other who we should have been all along? They did not call me to ask what had happened, and I did not call them to tell of it—I wanted one of them to care enough to ask. I wanted one of them to come to *my* rescue, finally. But they did not write, or call. They couldn't. This break threatened the most venerable of family fables—the myth that our improprieties were admirable acts of sophisticated rebellion, rather than crude, horrendous mistakes. They stayed away, propping up that notion as best as they could, I guessed, while I kept throwing out lines to the past, trying to make fresh sense of childhood chaos. I wrote a story called "The Curtain Birds," about old curtains that fly off their rods and veer in flocks across a backyard, and another called "Slenderina," about a prisoner who starves until she can fit out a cell crack.

T HREE YEARS LATER, after Anne and I had returned to Brooklyn to live, I got a call from Elizabeth's husband, Bill. I had not been invited to their wedding, which occurred after the break, but I had met Bill. He was the boyfriend who arrived at 15 Crestwood Terrace with fresh salad greens for the fridge, knowing that there would not be any otherwise. Bill was calling, at Elizabeth's urging, to tell me that my father had suffered a heart attack and was undergoing quintuple bypass surgery. I asked Bill the name of the hospital. It was the one where I had been born: St. Luke's. I called the hospital to check on my father's condition and got transferred to the acute-care floor. When I identified myself to the RN who answered, she said, "Wait a minute," and handed the phone to someone I at first thought was another nurse. "Yes!" the voice chirped like an RN not identifying herself…and then the panting. This was my mother, pretending, playing a game, wearing another mask out of fear or sheer perversity. I said: "I know it's you." And the line went dead.

D URING BILL'S PHONE CALL he had let drop a detail that disturbed me more than either my father's operation or my mother's latest charade. He said he had been looking forward to having me as a brother-in-law and that after a few Christmases, when my name was not mentioned, he couldn't stand it anymore and asked: "Where's Ben? Why won't anyone say his name?" It took a stranger to say my name in my family's house. In me simmered the image of Bill by a blinking tree from the Wisemen lot, staring at a wall of silent faces, asking where I was. It was a product of confusion—in the case of my siblings. I had been clear with my mother and my father about the gravity of the situation, but could see that I had not made enough of an effort to explain to my brothers and sisters why I had separated from the clan. I kept hoping one of them might contact me in concern when I did not return for the holidays—it would make it far easier for me to say what needed to be said. When no one called I was prey to feeling no one cared to know why I stayed away. Had my sisters and brothers grouped me in with my mother's sister, the chemist Deena, who—it had long been said—selfishly abandoned the Midwest for the high life on the coast? But I had not thrown my family over for the snide life, nor had she. I was, on that coast, haunted each day by my past, dwelling on it to a degree some found distasteful. I had not been subsumed by selfishness or greed. I had been subsumed by sorrow over what our family had been, and was still. I wanted our lives to be about more than the disastrous years. We each experienced our own private version of the domestic scenario; we were, all six of us, bitterly reexperiencing it. I was no freer of regret than any of them—though they could not know it. I may have raced to out-distance the darkness and reach the available light—the brightness of skyscrapers and graduate school—but those moments when a mother asked of a son what no son should ever be asked remained pivot points that defined my existence. A storm of chaos had been implanted deep in me then, and ever afterward it could strike and make of days, or weeks, total wreckage. My siblings deserved, I thought, to know exactly what had made a break at this point in my life not only inevitable, but right, despite its cost. Shut out, I had one option left, which was to invite them to join me where I was, to try to admit them into the realities I had lived and to hope that the desire for an imperfect but authentic connection could overcome the terror of silence.

In 1997 I SENT EACH BROTHER AND SISTER a copy of the same letter describing in detail the bedroom weirdness with my mother and its relation to my drastic weight loss in 1977. Twenty years it took me to get to the heart of the matter. I had exhausted all the metaphors for pain and burned up all the mist in which the ugliness might be stowed and briefly forgotten. Finally there was only the darkness on the page, the unvarnished nightmare, no buried moon, no tiger in the rose garden: the m-word. The verb a sister had long ago tried to pin on a neighbor boy who *tried something*. Every clinician had labeled the bedroom experiences I described with that term. Was it apt, warranted? I found the syllables sickening. It was not my word. But I had exhausted the list of other words. As I typed it I heard a girl's voice wail *mole-esther*. Household language contagion had revealed that even the most sacrosanct language—legal, poetic, scientific—could be manipulated to skirt levels of truth. Exploitable chinks existed in every word; holes could be blown in any story. Whatever I said, it would be my assertion against that of a parent, and no sorrier text existed than *he said, she said*. Regardless, a voice had to be raised, didn't it? More avoidance of the terrible events could only compound the disaster and make a mockery of any future reconciliation between my siblings and me. They needed to know how far I had been pushed. Whatever the right label for the years of bedroom weirdness, the effects were unmistakable. Her roughened hands and monologues had steered a sensitive boy to the edge, and over. Shattered him. I had spent much of my life picking up pieces. But like other serious attempts, the composing of the letter taught me that any available word was either too narrow or too broad, able only to faintly illuminate the roiled depths of reality. I was crying *mole-esther* ineptly as I spelled perfectly—falling short and going too far, simultaneously. I knew there was more to my mother than her bedtime betrayals. She was an entire war of elements, a cyclone of contradictions. Part of her was better than those nights, and, I hoped, ashamed of her actions. Maybe she had never done it to any of my brothers or sisters—maybe what they had suffered was limited to being abandoned by her when they needed a parent to watch over them. But she had done what she had done to me, and I was lucky to be alive. Half of me, in fact, had not made it out of the city alive. She had gone way too far, and she had never once assumed responsibility, apologized. She had instead cowered behind a golden shield of eccentricities calculated to make her look far more saintly, or helpless, than she actually was. And I had let her get away with it. I had excused her a thousand times in the name of pity or even respect. She had been incredibly helpful to the poor of the city. She had a sense of humor and had granted me a passion for many classic poems that I still reread, bask in, really, like sunshine. These aspects of her that I adored—doted on with a son's love—had protected her from any accusation for the longest time, even after the night I broke off. No child wants to state what I stated about my mother in that letter. No child wants to acknowledge that his worst moments on earth have been spent in the company of a parent he counts on to protect him from the world's evil. But when this happens, there is something to be said, no matter how long it takes for the words to arrive, or how awkward the delivery is. In front of the battered hall linen closet, when her face flushed and she asked if I wanted her to put on more medicine, I agreed. I did have rashes from the dirty sheets on my buttocks. The cold wet salve did feel good on the aching skin. But as I lay motionless on my fat belly, spread-eagled, it felt dizzyingly dangerous—her fingers down there, sliding, skating into crevices as the wind trickled in the screen window and her far-off Samaritan voice instructed me on what to do if I were attacked by a drifter . . . That kind of care was one reason I had no children of my own. I met my partner for life, a brilliant and tender partner, yet the idea of my adding any innocence to the world seemed patently ridiculous, or frightening. Innocence was intactness, and I lived in pieces. Knowing what could happen to children, I wouldn't have been able to let a son or daughter go anywhere, would I? Not that I put any of that in the 1997 letter. Into the letter I put the minimum for maximum impact. It was a real chance, I thought, to make five family members see what my skeleton had not made them see, nor my mysterious absence. The letter began: "I think it is important you know why I have not been home since 1991."

H OWARD RETURNED THE ENVELOPE torn up, writing on one of the tatters: *Please don't try to contact me again.* I heard nothing about my letter from Elizabeth, Nathan, or Nanette. Marianna, though, got back to me promptly. It amounted to the most direct—circularly direct—response to my account. She wrote:

> I more than welcome any cards or letters from you, but please refrain from any references to "MOTHER" and "FATHER." I have many thoughts and ideas exclusive of the family perhaps only you can understand. (I'm writing again!) I try very hard to progress as a person every day. To me, progression and forgiveness makes more sense than dwelling on shit that happened in the past. Ben, two years ago my despair was so great I overdosed. Technically, I died 3xs. I pulled through only after being in a coma for a week. I am here today for a reason. I don't think that it's anyone's—mine—or anyone's reason to be here to harbor anger. Think about it. Life is short. I'm here for you. I love you, Marianna.

I replied right away, and in that letter wondered if the suppression of anger was the best thing for any of us at this point. She took umbrage:

> In response to your letter of Dec. 15—you are certainly enti-
> tled to your feelings, I merely wish to establish contact with
> you on another level. I understand your hatred toward our
> parents, I don't need to hear about it constantly. If you are
> that consumed (so consumed that's all you can talk about)
> this entire correspondence is not only bogus, but pointless.
> Do you think I don't get what you've accused them of?
> You really needn't only speak, or write of that, for if that
> is your only facet left thanks, but no thanks, I don't need
> to hear any more of it. I chose to forgive and if you cannot
> accept that of me—see ya.

BUT I HAD NOT USED THE WORD HATRED in the letter—not come close to it. She had applied that word to my contention that our parents needed to accept responsibility and stop allow-ing we children to bear an unfair—and crushing—share of the burden for the family's failures. I worried more than ever about my sister Marianna who had died three times in order to live, but I didn't return that letter. I felt I had no way to reach her. I lacked the imagination to see us pulling off a relationship separate from house ordeals that, as she stated, allowed us to know things about each other that no one else knew. I could, though, see Elizabeth and me as still having something "separate." We had had that when we were little, with our "family of two," around the time we made the blood pact to be writers. Although she never responded specifically to my letter, we continued in our effort, begun in the early '90s, to exchange one annual letter—her telling me about her life of teaching Latin, me telling her about my life of writing and working bad jobs. She was better at casual chatter than I was. I got tangled up by the urge to slip in observations of the challenges we faced due to the past. The comments, though, were general. I was careful not to place her in the potentially hazardous role of family messenger. Things were dicey enough. I sometimes found it scary just to hold the letters she sent, infused as they were with my mother's Brook Farm tone of: *Aren't we a wonderful family for setting ourselves apart from others, living weirder?* On the envelope she would wreath my address, and hers, in tiny hand-drawn flowers. One letter described being involved in a three-car accident and yet still making it to school on time for the production of *Alice in Wonderland* that she was overseeing. The content was rife with the menace of our upbringing: its pathos and its cacophony. Still, I gave her credit for the effort to keep in touch even when I was unable to return her letters. She did it with a sense of mission. She did it, I think, out of loneliness. It went on year after year. During that time her two sons grew to be teenagers. She had also had a child, another boy, who had died in infancy of a heart condition. The disease had been discovered before birth and the baby was initially operated on in the womb. Elizabeth did everything she could to save that son. She lived in Cincinnati—apart from her family in Indiana—to receive specialized prenatal care during the late stages of pregnancy, following the surgery. After his birth, my nephew—named after an Irish playwright and prose writer—received the best care available, heroic aid, from Ohio doctors and his mother. A heart transplant was attempted as a last resort, but the child died forty-six days later. After the burial, which I later found out occurred on my birthday, Elizabeth sent a graphic account of the event that had permanently altered her life. In subsequent annual letters, sister wrote of candles lit nightly in the window. The two surviving boys posed with an ornament representing my lost nephew for their Christmas card. When the dead demand their space, they get it.

In 2000 MY FATHER SENT ME A LETTER. That business-size envelope contained a studio head-shot folded so that it would fit—his face quartered—and a note. In it he mentioned again my tendency to never come out of the rain. He said he was writing mysteries. He listed the writing conferences he was scheduled to attend in the upcoming summer. They were located all over the country— the most expensive conferences. (I recalled how he had refused to write me a twenty-dollar check to attend the Mississippi Valley Writers' Conference when I was in high school. Dr. Miller's widow, Opal, had died, I figured, and left him a lump sum.) He wrote that he planned to attend the Edgar Awards in New York, at the Hilton, and commingle with the best mystery writers the world had to offer. I sensed he was not traveling to get an award but to ogle the winners and hope their magic rubbed off. He offered to meet with me at the Hilton. But I couldn't meet him in a lobby of prefab pretensions. I did not want to play second fiddle to any Edgar Awards. If he couldn't commit words to paper to the effect that he was coming to see me, that it had been too long—if he must come for another reason and work me in on the side like a minor tourist attraction—well, I was busy. I avoided the loner who flew in from Iowa to attend the Edgar Awards and wait in line for the autographs of Anne Perry and Eliot Pattison.

On the day of the attacks of September 11, 2001, Robert Dana called from Iowa to see how I was doing. It meant everything to hear his strong baritone voice on that harrowing day when I, like tens of thousands, fled Manhattan on foot, walking downtown, toward the smoke and fire, to reach a bridge to Brooklyn. I described the dust-covered New Yorkers—the downtown refugees—and surgeons in scrubs waiting outside Bellevue for survivors not materializing. He described contacting an old Iowa Workshop friend of his, Donald Justice, to sort through the events. There were no calls that night from my family. I trusted that my mother, though, would closely check any printed list of victims for the name of her estranged oldest child. Several days after the attack, Marianna left a few words on my work voice mail. She sounded as if speaking through a pillow, half-smothered. She said she missed me. That Marianna—of them all—would be the one to call was astonishing. She was coping the worst of anyone with her difficult past. Yet she was the one to make the effort. It was all backward. It was all so strange. She did not leave a return number or say where she was. She sounded lost. From oblique references in Elizabeth's letters, I had gathered that Marianna's second marriage had fallen apart quick. She really did miss me and I missed her. What I did not miss was the situation that had done that to her once-vibrant voice, muted it and then all but silenced it. There were alternatives. I had found one. I had my own fragile life to keep clinging to.

Ten more years passed just like that. They passed like a freight train and every Christmas hit me hard, and every birthday, but I expected that. I had to face again, during those "family" holidays, that I had no safety net under me other than my wife, my in-laws, and a few friends. I had made it a point to keep my circle of friends small, small enough that I could do right by each one. These intimate acquaintances meant much to me, and, whether they knew it or not, bore an extra burden, because try as I might to avoid it, I did at times look to them for the support I should have been getting from my missing-in-action family. No one bore more of the burden, or bore it more gracefully, than my spouse. When I went into my holiday funks for the obvious reasons, Anne helped me through. We made a big thing of our anniversaries. We went to Montauk for the weekend, the winter ocean. We celebrated our fifteenth, and then twentieth, wedding anniversaries. The historic gas-lit restaurant where we were joined in matrimony had become an Arby's, but that was America, something to marvel at while wincing. Each year, on December 9, we slipped the nautical rope out of the green velvet bag and pulled on it, retightening our knot. We kept writing—while holding unrelated day jobs—and publishing in a myriad of small literary journals. We purchased an apartment at last, my in-laws providing the down payment. Having children was not the right decision for us, for many reasons, but we wanted to have books in the family, and in 2006 Anne's first book of poems, *Floating City*, was chosen by Kay Ryan as the winner of the Walt Whitman Award, given annually by the Academy of American Poets. We sent Elizabeth a copy and she was enthusiastic. Then, in the interest of nudging our correspondence in a possibly more fruitful, or honest, direction I sent Elizabeth a journal containing an early version of "Battle Hymn of the Iowa State Teachers College." She was enthusiastic about it as well. In July 2008 she wrote: "I could just feel in your account the loneliness, confusion and alienation that filled much of our elementary school years. It resonated with me, of course."

I had to think we were getting somewhere, very slowly. She was usually careful not to mention our brothers and sisters—careful to keep our "family of two" intact—but stuff slipped in. From her, over the years, I learned that Howard had made good on his childhood threat to run away to California, and had worked on LA film crews. I learned that Nanette had a job as a librarian, then married well and had many children. I learned that Nathan, like Grandpa Stanley, had become a civil engineer, and owned dogs. She was most careful never to relate any data about our mother. We sent Elizabeth's boys Christmas presents: notebooks, Astro-Pens, the anthology *Poem in Your Pocket*. We were sure they loved to read.

Because of these exchanges, I was unprepared for the events of December 22, 2011. It started with a grave phone message. "Is this the Ben Miller who grew up in the East Village of Davenport? If so, call me right away." When I dialed that evening, I reached a high school classmate to whom I had not spoken in nearly thirty years. Randy sat at a public library Googling the Ben Millers of New York City. He was prepared to call dozens, if he had to. We had been long distance runners on the track team and riding buddies on river valley cycling adventures. We had fallen out of touch when I went away to college. We had a minute or so of casual conversation, and then Randy reported that he had attended my father's funeral that day chiefly to see me, and, not seeing me, had asked my family members why I was not there. One of them—he did not say who—admitted I had not been informed of the death, and this brother or sister continued: "He wouldn't have wanted to come anyway." As I struggled to absorb that information, Randy went on: "And another thing, your sister Marianna is dead, too. She died a few months ago."

I REPEATED THE NEWS ALOUD to make sure I had it right, and my wife got up from the desk where she had been typing on her laptop and sat down next to me at our dining room table. "You did not know?" Randy said. "You should know." I agreed I should know. Randy offered his deep condolences. He said he was awfully sorry to be the one to break the news. I said I was sorry he had to do it, too. I told him that it was one of the most heroic things... Somehow sentences filled my mouth like over-large fruit sections. *He wouldn't have wanted to come anyway.* I heard the words in Nathan's soft, discouraged voice—the voice of our six-mile walks to nowhere. Randy asked, "Would you have gone?" I said I did not know. I might have. I... I was not crying. I was in shock, chilled. I told Randy that I had learned in the summer, in a letter from Elizabeth, that my middle sister was unable to care for herself. It sounded like she might be in a home of some kind, but the place was not identified. I had written back, asking for details, and still had gotten no response. Elizabeth would have returned from Marianna's funeral to find my letter, but had not answered it, though she knew I had no other way of knowing about our sister's death, since my mother would likely never call me, and likely no one else, either. Then my father had died two months later, and still she had failed to call. At the bottom of my last letter to Elizabeth, in October, I had jotted my phone number, just in case. I now had with Elizabeth what I had with the others, dead or alive. I had the darkness that relationships can escort into lives, wave by wave, until finally there exists only the darkness and no relationship—the night you have granted each other, night to superintend, to carry with you everywhere and get lost inside.

Randy was the crazy eight in this narrative whom no one had planned on. Randy on the phone with me now like an ache of light in the dark, wanting to tell me things about the events I had missed. Randy, another non-family member appearing out of nowhere to help me when I needed aid the most. Again and again, it had happened. The Iowa that had almost been the end of me had also saved me, cared for me. Mr. Hickey serving the fat boy the respect he hungered for. Murray Bischoff who, on hearing of my poetry award at fifteen, had bought me a gift subscription to the *New York Review of Books*. Blanche and the rest of Writers' Studio giving me a basket overflowing with notebooks, pens, and toiletries before I went off to college. I sat at a mission-style table, hunched, squeezing the receiver, astonished again by the improbable collision of curse and blessing. As horrible as it was to hear the news, not knowing was worse. Randy said Elizabeth had mentioned the name of the place where I worked, which made finding my number easier. I thanked him again for the brave, kind effort. What made Randy do it? A feeling lingering from those long bike tours we went on—that's all I could think. Sharing the duress of August sun and November wind, keeping pace with each other, hour after hour, keeping each other in sight, sharing the water bottle. We had had that bond in high school, and no girlfriends, and the home ordeals. (The one time I had met Randy's father had been one time too many.) We were the jittery misfits in exactly the wrong cut of clothing. The stress of biking...it fleetingly cleansed us of other stresses and expectations. On our rides we suffered for a reason—suffered to get stronger. We stretched the chains of our trouble across counties until we felt nearly unchained, almost free.

THE POOR FUNERAL ATTENDANCE, Randy said, indicated that
my father was an unpopular member of the law profession. I con-
curred. Randy was a declarative speaker. At times his speech had
an almost Tourettic rhythm and it could be wildly off-key. When I
told him my wife was a poet, I was hit with an Andrew Dice Clay
joke. Then he said: "I don't recall ever seeing your father." I said
a lot of people didn't recall seeing him during his lifetime. Randy
said that he had meant to go to Marianna's funeral but that he had
to work that day. He told me he was a history buff, a member of
the Quad City Archeological Society, and now jobless. After the
funeral he had gone to the library to work on his résumé, when it
hit him that he had to find me, let me know about my father and
Marianna. He said that he and his wife lived near the house Bix
Biederbecke had grown up in. Things kept coming together like
they always had for me. They came together by falling completely
apart. I don't know how much silence passed between us, but
then I heard Randy asking me if I was still there. I was. Randy
described his interactions with my brothers and sisters at the
funeral service and at the reception afterward. It sounded like he
had come to them in confusion and been alternately pandered
to and managed, dazzled and misdirected. I knew my family. I
knew where they came from. We were estranged but no strangers.
In their faces one hurt was lost in another hurt until they didn't
know why they hurt, until they could tell themselves they did not
hurt, and sometimes get away with it, as I had at times. Elizabeth,
Howard, Nanette, and Nathan were, like me, the children of a
father's smoke and a mother's steam—people whose stories had
vaporized. We were kids delivered to the school system from the
Outer Limits down the block. We were, each of us, shape-shifters
to one degree or another. That ability had allowed them, at least
on the surface, to swiftly accommodate to the contour of a family

lacking me, just as it allowed me to assume a place in a life lacking
them. If Randy was disgusted by their not calling me, he was impressed by the other elements of themselves that they put forward.
For a minute or two, each of us children could impress almost
anyone—that was part of our family curse. Elizabeth told Randy—
the child of the blue-collar west-side bungalow—about teaching
Latin and also about losing a child in infancy after the complicated surgeries. Randy learned of Howard's twenty-year stint in
the film industry in LA. With wonder, Randy went on to relate
that Howard was now selling vegetables in the summer on US 52.
Hollywood to tomatoes—not many people could manage a leap
like that. And what else did they have over Randy? Well, Randy
lacked the ability to imagine that I would not be there. They had
imaginations! And Randy, he had merely an ill-fated hunt for an
old friend. Just an affection for me that was deeply rooted in rivers
of light, and made him the fool asking: "Why didn't you call?"
Randy said Nanette fled the chapel after an argument with Elizabeth over funeral details. Randy told me that he had congratulated
Nathan on winning a statewide grilling competition. Randy was
an avid newspaper reader, trivia recaller. Nathan, the civil engineer, would have been the nicest to Randy, I guessed.

W E COULD NOT HOLD EACH OTHER. We kept finding new
ways to let each other go, though we had not seen each other in
decades. It truly felt like the last time I had seen Marianna was
outside the Blue and Gold Tavern the Thanksgiving night a man
had tried to buy her. It seemed that at twenty she had sneaked into
the rest of her life and rarely poked her head out, as I had sneaked
into mine and hunkered there, waiting. But that wasn't the last

time I saw her. I had been to her first wedding, after the New York visit. I recalled the gown without her in it. The night before the big event, my wife and I slept in the basement at 15 Crestwood Terrace, which had recently been renovated—in one corner. We slept on the floor of that "game room," where the dress hung like a mist rising off the carpet.

I COULD NOT LET GO of the phone and apparently Randy couldn't, either. He kept doggedly circling back to the issue of my having been locked out of my father's funeral. He had never known people to behave like this. For all the trouble he had with his father, they were not only in touch, but the man was helping his son through the hard economic time. "Betsy should have called you. Or Howard. I have Howard's cell number, want it?" I did not answer. The family rituals of avoidance and flight, of shunning responsibilities, worked against the interests of us all, but the longer it went on, the greater grew our worries over what confronting each other would mean. I heeded Howard's warning scrawled on the scrap of my letter he had torn up and returned. And besides, I told Randy, it was my mother's job to call me. It was her job, as head of the family, to do it. Once again, she had done no job. She had run away.

My MIND CAREENED with images, the downed timeline, its branches tangled and mangled and snapped. The cartons of Marlboro cigarettes father placed under the Christmas tree in later years for Marianna and Howard, the trio puffing away in the living

room strewn with wrapping paper and smelling of bacon fry-
ing. Marianna, at forty-four, bloated in her bed in the institution
where she had been sent when she could no longer take care of
herself. Father telling me after my wedding ceremony that he had
disliked the "rope shenanigans." Marianna writing in the late '90s
to proudly inform me that she had obtained a secretarial position
with a "conglomerate in Cincinnati." I couldn't help thinking
about the shell of her body separated from the blood and breath
of its story, the coffin and mourners filing past, pausing to look at
her made-up face, hinting either at the bloom of youth or desecration, depending on the viewer. Death did not end a person's vulnerability but eerily intensified it. Marianna was a memory pulled
like taffy into countless shapes, and that was true of my father also.
All who remain are guilty of grief's unavoidable outcome: remembering. I recalled the final glimpse of my father and my mother,
back before the break. It was at a Motel 6 in Madison, Wisconsin,
where they had driven to attend the wedding of a cousin of my
wife's. My parents had pressed me to get them invitations so we
could "all be together." But they wanted nothing to do with Anne
or her parents or relatives. My mother, at one point during that
sad weekend, held out her hand and said, "Let's you and me go
to the mall." She did not know which one but trusted she could
find one for our pseudo-tryst. I could not take her hand because I
knew by then all that it was attached to. My father demanded I get
up at seven to meet him at the breakfast bar in the stifling room
off the lobby. I had trouble getting up in time and heard about it.
I saw my mother stealing lotion packets from the maid's cart in
the hall, filling the gullet of the latest incarnation of Moby Purse.
At last it was over. There were surly good-byes in the parking lot.
My mother and father wedged themselves into their old car, and
my wife and I and her parents got in the shiny rental. Prior to our

turning off for the airport, on the neither-here-nor-there access road, I got the last of the last excruciating glimpses of my parents, two shadows in a vehicle burning oil. The lonely shade of a woman in the passenger's seat scooted over to be nearer the shade of a man in the driver's seat, or to get within reach of the steering wheel—it would be impossible to know which. The turbulence of her conflicts lent each choice multiple meanings so that none really had to be authentic.

*H*E WOULDN'T HAVE WANTED *to come anyway.* I kept trying to explain to Randy that our family had rarely come through for each other. It was our trope. It was our plot. I struggled, as usual, to efficiently convey the disaster without dumbing it down. I had come to question those books and articles that from family chaos purported to create something easy, even pleasing, for consumers to devour. The death of a family could have no happy ending. It could have survivors, possibly. In the end I fell back on the line Marianna had been the first to use, way back in 1989, when she met my wife-to-be and my mother-in-law in the Cellar at Macy's. "You know, there was violence in our family." Randy, because of his own past, assumed I was speaking about a father who beat my brains out. I said no, it was my father's fading from the picture that allowed my mother to lean on me with all her might, all her desire. And it was my father's fading away that allowed his six children to attack each other at will, in different ways. Randy blurted: "So the prick is dead now, huh?" My father, he meant. "She's so little!" My mother, he meant. Now she is, I thought. Randy indicated that Walcott Library patrons were now giving him looks. He said he would call me later. He asked for my e-mail address and street address. He asked once more if I wanted

Howard's number. I had much to do in the wake of this news, but calling him? Not on the list. I wasn't as valiant as Randy, though I wanted to be. I hadn't seen or talked to Howard since 1991, and in the decade before that we hardly spoke; mostly I heard stories about Howard—including the one about him killing the raccoon in our attic with a baseball bat to get cash for the pelt while I was away at college. Howard too had cracked under the strain of the family circus. He might have, in fact, been the first to crack. While mother and I were out, stuffing our faces at Big Boy, nine-year-old Howard, alone in a messy room, repeatedly played the hit single "Wild Thing" in a wolverine daze of electric upset. By then our parents had already labeled him "bad." They'd let him go, and he knew it. I had let him go, too, and he was smart enough to know it. When he let go of sister and a door shattered, more than one heart broke into jagged bits. The shards still need to be sorted out, the glitter cradled. There are as many forms of atonement as people. And what was mine—for not being there for my little brother or for Marianna in her time of greatest need, those months of institutionalization in whatever facility? No one—and no religion—could tell me.

O N THE LIST, IMMEDIATELY AFTER HANGING UP, was to print out two obituaries that had appeared in the *Quad-City Times*, each accompanied by a photograph. Marianna as a teenager, the game smile of the party girl, the shampoo glow around her head. Father in the last stage of his long life as a self-appointed savant: chimp grin, wire rims, buzz-cut. The obituary texts amply displayed the brio and balderdash of the family language contagion. I figured that my mother—maybe with Elizabeth's help—had written them. Not to be notified of either funeral, yet to be neatly noted as a surviving loved one ("Benjamin (Anna) [*sic*] Miller, New York City") counted as more weirdness. Natives reading my name there would naturally believe I had been notified of the deaths, and some of those present might well have assumed I chose not to attend due to disinterest, or spite. Whenever I returned to the area I would wear a new badge of shame unless the whole truth came out. I believed it existed—the whole truth. It arced like a rocky shore at the end of the furious current of imperfect words.

D‍AVID TRAVELED WIDELY, most memorably to Singapore and the Cape of Good Hope, South Africa. He had a scholar's grasp of history, art, and literature. He had a beautiful singing voice, occasionally bursting into song, and he was renowned for his whistling. He loved to take liberties with the English language to the amusement of his family. He was the author of numerous books...

... and one genuine masterpiece, cut from the bramble of doubt and imagination, named by his daughter Nanette: "Twigmas."

B‍ORN WITH AN ARTISTIC SOUL, Marianna had a gift for visual and creative arts. She enjoyed painting, drawing and writing, working for a time in the printing business. Known to all who loved her as "Mitzi," she was clever, quick-witted, silly, well-versed, intelligent, articulate and spunky.

Born an artistic soul. Burned—this artistic soul. It was suggested that mourners make contributions to the American Heart Association.

I DID NOT CALL ELIZABETH to ask why she had not called. I feared she'd want instantaneous forgiveness—or at least for me to excuse her actions—and I couldn't, not yet. Nor did I go out to a New York diner, order the greasiest meal, and, outside, in the appointed spot, chain-smoke Philip Morris Commander cigarettes to memorialize my father, who had reclined for one last time.

ON THE LIST ALSO was recalling my supposed rescue of Marianna at Duck Creek Plaza and other faux rescues, creeping across manicured lawns, at age thirteen and fifteen and seventeen, to wrest a sister from the claws of wealth or to be humiliated trying, while my coffee-breathing anthology-paging mother waited in the car. On the list was thinking about why I had let the East Coast visits of my brothers and sisters in the late '80s be among our last meetings as adults. I faced again the fact of how exhausted I had been at age twenty-two by the family murk and peril—that toxic mix of cynicism and sentiment, the desire for a togetherness that never materialized no matter how hard we dreamed to make it real. Even as the thrilling city visits played out, I was already on my way to being considered "the one who left and never came back." My love for my parents had been matched, then completely overrun, by my terror of becoming them, individuals whose slow-burn self-destruction was their largest achievement. In each of their pitiful postures lurked the taunt: *If I was not good enough to make it, how can you be?* On the list was rereading my last letter to Elizabeth, dated October 14, 2011, the day before Marianna died:

> We know how she was neglected when she was young—
> allowed to drop out of Central, allowed to take awful jobs

like the security guard position at the factory in downtown
Rock Island. (I will never forget going to pick her up one
night—the pale teenage figure coming across the vast
empty parking lot—ill-fitting uniform, ponytail gleaming in
the orange death light.) Too often our sister was dropped
off at places where she was likely to be preyed upon. Please,
if possible, let me know the name of the institution where
she is being kept. Who put her there? How compromised
is she? Can you bear visiting her? Does she ever get out?

I railed to Anne about that letter lying quarantined on the corner
of Elizabeth's desk—opened or unopened? My return address
sleeting across paper. How could the sister who had faithfully
written birthday letters be the same person who hadn't called
when my father and Marianna died? The mechanism that had
helped us summon the courage to keep in contact—that romantic
notion of a disinfected relationship apart from the family mire—
had in the end wrenched us free of our obligation to reality, made
unthinkable lapses in judgment possible. The letters, I understood now, were but a silky lining of the nightmare, more intelligent derangement. The next, and final, childish oath to be broken.
Possibly the fact that I had not included my phone number in a
letter for a decade prevented Elizabeth from seeing that scrawl at
the bottom of the page under my signature.

On the list, too, was appearing the next morning in my cube
at a reference publisher blocks from Madison Square Garden,
where I earned what they called a living and had deadlines to
meet, files to format. On the list was passing coworkers in the

hall, talking about holiday plans, exchanging small talk. If I told them about the deaths they would want to know why I was not with my family. If I told them why I was not with my family they would have the look of people hearing what no one wants to hear. I got through the day in serf mode—typing quick, robotic. Then, because I dwelled in the America of Gatsby and MasterCard, I left my stall to meet Anne at the bar of the St. Regis, a dark place of delight that Marianna would have liked. There we held a quiet teary wake in front of the absurdist King Cole mural painted by Maxfield Parrish. One martini, two... On the list—that weekend—was Christmas with my in-laws, receiving their embraces and their copious gifts of music, books, patient listening.

On the list, the next week, was waiting for a call from my mother or from Elizabeth. It did not come. The wizardry of technology purporting to connect all to all did not connect Millers to Millers. For those who are estranged, a disconnection predicated on deepest feelings can be less repulsive than instant connections glib around the edges, or eaten through with superficiality. On the list was bearing up under the generous onslaught of supportive e-mails Randy whipped off. He wrote in the peripatetic and blunt way that he spoke, the words unscrolling. *I met your deceased sister in 2003 again, and I did not recognize her. When she was in high school she was so hot, cigarettes and booze killed her. Such a tragedy. I was not happy that I had to break the news to you. I feel that Howard or Betsy should have called you. But that is life. And life is not fair. I have not received any job offers yet, but I may be getting on as a direct care provider for handicapped people at a social work place. I hope to make it out to New York some day to visit you.* Time that had torn everything apart—turn after turn— was also the only thing that could put it all back together. Randy, Class of '83, spilling the beans, my new eyes and ears in urban Iowa.

ON THE LIST IN THE TWO WEEKS that followed was writing. Writing had always been the most reliable way of making it through any crisis. The dark I had been dealt by the family must be tended to. It could not be tamed but layers could be captured, examined. It was what I had left to hold on to. I retyped my father's and my sister's obituary to reflect how I saw their lives. I retyped the last letter I had sent Elizabeth, the day before Marianna's death, reinserting the thoughts and emotions that had been pared almost to nothing in order to fit into the envelope and the template of our stilted and filtered correspondence. In a fury I typed the raw materials for a novel, *The Clouds*, which would involve cutting out the right sentences and pasting them into ragged clusters scudding across a horizontal page. Fathers and sons have such a genius for imitation.

IN FEBRUARY I CALLED RANDY. He mentioned applying to work on the second shift at a turkey slaughterhouse near Iowa City. The words *food pantry* came up. In the midst of his economic trial, however, he kept citing mine: "Betsy hasn't called you yet?" I said no, adding that it was unlikely she would at this point. Randy declared more amazement. I stated that Elizabeth was likely still so addled by the family static following the funerals that making a common-sense call to me would be one of the hardest things in the world. Even at a remove of a thousand miles I myself was addled by family static. Anyway, I emphasized, as before, that my mother should be the one calling. The trouble for Randy was that he didn't understand that shunning could be a family's modus operandi—that scapegoats must exist to absorb the sole blame for communal ruination. Howard and Marianna and father first. Elizabeth at many junctures—once simply because she had asked for Italian clogs. At last my own halo had slipped, becoming a collar of disgrace. No, I could not make real to a loyal person like Randy that family shutting out family was our family's only lasting tradition. It was my father lifting the newspaper whenever a child approached the easy chair. It was my mother putting the pedal to the metal to elude five children chasing the car down the alley. It went back generations. Grandpa Stanley slamming the door in my face and Nathan's after we had trudged across state lines to see him. Dr. Miller sending my birthday gift down to the parking lot with Grandmother Rose. Dr. Miller's father from Scotland, my great-grandfather, the Milwaukee road mechanic, refusing to let any kids into his white house in Wisconsin. I had a memory of picking grass outside on the front lawn, staring at a shut door. The engine of estrangement was love's engine slammed into reverse, and not incidentally. Estrangement was one of the few events in life that could not be a pure godchild of chance. We had done it to ourselves. Whether out of despair or malice or paranoia or ignorance, all of us had played a role. Had I called Elizabeth? I had not. I had started to feel empathy for her again. Who knew how many deaths she had died already? But that empathy didn't change what a phone call initiated by me would mean. Such a call would mean me again taking the lead on "patching things up" and I couldn't. I couldn't repair this ruined family on my own. Years of sorry attempts had only led to more wreckage. I'd wait for her to contact me. I'd see what she had to say for herself.

In AUGUST OF 2012, ten months after Marianna's death, I received word from Elizabeth. In her short letter, she wanted to know if I was upset with her for not calling. She wondered, out loud on the page, if she should have shared the news that our sister had died. If she didn't know the answer, I couldn't tell her. But after meditating on many angles of the December debacle, this much was clear: just how spooked Millers were by each other. When we got together, scary stuff generally happened. It was sick but true: all that really held us together was our inclusion in the same crisis that had blown us apart. And then there was that haunting snippet of funeral dialogue: *He wouldn't have wanted to come anyway.* Those who had failed to contact me after these two recent deaths had ample reason to fear what I myself had feared when I returned to Davenport in the summer of 2007, too aggrieved to stay away any longer yet unable to knock on doors. By then my sense of loss was such that I could not believe a family member would be there to let me in.

GRIEF BROUGHT ME all the way from 149th Street, in New York City, to the bottom of my childhood alley, but no farther. I stood there with my wife, who held the 35 mm camera I had asked her to carry. We had traveled to Davenport from Iowa City, where we had stayed a few days with Robert Dana, the poet yet afloat, publishing books, and now, in his seventh decade, the Poet Laurete of Iowa. The night before, after a deck cookout, he had recited fresh work to us and we to him. It was a warm, nice evening. Then this. Cars passed behind me on Jersey Ridge Road as my eyes followed the cracks of the alley, which had not been repaved in many decades. These cracks were history's EKG. My gaze followed the jagging rhythm upward to Crestwood Terrace. My feet shifted.

My chest throbbed, as in the bad stories of Writers' Studio that kept coming true. My head spun—as Norm or Gordon would have written. Sweating bullets would be next, according to Roy. Even the most flawed or dull art could mysteriously possess a rich ability to frame a life. Anne said it wouldn't be a good idea to go knock on the door—unannounced. I nodded. I had not seriously considered that. Being shut out by loved ones was most bearable when your back was turned to those locked doors—more tolerable, if no less real. I didn't need to step near that closed door to know that the place where a person most wants to belong can also be the place where he feels the most intense disaffection and disorientation—for there, in that cradle of origin, each tick and tock of change resounds the weirdest and the longest. I could have warned my parents about this visit, felt them out, but after all these years I could not have handled a receiver slamming down any more than I would be able to handle our eyes slamming together followed by the slamming shut of a door. Their silence up there on the hill was as packed with messages as anything I could ever say or write. They wanted no part of my life—present or past. Nothing to do with that fourteen-year-old skeleton on the stairs. He was troubling to see, I knew. But the longer he went unseen, and until secrets were revealed and examined, they would unfairly overshadow the rest of a family's complex saga.

I KNEW THE DOORS WERE EQUIPPED with working locks now. They hadn't been when I was a kid—constant escapes from each other broke those locks—but they had been replaced, finally. They had been fixed right before I broke off with my parents. It had nothing to do with me, though. It had to do with my mother getting a call from the bus station in Davenport. It was a woman, just arrived, requesting money. The story was mysterious and not filled in. But from what Nathan had told me more than a decade earlier—during a visit he paid to us in Vermont, the last time I'd seen him—and from what I learned later in bits and pieces from Elizabeth and Marianna, my mother had immediately gotten locks installed on the doors, and had then met with this woman at Riefe's Restaurant and given her cash to leave town. Aunt Julie was at that meeting to aid the effort to get rid of the blackmailing stranger. Who was she? She might well have been my half sister, and the reason there had been a baby bed, and related items, in the locked attic of the Stanley house. I saw it once, when devious Grandpa gave me the key. The maid, Beatrice, dusted up there. The bed rungs were clean. There was a pillow.

My wife walked back to the car. She knew what time it was. Time to go. I followed. We had other sights to see, places to claim. For if I had never stopped clinging to family riddles with one hand, I had with the other hand never stopped clinging to the alternative real estate of my childhood—its bridges, its neighborhoods, its downtowns; the idiot riddles and answers of place. I clung essay by essay, story by story. My writing—all of it—was one vast open letter to the past. I was driven in that work, consumed by the task of channeling the twisting rivers of feeling and thought back to their source, where they ran darkest and brightest. That wasn't easy, but what could be easy about a world achieving endlessness through mortality, a world revolving its deaths—between the generations—like births? There was nothing new unless something else died. Almost immediately we parked again, got out, and approached the school playground where an obese boy had made his weird last stand, pencil in hand.

An hour later, after checking in at the Holiday Inn in Rock Island (a river view, please), we walked a short distance down the deserted pedestrian mall to the site where I had attended my first Writers' Studio meetings in the tenement long since bulldozed. People hunting phantoms point, and I did, like ancient Mr. Rush had once pointed out the slough where he shot ducks. "Right there," I said to Anne. The buzzing Kelvinator. John Morgan haltingly reciting his haiku. Blanche giving Norm's railroad poems that grimace of nurturing disdain. David R. Collins, in the turtleneck, keeping order. Howard Koenig, the first member I'd met that first night, offering help. The fourteen-year-old sliver of me listening to each of them, relying on each of them, believing in all of them, believing fully in the power of their encouragement to change my life for the better. It was as if the mistrust that had infected the other areas of my existence had granted me a supernatural ability to trust in them and in Mr. Hickey—just like a deaf person's vision sharpens in recompense. "Right there it was," I said, "on that lot." The uneven floor, the tilting table, a circle that even when it existed seemed to me to be hovering in an oblivion that failed to swallow us only because we ignored its long teeth.

Within the hour I was on centennial bridge, heading back to Davenport as my wife napped in the room. I was the ant on a concrete deck high above this mighty river shattered into glitters. The low and gloomy Government Bridge shivered when traffic was heavy, but not this one. Centennial Bridge, formerly a toll bridge, now paid for, thrust its monumental arcs across the sky. In an ecstatic fashion the roadway spanned the rift between Iowa and Illinois without resolving it. I was one with the weather, the broiling sun. My eyes tripped over the sight of Davenport. The skyline looked like the old emaciated skyline on steroids. I got dizzy, conscious of, and somehow threatened by, the railing there to protect me. To think I had pedaled my bike over the same narrow path at twenty miles an hour, my entire body above the rail save for my knees! I shuffled, stared at the tops of my shoes for security, stealing periodic peeks at a vista that a Writers' Studio alumnus could describe only as "breathtaking." (Research indicated that Dick Stahl, of Writers' Studio days, had been appointed the area's first poet laureate, serving from 2002 until 2003.) The area had by now been firmly branded as "Quad Cities, USA." It was a funny designation. To my knowledge, it had never appeared on a birth, wedding, or death certificate. Stamps were cancelled with the phrase and it had for decades adorned event banners, but in a legal sense it had no population. Gogol territory. Quad Cities, USA, was the codification of an identity crisis, and maybe wisely, as the municipalities strung along this bend of the river were forever wavering on the issue of whether it was preferable to resist the sprawl as a defined entity or to succumb to the momentum of conglomeration and melt away. The math didn't come out right no matter how you added. At a minimum Quad Cities, USA, consisted of five communities—Davenport and Bettendorf on the Iowa side; Rock Island, Moline, and East Moline on the Illinois side—and to be accurate, to that list should be added Milan, Illinois, and a slew of Iowa towns that Davenport and Bettendorf had all but usurped—DeWitt, Mount Joy, Pleasant Valley, Walcott. The Octo Cities, I'd have called it. Towns lost in cities like days were lost in years and people in the river. Talented Jack Seier, president of my senior class, had drowned in the Mississippi. Jack decided to bag groceries and to play guitar in cafés rather than go to college. He dived off the levee during a kegger and didn't come out. Jack had once asked me for lyrics and I wrote a parody of a country song. "I'd rather be run over by a tractor / than visit that chiropractor." Jack and I had gone to McKinley Elementary together, and also Sudlow Junior High.

NEAR THE END OF THE BRIDGE, where it arched over land again, I felt safer and leaned on the railing, gazing down at the brick ballpark where, on the best July nights, father had taken us to see the farm team of the California Angels play rivals from Dubuque and Wisconsin. He was very proud that the man who owned the team, Harry Pell, also maintained an office in the Davenport Bank Building. He told us of riding up in the elevator with Harry Pell. At the ballpark he would forget to worry about mosquitoes or about how bleacher seats hurt his hip. He would forget he was broke, and we would get programs, and also food. The outfield grass was so green it was blinding, the infield dirt groomed in Van Gogh swirls. It was possible to get Olympia beer poured down your back by a rowdy fan—wonderful thing! Out beyond the outfield-wall ads for THE DOCK, SEAFOOD and ACRE SIDING flowed the Mississippi, with its Styx ambiance. It all came back to me. The chewy popcorn, the gritty hot dogs. Howard on his back watching nighthawks dive at the banks of lights. Me screaming: "Attabatterattabatter..." Marianna and Elizabeth huddled like twins. Foul balls to chase. We were father's family for a good two hours. He barked: "Get me a dog. Go get yourself another! More popcorn, too." The dollar bills were as warm as skin. His favorite scene in literature was Thomas Wolfe's descriptions of the St. Louis World's Fair bacchanal: tents, food, freaks, and hayseed crowds.

WHERE THE BRIDGE ENDED the YWCA was still there. I turned right and headed into the cluster of downtown buildings, old and new. At the first deserted intersection I waited for the light to change. The back-and-forth between place and mind was fast, the traffic of ghosts thick. I saw no one leave, or enter, any of the anonymous new towers that stood out dumbly, as if their purpose was to hasten the complete demise of downtown by stamping out the blocks where rebirth might have occurred, one small storefront at a time. Yet it had not worked. This downtown was a resilient fragility, and entities living on the brink of extinction had a certain remarkable ambiance. They engaged the imagination like almost nothing else. Below the new towers cornices floated in shadows, sailing the eyes from Now to Then, back again. The vintage downtown could not be stamped out—not completely. It crept like weeds in crevices between the new developments. It lived on rooftops. The KAHL marquee still stood atop the building where Mr. Hickey had sold real estate and insurance. The office where, on a slow day, he carried the camera to the window, snapped a shot of the river bend, and returned to his desk, having accomplished something. "How was the school week?" he would ask, bundling the days to give me a better chance to say something positive. Often all I could say, striving to be neutral rather than negative, was "At school they took attendance." I was taking attendance as I walked. I was calling out to familiar corners and they were answering. I had them left. I had whatever the sun would allow me, and it entered the street like it was a little room belonging to someone—like a shaft of light creases the air after a blind is pulled. The city had let me in.

I ENCOUNTERED SIGNAGE directing busloads of visitors to the riverfront, where chintz-bedecked gambling barges were moored. The Figge Art Museum stood blocks away from the levee, like a glass penitentiary where works of art served long sentences for a noble cause. Near the museum I passed another pedestrian. The awkwardness of being alone together on the street prevented us from saying hello. Reaching Main, I turned left, and walked a half block to the Putnam Building, where my mother had restarted her law career after a nearly twenty-year hiatus. The small gloomy Putnam lobby still smelled of onions, as it had when I was a teenager. The odor wafted from the lobby door that led directly into the still-operating Hungry Hobo sub shop. Legal Assistance was no longer listed on the tenant roster. Few names were. I had a memory of plunging three floors in a Putnam elevator. After that heart-stopping incident I had always climbed the marble stairs to visit my mother at her office heaped with client files and listen to her latest rebukes of the unfair System that demonized the poor, canonized the rich. I could see her jowls flapping like puppets going on with the show on a rainy day. I could see myself nodding. It was as she said—a tragedy. It was one bad old world, brother. I crossed the street, entering what used to be the tallest building downtown, once owned by Davenport Bank, which by now had been bought out. The art deco lobby was empty but shiny, well-maintained by the Wells Fargo organization. When I was in college my father had closed his office here to take a job administrating Iowa bankruptcies for the government. He had told no one he had applied for the job, he simply came home one day and told my mother he would now be home only on weekends. She was not shocked. For a few years after that he lived during the weekdays in single rooms in Des Moines and Cedar Rapids, and I visited these places: microwave, ashtrays, television, thumbed copy of the novel *Ironweed*. Then, in the late '80s, he returned on a Saturday to say he had been let go. Why? He said his boss had called him in and explained that there had been a mix-up during the hiring process—they had meant to hire a different David Miller. No one knew what that story meant. But he was back in Davenport to stay . . . On the way out of the former Davenport Bank Building I peeked into the nook where a German lady, Murilla, had once sold fruit-flavored Nesbitt's Soda out of an old-style cooler. In the 1970s Murilla had given our family some living room furniture that she no longer needed. My mother set the deal up. My father was against receiving "charity" of any type, and raged at the giver's "meddling," but he had no power to rebuff a blue couch halfway through the door. It got all the way in; the powder-blue chairs, too. And after that my poor father could not reach his office without passing a face he had received charity from. It was part of why my mother had set the deal up, I believed.

T o escape the heat again, I entered the Source, a used bookstore around the corner. It was another old place, alive and selling. Near the front of the deep dark cave of pulp, I combed through the local interest shelves, and found *Profiles in Leadership: Dynamic Men and Women of the Quad Cities*. It had been published in hardcover in 1981. I recognized the dust jacket drawing of a giant bald eagle's head hovering in orange dawn light over area bridges, the downtowns, and the bending Mississippi. David R. Collins and Howard Koenig had written most of the portraits, based on their interviews with that era's leading lights. I remembered them both talking about their work on the project at Writers' Studio meetings. I remembered thinking that they were wasting their talent on what sounded like a work of unbridled boosterism, but the book actually amounted to much more. For they somehow got these social and business leaders to eloquently, and rather courageously, reveal the doubts running neck and neck with the grand hopes for unity and cooperation between the cities and towns in two states. I left the store with that volume—a "tome" in the parlance of Writers' Studio—which contained this quote from Robert McGriff:

> When I moved here twenty years ago with my family, I didn't understand just how wide the Mississippi River really was. At least, I didn't know the effect it had as a separation between the Illinois and Iowa cities. That almost overwhelming feeling of division was one of the things I have endeavored to bridge with the Quad City Open.

I was soon across the street from the abrupt Government Bridge entrance. Vehicles made sharp turns off the road to enter or exit a span hooded by ironwork. I stood in the parking lot of the hotel once called the Clayton House and now defunct or undergoing renovation, I could not tell which. Out a back door stretched an industrial hose leaking green fluid across the warped and weedy asphalt. There was no breeze off the river. The water had a viral glow. To mind flashed a memory of once gravely informing my wife that I wanted a wet suit. This was in Vermont, soon after I called my parents to beseech them to get help—to tell them not to call me again until they had reckoned with the past. Instead of the wet suit, I had obtained what I actually needed— more therapy. Across the feverish Mississippi, on the Rock Island Arsenal military complex, I spotted the pale yellow limestone clock tower, still ticking. The TIME and TEMP sign had been removed from the roof of that windowless building upriver from the Civil War–era bridge, and the levee weed jungle was chopped down. Now there was a straight, narrow bike path. But there was no stopping time from continuing to grow wild over here, no stopping its minutes and hours and days from tripping over each other, tangling, lurching backward or forward or in both directions simultaneously. August light fell like snow on the gaunt bridge beams and uncoiled like silver Slinkys across the hood of a passing SUV. I remembered how in September of 1986 I had taken one final life-changing turn at this conjunction of bridge and Iowa, when the green Monte Carlo we had inherited from Grandpa Stanley veered off River Drive and headed for the Amtrak station in Galesburg, Illinois, where I meant to board a train for New York. My father drove and I sat in the front passenger's seat—others crowded in the back. He smoked and offered writing advice. Books, he said, were "systems of symbols," and I ought not to forget that. Later, as the train approached, my mother, in a loose dress, stood on the tracks, picking wildflowers and looking as if she was contemplating suicide. As often before, she decided against it. I got on the train and, face pressed to the window, waved at her and she waved back as if erasing a chalkboard or a nightmare image of my face pulling away. Was she flashing back suddenly to her own long ago year in New York—the one that, in conversation, she boiled down to a mournful sigh over a cup of Chock Full o' Nuts coffee? I had in my wallet some traveler's checks that would not last long. I had a notebook on my lap, and a pen tucked in the hoop of the spiral, and my own idea of what a writer was. It had nothing to do with material gain or fame, and nothing to do with any calculated and dry system of symbols. Writing for me was one way of living—of utilizing life's gift. It was transcribing your pulse, and reading as much as possible. And that aim was maybe the only ostensibly sane aspect of a plan to go to live on the East Coast when I had never before been east of Chicago. Finding a way each year to keep on working kept me attached to the glories and grief of a river bend, and eventually made me a New Yorker, and a husband. Writing had always been my best shot at synthesis, at regaining a happy wholeness lost to the strangest of circumstances, and that was still true. I had to get back at it. I must return to the hotel, and to Anne, and to whatever might come next for us. But for a little longer I lingered, toeing the hot pavement, holding the Source bag. I was both outcast and native son, met by too many memories to name or count.

T HAT SUMMER AFTERNOON as I started back to Rock Island on the Government Bridge, with the traffic vibrating around me, I knew my family had seldom been together in life. I'd never have guessed then, though, that we would not all convene to mourn one of our own—two of our own. Perhaps I should have, but I had much more to learn about the presence of absence in our lives and the mechanics of estrangement. Yet if there exists no way to leave a portrait of a family always missing one or more of its vital faces, it is also true that whenever as few as four of us showed up anywhere, a "family scene" followed with a noise level and choreography hinting so strongly at a whole that onlookers were persuaded. I'm thinking, in particular, of those Saturday afternoons when we time-traveled like Dr. Who, when the family junker on River Drive veered from a disco haze to the 1930s lunch phantasmagoria of Shannon's Cafeteria. Shannon's offered nothing to love but much to like if you were an out-of-step out-of-milk tribe. There

Mr. Hickey would have been a young buck. Steam and steam and more steam, liver and starch, hard chairs, goiters, hernias, dry-gulch glares, varicose umbrellas, three-knob canes, "Brother can you spare a dime?" bums, sour apples, wiseguys, sallow floozies, bedbugs, enigma coats, unfastened frowns, olive-leaf pennies, grease-creased shopping bags that had long outlived their stores of origin, a buzzing water fountain and its beard of white conical cups, the stench of cheap tobacco and insulin shots sweated out the neck. In comparison, the YWCA cafeteria in Rock Island was a five-star emporium—and there I had found a roach preserved in a cherry JELL-O cube. At Shannon's in the men's restroom I discovered a cigar in the toilet bowl—a five-cent cigar swollen like a diseased spleen, floating in urine. The paper towels had anemia: plum and peach. There we learned that communal dining could be an accident of trays crashing and that embolism socks could be worn on arms, and also that it was sometimes vital to remove an eye patch and air the puckered hole. At Shannon's nail clippers served nicely for surgery on the elbow, the toes, the girdle and corset. There was always a man with a weather system for a nose and a woman murmuring yummy-yum-yum. Always a magnifico wearing purple shades and a suit of three greens or four yellows. Here the baby-name book of 1912 was alive, if not well. Dimples-in-time named Ida, Hazel, Matilda, Ruthie, Dottie, Nola, Bertha, Mamie, Hildegaard. So much to say that they yelled nonstop or said nothing. They picked on each other in the worst way, sup-ported each other without question. They had voted for FDR four times and bragged about it. Any cough or sneeze prompted great worry. Frayed outfits were complimented again and again, although the outfits were the same as the day before, and the decade before that. Hats and brooches were complimented sepa-rately, with repetitive vehemence. If Jim Croce had been unlucky enough to wander through Shannon's in his formative years, he would have composed "Time in a Ketchup Bottle" and then died an unknown. Many of the customers dined only on condiments. One lady appeared to have swallowed a string bass. Stone soup would have been appreciated, but there was none—only tepid consommé more fluid than tap water. Why, then, was every customer dying of dehydration? Liquids were for spilling, that's why. And dentures for soaking, and hearts for wearing on collars and sleeves since there was not a second left for caviling, but a whole afternoon ahead for parrying and kvetching and coffee-klatching and calling money "scratch." Mother and I and Elizabeth and Marianna entered the gray bay of glaucoma as a band of seals barely seen but heard barking. "Benny!" "Yes, mama?" "Take your sister's hand! Watch out for bunions!" I took Marianna's hand and mother took Elizabeth's, and we watched out for bunions and marveled at how young our mother suddenly looked, her flushed wattle sagging more spryly than any of the sad surrounding faces, her discolored dress resembling the latest Parisian fashion compared to the biblical shrouds hanging off the skeletal shoulders of regulars. The two-rail tray line was a road to a tropical atmosphere. The steam of the food rose and rose and gave a mirage-like appearance to the hand-lettered wall signs with their prices in cents, and to the brown cartoons of coffee cups and the meat loaf, the scrambled-egg sandwiches. Canes plowed into the line at any point. The line with no beginning, nor any discernible end. Paper-hatted servers snickered, thin and swarthy, Typhoid Mary's favorite grandchildren. They too happily shoveled soggy potatoes, mushy lima beans, bleeding beets, rubbery meat, and limp noodles. Every plate and bowl and mug was webbed with cracks under its ceramic glaze. My favorite meal at Shannon's was the eerie Twenty-Piece Chicken Special, a heap of minuscule breaded drumsticks: tender two-inch meshes of gristle and grease that went down in delicious lip-drenching bites. Where did the tiny hens come from? Dinky Farms? Or was it not chicken, but rather a fried version of sea monkeys? On special days I could get this delight, and though many of our long and desultory days were mislabeled "special" in order to maintain morale, usually the specialness did not allow for me to enjoy an entrée of my own—often mother and I and my sisters would share roast—what was it?—au jus. And custard. At Shannon's custard could always be counted on, a speckled membrane sealing the cup full of shiny stuff the exact color of phlegm, but slippery, not sticky, smooth and rich. There were also gummy rolls with slit tops and pies with hard lardy edges that the baker had pinched his marital woes into. After mother filled the tray with sordid delights, we wound back through the maze of bunions, corns, kidney stones, and gallbladder surgery scars. A "good table" was one near the humid window and far from those Edgars who munched cigars that got wider and wetter and wider. The tables were chrome-edged and small. Each of us placed a symbolic body part underneath—knee or foot—and then screwed our torsos into a position amenable to shouted conversation and chewing. Flavor had been boiled or fried or mashed out of most every item, and the fruit cocktail was as white as a ghost of Eden. Mother dispensed portions to her "soldiers," as she called us at Shannon's and nowhere else. Gag, gag, gag as we kept an eye on Mr. Magnifico, who could well do something to your back that not even Spillane had thought of. Around him Ruthies crabbed, gabbed, grabbed. Their hours—like ours—were cobbled together roughly, one event barely following another. "Salt. He spilt salt. See! Salt!" We saw. We saw our future in these ancients made of loose thread and thrombosis. They were not lost, not quite yet. Like us, they were swimming against a tide of years that no levee wall, no matter how high, could repel—the decades pouring over the bricks and roofs and streets of the city belonging to all those who were not washed away.

PUBLICATION NOTES

A number of these chapters appeared, often in significantly different form, in the following publications: *AGNI*, *Alaska Quarterly Review*, the *Antioch Review*, *Ecotone*, *Gulf Coast*, the *Normal School*, *Raritan*, *Salmagundi*, and the *Yale Review*. Many thanks to the editors of those publications. A portion of the prologue titled "Bix and Flannery" was chosen by Louis Menand for *Best American Essays*, and numerous other chapters were selected as "Notable Essays" by the series editor, Robert Atwan.

ACKNOWLEDGMENTS

The author wishes to recognize the extraordinary and indefatigable efforts of Emily Louise Smith, Ben George, and Beth Staples that were required to bring this work to fruition. In addition, he expresses deepest gratitude to Jim and Gail Wiese, for their unfailing generosity and sweet encouragement.

ABOUT THE PHOTOGRAPHER

ROBERT CAMPAGNA
resides in Loveland, Colorado,
with special connections to his
lifelong home in Iowa. He teaches
film photography at the Loveland
Integrated School of the Arts.

Lookout Books

Lookout is more than a name—it's our
publishing philosophy. Founded as the
literary book imprint of the Department of
Creative Writing at the University of North
Carolina Wilmington, Lookout pledges to
seek out works by emerging and historically
underrepresented voices, as well as
overlooked gems by established writers.
In a publishing landscape increasingly
indifferent to literary innovation, Lookout
offers a haven for books that matter.

TEXT Monotype Bulmer 11.3/13.7
DISPLAY Monotype Bulmer Semibold 18